America's Greatest Brands ©

AN INSIGHT INTO 80 OF AMERICA'S STRONGEST BRANDS
VOLUME 1

America's Greatest Brands ©

Inc.

Publisher and Editor-in-Chief
Stephen P Smith

Associate Publishers
Peter McCutchen
Peter Richardson

Managing Editor
Robert T Gray

Design Management
Walter E Ratcliff

Production Manager
J Peter Thoeming

Published by America's Greatest Brands, Inc.
350 Theodore Fremd Avenue
Rye, New York 10580

Telephone (914) 921 3300
Facsimile (914) 921 3330
E-mail pm@americasgreatestbrands.com
www.americasgreatestbrands.com

Special thanks to Gene Bartley, Joseph Fisher,
Rich Hamilton, Jennifer Laing, James
McDowell, Keith Reinhard, Linda Srere, John C
Thomas, Bob Tomei, Marcel Knobil, David
Haigh, Bill Colegrave, Richard Thomas, Jean,
Sara, Peter, Mark Hofer, Maura Toller, Gerard
Wilson, Jake Wilson, Graham Hartmann, Annie
Richardson, Blair Hamilford, Jilly, Soraya, Cara,
Elizabeth Smith, Kevin Boland, Angela
Pumphrey, Bruce Connolly, David Goldschmidt,
Edwin & Agnes Fabiero, Ferdi Stolzenburg, Ray
Barnes, Jack Maisano, Jeff Palfreyman, Noel
Derby, Paul Gregory, Russell Yu, Steve Moss,
Peter Brack, Paul Ashby, Lindsay Birley, Victor
Jeffery, George Vastardis, Jim Saunders, Bruce
Johnston, Chris Mooney, Kerrie Lindsay, Peter
Ryall, David Ryan, Neville Young, Agnes, Jason,
Peter, Daniel, Sally, Jack, William, Sam, Espie,
Alexander, Georgina, Anne, Alix and Louise.

Printed in Hong Kong

ISBN 0-9706860-0-5

America's Greatest Brands ©

AN INSIGHT INTO 80 OF AMERICA'S STRONGEST BRANDS
VOLUME 1

This book is dedicated to the men and
women who build and protect
America's greatest brand assets.

www.americasgreatestbrands.com

CONTENTS

ABC
ABC, Incorporated
2040 Avenue of the Stars
Century City, CA 90067

ALLSTATE
Allstate Insurance Company
2775 Sanders Road, Suite F3
Northbrook, IL 60062

AMERICAN AIRLINES
American Airlines, Incorporated
4333 Amon Carter Boulevard
Fort Worth, TX 76155

AMERICAN EXPRESS
American Express Company
World Financial Center
New York, NY 10285

AMERICAN RED CROSS
American Red Cross
431 18th Street NW 5th Floor
Washington, DC 20006

ARROW
The Arrow Company
200 Madison Avenue
New York, NY 10016

AUDI
Audi of America, Incorporated
3800 Hamlin Road
Auburn Hills, MI 48326

BAYER
Bayer Corporation
36 Columbia Road
Morristown, NJ 07962

BLUE CROSS / BLUE SHIELD
Blue Cross Blue Shield Association
225 North Michigan Avenue
Chicago, IL 60601

CANADIAN CLUB
Allied Domecq Spirits and Wine North
America
355 Riverside Avenue
Westport, CT 06880

CATERPILLAR
Caterpillar, Incorporated
100 NE Adams Street
Peoria, IL 61629-8310

CENTURY 21
Century 21 Real Estate Corporation
6 Sylvan Way
Parsippany, NJ 07054

CHARLES SCHWAB
Charles Schwab & Company,
Incorporated
101 Montgomery Street
San Francisco, CA 94104

CLUB MED
Club Med Sales, Incorporated
75 Valencia Avenue
Coral Gables, FL 33134

COCA-COLA
The Coca-Cola Company
One Coca-Cola Plaza
Atlanta, GA 30313

CREST
The Procter & Gamble Company
One Procter & Gamble Plaza
Cincinnati, OH 45202

DIET COKE
The Coca-Cola Company
One Coca-Cola Plaza
Atlanta, GA 30313

DISNEY CHANNEL
ABC Cable Networks Group
3800 W. Alameda Avenue
Burbank, CA 91505

DORITOS
Frito-Lay, Incorporated
7701 Legacy Drive
Plano, TX 75024

ENERGIZER
Energizer Battery Company,
Incorporated
800 Chouteau Avenue
Saint Louis, MO 63102

E*TRADE
E*TRADE Group, Incorporated
4500 Bohannon Drive
Menlo Park, CA 94025

FARMERS
Farmers Insurance Group
4680 Wilshire Boulevard
Los Angeles, CA 90010

FEDEX
FedEx Corporation
2003 Corporate Avenue
Memphis, TN 38132

FORD
Ford Motor Company
The American Road
Dearborn, MI 48121

FRITOS
Frito-Lay, Incorporated
7701 Legacy Drive
Plano, TX 75024

FTD
FTD, Incorporated
3113 Woodcreek Drive
Downers Grove, IL 60515

FUJIFILM
Fuji Photo Film USA, Incorporated
555 Taxter Road
Elmsford, NY 10523

GATEWAY
Gateway, Incorporated
610 Gateway Drive
North Sioux City, SD 57049

HANES
Sara Lee Branded Apparel
1000 East Hanes Mill Road
Winston-Salem, NC 27105

HOOVER
The Hoover Company
101 E. Maple Street
North Canton, OH 44720

HUSH PUPPIES
Wolverine Worldwide, Incorporated
9341 Courtland Drive
Rockford, MI 49351

IBM
IBM Corporation
New Orchard Road
Armonk, NY 10504

JOCKEY
Jockey International, Incorporated
2300 60th Street
Kenosha, WI 53140

JOHN DEERE
Deere & Company
1 John Deere Place
Moline, IL 61265-8098

JVC
JVC Company of America
1700 Valley Road
Wayne, NJ 07470

KELLOGG'S
Kellogg Company
1 Kellogg Square
Battle Creek, MI 49016

KENMORE
Sears, Roebuck and Company
3333 Beverly Road
Hoffman Estates, IL 60179

KOOL
Brown & Williamson Tobacco
Corporation
200 Brown & Williamson Tower 401
S. 4th Street
Louisville, KY 40202

LIFESAVERS
Kraft Foods North America
100 DeForest Avenue
East Hanover, NJ 07936

LUCKY STRIKE
Brown & Williamson Tobacco
Corporation
200 Brown & Williamson Tower 401
S. 4th Street
Louisville, KY 40202

M&M's
Mars, Incorporated
800 High Street
Hackettstown, NJ 07840

MAIL BOXES ETC.
Mail Boxes Etc.
6060 Cornerstone Court W.
San Diego, CA 92121

MANPOWER
Manpower, Incorporated
5301 N. Ironwood Road
Milwaukee, WI 53217

MAXWELL HOUSE
Kraft Foods North America
555 South Broadway
Tarrytown, NY 10591

MAYTAG
Maytag Corporation
403 W. Fourth Street N.
Newton, IA 50208

MCDONALD'S
McDonald's Corporation
1 Kroc Drive
Oak Brook, IL 60523

MONOPOLY
Hasbro, Incorporated
443 Shaker Road
East Long Meadow, MA 01028

MR. COFFEE
Sunbeam Corporation
2381 Executive Center Drive
Boca Raton, FL 33431

NEW YORK STOCK EXCHANGE
The New York Stock Exchange,
Incorporated
11 Wall Street, 12th Floor
New York, NY 10005

NIKON
Nikon, Incorporated
1300 Walt Whitman Road
Melville, NY 11747

NUTRASWEET
The NutraSweet Company
10 South Wacker, Suite 3200
Chicago, IL 60606

OREO
Kraft Foods North America
100 DeForest Avenue
East Hanover, NJ 07936

PALL MALL
Brown & Williamson Tobacco
Corporation
200 Brown & Williamson Tower 401
S. 4th Street
Louisville, KY 40202

PANASONIC
Matsushita Electric Corporation
of America
One Panasonic Way
Secaucus, NJ 07094

PEPSI
Pepsi-Cola Company
700 Anderson Hill Road
Purchase, NY 10577

PITNEY BOWES
Pitney Bowes, Incorporated
One Elmcroft Road
Stamford, CT 06926

PRUDENTIAL
The Prudential Insurance Company
of America
751 Broad Street
Newark, NJ 07102

PURINA
Ralston Purina Company
901 Chouteau Avenue
Saint Louis, MO 63164

ROYAL DOULTON
The Royal Doulton Company
700 Cottontail Lane
Somerset, NJ 08873

SCOTTS
The Scotts Company
41 South High Street
Columbus, OH 43215

SNICKERS
Mars, Incorporated
800 High Street
Hackettstown, NJ 07840

SONY
Sony Corporation
One Sony Drive
Park Ridge, NJ 07656

SPRINT
Sprint Corporation
6330 Sprint Parkway
Overland Park, KS 66251

SPRITE
The Coca-Cola Company
One Coca-Cola Plaza
Atlanta, GA 30313

STANLEY
The Stanley Works
1000 Stanley Drive
New Britain, CT 06053

SUNKIST
Sunkist Growers, Incorporated
14130 Riverside Drive
Sherman Oaks, CA 91423

TABASCO
McIlhenny Company
Avery Island, LA 70513

TEXACO
Texaco, Incorporated
2000 Westchester Avenue
White Plains, NY 10650

T-FAL
T-Fal Corporation
25 Riverside Drive
Pine Brook, NJ 07058

THE NEW YORK TIMES
The New York Times Company
229 W. 43rd Street
New York, NY 10036

TOYOTA
Toyota Motor Sales USA, Incorporated
19001 S. Western Avenue
Torrance, CA 90509

TOYS "R" US
Toys "R" Us, Incorporated
461 From Road
Paramus, NJ 07652

TRUE VALUE
TruServ Corporation
8600 W. Bryn Mawr Avenue
Chicago, IL 60631

UNITED STATES MARINE CORPS
United States Marine Corps
3280 Russel Road
Quantico, VA 22134

**UNITED STATES POSTAL
SERVICE**
United States Postal Service
1735 North Lynn Street
Arlington, VA 22209-6057

USA TODAY
Gannett Company, Incorporated
1100 Wilson Boulevard
Arlington, VA 22229

VERIZON
Verizon Communications, Incorporated
1095 Avenue of the Americas
New York, NY 10036

WESTINGHOUSE
Westinghouse Electric Corporation
1515 Broadway
New York, NY 10036-5794

WWF
World Wrestling Federation
Entertainment, Incorporated
1241 E. Main Street
Stamford, CT 06902

YOPLAIT
General Mills, Incorporated
Number One General Mills Boulevard
Minneapolis, MN 55426

FOREWORD

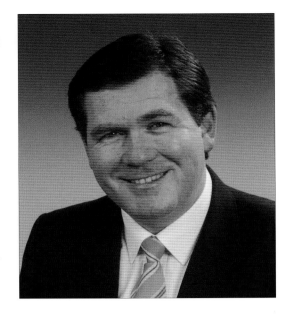

Stephen P Smith
Publisher
Chairman:
The American Brands Council

A great brand is not merely a maker's mark. It is almost an heraldic symbol, carrying with it a whole web of positive associations. We do well not to underestimate the power of symbols: put them on national flags and people die for them. And if consumers won't normally go quite that far for a particular brand of soap or sunglasses, they will certainly go to considerable lengths to buy the brand they have come to know and trust.

For the past 25 years I have been privileged to occupy a ringside seat looking directly into many of the world's great marketing organizations. My media and publishing work in more than 50 countries has brought me into contact with many leading international media companies, and through them with multinational firms boasting some of the biggest and best-known brand names in the world.

These companies have long recognized that their brands are powerful assets, but it is only recently that the true value of these great brands has found its way onto balance sheets. There has been dramatic, worldwide interest in brand values over recent years: a quest to discover exactly what it is that makes brands work, and what their true values are.

Recent surveys indicate that brands may account for 50 to 70 per cent of the total value of the company. In short, they can be worth billions of dollars. Studying the way these brands were started, then developed and maintained is not only a vital activity for anyone interested in the way the modern marketplace functions; it is also fascinating.

This is my fourth book in an international series on branding, and it contains fascinating stories about many of the great brands in America. It offers some intriguing insights into the creation and development of these brand icons with 130,000 words and nearly 500 pictures.

What makes a great brand? What creates the awareness, desirability and power that a truly great brand has? With the help of The American Brands Council and the companies themselves we have compiled the stories of some of America's, and the world's greatest brands, and the innovation and prestige that surround them.

In the following pages you will read about "what makes a great brand" by the members of The American Brands Council. The Council is made up of some of America's most eminent media and communications executives who each have a deep appreciation of what constitutes that rare and so-valuable thing — a truly great brand.

WHAT MAKES A GREAT BRAND?

BY THE AMERICAN BRANDS COUNCIL

**Mr Gene Bartley
Chief Executive
Officer,
Bozell Worldwide**

"Rather than give you some dry, precise definition of a brand in terms only an adman or woman would love, let's have some fun with this. Let's play a game that gets at the heart of what great brands are really about. I'll mention three things sequentially; you try and guess the brand they bring to mind.

"Adventure, the great outdoors and an all-terrain vehicle. You guessed it - Jeep. Fantasy, fun and big ears. Did I hear Disney? If so, you're right on the money. And finally, Coney Island, cotton candy and hot dogs. That's right - Nathan's hot dogs. (How could we talk about American brands without touching on hot dogs?)

"When a brand delivers, like the three knockouts above, you don't have to spend a lot of time figuring out how or why. They mean something very specific to anyone who has ever encountered them. They elicit feelings of warmth and confidence, a comfort level that's usually reserved for family or friends. That's what great brands and successful advertising are all about."

**Mr Joseph Fisher
President
and CEO,
Burson-Marsteller**

"A promise kept, simply stated, is what makes a great brand. Brand value doesn't exist in a marketer's plan or a company's portfolio. It exists solely within the minds of consumers or customers. Marketing programs make a promise, but fulfilment resides in the customer's experience. For that reason, great brands can't exist without a fundamental understanding by all those involved of the part they play in delivering on a promise. Great brands are those that enjoy universal internal understanding of a consistent promise and a commitment to always deliver externally. Identify almost any great brand and you will uncover an organization that understands what it takes to deliver on a promise."

**Mr Rich Hamilton
Chief Executive
Officer,
Zenith Media
Services Inc**

"Great brands have a life of their own. They are immortal; they stand for something.

"They are durable, simple, and elegant in design. They inspire loyalty. People pay more to buy them. Why? Because it's worth it!

"Who are they in America?

"They are brands like Cheerios, M&M's, Sony, Oreo, Coca-Cola, Ford, Disney and Kellogg's. There are many more.

"The companies that own these brands work to protect and indeed build them through innovation in product development, distribution and sales efforts, and all forms of marketing.

"Mars, Inc., owner of M&M's, conducted a sweepstakes which let consumers select the next new colour of M&M's. Consumers picked blue! A great example of leadership and consumer-focused marketing from the owner of a true brand icon."

Ms Jennifer Laing Chairman and CEO, Saatchi & Saatchi

"Great brands are just like competing products, yet we pay more for them because we have formed an emotional bond with them. Great brands are like good friends, we love them and we trust them.

"This place in our heart has been built through the skilful use of traditional media. Today, great brands, just like our friends, stay in touch via targeted messages, voice mail, web sites and e-mail. As we all become harder to reach, brands that fail to exploit new technologies will fall from consciousness.

"However, it is uncertain whether new media creates the same feelings of affection, trust and willingness to pay over the odds. Experimentation on the web is best matched by exploration of interactive TV, unconventional outdoor and transformational advertising ideas. Innovative use of old media may still prove the most potent when it comes to affairs of the heart."

Mr James McDowell Marketing Director, BMW of North America

"A brand is a consumer promise: it is an implied guarantee of having made the right choice.

"It promises and embodies a set of consumer expectations about important 'joy of ownership' and uses parameters such as performance, innovation, quality and longevity.

"A brand is partly defined by the people who use it and how they use it. The feeling that someone has when they use the product is very important. To the extent that this feeling is different than for competing products, the brand has attained true differentiation.

"To stand out in the marketplace, a brand has to stand for something. That means that while almost everyone will recognize and hopefully respect the brand, it probably won't be for everyone.

"If you are clever or lucky, a brand elicits passion and emotion. Strong brands often receive the spontaneous endorsement, 'This brand is perfect for a person like me. I wouldn't consider anything else'."

Mr Keith Reinhard Chairman and CEO, DDB Worldwide

"The twentieth-century Spanish philosopher Jose Ortega y Gasset counselled that 'the first act of any society is the selection of a point of view'. And so it is for brands. A great brand is distinguished by a passionately held point of view, from which evolves a relevant and compelling promise - the combination of which is conveyed with a distinctive style and personality.

"McDonald's point of view is that eating out is about more than food. It therefore promises a good time every time, always with a style that is warm and human. Volkswagen's point of view is that automotive excellence should be available to everyone. It is therefore expanding its line in order to promise the unique Volkswagen driving experience to people of all economic classes… but always with the same special style that launched the Beetle in 1959.

"A well-selected point of view, a compelling promise stated or implied, and a winning personality. These are the key elements of a great brand."

Ms Linda Srere Vice President/ Chairperson, Young & Rubicam, Inc

"That's way too big - and important - a question for this little space. But to understand what makes a great brand, I'd go to Y&R's brand definition as a starting point. A brand is a differentiating promise that links a product to its customer. The brand assures the customer of consistent quality plus superior value for which the customer is willing to give loyalty and pay a price that brings reasonable returns to the brand.

"Great brands take this relationship to greater heights. They create and inspire loyalty, even passion. Some brand relationships are downright romances. Just think about the way people feel about their Sony Discman or their iMac computer.

"The secret? Great brands share two essential characteristics -- differentiation and relevance. You have to be different and distinct to catch the consumer's eye. But you must also figure out what differentiates you and how you're relevant to today's consumers, then communicate that with simplicity and uniqueness. That's what truly makes a great and enduring brand."

Mr John C. Thomas Chairman, Adweek Magazines

"In the 1980s, we started a business magazine called MARKETING WEEK and thought we had a great idea and a great brand name that would appeal to an audience far broader and much larger than the discrete audience reached by ADWEEK.

"A few years into the mission, it occurred to our editors that marketing was more precisely about 'branding'. MARKETING WEEK became BRANDWEEK and the editorial focus became much clearer as did the appeal of the magazine.

"After all is said and done, a brand is only an idea - an implied promise that whatever you are buying or reading or watching or listening to satisfies what is ideal in your mind. A great brand must establish that ideal and the product must deliver it, over and over again."

Mr Bob Tomei Senior Vice President of Marketing, AC Nielsen

"A great brand is best defined by the equity and positioning it holds in the marketplace. Brand equity is defined by the price/value relationship it maintains among a specific target audience. Once a brand's equity is established in the market, its positioning and image must reinforce that price/value relationship over and over again. It is critical to maintain a consistent message over time that reinforces those attributes of a brand that consumers value. It is also important to not extend a brand beyond its defined equity and positioning. A great brand must deliver on its stated commitment to responsibly fulfil a specific consumer need or desire. The brand's packaging, promotion, advertising and positioning in the market needs to support that commitment. While it's relatively easy to 'refresh/update' a brand using repackaging or close-in line extensions, the real challenge lies in making it relevant over time to your target consumer."

THE MARKET

In a short period of time, the American television market has grown from a comfortable three-network landscape to a highly-competitive 200+ channel media environment, with each channel fighting for the leisure-time attention of an American public that finds itself with less and less of such time. The phenomenal

If TV's so bad for you, why is there one in every hospital room?

growth of VCRs and DVDs, video games, radio, movies, the Internet, and other new technology is also a major element in media competition. This ever-increasing proliferation of choices has created a marketplace of entertainment, news and sports programmers and suppliers who have become evermore dependent upon the growth and the strength of their brands and the connection their brands have with their consumers.

ACHIEVEMENTS

ABC is presently America's #1 Broadcasting Company due to the combined growth of its

diverse and distinctive programming and a unique, patient, and successful brand strategy.

ABC's quality mix of news, sports, daytime, children's, and primetime entertainment programs assures that no network reaches more Americans during primetime alone or the entire broadcast day than ABC does.

That success has deep roots. ABC developed ground-breaking program partnerships in the 1950s with the Walt Disney Company, which spawned programs like "Disneyland" and "The Mickey Mouse Club," and Warner Brothers, which produced the first-ever Hollywood film-styled action-western-adventure programs like "Cheyenne," "Kings Row," and "Wyatt Earp."

In the 1960s ABC achieved incredible success with aggressive risk-taking and pioneering broadcast and technological innovations like the first-ever separate AM and FM broadcast radio divisions. ABC pioneered in the 1970s such new program genre styles as made-for-television movies and the unique multi-part "novels for television" and mini-series forms with shows like "Rich Man, Poor Man" and the unprecedented 12-hour, eight-day television event, "Roots."

ABC also changed the way people watched television with new broad-reach, non-entertainment program innovations like "Monday Night Football," "The Wide World of Sports," and late-night's "ABC News: Nightline."

And ABC continues to stay ahead of the curve by being among the first broadcast networks to recognize the growth of the interactive online medium by developing aggressive Intertnet and enhanced television products.

HISTORY

The ABC Television Network evolved from events beginning in 1943, when Edward Noble, owner of the Rexall Drug Store chain, bought the National Broadcasting Company's Blue radio network after the U.S. government ordered that NBC sell one of its two radio networks. Noble named his new entity the American Broadcasting Company. It was

owned by United Paramount Theaters, headed by Leonard Goldenson and then by Capital Cities Communications before its acquisition in 1996 by its present owner, The Walt Disney Company.

It was the infusion of UPT money that enabled ABC to truly compete with the well-established NBC and the Columbia Broadcasting System (CBS). ABC quickly developed westerns, action/adventure series, sports properties and launched its highly successful, long-term programming partnership with Disney.

After early years of struggling, ABC eventually overtook its competitors in the mid-to-late 1970s. ABC's success came with a long string of successful urban, contemporary comedy and drama series like "Happy Days," "Laverne & Shirley," "Charlie's Angels," "Starsky & Hutch," and "Family," as well as "Monday Night Football," television's number one sports franchise.

Further success in ABC Sports and ABC News under the leadership of Roone Arledge brought the network to even greater prominence.

THE PRODUCT

The ABC Television Network is the broadcast network arm of ABC Inc., a division of the Walt Disney Company. Other ABC Inc. properties include cable networks such as ESPN and the Disney Channel and significant minority positions in other major cable networks, syndicated programming, production, and publishing.

ABC-TV's products appeal to all demographics and every member of the family. The ABC Entertainment lineup boasts such top-rated and audience favorite programs as *"Who Wants to be a Millionaire," "The Drew Carey Show," "Spin City," "Dharma & Greg," "NYPD Blue," "The Practice,"* and *"The Wonderful World of Disney."* ABC Daytime offers such leaders in serial dramas as *"General Hospital," "All My Children," "One Life to Live,"* and *"The View,"* featuring Barbara Walters.

ABC News features the most informative, most respected, most credible, and most intelligent journalists in broadcasting with Peter Jennings, Ted Koppel, Barbara Walters, Diane Sawyer, Charles Gibson, Sam Donaldson, and others.

ABC Sports' programming features high-profile, quality events—NFL's "Monday Night Football," Wild-Card Playoffs, NCAA College Football, the College Bowl Championship Series, NCAA Basketball, golf's PGA Tour events, the Indianapolis 500, NHL Hockey and Stanley Cup Playoffs, and U.S. and World Figure Skating Championships.

Disney's One Saturday Morning lineup features Disney animated character-based programs and lively, fun interstitial programming that reaches more American children on Saturday mornings than that of any other broadcast network.

RECENT DEVELOPMENTS

With the rise of the incredibly popular reality-based *"Who Wants to be a Millionaire"* hosted by Regis Philbin, and the growth of several of ABC's signature comedy and drama programs, ABC Entertainment's primetime schedule concluded the 1999-2000 season firmly in first place among television networks in households and key young adult demographics.

ABC News also experienced a resurgence in audience popularity, critical acclaim, and growth due to the immense success generated by the unprecedented ABC 2000 24-hour Millennium broadcast, the double-digit growth of *"Good Morning America"* from its brand-new state-of-the-art broadcast facility in Times Square, New York, and the continued success of the primetime news magazine series, *"20/20."*

ABC daytime programming remains #1 and continues to dominate the ratings target of women 18-49.

Further expansion at ABC Daytime included the recent launch of a new 24-hour cable channel called SoapNet. ABC Sports presented a string of the highest-rated sports programming on television that included Super Bowl

definitely abc

XXXIV as well as other top-rated sportscasts.

But a significant development beyond the programming was the parallel development of the ABC brand itself. ABC developed a distinct identity, graphic style, attitude, and brand personality.

PROMOTION

Distinctive promotion, marketing and branding, in concert with programming, have proven to be the driver of the ABC brand identity. In 1997, ABC began differentiating itself from its competitors by developing a personality-based brand identity. This also included unique look-and-feel style graphic packaging and a signature four-note sound environment that stood out from the clutter of current-day television brands.

Described initially by some as a sort of "anti-television" style, ABC's promotional approach and personality was built on a positive, emotional and "conversational" relationship with its audience.

This personality broke from traditional network television promotional tactics of hype, slogans, and screaming at viewers to "watch us more," to a new, warmer, and friendlier tone.

Oftentimes humorous and irreverent, the brand attitude developed first as a summer campaign celebrating the medium of television *"(TV is Good®)"*. It was wildly and instantly successful, spawning widespread critical acclaim, attention-getting controversy, imitations and parodies, and a significant place in the annals of media pop-culture history.

The campaign then moved to incorporate ABC's signature shows and stars, the most powerful elements of the ABC brand, all within that brand architecture and style, and infiltrating all of ABC's year-long traditional and ground-breaking nontraditional marketing, advertising and promotion efforts.

As for the distinctive packaging, ABC first introduced a signature flat "yellow and black" graphic environment for its corporate and primetime brand promotion and marketing. It featured an extensive library of original music all utilizing a recognizable four-note "signature" sting, black & white still photography of ABC programs and stars, and distinctive navigational screens informing viewers of upcoming ABC programming choices.

That ABC brand "look and feel" was then eventually expanded to include other ABC programming dayparts, each following the rules of the original brand formula, but at the same time allowing each program division to maintain its own unique identity within the ABC family—

blue for news, red for sports, yellow for all entertainment dayparts.

And, finally, that same graphic style was expanded across ABC's owned and affiliated local stations across the country to create a clearly distinguishable environment signaling, reinforcing, and promoting the ABC brand.

BRAND VALUES

ABC's core brand values are more recognized now than ever before. ABC is seen to be a network that is real, honest, diverse, fun, smart, confident, and understated in a world of hype. The programming is a genuine reflection of that brand attitude and a reflection of the diverse population that tunes in each day. The network distinguishes itself and prides itself in each of its programming dayparts on producing the best storytelling and delivering the highest quality programming from entertainment to news to sports to community service.

THINGS YOU DIDN'T KNOW ABOUT ABC

○ ABC's 1997 "We Love TV" brand campaign, design to reposition the Television Network, cost $4 million and generated almost $100 million of exposure in all media, including a parody commercial spot that NBC created and aired in their top rated program.

○ For the Millenium, ABC News created almost 24 hours of live programming celebrating the new century in every time zone. Over 175 million Americans watched the turn of the century as it happened, as did people in 66 other countries.

○ Saturday Morning television was reinvented when ABC's kids programming line-up became "Disney's One Saturday Morning." Tossing out conventional programming blocks and adding live action and short-form programming, the line-up went from fourth to first place in the ratings in its first season.

○ ABC's NFL Monday Night Football is ABC's longest running Prime Time Series, having premiered on September 21, 1970. It remains the #1 Sports franchise on television and has ranked among the top 10 programs over the past decade.

Allstate

You're in good hands.

THE MARKET

The Allstate Corporation appraises its market in clear-cut terms: Competition in the insurance and financial services segments is fierce with thousands of competitors; customers expect better, faster, and smarter service; and consumers often have ambivalent feelings about the insurance industry.

ACHIEVEMENTS

Allstate, which is based in Northbrook, IL, meets its competition and marketplace realities head on. The company writes policies on one of every eight autos and homes in the United States,

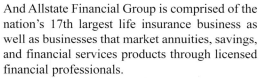

making it the second largest of such insurers with more than 30 million auto and property policies in force. Using different brand names, it is also one of the leading independent agency companies. And Allstate Financial Group is comprised of the nation's 17th largest life insurance business as well as businesses that market annuities, savings, and financial services products through licensed financial professionals.

Allstate has faced various competitors and forms of competition over the years. With the rapid advances of business technology in the 1990s, competitors have emerged that sell insurance directly through web sites or toll-free phone numbers. There has also been increased competition from other financial institutions selling insurance and from other insurance companies strengthened by mergers and acquisitions.

Allstate has responded to the competition and changing marketplace by recasting its business model. The company's new business model is actually a network of strategies that are centered around plans for growing exclusive agencies, leveraging state-of-the art technology, building customer-centric processes, and delivering enhanced competitive pricing for valued customer segments.

HISTORY

Innovation in meeting the changing needs and expectations of consumers has been a long tradition at Allstate. In fact, the company has its very roots in an innovative access and distribution idea—mail order insurance policies.

In 1930, on a commuter train to Chicago, insurance broker Carl Odell suggested to his neighbor, Sears, Roebuck and Company President Gen. Robert E. Wood, that Sears should start an auto insurance company and sell insurance by mail.

That idea became reality. Allstate Insurance Company was launched by Sears in 1931. The new insurance company was financed with $700,000 from the parent firm. The initial sales campaign consisted of mailing a half-million circulars that produced 40,000 inquiries.

In 1934, Sears began placing Allstate agents in its retail stores and five years later the company began tailoring auto insurance rates to the age of the driver and the type of use and mileage driven for the car—a move that was quickly copied by the industry.

Moving from its auto insurance origins, the company added residential fire coverage in 1954, and the Allstate Life Insurance Company was formed in 1957. Allstate expanded its market in 1960 to include financing for autos, boats, and recreational vehicles, mortgage banking, and mutual-fund management. A further evolution occurred in 1982, when Allstate became part of the Sears Financial Network.

In 1993, Sears sold nearly 20 percent of its interest in Allstate to the public and spun off the rest of its Allstate holdings to Sears stockholders in 1995. Today, The Allstate Corporation is the nation's largest publicly held personal lines insurance company.

THE PRODUCT

Allstate products offer security, protection, and peace of mind. The main business of The Allstate Corporation is the Allstate personal property and casualty insurance segment, with more than 14 million household customers. Specific products include auto, home, and business insurance, as well as coverage for boats, recreational vehicles,

and mobile homes. It also offers roadside assistance plans and mechanical-breakdown coverage for vehicles.

In addition, Allstate is one of the leading independent agency companies, through its purchase in 1999 of CNA Personal Insurance, since renamed Encompass Insurance. Through Encompass, Deerbrook (for non-standard auto risks), and Allstate independent agency affiliations, subsidiaries of The Allstate Corporation insure some 2 million customers who have elected to shop with independent agents.

Newly named to reflect its recently expanded product line, Allstate Financial Group markets a number of life insurance, savings products and annuities under a variety of brands. According to Allstate Financial Group, "We've moved beyond traditional life insurance to include financial products and services to help Americans achieve a secure financial future. The strong Allstate brand name gives us the leverage to provide these enhancements tailored to a customer's personal financial needs." Life insurance and financial services products are sold through Allstate agents, Personal Financial Representatives and a variety of other outlets that include brokers and banks.

RECENT DEVELOPMENTS

Allstate said in its 1999 annual report that the company had taken "bold steps to reposition itself for industry leadership—marked by a major commitment to technology and the Internet in an effort to make our agents more successful and productive and our customers more satisfied. Simply put, Allstate is taking the lead in transforming our industry and setting new standards for consumer choice and convenience."

The core of the repositioning strategy is the company's new business model, a fully integrated plan to grow exclusive agencies, leverage state-of-the art technology, build customer-centric processes, and deliver enhanced competitive pricing for valued customer segments.

A major component of the company's new business model is The Good Hands℠ Network. This initiative will give customers access to Allstate products, services, and information via the Internet (allstate.com), Customer Information Centers (1-800-Allstate), and local Allstate agents. The Good Hands℠ Network will, according to the company, "integrate ease of access with the reassuring presence of a local Allstate agent."

The three easy-to-use service options—Internet, phone and agent—serve customers and prospects when, where, and how they want. Allstate says, "All three offer a wealth of knowledge and professional attentiveness. All three are interconnected for fast, consistent service, so customers get the same great service no matter which method they choose. And all three are ready to help customers handle their insurance needs: file a claim, check the status of a claim, get a quote, buy a policy, add coverage, change coverage, renew their current policies, have questions answered, receive safety tips, and more."

In other developments, the company is targeting several major segments of the population for faster growth. They include ethnic markets, such as the Hispanic community, which is expected to be the largest ethnic market in America by 2010, and the 79 million U.S. baby boomers approaching retirement age.

PROMOTION

Allstate's "Good Hands" campaign is one of the most famous in the history of American business. A half-century old, the slogan was launched with a magazine ad campaign that featured the message, "You're In Good Hands With Allstate." The campaign was so successful that Allstate adopted the slogan as its service mark and combined it with an illustration of cupped hands holding an automobile. While fundamentally unchanged, the Allstate logo has been consistently updated over the years to reflect the company's expansion into other types of protection and evolving brand positioning.

Today, according to a recent study at a leading university, Allstate's famous slogan is among the most widely recognized slogans in business history. Allstate ad campaigns have won a number of awards through the years, with nearly all of them using the famous line.

BRAND VALUES

"You're In Good Hands With Allstate" is much more than a memorable slogan. It has come to convey a deeper meaning about the Allstate brand and what that brand means to consumers

and the company itself. Packed into those famous words is the firm's commitment to be a company of people who feel a personal responsibility to help their customers meet their needs today and in the future. To deliver service that responds to customers when, where and how they want. And to take the time to understand a customer's insurance and financial needs and, as those needs change over time, be there to help the customer with appropriate insurance coverages and financial solutions.

As timeless and powerful as that brand commitment is, Allstate expects to deepen and evolve it. This evolution will no doubt reflect the continued growth and product expansion of Allstate Financial Group, as it builds on its already impressive product portfolio, customer-focused marketing, and financial results.

THINGS YOU DIDN'T KNOW ABOUT ALLSTATE INSURANCE CO.

○ The company's legendary slogan, "You're In Good Hands With Allstate," was created by a sales manager in 1950. A proposed ad layout showing a pair of protective hands symbolizing the security of insurance coverage reminded him of his relief when a hospital nurse had told him that his seriously ill daughter "was in good hands."

○ The first automobile insured by Allstate was a 1930 Studebaker Dictator 8. The annual premium was $41.50. The car is now on display at company headquarters.

○ The first claim made under an Allstate policy was paid on the spot by employee Richard Roskam to a customer who walked into the company's office in 1931 holding an automobile door handle broken off in a theft attempt.

○ The first computer at Allstate, an Electrodata 30-203, was installed in 1953, and its performance was equivalent to that of a modern pocket calculator.

○ Allstate revolutionized the insurance industry in 1952 by opening the first drive-in claim office.

THE MARKET

For many years, U.S. airlines conducted business under the relatively benevolent regulation of the Civil Aeronautics Board, operating in an air travel market noted for its high costs, seasonality, and uncertain cycles of profitability. The CAB controlled everything from routes to pricing to service.

Airline deregulation in 1979 opened the door to a host of new competitors. Spunky start-up carriers, operating hand-me-down jetliners

and often paying lower wages, rushed into the market offering bargain-basement fares.

Many of those start-ups would soon fail. Nonetheless, they extracted a toll on traditional airlines, which had generally high operating costs. Some tradition-bound airlines, unable to keep pace with the changing times, collapsed into bankruptcy or sold out to competitors. Others pared employment or forced workers to accept pay cuts.

If deregulation traumatized the industry, its fierce price-cutting lured millions of travelers to climb aboard for the first time. Air travel became commonplace for Americans in the 1980s and 1990s. The nation's airlines now enplane more than 1.7 million passengers every day on 23,000 domestic and international flights. More than 646,000 employees work in the U.S. industry, which pours nearly $300 billion into the national economy each year.

ACHIEVEMENTS

Since its inception seven decades ago, American Airlines has prided itself on industry leadership in such critical areas as safety, advanced aircraft and top-notch training for employees. It opened the industry's first stewardess training center in 1957 on a Fort Worth campus where, in 1970, a new Flight Academy would begin to train pilots, with the help of realistic flight simulators.

The airline's marketing heritage includes

the industry's first fare-discounting plan, the first family fares, and AAdvantage, the world's first and still largest travel awards program, with more than 40 million members. AAdvantage was made possible in part by Sabre, American's sophisticated computer system. With Sabre's help, the airline has supported its flight crews and other employees with the latest in automation. American harnessed the power of computers to fill seats, and it now reaches a growing number of travelers through AA.com, the industry's most visited web site.

HISTORY

In 1930, a holding company called the Aviation Corporation (AVCO) cobbled together a hodgepodge of air-mail carriers to create American Airways. The company brought together a disparate collection of independent-minded aviation outfits such as Robertson Aircraft Corporation, whose first air-mail flight from Chicago to St. Louis on April 15, 1926—by a boyish aviator named Charles Lindbergh—is considered the first by an AA predecessor.

The consolidated company truly became a single airline only after it was restructured as American Airlines in 1934, with a young executive named C. R. Smith as its president. Affable yet tough, Smith would guide the airline until 1968, only to be called out of semi-retirement in 1973 to help get the airline back on track.

Under Smith, American became an industry pacesetter when it introduced the revolutionary DC-3 in 1936. By 1937, AA had become the first airline to fly a million passengers. Two years later, it opened the world's most advanced airline base at New York's new LaGuardia Airport. LaGuardia incorporated another AA marketing innovation—its first of more than 50 Admirals Clubs for loyal customers.

Even during the war years, when AA people and aircraft were serving around the world, American pioneered the first scheduled air cargo service. With peace, American was flying the fastest, safest and

most comfortable prop-liners in the skies. By 1949 it became the first U.S. airline with an all-postwar fleet of pressurized aircraft, some of which pioneered transatlantic routes for the American Overseas Airlines subsidiary.

By the late 1950s, AA inaugurated the first nonstop coast-to-coast service with new Boeing 707s. That jetliner, and those that followed, revolutionized air travel.

Deregulation came as a jolt to traditional carriers in 1979. CEO Al Casey's management assured American's survival by replacing its fleet with smaller, more fuel-efficient jets and moving corporate headquarters from New York to Dallas/Fort Worth, Texas.

Casey's successor, Bob Crandall, pushed the development of Sabre, not only as a superior reservations system, but as a productive marketing tool. Combined with the new science of yield management, Sabre made possible the

deeply discounted Super SAAver fares that opened air travel to virtually everyone.

During the 1980s, AA's "Growth Plan," based on driving down average costs, permitted an ambitious expansion that included revamping the fleet and expanding its hub network. American Eagle, the regional carrier, was created to connect the hubs and smaller cities. At the same time, AA expanded to Europe, South America and Japan.

Like the rest of the industry, AA suffered painful losses in the early 1990s as a worldwide recession hit the economy. The company trimmed its staff and fleet, discontinuing service in weaker markets while rapidly expanding profitable nonairline businesses.

With profits restored, American was ready to begin growing again by 1998, signing an agreement with the Boeing Co. that assured it a modern fleet for the next 20 years.

THE PRODUCT
Today, American's "Silverbirds"—its proudly polished fleet of more than 700 jetliners with their distinctive blue, white and red stripes—operate worldwide. Besides a broad domestic network, the airline provides scheduled service throughout the Western Hemisphere as well as to Europe and Asia.

American Eagle, AA's regional airline affiliate, has grown into a major airline in its own right. Its modern fleet is quickly being transformed by the arrival of new regional jets.

With a combined fleet numbering about 965, American and "the Eagle" carry almost 100 million passengers between about 240 destinations every year.

RECENT DEVELOPMENTS
Under the leadership of Don Carty, who fol-

lowed Crandall as chairman and CEO in 1998, American has renewed its focus on the airline business, divesting itself of many non-airline businesses that had grown up over a period of many years. That focus on airline operations is apparent in American's massive investment in new and upgraded aircraft and airport terminals. American took delivery of 45 new Boeing aircraft in 1999 alone, introducing two new types to its fleet—the Boeing 777 and 737— on the same day.

On the ground, it is constructing $1 billion terminals at both New York Kennedy and Miami, and upgrading facilities at other major airports.

To fill gaps in the domestic route network, American acquired Reno Air to strengthen operations on the West Coast and American Eagle added Business Express in the Northeast. AA solidified its international network by helping to launch **one**world, an alliance of outstanding international airlines. New bilateral alliances with other carriers also broadened the scope of destinations AA could offer.

In 2000, Carty and his marketing team took the bold step of actually removing two rows of seats from every plane in order to spread out the remaining rows and create additional legroom throughout the coach cabin. The effort won the business and praise of tens of thousands of customers.

PROMOTION
Through the years, American's advertising has kept the crucial business passenger in mind with tag lines such as "The Airline for Professional Travelers," "America's Leading Airline," "Doing What We Do Best," and "Something Special in the Air" are among its other memorable slogans. Its advertising has capitalized on a reputation for reliability, notably with its famous "On-Time Machine" campaign. In years past, corporate image television advertising focused on various professionals—pilots, flight attendants, mechanics—doing their jobs. That theme has been replaced by more targeted local campaigns, such as the "Based Here, Best Here" blitz at its DFW home. That campaign, and a "We Mean Business in Chicago" promotion, preceded market-specific efforts in New York and Boston. The New York campaign, playing to the importance of bridges to that city's commuters, positioned American as an "air bridge" to many destinations.

And, of course, with its new legroom configuration, the company has touted its "More Room Throughout Coach" amenities in print, broadcast, outdoor, collateral—and even a shiny silver "More Roommobile" that travels the country showing customers the advantages of more room.

BRAND VALUES
Throughout its history, American Airlines has projected an image of safety, service and professionalism.

Research through the years confirms that the airline stands for reliable, consistent service, with professional employees and high standards. Business travelers say AA does better than major competitors in solving problems courteously and professionally.

Even in recent years, when unprecedented traffic volume and an aging national air traffic control system have sometimes made it difficult to achieve those goals, AA has enjoyed travelers' respect. It is a brand that has commanded air travelers' loyalty for more than 70 years.

THINGS YOU DIDN'T KNOW ABOUT AMERICAN AIRLINES

○ American was the first airline in the world to carry a million passengers, a milestone it passed in February 1937.

○ Today AA and American Eagle carry 95 million travelers every year.

○ The jet fleet operated by American is the world's largest, with more than 700 jet aircraft averaging 2,400 flights a day.

○ Once a strictly domestic airline, AA now serves more than 50 countries, from Europe to Asia to the Caribbean and all of Latin America.

○ On an average day, AA will receive more than 338,000 reservations calls, handle over 293,000 pieces of luggage, dish up more than 200,000 meals and snacks, and change more than 85 airplane tires, more than 31,000 per year.

THE MARKET

American Express Company is the world's largest issuer of charge and credit cards, the world's largest travel agency, and a respected global financial services and network services provider. Founded in 1850, the company provides a full range of financial services and products to its customers—ranging from American Express Travelers Cheques (the company's oldest product) to charge and credit cards, financial planning services, mutual funds and other investment products, and global network services through its partnerships with banks and financial institutions worldwide.

Through its family of Corporate Card and business travel services, American Express helps companies manage their travel, entertainment and purchasing expenses. It provides investment management services to corporations and administers pension and other employee benefit plans. The company also offers accounting and tax preparation services to small businesses, as well as financial education services to employees at their places of work.

As the world's largest travel agency, American Express offers travel and related consulting services to individuals and corporations around the world. The company also provides private banking services and personal financial services to individuals outside the United States.

ACHIEVEMENTS

Few companies survive to celebrate their 150th anniversaries, as American Express Company did in 2000, and in the global financial services sector there are few globally recognized brands. American Express has not only survived, but continues to thrive in an increasingly competitive marketplace.

HISTORY

The express and freight forwarding business upon which American Express was founded in 1850 was an essential service, and the people who manned the stagecoaches, express wagons and railway cars were rugged individuals whose duties were frequently romanticized by the public.

During the latter half of the 19th century, as Americans developed an intense appetite for travel, the company expanded its freight forwarding services into Europe. Americans abroad began to rely on the company for travel advice, and American Express increasingly became a travel services company.

With the outbreak of World War I in 1914, American Express' international growth plans were quashed. When the United States entered the war several years later, the railroads were commandeered for government purposes, and the express and freight companies were consolidated into a single entity which took over the pooled equipment of all the express companies.

However, with its strong money order sales and the introduction of the travelers cheque in 1891, American Express had diversified its businesses enough to separate its growing travel and financial operations from the freight and express businesses. Although operations and the number of employees had to be pared down with the loss of its core business, the company thrived. The travel business flourished, and the company's financial businesses also performed well.

By the early 1950s, American Express had solidified its position as one of the world's premier travel companies. Its offices around the globe—like the famous 11, rue Scribe site in Paris—were every American traveler's "home away from home". The company's travelers cheques became (and remain) the best-selling product of their kind in the world. American Express' international banking business expanded,

and the company's contracts with the U.S. government to provide banking services to military personnel and their families stationed outside the United States following World War II helped build a broader customer base for the company.

But the 1950s also brought about another dramatic transformation of American Express. In 1958, American Express launched the American Express Card, which became the touchstone for the company's next transformation. The card business, which had been viewed as supplemental, quickly became the company's core business.

The advent of computers and other technological advancements during the 1960s helped spur the growth and streamline processes of the card business and the company's other businesses, as well. In the 1970s and early 1980s, American Express diversified its holdings through acquisitions and became what the business press dubbed a "financial supermarket". In a series of moves designed to broaden its earn-

ings base, the company acquired Shearson, IDS Financial Services and a Swiss private bank, Trade Development Bank.

During the early 1990s, the company survived a series of financial setbacks, divested its non-core businesses like its Shearson and Lehman Brothers subsidiaries, and went through

a lengthy period of re-engineering. The company focused single-mindedly on the brand and its application. The company's U.S. financial planning unit—long known as IDS Financial Services—was rebranded in 1995 as American Express Financial Advisors. Through re-engineering and market share gains in several of its businesses, American Express once again became a growth company.

THE PRODUCT

American Express' principal lines of business are organized into four groups: The Global Financial Services Group (which includes American Express Financial Advisors and American Express Bank); the U.S. Consumer and Small Business Services Group (which includes its credit and charge card businesses); the Global Corporate Services Group (which includes the company's Corporate Card and corporate travel businesses); and the Global Establishment Services and Travelers Cheque Group.

Through these four groups, American Express serves the broad needs of its global customer base. Whether for a cardmember, a financial planning client, an international private banking client, a student booking a tour through a travel service office or a small business owner, American Express provides customized service designed to meet each customer's unique needs.

RECENT DEVELOPMENTS

Over the past several years, the company has begun to more aggressively introduce new products and services into the marketplace. Building on the success of its ubiquitous green American Express Card, the company today increasingly offers products that are customized for its customers' diverse needs.

During 1999 alone, the company launched more than a dozen new credit and charge card products, including the ultra-premium Centurion Card which is available by invitation only and the revolutionary Blue from American Express with smart chip functionality.

The company has also expanded its presence internationally, both through the launch of its own card and financial services products and through its Global Network Services (GNS) business. Launched in 1996, GNS now provides card network services through partnerships with

banks and financial institutions in more than 70 countries around the world.

American Express has also reaffirmed its commitment to customer privacy—not just in the offline world, where it has long been an acknowledged leader, but also in the online world. In 2000, the company introduced Private Payments, which allows cardmembers to use a unique number designed for a single online purchase.

PROMOTION

American Express has long been known for its inventive advertising. Whether it was Karl Malden intoning "Don't leave home without them" on television in the 1960s, the "Do You Know Me?" campaign of the 1970s, the "Membership Has Its Privileges" campaign of the 1980s or the highly visible participation of

ARE YOU A CARDMEMBER?

American Express is a proud sponsor of the
World Golf Championships.
© 2000 American Express.

Jerry Seinfeld and Tiger Woods as American Express spokesmen in the 1990s and beyond, advertising has long played a role in American Express' sustained visibility.

But the power of advertising is only one component of the company's visibility. The

company also has leveraged the power of its Blue Box logo. Since its introduction in 1975, the logo has become one of the world's most familiar corporate identifiers. This is in part due to the global nature of American Express' business; the Blue Box appears on travelers cheques, travel and financial services locations and communications, as well as on a broad range of charge and credit card products.

It is also due in part to the extension of that identifier into new media. The American Express website—www.americanexpress.com—is anchored by the Blue Box, and provides the company's customers with access to a wide range of products and services. They may view their card account information, pay their American Express bills online, book travel reservations, conduct online brokerage and banking transactions, and access powerful financial research and planning tools.

BRAND VALUES

Ever since its days as a freight forwarding company, the American Express brand has exemplified trust, security, and exemplary customer service. Throughout the company's leadership in a number of industries—freight forwarding, travel and tourism, travelers cheques, credit and charge cards, financial services—the core attributes of the American Express brand have endured.

The past several years have been a time of rebirth for American Express, and the transformation the company has undergone is no less dramatic than its previous reinventions. Part of the reason for its current success is the focus on the American Express brand. The fundamental elements that made the company successful a hundred years earlier—values like trust, integrity, aspiration, quality and service—are still the basic tenets upon which all of its businesses are built.

Photograph of Jerry Seinfeld by Mark Seliger.
Archival photos courtesy of American Express Corporate Archives.

THINGS YOU DIDN'T KNOW ABOUT AMERICAN EXPRESS

○ Two of the three founders of American Express were Henry Wells and William Fargo—who also founded Wells Fargo.

○ One of the earliest emblems used to represent American Express was a photograph of a bulldog atop a locked strongbox—symbolizing trust, vigilance, and security.

○ An American Express employee named Marcellus Berry invented the travelers cheque, which the company introduced in 1891.

○ Following World War II, American Express was engaged by the U.S. government to help transport the belongings of soldiers stationed abroad, and one especially memorable initiative—Operation Pooch—involved shipping more than 10,000 adopted dogs back to the United States for reunions with their owners.

○ During the early 1980s, through a joint venture with Warner Communications, American Express helped fund the start-up of MTV.

American Red Cross
Together, we can save a life

THE MARKET

Every year, millions of Americans face life-threatening disasters, from huge hurricanes and floods that displace thousands to fires that rob a single family of a place called home. Such crises strike every day. Every two seconds, someone needs a blood transfusion. At home and at work, people suffer from heart attacks or need first aid.

Fortunately, there are also millions of Americans who want to help themselves, their families, and others prevent, prepare for and respond to life's emergencies. They are people who give their time, their money, even their blood, to save the life of someone down the street, across the country or around the world. The American Red Cross brings together people in the global community who are committed to help save lives.

ACHIEVEMENTS

The American Red Cross network of more than 1,000 chapters, Blood Services regions, and Armed Forces Emergency Services stations makes it the country's premier humanitarian services organization. With combined annual revenues exceeding $2 billion, including some $817 million in contributions in 1999, the Red

Cross consistently ranks among the nation's largest and most respected nonprofit humanitarian organizations.

Some 83,000 trained Red Cross volunteers respond to more than 63,000 disasters each year with immediate help such as food, clothing, shelter, and encouragement. These volunteers stay until all disaster-caused needs are met.

Through voluntary donations, the American Red Cross supplies almost half of the nation's blood and blood products. It also operates the Holland Laboratory, a $30 million national research facility in suburban Washington, D.C. The Holland Lab saves lives one by one through significant contributions to biomedical science, blood safety, plasma-derived therapeutics, and transfusion technology.

In 1999, the Red Cross trained 12 million people in such lifesaving skills as first aid, CPR, swimming and water safety, and today in such cutting-edge technology as Automatic External Defibrillators (AEDs).

An AED is a device that, when used during or shortly after cardiac arrest, can improve victim survival rates by 40 percent.

The American Red Cross also touches people in communities across the nation through the provision of nearly 25 million individual services. These services include food pantries and hot lunch programs, hospital and nursing home visitation programs, transportation to and from medical appointments, and transitional housing programs.

Long separations when a service member is stationed or deployed overseas can strain military families. The American Red Cross is there for them around the clock with emergency communications and assistance following the death or serious illness of a family member, the birth of a child, or other critical family matters.

As part of the International Red Cross and Red Crescent Movement, the American Red Cross works to alleviate human suffering around the world. During 1999 it linked or reunited U.S. families with loved ones in 115 countries on six continents. And the American Red Cross is expanding its involvement with other Red Cross and Red Crescent societies worldwide to bring urgently needed relief to the victims of disasters and armed conflicts in more than 30 countries around the world.

HISTORY

In 1862, Swiss businessman Henry Dunant wrote of witnessing 40,000 troops killed or wounded and left without help on a battlefield in Northern Italy. His concern ultimately led to the birth in 1863 of the International Committee of the Red Cross

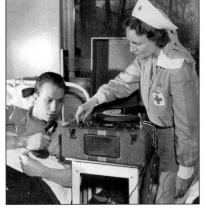

(ICRC) and, later, to the Geneva Conventions, a series of international treaties designed to protect victims of war and armed conflict. In honor of his vision and humanitarian contribution, Dunant was a co-recipient of the first Nobel Peace Prize in 1901.

During the American Civil War, the visionary Clara Barton cared for the wounded on battlefields; she learned about the Red Cross movement later while work-

ing in relief efforts for civilians during the Franco-Prussian War. Upon her return to the United States, Barton received assurance that the U.S. government would sign the Geneva Conventions. She founded the American Association of the Red Cross on May 21, 1881.

Barton led a group of nurses to Cuba during the Spanish-American War to provide care, medical supplies, and food to civilians and troops. But among Barton's most unique contributions to the growing worldwide Red Cross Movement was organizing volunteers to help disaster victims.

The U.S. Congress granted the American Red Cross its first charter in 1900, later revised in 1905, making it responsible for providing services to members of the armed forces and relief to disaster victims at home and abroad.

In 1910 the Red Cross responded to a rash of industrial accidents by instituting first aid training; four years later, it sought to combat the soaring number of accidental drownings by introducing water safety instruction.

During World War I, the Red Cross was transformed into a huge humanitarian organization raising more than $400 million in supplies and donations to support its services.

In early 1941, under the direction of Dr. Charles Drew, a pioneer in the development of plasma, the Red Cross laid the groundwork for a national blood program called Blood Donor Services. During World War II, Red Cross volunteers served on the battlefield and in hospitals, recruited blood donors, provided recreational activities for the troops, and supplied 27 million food parcels weekly to United States and Allied prisoners of war. Similar heroic services

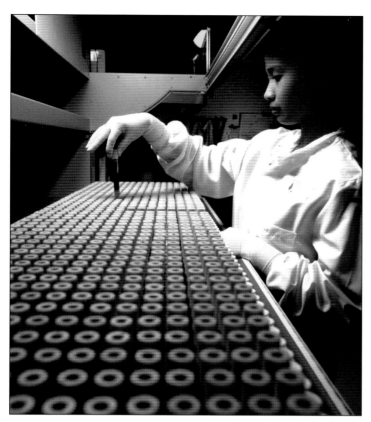

were carried out during the Korean and Vietnam wars.

Today's Red Cross is a far more comprehensive and professional organization, yet it continues to advance the same humanitarian mission under the principles championed by Dunant and Barton.

THE PRODUCT

The American Red Cross provides basic services—disaster relief, blood and biomedical services, health and safety training, assistance to military families, international services—as it seeks to find additional ways to enhance personal safety and security and help save lives in every community.

Operating a 24-hour Disaster Operations Center, the Red Cross can deploy workers, equipment, and supplies nationwide at a moment's notice. The Blood and Biomedical Services program of the Red Cross is the nation's largest supplier of blood, plasma, and human-tissue products, enhancing and saving the lives of countless Americans.

The Red Cross presence is felt globally by military personnel through the services of more than 40,000 volunteers. Often with the International Red Cross and Red Crescent Movement, the American Red Cross responds to international emergencies while promoting self-sufficiency and building emerging relief and development capacities of other national societies.

RECENT DEVELOPMENTS

The American Red Cross continually harnesses the power of innovative technology to find bet-

ter ways of serving communities, with the goal of saving more lives.

Led by Dr. Bernadine Healy, president and chief executive officer of the American Red Cross, the organization is identifying more effective ways of providing international relief and continued blood safety improvements.

To better serve military families, the Red Cross recently completed a three-year modernization of its Armed Forces Emergency Services, increasing efficiency and reducing operating costs by consolidating the emergency communications work from military installations into a small number of centers.

PROMOTION

The American Red Cross is uniquely positioned, largely through its high visibility, when disaster strikes and through its lifesaving blood system. In addition, by presidential proclamation every year since 1943, March is Red Cross Month, an opportunity for chapters and blood regions to spotlight their services in communities nationwide. Market research consistently indicates that the Red Cross is ranked by consumers as first among nonprofit organizations in terms of favorability (76 percent) and trust (80 percent).

The American Red Cross creates award-winning multimedia advertising campaigns to promote its brand to the American public. These advertisements are run by broadcast, print, and new media as a public service and generate an estimated $40-$60 million worth of donated visibility each year.

Over the years numerous celebrities from Shirley Temple to Harrison Ford have lent their names to Red Cross messages to add impact to the charity's communications. The Red Cross also enjoys strong cooperation from corporations that help sponsor or secure Red Cross advertising placements.

Target Corporation and Federal Express Corporation are among the founding members of the Annual Disaster Giving Program, in which companies make significant contributions to disaster relief efforts and are then recognized nationally, regionally, and locally following major disasters. Retail giants, including Lowe's Home Improvement Warehouse and the Food Lion grocery chain, have helped disaster victims and local Red Cross chapters by donating money and products. A number of initiatives with Internet companies such as America Online and Yahoo! help promote visibility online every day.

BRAND VALUES

Throughout all its messages, the American Red Cross reinforces the deep trust and respect the American public has for an organization that, as research demonstrates, people trust to help save lives and to enhance their personal safety and security. The new American Red Cross slogan, "Together, we can save a life," highlights the personal satisfaction that supporters feel in partnering with this great organization to save lives.

THINGS YOU DIDN'T KNOW ABOUT AMERICAN RED CROSS

❍ In 1999, the American Red Cross collected more than 6.1 million units of blood from approximately 4.5 million people.

❍ The American Red Cross Holocaust and War Victims Tracing and Information Center opened in 1990 after captured Nazi documents from the archives of the former Soviet Union were released, enabling the Red Cross to trace the fate of thousands of victims.

❍ The news of founder Clara Barton's death on April 12, 1912 was overshadowed by coverage of the sinking of RMS Titanic. Appropriately enough, the American Red Cross Emergency Relief Committee received the Titanic survivors from the Carpathia and processed assistance of over $150,000 to families and survivors of those lost at sea.

❍ Five-time Olympic gold medallist swimmer Johnny Weissmuller, perhaps even better known as the star of 19 "Tarzan" movies in the 1930s and 1940s, often volunteered at American Red Cross aquatic schools.

ARROW

THE MARKET

The men's apparel market is continually evolving as it strives to satisfy a diversity of fashion trends. Over the past several years, the industry has experienced a shift in the workplace dress code, with business casual wear on the rise. Although the dress shirt market has experienced a decline over the last several years, this segment now appears to be stabilizing. A dressier casual look has sparked a fashion resurgence, and experimentation with various fabrications, style, and color has resulted in renewed interest. The sportswear market continues to enjoy an upward trend, with both woven and knit shirts experiencing increased sales. With the turn of the century, advancements in technology will certainly influence the apparel manufacturer. So, too, the changing lifestyle of the consumer will transform this industry.

ACHIEVEMENTS

Founded in 1851, The Arrow Company will soon celebrate its 150th anniversary. Withstanding the test of time, Arrow commands extraordinary brand recognition. In 1876 at a ceremony celebrating the United States' centennial, Arrow was awarded a bronze medal as a symbol of its commitment to quality and in recognition for its outstanding influence on American men's fashion. Early in the twentieth century, Arrow became the dominant shirt maker in North America. By the 1950s, it was one of the five most recognized American brands in the world.

The Arrow Company is committed to producing quality merchandise and it designs apparel that is fashionable yet provides comfort and functionality. With these goals in mind, Arrow was the first menswear company to introduce the wrinkle-free dress shirt. This revolutionary fabric proved to be a consumer favorite and continues to be a best seller. As fashion trends change, Arrow continues to be a mainstay of the men's apparel industry. Sold throughout the world, Arrow products can be found in over seventy countries.

HISTORY

In the mid-1800s, a small manufacturer of men's detachable collars opened in Troy, New York. This modest beginning would lead to the emergence of the Arrow brand as a leader in men's fashion. By the turn of the century, Cluett, Peabody & Company owned the Arrow trademark, and Frederick Peabody had turned Arrow into a household name.

In 1905, commercial artist J. C. Leyendecker created the

Arrow Collar Man, an image that appeared in advertisements across the country. So popular was this figure, that the Arrow Collar Man became the symbol of the ideal American male and was the recipient of fan mail as well as marriage proposals. The Arrow Collar Man became synonymous with style. As the times changed, every new model that the Arrow Collar Man wore became the height of fashion. Arrow's business was booming, with over 400 different collar styles being manufactured. By the end of World War I, however, the detachable collar was virtually obsolete. Returning soldiers had grown accustomed to the softer, attached collars of their uniforms. Answering their demands, Arrow introduced "Trump" in the late 1920s as the brand's first dress shirt and within several years had introduced dress shirts in a variety of colors and stripes. By the early 1930s, Arrow had successfully entered the sportswear market. By the 1940s dress shirts were loose fitting and sport shirts were designed in bright colors and floral patterns.

Throughout the years, Arrow has continued to respond to shifting fashion trends. As the stability of the 1950s gave way to the turbulent 1960s, Arrow replaced its conventional white dress shirt with colorful, more flamboyant designs. By 1968, less than half of Arrow shirts sold were solid white. During the 1970s and '80s, Arrow redesigned its line, appealing to the renewed conservatism of the

ARROW COLLARS & SHIRTS FOR DRESS

Extroverted Shirts. If you're fat and forty, forget it.

All of a sudden, it's Spring. And along comes Arrow with flowers in every color except Shrinking Violet. Shirts that can stop — as well as start — any conversation. High-band, 4½ inch collars, rounded double- and triple-button cuffs, in a taper that's measured in ounces, not pounds. Introverts, beware. These shirts are not really for every one. Or at least, not for every body. **-Arrow-**

Mach II by Arrow

young, urban professional with a resurgence of classic tailoring and natural fibers, as well as the synthetic fabrics, tapering darts, and oversized collars of the disco-inspired look. The downswing in the dress shirt market during the 1990s has abated as the millennium brings renewed interest to this market segment. Arrow has forged a remarkable record since its humble beginning; and with the advent of the twenty-first century, it continues to be regarded as a leader in American men's fashion.

THE PRODUCT

The Arrow brand name is featured on a variety of men's and boys' apparel. Its products not only include sportswear and dress shirts, but encompass sweaters, pants, shorts, underwear, neck-

wear and socks, as well. Both sport and dress shirts are also offered in a variety of big and tall styles to satisfy this specific market segment. Focusing on the consumers' demand for clothing that conforms to their lifestyle needs, Arrow is committed to providing comfort and functionality in its design.

The sportswear line is predominated by the Arrow's Khaki Label, the number one selling moderate priced sportswear brand in the United States. Launched in February of 1999, its popularity has led to a complete collection including woven shirts, knits, vests, sweaters, jackets, pants, and shorts. Constructed of soft, cotton fabrics, the Arrow's Khaki Label is recognized for its comfort, fashion and wide array of styles.

Arrow's Blue label, a new sportswear line, will be introduced in the Spring of 2002. This denim driven line will be a complement to the Arrow's Khaki label. the collection will consist of T-shirts, knits, woven, and vests. Arrow's Blue label will be geared toward the more cool, comfortable and casual lifestyle.

The Arrow dress shirt line is well known for its mainstream staples of oxford and broadcloth styles. The brand, however, has recently debuted a line featuring technical fabrics such as stretch, microfiber, and Tencel. These superior fabrics offer the ultimate in ease and function, featuring smooth, lustrous finishes, and extra softness. Arrow dress shirts also feature a variety of textures and colors. Today's Arrow shirt line features a mix of traditional styles, as well as a fresh, new approach to the dress shirt business.

RECENT DEVELOPMENTS

An official sponsor of The National Archery Association, Arrow is the exclusive supplier of apparel for both the Senior and Junior United States Archery Teams. The Arrow Company is proud to be associated with this fine organization and its deserving athletes.

In recent months, the Phillips-Van Heusen Corporation has licensed the Arrow brand name from Cluett, Peabody & Co., Inc. The merging of these two well-established shirt manufacturers will have significant impact on the men's apparel business.

PROMOTION

The Arrow Company promotes its products through innovative point of sale displays, magazine and newspaper advertisements, fixture design, and in-store presentations. Together with its retail partners, Arrow develops promotional events tailored specifically for the customer on a regional and national basis. The Arrow Company invests in sponsorships, as well. During the 1960s, the company was an official sponsor of the prestigious Masters Golf Tournament in Augusta, Georgia. Most recently, Arrow has become a sponsor as well as the exclusive supplier of attire for the National Archery Association competitions.

BRAND VALUES

The Arrow Company is committed to manufacturing a quality product that is stylish and affordable and the success of the Arrow brand can be attributed to its name recognition and attention to detail. Through its research and development, The Arrow Company focuses on the needs of the consumer, resulting in high brand awareness and customer loyalty. As a result, Arrow remains in the forefront of the men's apparel industry.

THINGS YOU DIDN'T KNOW ABOUT ARROW

❍ In 1923, the Arrow Collar Man became the subject of a Broadway musical by George S. Kaufman and Marc Connelly entitled "Helen of Troy, New York," featuring the show-stopping number, "My Arrow Collar Man."

❍ Mrs. Orlando Montague, the wife of a fastidious blacksmith who demanded a clean shirt for his frequent evening engagements, invented the detachable collar in 1820. Tired of laundering numerous shirts, she removed the collars, hemmed the edges, and attached strings to hold them in place, making it easy for her husband to have a fresh collar each evening.

❍ At the height of the detachable collar craze, the well-dressed man had charts denoting the appropriate collar to wear at every time of the day and for every occasion.

❍ The shrinkage problem in men's shirts was solved in 1928 by Sanford L. Cluett who developed a patent to significantly minimize the shrinkage in cotton fabric. This process, called "Sanforizing," continues to be used today by cotton finishers worldwide.

❍ Over the years, celebrities such as singer Tony Bennett, magician David Copperfield, model Fabio, football stars Joe Namath and Fran Tarkenton, and tennis champion Jim Courier, have promoted the Arrow product.

Audi

THE MARKET

Even as car and light truck sales in the United States have experienced steady year-over-year growth since 1995, the market for premium and luxury cars has grown even more. Within this segment, no brand has achieved faster growth than Audi. With consecutive double-digit sales gains every year since 1995, Audi has rapidly established an influential position in one of the market's most competitive segments.

The lucrative premium segment continues to attract new entries and spawn new products, assuring that the level of competition will remain intense. In this environment, Audi's well-engineered automobiles led the company to best-ever sales in 2000 with the prospect of greater success in years to come.

ACHIEVEMENTS

Audi's history is one of pioneering innovations and breakthrough products. This continues today with such cars as the much-coveted TT Coupe and Roadster, the high-performance S4 sedan and the Audi allroad quattro, a vehicle that will set new standards for on- and off-road performance and versatility.

From the beginning, Audi built cars to succeed in motor sports. August Horch, founder of the company, was at the wheel when his Audi won the prestigious Austrian Alpine Run in 1911. In the thirties the innovative Auto Union Silver Arrow race cars thundered to scores of victories in events ranging from Grand Prix races to hill climbs and land speed records. More recently, the revolutionary quattro® all-wheel drive system was so successful in international rallying and touring car racing through the 80s and 90s that it was eventually banned, ostensibly as an "unfair advantage." And most recently, in June 2000, Audi's R8 sports cars swept to a dominating 1-2-3 finish at the world-famous Le Mans 24-hour endurance race in France.

Audi continues to pioneer concepts that set new standards for innovation and customer acceptance. Its production cars benefit directly from technology originally engineered for motor sports. The quattro all-wheel drive system, while banned from racing, is available on the full range of Audi models. The engines in all U.S. Audi models employ a unique five-valve technology first tested in Audi race cars built for long-distance endurance record setting.

HISTORY

August Horch started an automobile business under his own name in 1899, but 10 years later, the gifted but headstrong founder was forced out by company directors who objected, among other things, to the time he spent on the company's racing cars.

Horch immediately established a second company, eventually calling it Audi, a Latin derivation of his own surname. True to his original concept, the firm produced well-equipped cars that proved quite successful in the market and in competitive events.

The Horch and Audi firms joined forces in 1932 with DKW and Wanderer to form Auto Union, which later became today's Audi AG. The 1969 merger with NSU, a respected innovator in its own right, brought the company to its current state. In 1999, Audi celebrated 100 years of automotive tradition in the headquarters city of Ingolstadt, Germany.

Audi exports to the U.S. market began in 1970 with two models and the sale of some 7,600 cars. Over one million cars later, Audi of America has grown to become a leader in the luxury segment and a company recognized for performance, advanced technology, and attractive designs.

As a global producer of premium automobiles, Audi operates worldwide with production facilities on four continents. In 2000, sales amounted to approximately 650,000 cars and over 1.1 million engines. Additional capacity and favorable acceptance in over 100 countries around the world bode well for more growth.

THE PRODUCT

In recent years, Audi introduced a broad range of luxurious and high-performance cars and, most recently, the allroad quattro, an on- and off-road performer with unparalleled capability.

Audi's return to prominence in America was anchored by the A4 range. Now comprised of two sedans and two Avant models—Audi's term for its wagons—the A4s combine sporting dynamics with a level of refinement unexpected in this class. These are the most accessible Audi models and have introduced tens of thousands of new owners to the brand.

The sporting capabilities of the A4 range received a pronounced boost with the quattro-equipped S4 biturbo model. This powerful sports sedan has been joined by an Avant companion to offer driving enthusiasts a healthy dose of power and dynamic capability with a choice of two body styles.

Audi's award-winning designs frequently lead the industry in new directions. The A6 could be the signature model for this position-

ing. With a sleek Avant model and three power trains for the sedans, the A6 offers arguably the most expressive and attractive range of premium automobiles.

A good part of the attraction in a prestige car lies in its exclusivity, a high level of performance, and generous equipment. The groundbreaking Audi A8 sedan adds an unprecedented level of technology and safety to that established formula. Its high-tech all-aluminum Audi Space Frame construction (ASF®) has proven its merit with best-in-class crash test results. In 2001 Audi added an S8 version to crown the range with both high-performance and outstanding equipment.

The now available TT Coupe and Roadster have created a sensation of design purity.

Finally, Audi is about to change the rules for those who might consider a sport utility vehicle.

The allroad is a new cross-over concept that brings together the best of both worlds. Luxury and high-performance on-the-road manners are combined with the kind of off-road capability previously reserved for truck-based SUVs.

RECENT DEVELOPMENTS

Audi's renaissance over the past half-dozen years is due in equal part to exciting, attractive products and a dedication to the needs of its clients. Even before the current range achieved its acclaim, Audi was the first carmaker to introduce a vehicle warranty so comprehensive that it even covered the cost of all required service during the warranty term. This level of customer care is now widely imitated but rarely so comprehensively applied as by Audi.

After securely establishing a product range and progressive customer treatment policies that have been met with wide acclaim, Audi is moving on to integrate its brand values into all aspects of the ownership experience. This will manifest itself in many ways: new retail facilities that express a New World of Audi, personal client contacts and experiences that build strong relationships, a high degree of consistency in the brand's messages and new ways of reaching owners and those who aspire to the brand.

PROMOTION

Communicating Audi's message is a multi-faceted task that takes in traditional media, new media and other forms of communication and sponsorship. In the belief that any of these experiences represents the brand, Audi's goal is to make the message consistent across all media, all materials and all markets.

Within its message Audi regularly challenges conventional thinking and employs the value of understatement to make a stronger presentation. The promise of surpassing performance and surpassed expectations is delivered with charm—perhaps a twinkle in the eye —rather than with superlatives or claims.

Audi's advertising partner is the Raleigh, N.C., based agency McKinney & Silver. With stylish and sophisticated executions, the materials developed form an integrated whole, including television work as well as print for a range of magazines and newspapers. The television tonality conveys the essence of the automobile and brand while print executions often take a more direct tack in presenting specific details and offers.

In a less traditional medium, the company's web site—www.audiusa.com—provides a place for interested parties to linger over rich information and to explore specific cars, financing options, and competitive information.

BRAND VALUES

Defining those things that are the essence of Audi's products — Advanced Technology, Design, Performance, Emotion—leads to greater clarity in establishing the values of the Audi brand. This requires going beyond the hardware side of the equation and leads to the conclusion that it is actually people who give life to the brand. At its core, the Audi brand is characterized by the words human, passionate, leading and visionary. More than simply words, these terms give definition to the character and practices of Audi—and of its people—in interactions with clients and others who are attracted to the brand. The ability to experience the brand in this way determines how people think and feel when interacting in everyday situations.

THINGS YOU DIDN'T KNOW ABOUT AUDI

○ The well-recognized Audi four rings logo symbolizes the four distinct brands that merged in 1932 to form Auto Union, predecessor to today's Audi AG. The companies are Audi, DKW, Horch, and Wanderer.

○ Audi is one of only a handful of automotive firms able to draw upon more than a century of tradition. Founder August Horch established his first automobile company in Germany in 1899.

○ Audi subsidiaries Lamborghini S.p.A. in Italy and Cosworth Technology Ltd. in the UK are world renowned for, respectively, exotic sports cars and advanced vehicle powertrains and research.

○ Audi draws on over two decades of experience in all-wheel drive cars. In the U.S. market, about 80 percent of today's Audis are equipped with quattro® all-wheel drive.

THE MARKET

Bayer Corporation's Consumer Care Division, based in Morris Township, N.J., produces many of the most trusted and best-known medical products in the world: Bayer® Aspirin, Alka-Seltzer®, and Phillips'® Milk of Magnesia. All have maintained that status with generation after generation of consumers, despite unrelenting challenges from competitors who have entered the same markets, often advertising that their newer products were better than the long-established brands. Bayer Aspirin alone has more than 100 competitors.

ACHIEVEMENTS

The Bayer Consumer Care Division is among the largest manufacturers of over-the-counter medications in the world. Three of its major brands—Bayer Aspirin, Alka-Seltzer, and Phillips' Milk of Magnesia—originated with a

single product and each is now offered in a variety of choices to meet consumers' specific requirements.

HISTORY

Bayer Aspirin, Alka-Seltzer, and Phillips' Milk of Magnesia all have long and distinguished histories.

In the late 1890s, a chemist at Friedrich Bayer and Company who was seeking a way to relieve his father's arthritic pain, began looking into acetylsalicylic acid (ASA). He developed a stable form of ASA powder, and the compound became the active ingredient in a new pain-reliever that the company called "aspirin."

The name was derived by using the "a" from acetyl and "spirea," a plant that is a natural source of salicin.

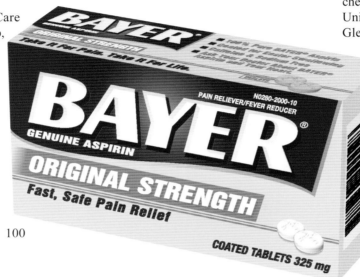

Bayer began providing aspirin in powder form to physicians for dispensing to their patients, and it quickly became the most widely used pain reliever in the world. In 1900, the product became one of the first major drugs to be offered in a convenient tablet form.

Aspirin gained vastly increased medical significance as a result of a physician's research that showed that a group of men who took it regularly had a substantially decreased incidence of heart attacks. The findings led Bayer to the exploration of the cardiovascular benefits of aspirin.

Alka-Seltzer was created in 1928 by the Dr. Miles Laboratories of Elkhart, Ind., in response to a widespread influenza epidemic. The company had already produced medicines in effervescent form. Its ease of use and ability to deal with a wide range of aches, pains, colds, upset stomach, and overindulgence made it highly popular. Sales of the effervescent, alkalizing tablet exceeded all expectations. (A company official who had purchased five pounds of cotton to make the small wads that would be stuffed into each bottle worried that he had over-estimated the need).

Phillips' Milk of Magnesia first reached the market in 1873 and quickly became a staple in American medicine cabinets. While magnesia had long been used as a remedy, its use was declining because of two factors—impurities in the commercial products then available and the difficulty of ingesting it in powder form. Charles H. Phillips, an English

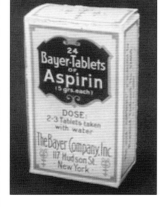

chemist (pharmacist) who had migrated to the United States and established a laboratory in Glenbrook, Conn., overcame both of those problems in developing Phillips' Milk of Magnesia.

The Bayer Consumer Care Division was created in 1995 following Bayer's $1 billion purchase of the North American over-the-counter business of Sterling Winthrop. In that transaction, Bayer regained the North American rights to its flagship aspirin brand. Germany-based Bayer had lost those rights in 1918 when they were sold at auction because the U.S. and Germany were at war.

Phillips' was also a part of Sterling and Bayer had previously acquired Alka-Seltzer in the purchase of Miles Laboratories.

THE PRODUCT

Bayer Aspirin offers its product in original, extra, and children's strengths while another choice is Aspirin Regimen to help prevent cardiovascular disease.

Alka-Seltzer offers a wide range of product choices for heartburn, acid indigestion, sour stomach with headache, body aches, and other pains and for sleeplessness accompanied by pain.

Phillips' has expanded its original line and now offers its Milk of Magnesia products in the Original, Mint, and Cherry flavors and in chewable mint-flavor tablets; Fiber Caps, a bulk-forming fiber laxative; and Liqui-Gels, a stool-softener laxative.

RECENT DEVELOPMENTS

During the past 12 years, physicians have placed more than 50 million Americans on aspirin therapy for prevention of a second heart attack, a move that could potentially prevent 210,000 heart attacks a year. In addition, the Food and Drug Administration has recognized aspirin's potential to reduce the risk of death by as much as 23 percent if taken as directed by a physician as soon as a heart attack is suspected.

Bayer points out that the product introduced more than a century ago as a pain killer is today "not only known for its effect on the heart, but it is generally regarded as one of the safest, most important, and cost-effective tools in the fight against cardiovascular disease, the world's number one killer."

The company has also embarked on a continuing research project to explore links between aspirin and pre-

vention of other diseases that include some cancers, diabetes, migraine headaches, and Alzheimer's Disease.

New Alka-Seltzer products include "Heartburn Relief" to reach the 25 million Americans who suffer from heartburn every day.

PROMOTION

In 1997, Bayer celebrated aspirin's 100th anniversary with an event that drew worldwide publicity—30 mountaineers wrapped the company's high-rise administration building in Leverkusen, Germany, with 32 strips of cloth, weighting 8.8 tons, that made the structure resemble the largest package of Aspirin® ever

created. More than 200,000 visitors came to see the attraction.

Bayer Aspirin, in cooperation with the American Stroke Association, sponsors the American Stroke Challenge, a national stroke awareness and fund-raising initiative. The 2000 and 2001 events included a $1-million hole-in-one golf contest in which golf courses throughout the country participated.

Alka-Seltzer's promotions since the product first hit the market have included some of the most memorable advertising campaigns in business history.

Among them: the "Speedy" Alka-Seltzer character, "Plop, plop, fizz, fizz," "Relief is only a swallow away," "Try it, you'll like it," "I can't believe I ate the whole thing," "One spicy meatball," and the famous "stomachs" campaign. Many of the company's themes have come into popular use as part of the American language and culture.

Phillips' Milk of Magnesia relies primarily on television in its promotion campaigns. The company occasionally uses free-standing inserts in major newspapers to put money-saving coupons in the hands of potential purchasers but does not otherwise rely on print advertising.

BRAND VALUES

All three of the products of the Bayer Company have long been staples of medicine cabinets throughout the nation because of their reputations associated with their names.

"Genuine Bayer Aspirin," the company says, "is the most trusted name in aspirin," providing "fast, safe, effective pain relief." This allows consumers to trust in its slogan "Take it for pain. Take it for life."

The strength of the Phillips' brand is still based on the same foundation described by an official at the midpoint of the product's 127-year history:

"(The company) moves securely onward, firm in the knowledge that the substantial products of its laboratories, backed by years of experience, will always have a ready acceptance and merited popularity."

Phillips' Milk of Magnesia's strongest brand value is its 127-year history as a trusted product for solving constipation and regularity problems. It has held the trust of succeeding generations of consumers seeking relief from constipation. The reason behind that enduring popularity is summed up in the brand slogan: "Effective

Relief Without Harsh Stimulants."

The Alka-Seltzer brand, now in its 70th year, has long been recognized as one of the greatest home remedies of all time. It is one of the most visible products of its type.

Consumer loyalty is so strong that a citrus flavored formula offered in the early 1960s was dropped when tests showed that regular users preferred the original product.

The brand succeeded, its maker says, "because it worked and it was superbly promoted."

Alka-Seltzer's "Heartburn Relief" was added to the line to provide fast relief for heartburn and acid indigestion while neutralizing more acid than the original Alka-Seltzer.

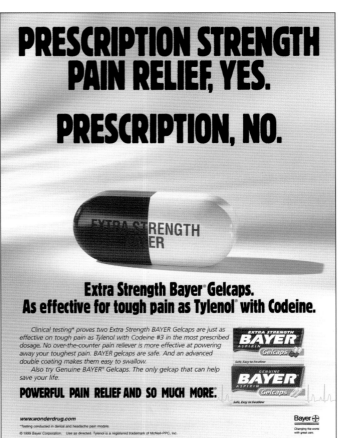

THINGS YOU DIDN'T KNOW ABOUT BAYER

○ Aspirin can reduce the risk of death by up to 23 percent if administered when a heart attack is suspected and for 30 days thereafter as directed by a doctor.

○ When Bayer first marketed the product, they used the following formula to derive the name "aspirin": The "A" comes from acetyl chloride, "SPIR" comes from Spiraea ulmaria, the plant salicylic acid is derived from, and the "IN" was a common ending for medicines at the turn of the century.

○ Phillips' Milk of Magnesia can also relieve acid indigestion and heartburn.

○ Phillips' used to make toothpaste.

○ The Alka-Seltzer formula was originally developed to help combat a 1928 influenza epidemic that affected 25 percent of Alka-Seltzer's laboratory staff.

○ In 1968, Alka-Seltzer launched Alka-Seltzer Plus to fight the symptoms of cold and flu, and the product was one of the most successful line extensions in U.S. history.

BlueCross®
BlueShield®

THE MARKET

The Blue Cross and Blue Shield System's unique connection to consumers, based on trust, peace of mind and service to local communities, has served it well for more than 70 years. Ongoing marketplace changes and the rise of consumerism, combined with the power of the Internet, are offering exciting new challenges and opportunities to virtually every business sector, and health care insurance is no exception.

The Blue Cross and Blue Shield Association and its Member Plans nationwide are dedicated to bringing meaningful change and meaningful advances to the health care delivery system in America, taking a lead role in striving for solutions to important consumer issues. The Blue Cross and Blue Shield Association and Blue Plans around the country are working to meet these challenges, including partnering with Internet companies to leverage new technologies and provide personalized, real-time services and information for consumers.

ACHIEVEMENTS

The Blue Cross and Blue Shield Association and its Member Plans, which lead the health insurance industry, are committed to consumer satisfaction. Americans rely on the Blue Cross and Blue Shield System, as originators and continuing innovators of health insurance, to provide them and their families with security, protection and peace of mind when it is needed most. Blue Cross and Blue Shield Plans have responded by consistently meeting and exceeding consumer

expectations with high-quality, affordable health care insurance. They currently cover more than 80 million Americans, over one quarter of the U.S. population.

The Blue Cross and Blue Shield Federal Employee Program (FEP) is the largest insured group underwritten jointly by participating Blue Cross and Blue Shield Plans. Forty-eight percent of all federal employees and retirees in the government's Federal Employees Health Benefits Program, more than 4 million, are members of FEP and receive health coverage through Blue Plans. FEP's innovative Blue Health Connection, a 24-hour, seven-days-a-

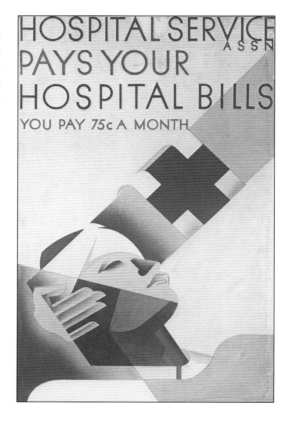

week, toll-free nurse triage telephone and Web site service, provides health advice and information to its members.

Created in 1985, the Blue Cross and Blue Shield Association's Technology Evaluation Center (TEC) evaluates the safety and efficacy of new medical technologies to determine whether they improve patient health outcomes, such as quality of life, length of life, and functional ability. TEC has been widely recognized for its leadership in producing evidence-based technology assessments, and is one of only 12 centers nationwide contracted by the federal government to conduct research on these topics.

HISTORY

Blue Cross: In 1929, Baylor University's Justin Ford Kimball introduced a plan to guarantee school teachers 21 days of hospital care for $6 a year. In 1933, E.A. van Steenwyk, an executive with the forerunner of Blue Cross

and Blue Shield of Minnesota, began to identify his hospital-care program with a blue cross. Other groups across the country followed suit. In 1939, a commission of the American Hospital Association (AHA) officially adopted the Blue Cross symbol as the emblem for health plans that met their standards. In 1960, the AHA commission was replaced by the Blue Cross Association, and in 1972, the Blue Cross Association became independent of the AHA.

Blue Shield: The Blue Shield's history dates back to the lumber and mining camps of the Pacific Northwest. Employers who wanted to provide medical care for their workers made arrangements with physicians, paying them a monthly fee for their services. This led to the creation of medical service bureaus composed of groups of physicians. The first such group was organized in 1917 in Tacoma, Wash., by Pierce County physicians, and the first Blue Shield Plan was formed in California in 1939. The Blue Shield was informally adopted in 1948 by a group of nine plans that eventually became the National Association of Blue Shield Plans.

Blue Cross and Blue Shield Association: The 1982 merger of the Blue Cross Association and the Blue Shield Association created the Blue Cross and Blue Shield Association, serving the federation of independent, locally operated Blue

Carefree is a place I want my family to live.
Where I am the gardener with all
the tools I need to help them grow.
With my Blue Cross and Blue Shield Plan
I have more health care choices
to ensure that my family blooms.
This is my plan.
To take care of...

Their mind. Their body. Their spirit. Their health.

For more information, visit our Web site at www.BCBS.com.

BlueCross BlueShield

©2000 Blue Cross and Blue Shield Association, an Association of Independent Blue Cross and Blue Shield Plans.

Plans. The Association owns the Blue Cross and Blue Shield trade names and service marks, and licenses their use to the independent Blue Plans.

THE PRODUCT

Blue Cross and Blue Shield Plans offer a wide variety of individual health insurance plans and innovative health programs for consumers in every state across the country. Because each Blue Plan is independent and locally owned, it is in the position of being able to respond to the unique needs of its local community.

The BlueCard Program enables Blue Cross and Blue Shield Plan members to obtain health care services while traveling anywhere in the United States, receiving the same benefits they would at home. The program links participating health care providers and the independent Blue Cross and Blue Shield Plans across the country through a single, effective electronic network for processing claims.

For world travelers, BlueCard Worldwide provides Blue Plan members with coverage in more than 200 countries around the globe. Services include referrals to inpatient, outpatient, and professional services; medical assessments by medical professionals, and translation services.

RECENT DEVELOPMENTS

The Blue Cross and Blue Shield Association helped establish the independent, non-profit organization, RxIntelligence, which gathers, reviews and disseminates information designed to aid consumers and decision-makers in evaluating new medicines and comparing the effectiveness of existing and new drugs. Specific services offered by RxIntelligence include "early alert" analyses of drugs approaching final FDA approval, evaluation of therapeutic interchangeability and cost-effectiveness studies.

BCBS.com, the Association's main public Web site, offers one of the largest on-line physician directories in the United States, as well as a directory of international hospitals that are part of the BlueCard Worldwide program.

The Blue Cross and Blue Shield Association's Healthy Competition Foundation leads the way in educating young people and their families, as well as coaches and teachers, about the potential health dangers of performance-enhancing drugs and strives to eliminate their use at all levels of sports. The Foundation complements and supports the Blue System's long-standing U.S. Olympic Team sponsorship.

The Association's BCBSHealthIssues.com communicates the Blue System's point of view on important public issues and also features some of the best pro and con thinking from other leading experts. Using a search engine that regularly scans thousands of public policy Web sites, BCBSHealthIssues.com provides easy access to an extensive range of credible consumer health care issues information.

PROMOTION

The Blue Cross and Blue Shield Association and the Blue Cross and Blue Shield Plans have served as official health insurance sponsors of the U.S. Olympic Team since 1988—and will be sponsors in 2002 and 2004. Over the years, the U. S. Olympic Team sponsorship has led to groundbreaking new initiatives, including the Blue Cross and Blue Shield Adopt-an-Athlete program. This innovative program began with 20 Blue Cross and Blue Shield Plans sponsoring more than 40 athletes. It was expanded nationwide in 1992 under the auspices of the U.S. Olympic Committee.

Other major Olympic initiatives include sponsorship of the first Olympic Congressional Dinner in conjunction with the U.S. Olympic Committee, a school curriculum program, a series of health and wellness seminars, an Olympic Games spectators' wellness guide and the Caring for the Human Spirit Tour, bringing the Olympic spirit to local communities across America.

Although Blue Cross and Blue Shield Plans promote their products and services directly in their local markets, the Plans and the Blue Cross and Blue Shield Association share responsibility for enhancing the Blue Brands. The main vehicles used to promote the Brands on a national level are TV and print advertising. The most recent campaign reflects Blue Cross and Blue Shield's commitment to empowering consumers and helping them achieve good health—captured in the tagline, "Your mind...Your body...Your spirit...Your health."

BRAND VALUES

The Blue Cross and Blue Shield Brands are synonymous with health insurance in America. The familiar Blue Cross and Blue Shield card is recognized by consumers as a symbol of quality because of its distinguished heritage, and because it represents a wide choice of doctors, hospitals and other providers and ease of use anywhere in the world.

A comprehensive research program, unparalleled in other service industries, helps identify the needs of consumers and how to best respond to those needs. Ongoing, fact-based research measures the success of programs and anticipates further changes in consumer expectations. This enables the Blue Cross and Blue Shield System to respond proactively to consumers' needs and concerns locally, nationally and worldwide.

Preparing for an even more consumer-driven market, the Blues are well positioned to leverage their competitive advantage by effectively meeting and exceeding customer expectations—further enhancing Blue Cross and Blue Shield as the Brand of Choice.

THINGS YOU DIDN'T KNOW ABOUT BLUE CROSS/BLUE SHIELD

○ Eighty percent of doctors and 90 percent of hospitals in America honor Blue Cross and Blue Shield cards.

○ The human figure in the center of the Blue Cross symbol represents the spirit of the traditional Blue Cross concept—helping people to achieve and maintain good health.

○ The symbol in the center of the Blue Shield is a staff of Aesculapius, a symbol of the medical profession linked with the Greek and early Roman gods of medicine, and a classic symbol of protection.

○ If all 80 million Americans insured through Blue Cross and Blue Shield Plans held hands, they could circle the Earth three and one-half times.

○ With more than 150,000 employees, the Blue Cross and Blue Shield Plans collectively are one of the largest employers in the United States.

THE MARKET

There are 11,000 brands of domestic and imported distilled spirits sold in the United States, and Canadian Club ranks at the very top of the most widely recognized and respected of these products.

ACHIEVEMENTS

Canadian Club Whisky, which is now sold in 150 countries, has been the world's favorite since 1858. In 1898, Hiram Walker & Son became the first North American whisky distiller to receive a royal warrant from the Royal Family of Great Britain.

HISTORY

Hiram Walker was raised on a Massachusetts farm but left to pursue a different type of career. In 1836, at the age of 20, he left the farm for Boston and two years later moved on to what was then the bustling frontier city of Detroit, Mich., which then had approximately 3,000 people. But the business success he sought eluded him for 20 years as he failed in several businesses. He was a successful storeowner, a tanner, and a wholesale grocer. He eventually became as a one-man conglomerate—vinegar manufacturer, grain buyer, grocery-store owner, and real-estate

investor. By 1856, Walker had saved the princely sum, for that time, of $40,000. He decided to use it to build a flour grain mill and distillery and settled on a 486-acre parcel of timberland that was across the Detroit River in Canada.

Two factors were behind that decision. Walker's wholesale and retail experience had shown him that whisky was a high-profit item and, secondly, Michigan had three years earlier passed a tough prohibition law that allowed only druggists to sell liquor and set tight restrictions on such sales.

The Walker flour mill opened in 1858 and distilling operations began the same year. By the end of the year, Walker was producing a unique and distinctive whisky. He called it his "Club Whisky" because of its popularity in the men's clubs and better hotels of the day. American distillers, wanting to distinguish the domestic origin of their own brands from that of Walker's, insisted that he identify it as "Canadian" and the product became "Canadian Club."

It also became highly popular in the United States and in overseas countries.

Sales of the product boomed when prohibition in the United States closed down its distilleries. By that time, Hiram Walker's grandsons were running the company. As wealthy citizens of the United States and prominent members of

Detroit society, they decided in 1926 to get out of the liquor business.

Henry C. Hatch bought the company in 1926, and in 1936 he purchased Ballantines Scotch, which marked the beginning of the company's portfolio of distinguished global brands.

The Allied-Lyons company acquired Hiram Walker in 1987 and that company, now Allied Domecq PLC, is the second largest beverage alcohol company in the world.

THE PRODUCT

The Atlantic Ocean represents a major division in the world of whisky distilling. Scotch and Irish whiskies dominate one side, American and Canadian the other. American whiskies like bourbon have a strong color and flavor derived from their predominately corn bases and use of brand new White American Oak barrels. Ordinary Canadian whiskies have a light taste and appearance resulting from their blend of rye, corn, and barley. Canadian distillers are allowed to use the barrels over and over, hence producing a light, sweet, and very well balanced whisky.

But the biggest difference is between ordinary whiskies and the one that by its history and culture stands apart–Canadian Club.

Canadian Club is distinguished by the vision and special techniques of Hiram Walker, by the choice and quality of yeasts, by the softness of the water used in its manufacture, and by a pre-blending proprietary process that allows the various blends of distillates to "marry." Finally, aging that lasts up to six years helps to develop maturity, smoothness, and a uniquely satisfying flavor which has made Canadian Club truly a global brand.

Nothing is left to chance. Selection of ingredients, not only the experience but also the special know-how of the distillers, and modern facilities and controls make the difference.

From the receipt of grain to aged whisky

poured into the bottle, there are more than 150 quality control checks to ensure that the high-quality standards Hiram Walker established still exist today.

The grains and malts are sampled and tested to assure that strict quality standards for starch, odor, and moisture are met. This is where it all begins—with excellent quality grains. A special distillation process ensures that Canadian Club whisky is one of the lightest whiskies in the world. It is matured in once-used white oak barrels from their bourbon neighbors in the U.S.A. The barrels are charred to burn off the bourbon flavor and also to expose the wood sugars. During that long, six-year maturation period in temperature-controlled warehouses, the pre-barrel, blended distillates obtain a distinctive light, rich, amber color, mellowness, and flavors such as caramel, toffee, oak, and vanilla.

Prior to being released for bottling, the whisky must pass an "organoleptic" panel that detects any variations in flavor, color, and bouquet.

During the entire process, more than 150 quality-control standards must be met.

The end result is a family of whiskies, each with its own distinctive character and flavor. Those sold in the United States include the traditional Canadian Club plus Canadian Club 100% proof, Canadian Club Reserve 10 yr, and Canadian Club Sherry Cask. The company says of its 100-proof selection: "This is the finest-tasting, smoothest, high-proof whisky made–period." On Sept. 11, 2000, Canadian Club 100 Proof won the Gold Medal in the International Wine & Spirits Competition.

RECENT DEVELOPMENTS

Canadian Club has developed a marketing campaign designed to counter increased competition in the United States from vodka and wine.

While that competition has affected sales of all Canadian whiskys in the U.S., Canadian Club's campaign is being designed to set its brand apart from all others. The campaign will challenge consumers with the intriguing question: "CAN YOU.HANDLE.A.WHISKY.DRINK-ING.WOMAN?"

The strategy included test marketing in Tampa, Fla., Hartford, Conn., and Milwaukee, Wis., where the response exceeded all expectations, the company reports.

In the campaign, patrons are asked to become involved in a game of billiards and local contests are arranged, with winners going on to the state level and then to national competition. The grand prize is an opportunity to play with The Black Widow in Las Vegas, Nev., for a prize of $1 million.

Canadian Club says "This is a very aggressive campaign to make the brand relevant to the consumer in a fun environment at their favorite establishment, with friends and people they like to be with,"

while drinking their favorite brand: Canadian Club Whisky.

PROMOTION

Innovative advertising has been a hallmark of Hiram Walker since its earliest days. All whisky had previously been sold in large, unmarked kegs. Hiram Walker put his product into small kegs and earthenware jugs, with all clearly marked as "Walker's." Because his smooth product was unlike that of his competitors, his use of his own name to identify his whisky was a masterstroke of promotion.

As the 19th century ended, Walker advertising ranged from a broadside against "three rascally saloon-keepers" identified by name and accused of selling a product falsely labeled as Canadian Rye Whisky to a dignified ad showing the classical-style entrance to the new company headquarters in Walkerville, Canada.

As electricity enabled more impressive advertising displays, Canadian Club erected at its plant in 1900 what was then the world's largest electric sign. It was 150 feet wide by 60 feet high and had 4,300 light bulbs.

To mark the end of prohibition, the company erected the largest neon sign ever seen in New York City's famed Times Square, and it stood for 16 years. The return of legal alcohol sales also marked the launching of a Canadian Club print campaign to regain markets.

The year 1935 saw the advent of the Adventure Series campaign, which was to go into the Guinness Book of Records as the longest-running ad campaign ever. It featured Canadian Club as the preferred drink of travelers to exotic locales. Continuing into the 1960s, it showed skydivers in free fall and a caption that asked: "Isn't there an easier way to earn my Canadian Club?" and answered: "No."

From 1967 through 1981 Canadian Club advertising was geared to the "Hide A Case" theme, and it provided clues to the location of boxes of the product hidden in such places as the North Pole. The 1980s saw contemporary ads urging consumers to make Canadian Club part of their lifestyles. The modern theme carried into the 1990s in "The World's Favourite Club" campaign, with bottles of Canadian Club reflecting such headlines as "Jazz Club," "Night Club," and "Ski Club," enticing consumers to become Part of the Club.

Whatever the theme of a particular campaign, all reflected Hiram Walker's original determination that his distinctive whisky deserved a distinctive advertising message.

BRAND VALUES

Canadian Club's brand values derive from the fact that, for more than 140 years, master blenders at Hiram Walker & Sons Ltd. have

been making whisky exactly as he did—with the best ingredients, a time-tested recipe, pre-barrel blending, and plenty of patience. The distillation process is long and intense. It takes out the harshness and leaves behind the delicate character of the spirit. Bottled since 1858, Canadian Club has historically been recognized as an authentic Canadian whisky.

THINGS YOU DIDN'T KNOW ABOUT CANADIAN CLUB

❍ Hiram Walker was a resident of Detroit, Mich., when he built his distillery in Canada just over the Detroit River because Michigan had become a dry state. An international commuter, he traveled from his home to his factory every day by ferry and stagecoach.

❍ One of the yeasts used today in the fermentation of the flavoring grains for the manufacture of Canadian Club is a descendant of the pure culture yeast that Hiram Walker used in his original production.

❍ It was not long after the introduction of Canadian Club that a Detroit newspaper wrote: "Wherever you ask for American whisky today, in Europe, Asia, or Africa, you are offered not Yankee spirits but Walker's Club."

❍ In 1926, when Henry C. Hatch purchased the business from the sons of Hiram Walker, he paid $14 million. Of that amount, $5 million was for the company's assets and the balance, some two-thirds of the total, was for the name and good will of the Canadian Club brand.

CATERPILLAR®

THE MARKET

Big. Strong. Yellow. You know one when you see one. Those giant, powerful machines that literally move mountains have become universal symbols—at least in the public's eye—of the heavy machinery industry. Now that's a brand with real power.

But if you only see heavy machinery, you're not seeing the big Caterpillar picture. Through diversification, Caterpillar product lines include not only the heavy construction and agriculture sectors, but also road building, mining, quarry, forestry, and industrial waste handling. The company also makes light construction machinery; diesel and natural gas engines; and industrial gas turbines, which satisfy an ever-growing need for power sources in the marketplace.

Caterpillar has built one of the industry's and the world's most efficient and responsive parts, service, and support organizations. It also develops and produces fluids for its machines, provides financial services to its customers, re-manufactures used machines, has developed an equipment rental business; and has established Caterpillar Logistics Services, Inc. to offer logistics management services worldwide.

ACHIEVEMENTS

In 2000, as the company celebrated its 75th anniversary, Caterpillar—one of the Fortune 100—stood atop its industry with worldwide revenues of more than $20 billion.

But the financial side doesn't paint the full picture. Caterpillar attributes much of its success to aligning itself with the work its customers do rather than with the products they own—and to helping them by solving problems, providing support, and offering financial and technical expertise. The company prides itself on its track record of keeping its customers up and running, maximizing their productivity, and reducing their cost of operation through a global dealer network that provides customer support, parts, and service in nearly 200 countries literally overnight.

HISTORY

Caterpillar leads its industry for good reason. It literally invented that industry in 1904 with the introduction of the first tracked machine that

could lay down its own roadbed, allowing farmers to work in slippery fields without getting stuck up to their axles in mud. The product took hold, and Caterpillar endured.

The history of Caterpillar reads like a page out of the history of world events for the past three-quarters of a century. Caterpillar products have played a significant role in helping to shape those events. The company's machines have literally gone to war — in Europe and the Pacific Rim in World War II, in Vietnam, and in the Gulf War, helping to extinguish the blazing oil fields in Kuwait.

More often, Caterpillar products are at work to make progress around the world possible. That work is most publicly visible in such high-profile projects as the new Hong Kong airport, Egypt's massive efforts to green its vast deserts, and the building of the Three Gorges Dam in China. While some of those projects come with their

own measure of controversy, people also see Caterpillar at work in helping to develop sustainable techniques in the tropical rainforests and in bringing new-found prosperity and growth opportunities to communities as far flung as Piracicaba, Brazil, and Xuzhou, China. It's a big world. And Caterpillar puts its strength behind helping to make it a better one.

THE PRODUCT

Caterpillar manufactures more than 300 different types of machines. It also makes engines, power systems and solar turbines, provides parts, services, OEM components, and work tools. Caterpillar also offers a line of clothing and work boots bearing the company's brand. Its equipment and other products are used throughout the world across a wide range of major industries as well as by governments and military forces.

RECENT DEVELOPMENTS

At least within the company, referring to Cat or Caterpillar as a brand is unfamiliar language. Most think of Caterpillar as a business-to-business company, not a consumer products one. Caterpillar's products actually do something. They work hard.

But it's that work-related connotation that has allowed Caterpillar to successfully extend its brands to other products, even into consumer markets. And because of the company's reputation for high-quality, durable products, those attributes carry over into other product lines.

Perhaps the most successful extension of the Cat brand has been into the work boot market. "What's a company like Caterpillar doing in footwear?" you might ask. About $900 million a year in sales of Cat branded boots and other licensed merchandise, that's what.

Caterpillar's Mark Jostes, who manages the company's mass retail merchandise marketing, acknowledges that many both within and outside the company have expressed surprise, and not always delight, at Caterpillar's move into such a non-traditional market. He counters, however, by pointing out that the company keeps its merchandising strategy strictly in line with its brand image.

"We sell roughly 200,000 pieces of equipment a year. That's a lot in our business, especially when you

consider that replacing an undercarriage on some machines could cost upwards of $30,000. But that also means, at least in our core businesses, we have a somewhat limited primary customer base. When you consider that we've sold more than 40 million pairs of Cat branded boots since 1994, it gives a whole new meaning to brand awareness."

PROMOTION

The Peoria, Illinois-based corporation faces a dual challenge in representing itself publicly. Although the corporate name is Caterpillar Inc., many simply refer to the company as Cat. Caterpillar has seen the value in flexing its brand, rather than trying to rigidly insist that only its corporate name be used.

As a result, it uses both the Cat and Caterpillar names to identify the company and its products and services. Both are used interchangeably, but in general, the name "Caterpillar" refers to the company as a whole, and the name "Cat" applies to products, services, and dealers.

Having two equally established names was an important factor in the redesign of the company's logo in 1989. As a result, Caterpillar has two design marks, one incorporating the longer version of the name and one using the shorter version. While both are used to mark Caterpillar products, the flexibility of having a shorter version allows it to be represented in a larger, more visible size. Therefore, the Cat brand usually

takes the more dominant position in product promotion and identification.

BRAND VALUES

Caterpillar has a highly developed sense of who it is and what it stands for. When the company reorganized in the early 1990s, it wanted to make sure its corporate image was well defined and consistently communicated. Caterpillar works hard to instill a common understanding of its strategy and objectives not only to employees, but throughout its worldwide dealer network and its allied organizations.

The message comes through loud and clear in the company's statement of its attributes:

Down-to-earth. Straightforward. Gritty and rugged. Enduring. Accessible. Honest. Responsive. Global. Serious, thorough, and industrious. Commanding. Highest quality. Competitive. Industry leader.

Bonnie Briggs, Caterpillar's Manager of Corporate Identity and Communication, travels the globe to spread the message of the importance

of protecting and enhancing the brands' strength and value. She says, "brands should stand for something. To be believed, they must be lived." Caterpillar's more than 68,000 employees worldwide certainly understand what "living" Caterpillar means. Many often refer to themselves as having "yellow blood", a metaphor that sums up the pride they take in their company and their individual contributions to it.

In some cases, the strong work heritage associated with "yellow blood" has been passed from one generation to another. Kim Neible, Manager of Caterpillar's Global Brand Management Group, says, "I grew up with Cat. Everyone in my family has worked for this company at one time or another—my father retired after 37 years of service. So, what Caterpillar represents and our values are almost instinctive to me. This long-standing culture defined by our attributes is as prevalent within the organization as those yellow machines and engines in our factories. It sets our standards, drives our performance, and differentiates us from the rest of the industry."

THE MARKET

According to a United States Postal Service study, 17 percent of Americans—43 million people—change addresses annually. Many of those buyers and sellers turn to a real estate professional to help them navigate the tricky twists and turns of the real estate transaction, often choosing a real estate professional from a franchised office in their community or an independent brokerage.

Among those choices, Century 21 Real Estate Corporation, franchisor of the world's largest residential real estate sales organization, is one of the most well-known and preferred brands. It has the largest broker network and greater global coverage than any organization of its kind. In fact, it is the only real estate sales network to accumulate more than a trillion dollars in home and property sales.

ACHIEVEMENTS

Century 21 Real Estate Corporation has grown from a small California-based start-up business to the largest residential real estate sales organization in the world. It boasts 6,300 offices and 110,000 brokers and sales associates in 28 countries and territories worldwide. In fact, in 1999 sales of franchised offices increased seven percent over 1998, far surpassing the industry's average growth rate.

In addition, the CENTURY 21® System enjoys the greatest level of brand recognition in the real estate industry. According to a 1999 advertising tracking study, when asked to name a real estate company, 35 percent of consumers mentioned the CENTURY 21 System first, before any other real estate brand. The same study showed that the CENTURY 21 System is recognized nearly twice as often as the next competing brand.

HISTORY

Century 21 Real Estate Corporation was founded in 1971 by California real estate brokers Art Bartlett and Marsh Fisher, who had a vision of creating a national real estate sales organization. By the end of the year, the first broker had affiliated and, in 1975, combined sales of all CENTURY 21 companies topped $1 billion. In 1977, the company went public and began reacquiring the independently owned regions, which were originally sold as "master franchises."

Three years later, a merger between the company and TransWorld Corporation was approved and in 1985, Metropolitan Life Insurance Company purchased the organization. During the 1980s and early 1990s, Century 21 Real Estate Corporation became the first franchised

real estate organization to create a quality service program and is still the only real estate sales organization to systematically survey every buyer and seller that uses a CENTURY 21 broker or sales associate.

In 1995, Hospitality Franchise Systems, Inc. (HFS) acquired the corporation and two years later, HFS merged with CUC International to form Cendant Corporation (NYSE: CD). Century 21 Real Estate Corporation remains a subsidiary of Cendant Corporation today.

During its 30-year history, Century 21 Real Estate Corporation has developed a significant international presence that began in April of 1975, when Canada became the first international region. Global expansion brought the company into 28 countries and territories in the succeeding years. Most recently, the System signed a master franchise to bring the CENTURY 21 brand name to Kuwait and also opened its first office in Beijing, China.

THE PRODUCT

As a franchise organization, Century 21 Real Estate Corporation strives to provide its brokers and sales associates with the knowledge, skills and tools they need to help their clients have the most successful real estate experience possible. The vision of Century 21 Real Estate Corporation is to provide its members with the best marketing, technology and franchise support programs available in the industry.

For CENTURY 21 real estate professionals, the goal is always to provide exemplary customer service. CENTURY 21 System members aim to use their talents and skills to eliminate the anxiety or apprehension often associated with the real estate buying or selling experience. The ultimate goal is to give clients "peace of mind" during their real estate transaction.

In addition to residential real estate, CENTURY 21 offices also specialize in commercial, luxury, new construction and recreational real estate, as well as relocation services.

RECENT DEVELOPMENTS

By capitalizing on recent technological developments, Century 21 Real Estate Corporation has positioned itself to lead the industry in the new millennium. The System Web site,

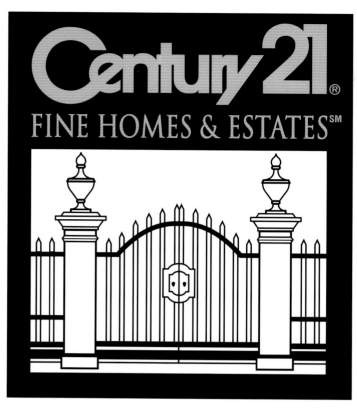

Century21.com, is a valuable resource for home buyers and sellers. It features more than 200,000 property listings, virtual tours, mortgage information, a home planner and links to agent and office profiles. The site receives approximately two million visitors per month and is recognized as one of the leading sites in its category.

Other technology resources developed by Century 21 Real Estate Corporation include an Internet-based referral network that links all CENTURY 21® offices around the world with other franchised real estate offices.

In addition, the System has developed a technology-based training program. The CENTURY 21 Learning System℠ (CLS) uses the Internet to make course offerings more affordable and accessible for its members.

The last decade has also seen an increase in new products for the CENTURY 21 System. Several brand extensions are available to help brokers and agents target and service specialty markets. Those programs include: CENTURY 21 Fine Homes & Estates℠ for luxury properties, CENTURY 21 Recreational Properties℠ for vacation and second homes, the CENTURY 21 Commercial Investment Network® for commercial and investment properties and CENTURY 21 Builder Connections℠ for the new construction market.

Century 21 Real Estate Corporation also knows that consumers are busier than ever before. That is why it has formed strategic relationships with leading companies that provide clients with time- and money-saving offers. The program, called CENTURY 21 Connections℠, "connects"

clients with everything from mortgages and home warranties to home security systems and satellite television systems. The goal of the CENTURY 21 Connections℠ program is to simplify the total home experience.

PROMOTION

A unique combination of advertising and promotional programs has helped Century 21 Real Estate Corporation build its brand awareness and earn a place in the hearts and minds of consumers.

In 1999, the CENTURY 21 System debuted its award-winning "Real Estate for the Real World®" advertising campaign. This campaign uses satire and humor to show consumers that CENTURY 21 real estate professionals understand the trials and tribulations of the home buying and selling experience. Noted celebrities such as Ringo Starr, psychologist Dr. Joyce Brothers, New York Yankees' baseball manager Joe Torre, renowned celebrity chef Emeril Lagasse, and Major League Baseball® legend Cal Ripken, Jr. have all been featured in the campaign.

In 1999, Century 21 Real Estate Corporation also joined Major League Baseball (MLB) as the "Official Real Estate Organization of Major League Baseball®," its first major event sponsorship. As part of the alliance, the CENTURY 21 System is the title sponsor of Major League Baseball's Home Run Derby™ competition, the most-watched sporting event, outside of NFL football, on ESPN.

In association with Major League Baseball's *Home Run Derby,* Century 21 Real Estate Corporation sponsors the "CENTURY 21 Home Run Derby All-Star Sweepstakes," which gives

consumers a chance to win a trip to All-Star Week and $250,000 towards a new home.

The CENTURY 21 Fine Homes & Estates brand extension is a sponsor of the Ladies Professional Golf Association (LPGA), which includes onsite sponsorship at selected tournaments and Golf Clinics for Women. As the "Official Luxury Real Estate Organization of the LPGA," the brand extension is also sponsoring the CENTURY 21 Fine Homes & Estates "Move of the Month" award recognizing excellence and consistency among LPGA players.

"The CENTURY 21 System also sponsors a National Hot Rod Association (NHRA) Pro-Stock car and its driver, Tom Martino. In collaboration with Pontiac, the System is the proud sponsor of the CENTURY 21 "Drive It Home Sweepstakes."

The CENTURY 21 System was also the title sponsor of the "Century21.com Presents Ringo Starr & His All-Starr Band Connections Tour 2000." The nationwide tour maximized visibility of Century21.com and promoted the CENTURY 21 *Connections* program.

BRAND VALUES

Century 21 Real Estate Corporation is dedicated to "reinventing the real estate experience" by providing its brokers and sales associates with the technology and marketing tools, as well as the franchise support services, they need to succeed.

On the local level, each CENTURY 21 broker and sales associate is dedicated to providing top-notch customer service by using their real estate experience and skills to reduce the anxiety and apprehension often associated with the real estate transaction. While the CENTURY 21 System may be the largest organization of its kind, it also understands that each home transaction needs special attention and care. The System's mixture of industry-leading resources and commitment to quality has proven to be an unbeatable combination.

THINGS YOU DIDN'T KNOW ABOUT CENTURY 21

○ The CENTURY 21 System's first-time entry into the 1990 Tournament of Roses parade won the coveted Sweepstakes Trophy as the event's most beautiful float.

○ The CENTURY 21 System updated and sharpened its identifiers, including its logo and colors (to black, gold and white from brown and gold), in March 1991.

○ In 1997, CENTURY 21 MoneyWorld gained international attention when it listed boxer Mike Tyson's 56,000 square-foot, 17-acre Farmington, Conn., estate for $22 million. The home featured 60 rooms, 24 bathrooms, 20 bedrooms, seven kitchens, a dance club, and a NBA regulation-size basketball court.

○ During its 21-year relationship with Easter Seals, the CENTURY 21 System has raised more than $66 million for the organization, making it one of Easter Seals, all-time leading corporate sponsors.

Charles Schwab

THE MARKET

The brokerage business has become a hotbed of competition. The rise of the Internet created discounted web-only trading. The repeal of the Depression-era Glass-Steagall Act in 1999 opened the industry to banks and insurance companies. Traditional brokers have remained a strong presence, serving clients who want brokers to help manage their money and perform the majority of their research and investing.

Charles Schwab & Co., Inc., in planning for its future, decided to combine the best of what's available in the market into a new financial model.

Recognizing the Internet would profoundly change the industry, the company made the Internet a priority. Schwab was the first major financial services company to provide trading and account services via the Internet. By June of 1999, Schwab had 42% of all industry-wide online account assets and was doing one out of every four industry-wide Internet trades. At the same time, the company was opening additional branches, implementing tiered pricing and service levels and increasing its advice offerings while the parent company, The Charles Schwab Corporation, was growing internationally.

As a result, the company distinguished itself from full-commission brokers and deep discounters and succeeded in creating a new model for full-service investing, a model described as "clicks and mortar" by president and co-CEO David Pottruck.

ACHIEVEMENTS

Charles Schwab & Co., Inc. has widely been recognized as an innovator in the brokerage business, pioneering many of today's accepted and expected practices. Since its beginning, the company has been an advocate for the individual investor. Schwab's strategy is to combine quality services with competitive pricing, to give customers what they want, when and how they want it. The company founded the multi-channel approach to customer service, integrating web, branch and phone service.

In 1982, Schwab offered 24-hour, seven-day-a-week order-entry and quote services, which grew into TeleBroker®, a fully automated telephone trading system. TeleBroker is still widely used, handling more than 80% of the company's 600,000 average daily calls.

A decade before the popularization of the Internet, Schwab introduced its Equalizer software. Equalizer let customers place trade orders through Schwab online and was a groundbreaking retail customer product, providing timely account information and third-party data from entities such as Standard & Poor's Marketscope.

In 1992, Schwab started the revolutionary Mutual Fund OneSource® service, the first ever no-transaction-fee "supermarket" of mutual funds. In the same year, Schwab dropped the annual fee on its Individual Retirement Accounts, making it easier for investors to save for the future. As a result of this decision, Schwab's IRA assets doubled by 1994 to $33 billion. In 1993, Schwab upgraded Equalizer to StreetSmart®, designed for online portfolio management, and by 1999, Schwab had become the largest online broker, with its website handling $25 billion worth of transactions weekly. Schwab adapted its business so well to the web, it became widely recognized as the only retail operation to do so successfully—and was ranked the number one e-broker by Gomez Advisors in 2000.

Schwab reached an impressive milestone that same year. Assets held in client accounts surpassed $1 trillion—five years ahead of the company's stated business goal. In 2000, *Forbes* named Schwab its Company of the Year, and *Fortune* ranked Schwab number five on its 100 Best Companies to Work For list. Also in 2000, *Forbes* named Dawn Lepore, Schwab's vice chairman and CIO, one of the most powerful women in business.

HISTORY

Charles Schwab started his brokerage company in San Francisco in 1971. By 1975, the SEC had deregulated the industry, allowing securities firms to set their own prices for trades. Schwab saw deregulation as a chance to begin a brokerage business that could act in the best interest of customers. He lowered his company's commissions, while the remainder of the industry raised theirs, and began what became known as discount brokerage.

Charles Schwab & Co., Inc. revolutionized the discount brokerage business by providing customers with the combination of low prices; timely, efficient order execution; and third-party investment products. Its formula paid off. Company revenues climbed from less than $5 million in 1975 to more than $126 million in 1982.

In 1983, Bank of America bought Schwab for $57 million. For four years, the company's entrepreneurial spirit seemed out of sync with the bank's conservative culture, prompting Charles Schwab himself, in 1987, to lead a $280 million management buy-back of his company. Charles Schwab & Co., Inc. went public that same year in an IPO valued at $450 million.

Seeing a combination of customer need and competitive advantage, Charles Schwab & Co., Inc. was willing to place big bets on the power of the Internet. By the end of 1998, schwab.com—the company's retail website—accounted for over 60% of the company's trades, and that number climbed to over 80% by 2000.

Schwab.com continues to be a vital part of Schwab's business—providing a critical access channel in conjunction with phone and branch services. The site also offers unprecedented research capabilities.

THE PRODUCT

Schwab offers a full range of innovative products and services to meet the needs of investors at every level.

Schwab's Mutual Fund OneSource® service

David Pottruck

Charles Schwab

Not Business As Usual.

Linnet Deily
Vice Chairman,
Office of the President

Dawn Lepore
Vice Chairman and
Chief Information Officer

Karen Chang
Enterprise President,
Retail Business Development
and Branch Network

Carrie Dwyer
General Counsel and
Executive Vice President,
Corporate Oversight

Susanne Lyons
Chief Marketing Officer

Beth Sawi
Executive Vice President and
Chief Administrative Officer

Innovating At Charles Schwab, we do things differently. From founding the first discount brokerage firm to pioneering the mutual fund supermarket to leading the revolution in online investing, Schwab is built on a tradition of innovation.

Listening Innovation has come from listening to what our customers want. By providing individual investors with the tools they need to take charge of their financial futures, Schwab has helped to level the playing field for every investor and changed the way Wall Street does business.

Leading Schwab is also changing the face of leadership on Wall Street. Women play a significant role in our business by fostering an environment of unlimited potential and opportunity. The result is a culture that's not focused on how things have always been done, but how they should be.

CharlesSchwab
creating a world of smarter investors™

continues to be a leader in the industry, allowing customers to invest in over 1,900 mutual funds from 275 fund families.

Schwab's Portfolio Answers provide investors with the amount of help and advice they want through the channel they prefer. For example, Schwab's Portfolio Consultation™ affords customers the opportunity for a personal evaluation of their portfolio by a Schwab Registered Investment Specialist. Self-directed customers can take advantage of products such as the popular Mutual Fund Select List® and services such as investing workshops and online courses. Schwab's AdvisorSource refers customers to third-party, fee-based advisors who help with investment management and financial planning.

Schwab continues to develop products and services to meet the growing needs of its customers. Schwab's active traders can take advantage of competitive tiered pricing and trading through Schwab's proprietary desktop software, Velocity™. The Schwab Access™ account for Schwab Signature Services™ clients features cash-management services such as checkwriting and automatic online bill payment. Schwab Signature Services itself offers three levels of premium service to clients based on trades per year and asset levels.

Schwab also has an enviable institutional business. Schwab Retirement Plan Services, Inc. performs recordkeeping and trust services for corporate retirement plans. Schwab Capital Markets, L.P. is one of the country's largest over-the-counter market makers. Schwab Institutional® provides support and trading services for independent fee-based investment advisors who hold client accounts at Schwab— assets that make up 25% of Schwab's total customer assets.

RECENT DEVELOPMENTS
The Charles Schwab Corporation has made significant international strides by leveraging its successful U.S. business model. Already a market presence in Britain, the company recently opened operations in Hong Kong, Australia and Japan. In 2000, Charles Schwab Canada Co. was ranked the number one online Canadian broker by *The Globe and Mail,* and Charles Schwab Europe became the first U.S. broker to surpass the one million mark in online trades.

In 2000, The Charles Schwab Corporation pur-

chased U.S. Trust®, a wealth management firm that provides private banking and tax and estate planning. With this acquisition, the company gained $90 billion in managed assets and can now extend services to affluent investors.

With the purchase of CyBerCorp®, The Charles Schwab Corporation gained a leader in direct-access trading. By purchasing a start-up firm geared to the needs of the very active trader, the corporation remains on the forefront of technology, excelling in its support of this important customer base.

PROMOTION
Schwab advertising has gone from no-nonsense, direct-response-driven print ads starring Charles Schwab himself to high-profile, brand image, national print and television campaigns. Throughout its promotional evolution, Schwab has portrayed itself as an investor advocate, bringing innovative products and services to customers' needs.

Shannon Sharpe
Schwab Investor

CharlesSchwab
creating a world of smarter investors™

In 1977, the company ran its first full-page ad in *Barron's.* In 1980, the company began calling itself "America's largest discount broker."

In 1991, the company ran its first network television ad with the tagline "Helping investors help themselves"—a line the company used successfully for close to five years.

Schwab broke creative ground with its "Smarter Investor" advertising in 1999. Designed to leverage Schwab's friendly, accessible brand, the campaign starred mostly sports personalities and positioned the company as a different kind of brokerage firm: a place everyone can become smarter about investing.

ADWEEK named the Anna Kournikova "Tennis" spot one of the 50 best commercials of 1999, and "Retirement," featuring ice skater Tara Lapinski, basketball great Charles Barkley and football coach Mike Ditka, among others, earned the 2000 Cannes Silver Lion award.

In 2000, the company went after a more expansive audience, placing Ringo Starr in a

spot that premiered during the Super Bowl and Sally Field in a spot that debuted during the Academy Awards.

While featuring high-profile celebrities, the campaign still managed to remain in line with the company's overall brand, positioning Schwab as a company that empowers investors to take control of their own financial futures.

BRAND VALUES
A significant part of the success story of this dynamic financial services firm is based on the founding vision of chairman and co-CEO Charles R. Schwab, who continues to be the company's visionary and soul. Schwab built the company on the unique premise of providing customers something he believed they weren't getting from Wall Street—useful, ethical financial services at fair prices.

The company's drive to do what's best for customers shapes employee relations, too. Schwab places a premium on corporate culture, believing if it takes care of its employees, its employees will take care of the customers.

The company has tailored its programs and policies to respect employees' lifestyles and has provided exciting, rewarding careers to thousands of people. By sponsoring programs such as School to Careers, Balancing Work/Life, Diversity of Style and Women's Interactive Network, among numerous others, Schwab has created a supportive, productive work environment that is rich with opportunity and embodies the values of the company.

The philosophy of customer-first has differentiated Schwab from the very beginning. This unique proposition keeps this powerful company and its strong brand ahead of the competition in technology, product offerings and customer service.

THINGS YOU DIDN'T KNOW ABOUT SCHWAB

❍ Schwab.com receives 76 million hits per day and has handled up to 100,000 logons simultaneously.

❍ Women represent 40% of the total work force at the company, and 40% of its vice presidents are women.

❍ Nearly 60% of Schwab employees invest time and resources in their communities through volunteer activities or the company's Matching Gift Program.

❍ First Commander Corporation was the company's first name before it was changed to Charles Schwab & Co., Inc.

Club Med ॐ

THE MARKET

In the early years, adventurous young people were Club Med's most enthusiastic members. And they still love Club Med. But today's typical Club Med vacationer is thirty something; two out of three come as part of a family. Most villages offer a Mini Club program for children 4 to 11. Some also offer a Baby Club for infants and toddlers (from 4 months old) and a Petit Club for two and three year olds. In addition, Club Med is reaching out to the growing number of lone travelers, single parents, and mature vacationers. Whatever their age, a very high proportion of Club members—about 70 percent—return year after year to soak up the sun, meet like-minded people, indulge in some golf, tennis, or water sports, whiz down the ski slopes, or try a new, extreme sport for the first time.

ACHIEVEMENTS

Club Med is dedicated to renewing its own capacities, building a great future on a foundation of enduring values. Since 1998, the company has fortified its financial position and made long strides toward the goal of moving from a hotel company to a service organization rooted in the concept of "Club" and in the sense

of belonging which that key word conveys.

Today, Club Med has 120 village resorts around the world, including 29 winter sports destinations, plus Club Med 2, which is the world's largest sailing cruise ship. It sails the Mediterranean all summer and the Caribbean all winter.

Club Med now has a total of 16 Club Med villages in the U.S., Bahamas, Caribbean, and Mexico. It would be hard to overstate the importance of the U.S. market today, or its potential for the future. After France—Club Med's historic home—the U.S. is the second biggest market, and thanks to a very aggressive marketing program, it may well become the number one market within a few short years.

And Club Med feels completely at home in the U.S. To the French recipe for gracious living, Club Med has added a measure of American vitality, a dash of Americans' love for action, and a little zest borrowed from Broadway and Hollywood. On the continental U.S., Club Med has three unique villages—Sandpiper in Florida, and two ski villages in the Rockies: Copper Mountain and Crested Butte. The newest U.S. village, Crested Butte, is a one-of-a-kind ski-in/ski-out village in Colorado.

HISTORY

Club Med invented—and continues to embody—the concept of the all-inclusive getaway. The year 2000 capped 50 years of Club Med history. The Club Med concept was born in 1950, when, during a camping trip with friends, Belgian sportsman Gerard Blitz recognized the need for a unique escape from the hardships of postwar Europe. He placed two small advertisements, announcing the first all-inclusive vacation on the exotic island of Majorca. The response was overwhelming—and Club Mediterranee was born. The very first village consisted of a number of army surplus tents in Alcudia, on the Balearic Island of Majorca. The first of Club Med's famous straw hut villages opened

in 1952 on the island of Corfu, Greece. Five years later, Club Med opened its first ski village in Leysin, Switzerland, becoming one of the world's first ski tour operators.

THE PRODUCT

Club Med offers dream destinations—but is just as concerned about the dreams as the destinations. At Club Med, "Renew" is not simply a campaign slogan. It is a deep philosophical commitment. The company's wide array of services and products all have a bottom-line commitment to re-energizing Club Med's members and reawakening their senses. At Club Med, members rediscover what's really important, and reconnect with themselves and their families.

Club Med is the original, the largest, and the most comprehensive of the world's all-inclusive vacation organizations. One price covers round-trip airfare and transfers, accommodations, all meals with complimentary beer, wine, and soft drinks with lunch and dinner. It also includes most sports and activities with daily lessons, Mini Club programs, and nightly entertainment. Winter sports vacations also include lift tickets and daily ski and snowboard lessons for the whole family.

Club Med has renewed all of the pleasures its members have come to expect, updating and improving its matchless array of 64 sports activities—everything from sailing and golf to inline skating and tai chi. Winter destinations offer many activities and excursions, including horse-drawn sleigh rides, dog sled tours, or snowmobile rides.

Of course, Club Med continues to offer more traditional activities, including golf and tennis. And when it's time to relax, there are fabulous meals and spectacular shows. Special events called Forums for arts enthusiasts are themed around literature, music, and photography.

The Club Med brand now encompasses cosmetics and sportswear, and may expand to include insurance, television, a magazine, entertainment, music, sports... The possibilities are endless.

As the leisure industry grows in coming years, Club Med is poised to play a major role in shaping not only travelers' leisure activities, but also their way of thinking about leisure.

Club Med's unique model makes it much more than just another tour operator or hotel organization. To book a Club Med vacation, guests become Club Members or Gentils Membres (G.M.s), making Club Med the world's largest and most cosmopolitan Club in the world!

The founders invented the notion of the "Gentil Organizateur" (G.O.)—a term that translates roughly as friendly host. More than half of Club Med's 25,000 employees are G.O.s, and they are hosts, guides, friends, and coaches, combining a commitment to service with specialized skills and talents.

RECENT DEVELOPMENTS
Expansion continues: eight new villages opened in 2000-01 including Crested Butte, Colorado; Beldi in Turkey, Djerba La Fidele and Djerba La Nomade in Tunisia, Meribel Le Chalet, Meribel Antares, and Serre Chevalier in France, along with two in Greece. Ten more will open by 2003.

More than 70 of the 120 Club Med villages

worldwide have been renovated and updated. Those who seek the simplicity and adventure of the original Club Med can still choose a straw hut village, but most villages provide a higher level of comfort.

Marketing innovations have made Club Med more "user-friendly"—with four comfort ratings that help members find the village that best meets their needs and budgets. Club Med has also designated villages for adults, families, and "everyone." More than $100 million has been invested in a new worldwide reservations system, allowing sales staff to respond more quickly to customers' requests.

As the leisure industry grows in coming years, Club Med is poised to play a major role in shaping not only travelers' leisure activities, but also their way of thinking about leisure. The company is extending the Club Med brand, moving in many directions at once. One exciting new venture is Club Med World—a neighborhood Club Med designed for an era when many city dwellers are struggling to balance work and personal time.

Club Med World represents a whole new way to spend free time right down the block—a place where members can chat, have fun for an hour, an afternoon or all evening long, have a fabulous meal, and, while they're at it, climb a wall or swing on a flying trapeze. The first Club Med World opened in Paris in mid-2000, and has been a great success. By mid-decade there will be as many as ten Club Med Worlds around the globe.

PROMOTION
Club Med is reaching new members with an integrated global communications strategy, including the Re-New ad campaign, which was designed to clarify Club Med's offerings and focus on its benefits. The Club Med brochure, The Trident, is available in ten languages and has a huge print circulation as well as a strong Internet presence. Promotional efforts have been intensified by means of international partnerships, such as those signed with Coca-Cola, Dannon, Hertz and COTY.

In addition, Club Med On Line, a wholly-owned subsidiary of Club Mediterranee, aims to be a major international internet player in the area of e-commerce and to develop sales of vacations, products, and complementary vacation and leisure services. Club Med On Line is responsible for all group internet activities worldwide. A completely updated website, featuring on line booking, allows the company to create a Club community and is an extraordinary sales channel. The web site, www.clubmed.com, now accounts for two percent of Group revenues in France and five percent in the U.S.

BRAND VALUES
A key to understanding the Club Med brand is realizing that the company is committed to redefining what it means to have or be a "brand." Club Med is not a destination—it is an identity. It is not a place people go to; it is something they become part of, and that becomes part of them. Club Med is an experience; a way of life; an attitude; an adventure. It is about being oneself and enjoying every experience to the fullest. These are the essential values that define the Club Med brand.

Club Med is dedicated to constant improvement and innovation, building on its three strategic assets: its members, its G.O.s, and its brand. The goal is nothing less than total transformation, with a view toward achieving strong growth in all aspects of leisure, relaxation, sports, and holiday enjoyment.

THINGS YOU DIDN'T KNOW ABOUT CLUB MED

- Club Med is the only tourism group integrated under a single brand name worldwide.

- With 36 village resorts featuring golf facilities and more than 150 golf professionals, Club Med is the largest Golf Club in the world. It is also the largest Tennis Club, with more than 800 courts and 300 instructors.

- Club Med is truly multicultural. Its team of G.O.s (Club Med office and village employees) represent 60 nationalities, and speak at least 40 different languages.

- Circus schools, complete with flying trapeze, are available to adults and children at 23 villages worldwide.

- Crested Butte, Club Med's newest U.S. village, is set in an authentic Colorado mining town founded in the 1880's and provides an ideal winter getaway for families.

THE MARKET

Americans consume some 15 billion gallons of soft drinks per year, which is 27 percent of the nation's total consumption of beverages. They have a choice of nearly 450 different types of soft drinks. Some 95 percent of Americans consume soft drinks, and they annually spend $60 billion on that product. There are approximately 500 bottlers producing soft drinks across the country, and modern plants can turn out more than 2,000 such drinks a minute on each operating line.

ACHIEVEMENTS

Coca-Cola, the flagship brand of The Coca-Cola Company, has long been the No. 1 selling soft-drink brand worldwide and is among the most recognized trademarks around the globe. The familiar shape of the bottle and the flowing script of its trademark are among the world's most widely recognized commercial symbols.

Although The Coca-Cola Company is still headquartered in its birthplace in Atlanta, Ga., it now operates daily in nearly 200 countries. Coca-Cola is enjoyed hundreds of millions of times a day by people all over the globe.

Coca-Cola's memorable achievements also include its all-out, highly successful effort to assure that every member of the U.S. armed services in World War II was able to obtain a Coke for five cents regardless of the remoteness of his duty station or the cost to the company. To fulfill that pledge, the company shipped and

assembled bottling plants in 64 locations in Europe, Africa, and the Pacific area. By the end of the war, military personnel overseas had enjoyed more than five billion bottles of Coke.

In addition, Coca-Cola had extended its reach into the areas where the war had been fought, positioning the company for postwar worldwide growth.

HISTORY

On May 8, 1886, pharmacist John Stith Pemberton made a caramel-colored syrup and offered it to the largest drugstore in Atlanta, Ga. But first-year sales averaged only nine a day. Pemberton died in 1888, the same year in which Atlanta businessman Asa G. Candler began to buy outstanding shares of Coca-Cola.

Within three years, he and his associates controlled the young company through a total investment of $2,300. The company registered the trademark "Coca-Cola" with the U.S. Patent Office in 1893 and has renewed it since. ("Coke" has been a trademark name since 1945.)

By 1895, the first syrup-manufacturing plants outside Atlanta had been opened in Dallas, Tex., Chicago, Ill., and Los Angeles, Calif. Candler reported to shareholders that Coca-Cola was being sold "in every state and territory of the United States."

As fountain sales expanded, entrepreneurs sought additional sales by offering the drink in bottles.

Large-scale bottling began when Benjamin F. Thomas and Joseph B. Whitehead of Chattanooga, Tenn., secured from Asa Candler exclusive rights to bottle and sell Coca-Cola in nearly all of the country. They gave other individuals exclusive territories for community bot-

tling operations. Those efforts laid the groundwork for what became a worldwide network of Coca-Cola bottling companies.

The company's response to the imitators who quickly arose included the adoption of one of the most famous product containers ever developed—the unique, contour Coca-Cola bottle. It was created in 1915 by the Root Glass Company of Indiana and approved as standard by the company's bottlers in the following year.

In 1919, a group of investors headed by Ernest Woodruff, an Atlanta banker, purchased The Coca-Cola Company from the Candler interests. Four years later, Robert W. Woodruff, Ernest's 33-year-old son, became president of the company and led it into a new era of domestic and global growth over the next six decades.

In keeping with its strategy to "think local, act local," the company has developed a broad philanthropic program of support of institutions and activities in communities in which it operates. A recent major manifestation of this program was The Coca-Cola Company's five-year, $1 billion commitment to diversity through a comprehensive empowerment and entrepreneurship program.

THE PRODUCT

Life is a series of special moments, and each is an opportunity for Coca-Cola to add its bit of magic.

From the look and feel of the bottle to the sound of effervescence, the tickle of fizz on the nose and tongue and, of course, the unique flavor, Coca-Cola is a sensory experience. But consumer emotions, memories, and values are even more powerful.

People love to speculate about the secret ingredient in Coke. One secret is indeed locked away in a secured vault. But another is readily available—it is the consistent quality of Coca-Cola. The Coca-Cola system adheres not only to local, state, and federal laws on food processing but also to its own strict standards for exceptional quality. From the selection of ingredients to the delivery of finished products, every phase of the process reflects a commitment to the highest-quality products.

The syrups start with pure, fresh water treated by using a multiple barrier filtration process to ensure its quality. The final step is testing of syrups for taste and adherence to their formulas. Bottlers then bring the syrup together with water and carbon dioxide and transform them into the essence of refreshment. Those bottlers undergo constant training and retraining in quality-assurance methods.

RECENT DEVELOPMENTS

In April 2001, the company launched "a new celebratory campaign that reclaims the Coca-Cola brand's roots, its values, its sensitivity, and its rightful place in the minds and hearts of people.

With the theme "Life Tastes Good," the campaign depicts a wide range of people, moods, and situations.

Steve Jones, chief marketing officer for the Coca-Cola Company, said that the commercials show that "Coca-Cola belongs in stories about the true soul of everyday life. These stories express feelings of optimism, of brightness, of spirit."

The campaign, Jones points out, includes TV, radio, outdoor and print executions "featuring people telling stories about special moments in their lives where Coke enriched and enhanced those experiences."

In new product initiatives, The Coca-Cola

Company has launched its own brand of bottled water, Dasani, and has introduced several other new beverages including an energy drink called KMX. In other recent major initiatives, the Company teamed up with America Online in a marketing agreement in which each company will use the other's brand and distribution channels to promote their products and services.

In the Coke-AOL agreement, Coke will draw on the Internet firm's extensive marketing experience, while AOL's name, advertisements, and physical products will reach the billions of Coke consumers worldwide.

A broad overview of the history, growth, and contemporary activities of The Coca-Cola Company is available on the Internet at www.cocacola.com.

PROMOTION

Coca-Cola's promotional efforts began with an oilcloth sign on the awning of the drugstore where the beverage was first offered. It read: "Drink Coca-Cola." Asa Candler put the newly trademarked name not only on syrup urns at soda fountains but on such novelty items as fans, calendars, and clocks.

Since those days, marketing and promotional efforts combined with a top-quality product have made the Coca-Cola trademark among the most admired and best-known in the world.

The book "New and Improved: The Story of Mass Marketing" in A m e r i c a declares:

"Coca-Cola stands today as the second most widely understood term in the world, after okay." The brand achieved such legendary status through a relentless focus on marketing. Such beloved artists as Norman Rockwell and

Haddon Sundblom illustrated Coca-Cola ads that appeared in leading magazines. They included "The Saturday Evening Post," where the famous slogan "The Pause That Refreshes" made its debut in 1929.

Coca-Cola was one of the first commercial sponsors as radio became a popular medium in the early 1930s and the company moved into television with sponsorship of a Thanksgiving Day live program featuring Edgar Bergen and Charlie McCarthy in 1950. Its many, legendary television ads include the international group singing "I'd Like To Buy The World A Coke" and the "Mean Joe Greene" ad featuring the famed football star and the boy who is rewarded with his jersey after giving him a Coke.

Whatever the medium, advertising for Coca-Cola has always reflected the mood and the look of the time.

The Company also has extensive affiliations with the world of sports. As far back as 1903, its advertising featured famous major-league baseball players drinking Coca-Cola. One of the most notable and long-lasting sports affiliations is the company's 72-year association with the Olympic Games. The company is, in many ways, more than a sponsor; it is a partner in the Olympic movement.

The company has had a long relationship with World Cup soccer, the Special Olympics, the Rugby World Cup, NASCAR®, the National Football League, National Basketball Association, and the National Hockey League.

BRAND VALUES

The Coca-Cola brand stands for the most successful product in the history of commerce and for the people responsible for its unique appeal. Each day, Coca-Cola strengths its position as the world's soft drink. Through more than a century of change and into a new era that promises even more change, Coca-Cola remains a timeless symbol of quality refreshment... always.

THINGS YOU DIDN'T KNOW ABOUT COCA-COLA

❍ If all the Coca-Cola ever produced was in eight-ounce bottles on average-sized delivery trucks, it would take six years, four months, and seven days for those trucks to pass a given point driven bumper to bumper at 65 miles an hour.

❍ If those bottles were assembled, there would be more than 13 trillion of them.

❍ Stacked on an American football field, they would form a pile 346 miles high, 70 times the height of Mount Everest, the highest mountain in the world.

❍ The slogan, "Good To The Last Drop," long associated with a coffee brand, was actually used first by Coca-Cola in 1908.

❍ The Coca-Cola trademark is recognized in countries containing 98 percent of the world's population.

❍ The two countries in which per-person consumption of Coca-Cola is highest have little else in common, particularly climate. They are Iceland and Mexico.

THE MARKET

The United States dentifrice market is highly competitive, fueled by improved benefits and new product introductions. In 1999, the dentifrice market accounted for nearly $2 billion in sales and grew at a rate of 4 percent.

The market is segmented into base and premium, with base products offering cavity and tartar protection and premium products offering multiple benefits and whitening. The premium segment is driving category growth as consumers seek new and improved products.

ACHIEVEMENTS

Crest has been a leader in oral care innovations since its introduction in 1955 and has been the leading toothpaste brand in the United States over the past 45 years. It was the first dentifrice to be recognized by the American Dental Association and the first authorized to use the ADA name in advertising.

In 1976, the American Chemical Society recognized Crest with fluoride as one of the 100 greatest discoveries of the previous 100 years. Crest was the first whitening toothpaste to receive the ADA Seal of Acceptance for effectively whitening teeth by gently polishing away surface stains. That recognition was given in 1999.

HISTORY

In 1928, natural fluoride in water was identified as a major factor in the reduction of tooth decay. However, the development of a fluoride toothpaste actually began in the early 1940s, when Procter & Gamble started a research program to find ingredients that would reduce tooth decay when added to a dentifrice. At that time, it was estimated that Americans developed more than 700 million cavities a year, making dental disease one of the most prevalent problems in the United States.

In 1950, Procter & Gamble developed a joint research project team headed by Dr. Joseph Muhler at Indiana University. In 1952,

Dr. Muhler and his research team began the first clinical tests of the new toothpaste. The results of the tests were startling. One test among children aged 6 to 16 showed an average 49 percent reduction in cavities. Furthermore, the toothpaste also reduced the tooth decay for adults to almost the same degree. In 1954, Procter & Gamble submitted the results of its extensive testing to the American Dental Association, which accepted the findings.

Test marketing of Crest with Fluoristan began in 1955. Though initial sales were disappointing, the company maintained confidence in the product, launching it nationally in January, 1956. But consumers did not recognize Crest's unique advantage. A way to convince them that they were indeed benefiting from the product's decay-preventing quality was needed. Since consumers could not see the benefit, they needed to hear it from an authority they would believe.

Early in the development of Crest, it was recognized that the American Dental Association could grant such recognition. Beginning in 1954, P&G submitted to the ADA the results of the company's extensive clinical tests. The ADA, however, had never before recognized a toothpaste and had developed an attitude of suspicion toward dentifrice advertising. To its credit, the ADA maintained an open mind on the Crest presentation. As P&G's clinical evidence mounted, the ADA evaluated it carefully and asked for more data.

On Aug. 1, 1960, the association reported: "Crest has been shown to be an effective anti-caries (decay preventive) dentifrice that can be of significant value when used in a conscientiously applied program of oral hygiene and regular professional cares."

The ADA did not merely recognize Crest's benefits, it went further. For the first time in its history, it granted the use of its name in consumer advertising for a commercial product. The response was electric. Within a year, Crest's sales nearly doubled. By 1962, they had nearly tripled, pushing Crest well ahead as the best-selling toothpaste in the United States.

THE PRODUCT

Crest's heritage is grounded in the dentifrice market, but the company has expanded into

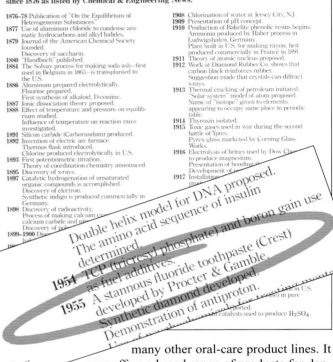

many other oral-care product lines. It now offers a broad range of products for dental needs and conducts the nation's best-known activities on behalf of good dental practices among children.

RECENT DEVELOPMENTS

The Crest brand reached major milestones in 2001.

Crest Extra Whitening recently became the first whitening toothpaste to be granted the prestigious Seal of Acceptance of the American Dental Association (ADA). Previously, the only tooth whitening products that carried the ADA seal were those available through dentists.

Members of that profession and consumers have long recognized the ADA Seal of Acceptance as an important symbol of a dental product's effectiveness and safety.

Another landmark development was the launching of "HEALTHY SMILES 2010," which will target what the U.S. Surgeon General David Satcher called "the silent epidemic" of oral-health disease among children and other members of low-income families in America.

With the goal of eliminating disparities between dental care available to low-income and other families, HEALTHY SMILES 2010

RIDGEWOOD DENTAL CLINIC
To the parents of: _Johnny Bitten_
I have examined Johnny's teeth and find no new cavities.
NBN D.D.S.

"Look, Mom—no cavities!"

Crest Toothpaste with fluoride means far fewer cavities for every member of the family—including children of all ages.

Crest's fluoride is the same decay fighter that dentists apply directly on teeth. Ask your dentist about Crest.

Crest TOOTH PASTE with fluoristan

You can't go too far to make a child smile.

Crest is going all the way to Zimbabwe. And Brazil. And India. And Vietnam. Since 1994, Crest has provided educational materials to Health Volunteers Overseas. It's helped bring oral health to countries where dental care is hard to find. So for the children of Chegutu village, the world is no wider than a smile.

Creating smiles every day   Crest

will provide education, oral-care tools, and increased access to dental professionals to the former group.

The campaign expects to reach 50 million members of low-income families.

The Surgeon General said of the campaign: "Creating public-private partnerships, such as Crest HEALTHY SMILES 2010, can help effect change in the oral health of our country. These collective efforts can help educate both the public and health professionals, as well as provide the health care services and oral care tools needed to help end the current disparity in our nation's oral health."

Acting on the principle that oral health is integral to overall health, HEALTHY SMILES 2010 will combine the passionate vision of Crest with the resources of the Boys & Girls Clubs of America, the For All Kids Foundation established by television personality Rosie O'Donnell, and leading members of the dental community to effect real change in oral health by the target year of 2010.

In yet another major step, The Procter & Gamble Company has purchased Dr. Johns Products, Ltd., makers of the Dr. Johns SpinBrush—a high-performance, battery-operated toothbrush priced within a dollar or two of manual brushes. It is being renamed the Crest SpinBrush.

The SpinBrush, says Michael Kehoe, P&G's vice president/general manager for global oral care, has "become the most popular power brush in America in less than one year and is leading the conversion of manual brush users to powered brushes."

The price of the brush ranges from $4.99 to $5.99, which makes it affordable for most families, Kehoe said.

PROMOTION

The advertising campaign that launched the Crest brand has become one of the most memorable in marketing history. In television commercials, smiling children proudly proclaimed: "Look, mom. No cavities." Along with the TV campaign, print ads illustrated by Norman Rockwell became classics.

In recent years, Crest has expanded its advertising efforts beyond the product to highlight the brand's commitment to promoting good oral health around the world. This breakthrough equity campaign has showcased Crest's support of such key areas as dental education for children, geriatric dentistry, and professional dental education.

Both ethnic and interactive marketing have received increased attention in recent years. Crest has taken its marketing message to the growing Hispanic community, developing culturally relevant Spanish-language advertising that features as spokesperson Maite Delgardo, a popular Hispanic talk-show host. To bring its message of good oral health online, Crest developed the innovative Sparkle City web site. Designed as an interactive teaching tool, Sparkle City supports the efforts of teachers, parents, and dental professionals to instill in children good dental habits that will last a lifetime.

BRAND VALUES

Crest is a brand that has continually pushed to improve oral health. Crest is among the most trusted household brands, a value reinforced by the continued recognition of its products by the American Dental Association.

Crest is committed to opening up the smiles of consumers around the world. Through innovative products and community outreach efforts, Crest is combining education with the proper tools to get things done.

THE MARKET

With The Coca-Cola Company's long and proud tradition behind it and its own qualities of unmatched taste and enjoyment, diet Coke is the leading low-calorie soft drink in the U.S. and worldwide. Clearly, the low-calorie soft drink market will continue to expand very strongly, providing substantial and continuing growth for diet Coke as the market's outstanding brand.

ACHIEVEMENTS

The heritage of diet Coke stems directly from Coca-Cola, the most valuable brand in the world, but diet Coke has achieved spectacular success in its own right as a very substantial brand. A focused strategy to position diet Coke as a stand-alone, carbonated soft drink brand and not a line extension of the parent brand has ensured that diet Coke has its own clear brand image and dedicated following.

Double-digit volume growth since launch and the highest per capita consumption in the world have made diet Coke the number one low-calorie soft drink internationally.

HISTORY

As lifestyles grew more diverse, The Coca-Cola Company recognized that consumers' needs were changing and that their demands for soft drinks to satisfy their thirsts were also differentiating. In 1979–81, a major project in product formulation and consumer market research led to the decision to launch a new, low-calorie cola carbonated soft drink. It was decided that it would be called "diet Coke." The trademark "Coke" had been granted to The Coca-Cola Company as long ago as 1945.

In July 1982, The Coca-Cola Company held a news conference in New York to an-

Monumental Taste.

Mt. Tastemore, South Dacola— the most refreshing tourist attraction in America.

Just for the ^monumental^ taste of it! **diet Coke**

nounce the introduction of diet Coke to U.S. consumers. This was a true milestone—the first ever extension of the company's basic trademark to another product, after almost a century of Coca-Cola.

The international rollout of diet Coke began in January 1983, and by December of that year it was available in 31 markets in 19 countries. In some overseas markets the product is knows as Coca-Cola light.

As a result of continuous research and growing insights into changing consumer needs and demands, the company launched caffeine-free diet Coke very soon afterwards, at the end of April 1983. Fountain sales of diet Coke began that same year.

Within a year of its introduction in the United States, diet Coke had become the biggest-selling low-calorie soft drink in the country. The brand received impressive recognition from The Coca-Cola Company when the company's famous Times Square electronic billboard was reconfigured to alternate its display between Coca-Cola and diet Coke.

RECENT DEVELOPMENTS

Diet Coke recently launched its Web site, dietcoke.com, featuring an exclusive online TV series called "What's Your 20?" The innovative, 13-episode broadband series follows one diet Coke fan as she pursues her lifelong dream of making it in the movie business. Dietcoke.com was created to be a connector to all things entertainment. The site is affiliated with a number of the Internet's top-tier entertainment sites through sponsorships, sweepstakes and special content.

PROMOTION

Coca-Cola advertising had long enjoyed legendary success throughout the world long before diet Coke was introduced. However, diet Coke advertising represented a major change in consumer communication and the use of celebrities catapulted the brand to international status.

Entertainment has been a part of diet Coke's heritage since it was launched in 1982. Numerous celebrities have appeared in diet Coke advertising, including Sharon Stone, Demi Moore, Pierce Brosnan, Paul Abdul, Whitney Houston, Elton John, George Michael, Evander Holyfield, and Katarina Witt, to name a few. Through the 1980s, the primary message to consumers about diet Coke was the "one calorie" theme along with images of fitness, shapeliness, and

Choose your refreshment.

©1997 The Coca-Cola Company. "Coca-Cola," "diet Coke," "Sprite" and the Contour Bottle design are registered trademarks of The Coca-Cola Company.

looking good. In the early 1990s, diet Coke introduced its "diet Coke break" commercial featuring Lucky Vanous. The diet coke break spots were extremely popular, helping to launch Vanous's career in filmmaking. Changes in brand positioning resulted in a focus on the "just for the taste of it approach" and the use of entertainment personalities conveyed the fun and enjoyment of drinking diet Coke.

In March 2001, diet Coke launched a new advertising campaign with the tagline "That Certain Something.", a campaign celebrating the real and human attributes that make people attractive and alluring in the eyes of another. The campaign featured the voices of five of the hottest stars from the silver screen—Renee Zellweger, Ed Burns, Ben Affleck, Matthew McConaughey and Ashley Judd. Shot from the narrator's point of view, these celebrity voiceovers were used to add a subtly recognizable, yet intriguing, feel to the spots, while also reinforcing the longstanding connection between diet Coke and the world of entertainment, which has been a part of the brand's heritage since its inception.

BRAND VALUES

Diet Coke is the soft drink of choice for adults—it tastes great and exudes spirit and sophistication. People drink diet Coke because it is more than a beverage; they see it as an exten-

sion of their personality that mirrors how they feel about themselves both inside and out—confident, energetic, and appealing. Diet Coke is one of those great brands that recognizes that attractiveness today goes beyond the surface—it's that indescribable, "certain something" on the inside that shines through.

THINGS YOU DIDN'T KNOW ABOUT DIET COKE

○ Diet Coke is the biggest selling diet carbonated soft drink in the world.

○ Diet Coke is currently sold in 149 countries. In 46 of them, it is known as "Coca-Cola light."

○ Diet Coke is The Coca-Cola Company's third biggest-selling brand in the United States. Coca-Cola is number one and Sprite is number two.

○ Coca-Cola, Coca-Cola light, Coke, and diet Coke, and the design of the Coke contour bottle are all trademarks of The Coca-Cola Company.

○ Diet Coke was named "Brand of the Decade" by the publication *Advertising Age* in December 1990.

CHANNEL

THE MARKET

The U.S. cable television marketplace is experiencing tremendous growth in both size and scope. By 2004, the cable industry will realize $86.4 billion in annual revenues, compared to just $39.0 billion for the web and $48.2 billion for broadcast television, according to Veronis, Suhler & Associates.

Cable affiliates offer customers a variety of services, from analog cable television programming, to digital-cable tiers with hundreds of channels, to pay-per-view movies and specials, to high-speed data service for at-home Internet access, to telephony. Television viewing remains the number-one leisure time activity, cited by 98 percent of all consumers.

ACHIEVEMENTS

Disney Channel is available in over 70 million U.S. homes on basic cable and satellite service. The channel is top-rated on the basic cable network in prime-time among "tweens" 9–14. Disney Channel consistently has 20 or more of the top 25 basic cable movies among these viewers.

Disney Channel ranks first in importance for the enjoyment of cable or satellite TV among subscribers with kids under 13, according to Beta.

Online, the Zoog Disney web site (ZoogDisney.com) has reached an all-time record of 87,000 daily unique visitors, accounting for a record 1.1 million daily page requests.

HISTORY

Walt Disney, the man who gave the world the first sound cartoon and its first full-length animated movie, "Snow White and the Seven Dwarfs", was a pioneer in the new medium of television as well. He produced TV Christmas specials as early as 1950 and 1951, and his first, long-running, television anthology series, "Disneyland," debuted in 1954 on the fledgling ABC television network.

His first-season show, "Operation Undersea", took viewers behind the scenes of his upcoming movie "20,000 Leagues Under the Sea" and Walt collected an Emmy for "Best Individual Show". With such programs and

nature shows, Disney movies, and even Disney animation created for the series, Walt had produced a new mix of family entertainment. The Disney anthology approach endures today with the program bearing "The Wonderful World of Disney" name.

Disney Channel, with an unparalleled library resulting from decades of television programming and movie production, was founded in 1983 as a pay-cable television channel. After only 18 weeks, Disney Channel was available on cable systems in all 50 U.S. states. After the first year, it had more than one million householder subscribers.

The 1980s saw Disney Channel delivering world television premieres of animated classics and developing original movie productions. A new-and-updated "Mickey Mouse Club" series was launched in 1989, and the second-generation Mouseketeers included future music sensations Britney Spears, Christina Aguilera and Justin Timberlake of the group 'NSYNC.

By 1990, Disney Channel had more than five million U.S. household subscribers, and was delivering world television premieres of Disney animated classics including several Emmy® Award-winning programs. The channel shifted from a pay-cable service to a basic cable service to prevent subscriber erosion to satellite providers.

Later in the decade, Disney Channel charted a course that reflected the shift in viewing habits in a multi-channel, multi-media universe. When research revealed that kids wanted to

spend more time with their parents, and families wanted to be together, Disney Channel answered the call. *The New York Times* noted "(t)hat is very different from the 'kids rule' irreverence [of] Disney's competitors...."

THE PRODUCT

The Walt Disney Company is a diversified worldwide entertainment company with operations in five business segments: Media Networks, Studio Entertainment, Parks & Resorts, Consumer Products, and the Disney Internet Group.

Disney Channel is the first full-time general entertainment television network designed for kids and families. It resides in the Media Networks segment of The Walt Disney Company. Media Networks operates the ABC Television Network and owns television and radio stations. It also operates cable programming services through subsidiaries, including ESPN-branded networks, Disney Channel International and SoapNet.

Although Mickey Mouse is no longer a programming focus of Disney Channel, he remains its corporate "host" and appears in Disney Channel's brand logo off-air. The silhouette of the logo is a combination of his universally recognized ears and the box shape of a television set. In this high-tech future, the box shape also symbolizes a personal computer.

"Playhouse Disney" is now the morning programming block on Disney Channel, dedicated to kids 2–5 and their parents and caregivers, with the brand promise of "learning powered by imagination". Original series include the Emmy® Award-winning winning "Bear in the Big Blue House" from Jim Henson Television, "Out of the Box", Disney's "PB&J Otter" and "Rolie Polie Olie".

New in 2001 are "The Book of Pooh", the first TV series to combine the 300-year-old art of Japanese "bunraku" puppetry with newly-developed computer-generated virtual sets, and "Stanley", an animated series.

The afternoon and evening programming block on Disney Channel is now "Zoog Disney", dedicated to kids 9–14 ("tweens") and their viewing and Internet-use habits. The brand promise of Zoog Disney is "TV you do"—convergence of the on-air experience with online features and enhancement at ZoogDisney.com.

Programming is a tween-dedicated mix of original movies, series and specials.

Original movies have included "Miracle in Lane 2", starring Frankie Muniz; "Zenon" and "Zenon the Zequel", starring Kirsten Storms, "Horse Sense", starring Joey and Andy Lawrence, and "Jett Jackson: The Movie", starring Lee Thompson Young.

Original narrative series on Zoog Disney currently include "The Famous Jett Jackson", "The Jersey", and "So Weird". New in 2001 is a stronger focus on comedies, with "Lizzie McGuire", new episodes of "Even Stevens" and the premiere of the animated series "The Proud Family".

Original reality series on Zoog Disney include "Bug Juice", (the adventures of kids at summer camp), "Totally Hoops" (the adventures of a girls' basketball team); and "Totally Circus" (the adventures of kids at a real-life camp for teen circus performers).

Each night, the rich history of the Walt Disney Company is tapped in "Vault Disney", an overnight programming block dedicated to nostalgic adults and families.

RECENT DEVELOPMENTS

Times have changed yet again, and once more Disney Channel has changed, evolving from its appeal to adults, to whole families and on to its current positioning—a kid's brand accessible to parents.

"A great way to win is to know your brand, and identify a niche in the marketplace and an audience you're going to commit that brand to," said Anne Sweeney, president of Disney Channel Worldwide.

Research confirmed to Disney Channel executives the national trend away from "co-viewing" by all family members simultaneously. Further, they recognized the unique viewing habits of kids versus parents, and younger versus older kids.

© Disney

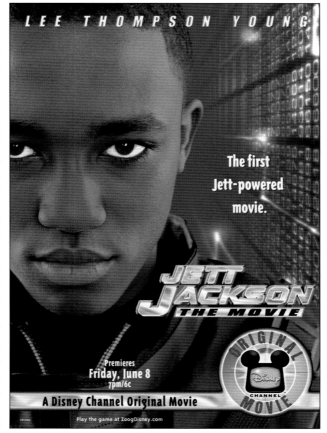

LEE THOMPSON YOUNG

The first Jett-powered movie.

JETT JACKSON THE MOVIE

Premieres
Friday, June 8
7pm/6c

A Disney Channel Original Movie

ORIGINAL MOVIE

Play the game at ZoogDisney.com

The result is the new comprehensive sub-branding strategy dividing the on-air experience into the three distinct blocks described above.

Disney Channel is a global brand and is available worldwide in places like the United Kingdom, Germany, Spain, Australia, Singapore, Taiwan, the Middle East and Latin American countries.

PROMOTION

Disney Channel is promoted nationwide via comprehensive marketing campaigns, employing TV, print and radio advertising; promotional offers; local events; online experiences; direct mail efforts and more.

National tours are an important part of this marketing mix—including "PremEARS in the Park", "Playhouse Disney Live!" and Toon Disney's "Most Animated Kid Search".

Off-air extensions are also important. For example, Disney Channel's "Bear in the Big Blue House" product is available as plush dolls, a nationwide tour event, a home video series, books, a music CD and so on.

Another promotional accomplishment is the success of Disney Channel's brand extension "Toon Disney". This 24-hour channel of Disney animation was launched in the U.S. in 1998. At the beginning of 2001, Toon Disney was already available in more than 15 million households nationwide.

BRAND VALUES

The Disney brand provides quality entertainment embodying magic, fantasy, creativity, trust and values such as decency, optimism and community spirit.

Disney Channel's brand vision is to become the first-choice television brand for kids, offering relevant original programming specific to age groups and converging with experiences that touch their lives off-air and online.

Focus groups have confirmed that the channel is known for such virtues as trust, quality and safety.

THE MARKET

Did you know that the average person in the U.S. consumes almost 15 pounds of salty snacks each year? That is worth over $11 billion in retail sales for the salty snack industry, made up predominantly of potato chips (40 percent) and tortilla chips (25 percent), but also comprising corn chips (5 percent), pretzels (8 percent), cheese puffs (7 percent), pre-popped popcorn (4 percent), and other segments (11 percent).

Salty snack consumers are largely impulse purchasers, and therefore value, visibility and variety are key to driving sales. Variety is especially important to younger consumers, who are proportionately the largest consumers of flavored salty snacks. Flavored tortilla chips are a big part of variety-seekers' "diet," and are a $2 billion category, which has grown at approximately 8 percent per year over the past 5 years. Frito-Lay introduced flavored tortilla chips to Americans with its Doritos® brand, and today Doritos® remains the only national player in the flavored tortilla chip category.

ACHIEVEMENTS

Doritos® is the second largest dry edible brand in the U.S.—second only to its sister product Lay's® Potato Chips. Frito-Lay's constant innovation, unique advertising and positioning, and world-class sales and distribution system have allowed the Doritos® brand to grow steadily since its 1964 introduction, with sales almost doubling over the past decade. The Doritos® flagship flavor, Nacho Cheesier®, is the number one selling item within Frito-Lay North America year after year.

On the brand equity front, Doritos® steps out of the world of food to play among popular fashion brands. Doritos® has the third highest brand equity (as defined by Frito-Lay internal measures) among the general U.S. population after benchmark brands Nike and Levi's, and ranks ahead of Coca-Cola, Oreos, and Reebok. Among teens, Doritos® ranks number two on brand equity. Doritos® chips receive high marks from teens on other attributes as well, being their #1 consumed snack and the "coolest" snack as measured by the 2000 Teen Research Unlimited "Coolest Brands" meter.

HISTORY

In the early 1960s, Frito-Lay already manufactured the Lay's®, Ruffles® and Fritos® brands,

but was on the lookout for an opportunity to innovate. The opportunity appeared in Doritos® tortilla chips, which were first introduced to the West Coast in 1964 by Alex Foods. Frito-Lay purchased the brand one year later, and by 1966, the original Toasted Corn flavor could be found nationwide. In those early days, Doritos® tortilla chips were positioned as a "unique Latin snack," which had appeal far beyond the Latino population. The trademark "Doritos®" is suggestive of the Latin word "do-ra-dos" meaning 'golden' – which the brand has certainly been for Frito-Lay.

The Doritos® brand story is one of constant improvement, innovation, and variety. In 1969, Taco flavor was introduced, which still exists in regions today, but the big hit came with the launch of the Nacho Cheese flavor in 1972.

While this flavor got off to a slow start, the focus of marketing dollars in the first few years made sales skyrocket. The flavor was continuously improved over the years, with a major relaunch as Nacho Cheesier® in 1992, and with each improvement sales grew. Today, with eleven flavors in the Doritos® brand portfolio, Nacho Cheesier® continues to be the top seller.

Over the years, many other new flavors of Doritos® chips were introduced. In 1986, Cool Ranch was introduced, and improved to Cooler Ranch® in 1994. Subsequent flavors Sour Cream and Onion, Salsa Rio, Jumpin' Jack Flash, Pizza Cravers and Smokey Red BBQ™ are part of the Doritos® brand history and, who knows, may reappear some day. Salsa Verde, Spicier Nacho®, Sonic Sour Cream™ and Baja Picante™ are among those flavors that are still available today.

Different product forms of the Doritos® brand have also been introduced to target new consumption occasions. A variety of lighter products was introduced in the '80s and '90s, with the most recent being the launch of the Doritos® Wow!® brand, which utilizes the fat-substitute Olestra. Doritos®3D's® puffed corn snacks were introduced nationally in 1998, and today are available in 2 flavors: Nacho Cheesier® and Jalapeño Cheddar.

Frito-Lay will continue to combine product innovation and improvement with superior selling and marketing to deliver continued growth for the Doritos® brand in the years to come.

THE PRODUCT

Doritos® chips are known for their triangular shape, satisfying crunch, and bold flavors. The product is made of yellow corn, and has very specific quality standards, which include the size and thickness of the chip, the roundness of the corners, the perfection of "blisters" (air bubbles) and "toast points" on the chip.

In the quest for continually improved product quality, Doritos® were introduced in a new metallized packaging in early 2000. This pack-

aging makes the chips taste fresher longer, so fans receive the best tasting product, and gives the brand a modern, eye-catching appeal.

Doritos® chips are currently available in five flavors nation-wide—Nacho Cheesier®, Cooler Ranch®, Four Cheese, Nacho Cheesier® 3D's® and Jalapeño Cheddar 3D's®. Regionally, the variety-seeking consumer can also find Salsa Verde, Spicier Nacho®, Baja Picante™, Sonic Sour Cream™, Taco, Toasted Corn, and a variety of Doritos® Wow!® flavors. Doritos® chips come in various sizes from a 1 oz. kids lunch bag to a 25 oz. supersize.

RECENT DEVELOPMENTS

Frito-Lay continuously strives to improve the Doritos® flagship flavor, Nacho Cheesier®, and in 2001, consumers are getting even more of the nacho cheese flavor they love. The product improvement is accompanied by a new advertising campaign and significant marketing support.

In addition, 2001 welcomes a new Four Cheese flavor, in honor of Doritos® strong cheese heritage. The four cheeses in the flavor are Monterey Jack, Parmesan, Cheddar and American, and combined with just the right spices, these chips will remind consumers that no one does cheese like the Doritos® brand.

The next significant innovation on the brand will be Doritos® Extreme™ — an extra thick, extra crunchy Doritos® made with a coarser grind of corn, for a bolder, more rugged teen snack. Doritos® Extreme™ will be introduced in August of 2001 in two bold flavors: Zesty Sour Cream & Cheddar and Bold BBQ.

PROMOTION

Since the beginning, brand-building advertising has been a core element of Frito-Lay's strategy for the Doritos® brand, and the first campaign for the brand, "The new beat in things to eat," set the stage for a long-term relationship with music. Over the years Doritos® brand advertising has featured many famous faces. Avery Schreiber in the early '70s claimed that "One good crunch deserves another." Jay Leno starred in the first spots to switch focus from purchasers (moms) to consumers (teens) in 1986. Chevy Chase rescued a bag of Doritos® chips from being steam-rolled in 1993 and Ali Landry captured the hearts of many Americans with her acrobatics for Doritos® 3D's® in 1998. The most recent campaign for Doritos®, "The

Loudest Taste on Earth," created in 1997 by BBDO Worldwide, won the coveted Silver Effie, and continued Doritos® long-standing relationship with American teens. 2001 sees the return of Ali Landry, as well as new advertising later in the year that celebrates the Doritos® experience.

Frito-Lay believes that to be seen as a big brand, it is necessary to act like a big brand, and therefore, broad-scale visibility for Doritos® is critical. In the early 1990's, Doritos® chips were advertised on the Super Bowl and sponsored the half-time show. In the summer of 2000, Frito-Lay tied Doritos® in with the CBS hit "Survivor," and continued this relationship with "Survivor II" in early 2001.

In-store presence is another key factor in the success of an impulse product like Doritos® chips, and over the years Frito-Lay has been known for the innovative and impactful "retail theatre" and consumer promotions which usually feature the Doritos® brand. Doritos® have been featured on lobby displays themed with the Super Bowl and the NFL, Disney, NCAA basketball, and many other crowd-pleasing associations. The most memorable of these may be PepsiCo's on-going relationship with Star Wars, which has driven unprecedented consumer excitement. The innovative way that Frito-Lay and its promotional agency, Frankel, brought Star Wars alive in-store through point of sale materials earned them a PRO Award in 2000 for promotional excellence.

Frito-Lay's focus for Doritos® over the next years will be on continuing to deliver breakthrough advertising and marketing ideas that set the standard in the snack food industry and that deliver high consumer involvement.

BRAND VALUES

Doritos® chips appeal to consumers young and old, but the heaviest users are teens and young adults. Frito-Lay aims to understand the teen and young adult life experience, and to enhance that experience in a way that makes the Doritos® brand an integral part of teen Americana.

(Sources: Data is derived predominantly from internal sources and from Information Resources, Inc.)

THINGS YOU DIDN'T KNOW ABOUT DORITOS® CHIPS

○ Over 5 million bags of Doritos® chips are sold every day in the U.S.

○ It takes 10,000 dairy cows to make all the cheese and dairy products used for 1 year of Doritos® sales!

○ If Frito-Lay laid out the packaging of all of the Doritos® bags it sells each year, end to end, the packaging would stretch around the earth more than 15 times (at the equator)!

○ In 1991, 250 million bags of Doritos® chips were airlifted to troops in Saudi Arabia who had requested them by name.

○ 98 percent of adults (and 99 percent of teens) are aware of Doritos® chips, and 69 percent of Americans claim to have eaten them in the past 4 weeks.

Energizer

THE MARKET

Americans are unplugged. They play, communicate, calculate and plan all with the help of portable power. Energizer® batteries power the lifestyle of this on-the-go society. In fact, the average American household owns more than 17 battery-operated devices, and that number continues to climb. In a technological game of leapfrog, devices evolve as battery power improves and battery power improves to make way for the next evolution of gadgets and gizmos.

More devices with added bells and whistles are certainly one trend that drives the category. Smaller devices are another. For example, music machines once the size of a small suitcase now fit in the palm of your hand. This trend toward miniaturization has made AA and AAA size batteries the workhorses of the category. Of the more than five billion batteries sold each year, 80 percent of them are AA or AAA sizes, according to A.C. Nielsen.

In short, there is an ever-increasing demand for reliable batteries that can keep pace with today's mobile lifestyles. *Energizer* continues to be the leading premium alkaline power source that keeps families "going…and going …and going…."

ACHIEVEMENTS

Energizer invented alkaline batteries in the late 1950s and has continued to enhance them over the years. Since 1960, the service life of an *Energizer* battery has improved dramatically. Anticipating the trend toward high-tech devices, *Energizer* led the industry in designing batteries to meet the power requirements of these sophisticated devices.

The company continues to innovate in all segments of the battery category. *Energizer* was the first company to:

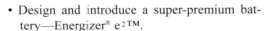

™

- Design and introduce a super-premium battery—Energizer® e2™.
- Harness the power of lithium in a AA cell size.
- Revolutionize the rechargeable category when it introduced a full line of high-powered Nickel Metal Hydride (NiMH) cells—Energizer® ACCU Rechargeable™ batteries.
- Offer consumers an on-battery tester to check the remaining power in the battery.

Energizer is the world's largest manufacturer of batteries and portable lighting products.

Energizer products are distributed in more than 160 countries. In the U.S. alone, *Energizer* sells more than 3.5 million batteries per day. *Energizer* manufactures nearly one out of three batteries sold in the world.

HISTORY

The country was alive with the spirit of discovery in the 1890s, when Joshua Lionel Cohen began selling his latest invention, a tiny battery-and-bulb device used to illuminate flowers in a pot. Conrad Hubert, who operated a New York City restaurant, was so impressed that he quit his job to sell the devices for Cowen. When the power failed in a restaurant where Hubert had just installed the flowerpots, he had an inspiration—put the "flowerpot lights" in people's hands. And the seeds for Eveready Battery Company—and portable power—were planted.

Hubert acquired the patent for the first Eveready® "electric hand torch" in 1898. His first flashlights were handmade, consisting of a dry cell battery, a bulb, and a rough brass reflector inside a paper tube. By 1900, his flashlights were sold in London, Montreal, Paris, Berlin, and Sydney, Australia.

Hubert's company, the American Electrical Novelty and Manufacturing Company, became American Ever Ready in 1905 to emphasize the dependability of its flashlight products. American Ever Ready merged in 1914 with National Carbon Company, whose six-inch tall "Columbia" battery was the first used to power home telephones.

The newly formed company, which was the only manufacturer specializing in both battery and lighting products, merged with Union Carbide Company three years later, and, as it expanded, the company's *"Eveready"* brand name became synonymous with power and reliability.

THE PRODUCT

Energizer offers a unique, complete portfolio of products designed to meet the distinct needs and expectations of different consumer groups. The flagship brand, *Energizer*, offers premium, long-lasting battery performance fueled by a continuous commitment to product improvement.

On the high end, *Energizer e2* established the super-premium category. Advanced titanium technology and cell construction resulted in a super long-lasting battery. The company also offers a value brand, Eveready Alkaline, for consumers seeking both a lower price and a dependable brand name they can trust.

In addition to primary batteries, *Energizer* manufactures miniature batteries for hearing aids, watches, wireless remotes, and other devices. In the rechargeable battery segment, *Energizer* provides both round cells and power packs for cordless phones and camcorders.

Energizer ACCU Rechargeable batteries are on the cutting edge of technology, providing the highest capacity cell in the marketplace. The reusable, renewable batteries can be charged up to 1,000 times, which makes them an exceptional value over time.

RECENT DEVELOPMENTS

Over the course of several decades, the company continued to grow, focusing upon its strong reputation as the dependable battery that you can trust. The batteries were certainly reliable, but one young, persistent scientist knew they could be better, and his work launched a new era for the company.

Assigned to an existing *Eveready* division in 1957, Lew Urry soon began to focus on an entirely new chemical system—a system known today as alkaline. Urry made a mock-up of an alkaline battery from an empty flashlight shaft, inserted it into a toy car and tested it on the cafeteria floor. The Vice President of Technology at the time brought two flashlights to the then-head of the Consumer Products Division and asked him to leave both on overnight. One light contained carbon zinc batteries and the other, alkaline batteries. To their surprise, the alkaline-powered flashlight was "still going" in the morning, while the carbon zinc-powered light had gone dead. The rest, you could say, is history. Alkaline batteries now make up 91 percent of all batteries sold in the U.S., according to A.C. Nielsen. And, just a few years ago, the company began using *Energizer*

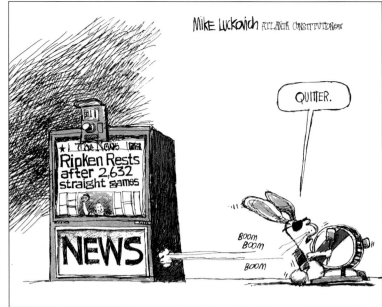

world. Urry's prototype cell is displayed at the Smithsonian Museum of Natural History.

PROMOTION

Energizer—the battery with the power to keep you going...and going.... This long-lasting power is embodied by the Energizer Bunny®, the likeable, infamous, battery-operated toy, one of the most recognizable symbols of perseverance and determination. The pink, furry Energizer Bunny with flip-flops and oversized sunglasses began marching across television screens in 1989 and drumming up quite a "bang" for *Energizer* batteries.

He first appeared in a parody of a competitor's "Toys" campaign in which he not only lasted longer than toys powered by the competitor's batteries but kept "going...and going..." right off the commercial set as an off-camera voice yelled, "Stop the Bunny!" Since that time he has appeared in more than 110 TV spots, always with an element of fun, an element of surprise, and a message of long-lasting power. The campaign has generated more than 119 billion consumer impressions since it was introduced.

Today, the Energizer Bunny has earned pop-culture icon status and is a favorite character to millions of Americans. The Energizer Bunny is so popular he has been invited to appear at weddings, class reunions, birthday parties, and even church services. His photo sits by the bedside of critically ill children whose parents are looking for a symbol of encouragement.

The Energizer Bunny's tagline, "keeps going...and going...and going...", a now famous trademark of *Energizer*, has become so popular that it is used to describe perennially successful sports, entertainment, and political figures. The Energizer Bunny campaign itself has won several dozen television advertising awards and consistently ranks among America's top 10 favorite advertising campaigns in annual polls.

The Energizer Bunny not only uses his notoriety to promote the brand, he also uses it to advance important causes. He leads the crusade for home fire-safety through the company's "Change Your Clock, Change Your Battery™"

program, through sales promotion, on the web, and in classrooms across the country, where he takes the message directly to children who are five times more likely to be critically hurt in a home fire.

The program is conducted in partnership with the International Association of Fire Chiefs and is attributed with helping to reduce U.S. home-fire deaths by 50 percent over the last decade.

BRAND VALUES

Energizer has a unique approach to the marketplace. Its goal is to match consumer wants and needs with the most meaningful, reliable, long-lasting product offerings. As a result, *Energizer* offers the broadest product line-up in the industry. The company's primary brand, *Energizer*, provides long-lasting power that keeps going ...and going...and going.... It is the battery families depend on to keep their fun going... and going...and going....

Energizer, e², Energizer Bunny, *Energizer ACCU Rechargeable*, and "Change Your Clock, Change Your Battery," are trademarks of Eveready Battery Company, Inc.

---

as its trade name to emphasize the alkaline focus and the flagship brand.

Lew Urry, a 40-year veteran at *Energizer*, is a highly respected senior fellow at the company, where he is known as "the father of alkaline." He holds over 50 patents covering battery designs and systems, but his invention of the first commercially viable alkaline battery remains a shining success story to *Energizer*, who brought the first alkaline batteries to the

E✳TRADE
It's your money.

THE MARKET

The growth of online trading has been explosive. NASDAQ reports that 20 percent of all retail securities trades are now processed online, and the number of online brokers has grown from 27 just four years ago to 150 at the beginning of this year.

The leaders in this historical development include E*TRADE, which began offering electronic trading services in 1992 and is now among the top three online securities firms, according to Gomez, Inc., a leading e-commerce analyst. Charles Schwab & Co., Fidelity, and E*TRADE were the only three electronic trading firms to earn a score of 7+, out of a possible 10, in the Gomez Spring 2001 listing.

Despite its rapid emergence as a leader in its field, E*TRADE still faces challenges. The major one, according to *Business Week* magazine, is for the firm "to establish itself as the top online financial services operation while fighting off cut-rate, bare-bone competition and do all that before the financial-services industry's giants, like Merrill Lynch & Co., bring all their marketing muscle to bear on the Web."

ACHIEVEMENTS

E*TRADE has become a global leader in online, personal financial services with branded Web sites around the world. It has become the No. 1 global online broker, serving investors in 13 countries, and operates the world's largest Internet bank.

It has created an innovative, low-cost alternative for the individual investor to 'bricks and mortar' institutions. The company was the first securities and financial services firm to be awarded the CPA Web Trust seal of assurance by the American Institute of Certified Public Accountants.

In March 2000, E*TRADE earned the No. 1 overall ranking in Gomez Advisors' Internet Broker Scorecard™ for the sixth time in eight quarters. The company was named the No. 1 online investing site by the Lafferty Information & Research Group in its Lafferty Internet Ratings Web-based financial-services report.

A 1999 survey by NFO Market Research found that E*TRADE's top-of-mind brand awareness is greater than that of its competitors combined.

And Opinion Research Corp. ranked E*TRADE among the top four most recognized blue-chip Internet brands, along with Amazon.com, eBay, and Priceline.com

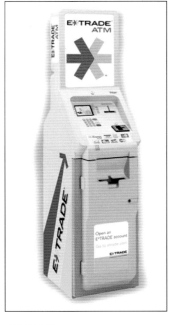

HISTORY

E*TRADE's forerunner, TRADEPLUS was founded as a service bureau in 1982 by Bill Porter, a physicist and inventor with more than a dozen patents to his credit. The company originally provided online quote and trading services to Fidelity, Charles Schwab, and Quick & Reilly.

Porter began wondering why, as an individual investor, he had to pay a broker hundreds of dollars for stock transactions. He envisioned the ultimate solution: investors using their personal computers to make their own purchases.

Porter started E*TRADE Securities, Incorporated, in 1992 as an all-electronic brokerage that offered online investing services through America Online and CompuServe.

Two key events in 1996 marked the beginning of the explosive growth that made E*TRADE the giant it is today: Christos M. Cotsakos became Chairman of the Board and CEO of the company and www.etrade.com was launched, which generated explosive demand for E*TRADE services.

Cotsakos, who had earned the Bronze Star, Army and Commendation Medal for Valor, the Air Medal and a Purple Heart in Vietnam War combat, amongst other citations and ribbons during his years of service, had 20 years of top management experience at Federal Express and A.C. Neilsen, prior to joining E*TRADE.

THE PRODUCT

A leading branded provider of online investing services, E*TRADE has established a popular destination web site for self-directed investors.

The company offers independent investors the convenience and control across a variety of brokerage, banking, insurance and wealth management services. E*TRADE offers investing opportunities that include stocks, options, initial public offerings (IPOs), mutual funds, and bonds. It also delivers a wide range of financial services that cover banking, bill management, advice, retirement planning, college savings planning, mortgage, real estate, insurance, and taxes. It sells shares in about 5,200 mutual funds and has 10 in-house branded index funds.

In addition, E*TRADE has a suite of value-added products and services that can be personalized. They include portfolio tracking, real-time stock quotes, Smart Alerts, market commentary and analysis, news, investor community areas, Power E*TRADE, the Knowledge Center, and other services.

The tools and services provided through Power E*TRADE include MarketTrader, where investors can view and manage their daily trading activities; as well as access real-time, level II quotes and charts; real-time balances, positions, and buying power; news, information, and investment ideas, and priority customer services.

The Knowledge Center contains advice on the basics of investing, advanced strategies, taxes that affect investment activity, and on reading financial statements.

RECENT DEVELOPMENTS

E*TRADE's net revenues for its 2000 fiscal year were $1.4 billion, representing growth of 104 percent, and customer assets went up to $66 billion.

The company reached 3.3 three million customer accounts, seven times the total just two years earlier. Working toward its goal of becoming a financial supermarket, E*TRADE acquired a bank that offers federally insured CDs and

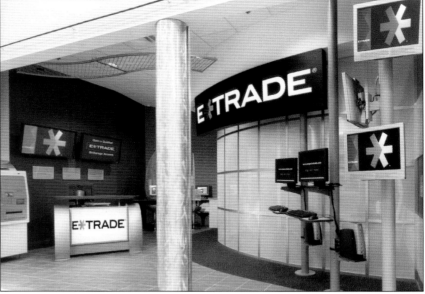

savings, checking, and money-market accounts, and also bought the nation's third largest ATM network, which it plans to continue expanding substantially. Additionally, E*TRADE acquired one of the nation's leading and largest online mortgage originators in January 2001, allowing the company to create its own mortgage origination platform that integrates both banking and brokerage.

E*TRADE reached a milestone during 2001 with the opening of E*TRADE Center in New York. Over 30,000 square feet, E*TRADE Center provides visitors with the ability to make financial transactions in their E*TRADE brokerage and bank accounts, participate in educational seminars, interact with financial service associates, browse through financial books, purchase items at the E*TRADE gift store and dine in the Mangia Café. The Center also contains a full service production studio where E*TRADE broadcasts E*TRADE On Air, featuring daily live audio and video financial news to keep investors apprised of current financial markets. The Center is the next phase of the company's physical presence approach, including its E*TRADE Zones concept which will be rolled out in 20 new locations across the nation.

It has also enhanced its visibility through partnerships with major Internet and other companies that include *Target Stores, Yahoo! Microsoft, Intuit, United Airlines, Delta Airlines, and Ernst & Young.*

E*TRADE has also introduced extended-hours trading that enables investors to obtain quotes and place orders before and after regular trading hours, enabling individuals to react to market-moving news that develops outside traditional trading periods.

Other innovations include the launching of an integrated wireless banking platform enabling customers to access their balances, to transfer funds, and pay bills at anytime, anywhere.

Additionally, the company has expanded its wireless strategy through carrier agreements with Sprint PCS and Nextel Communications in addition to existing agreements with Verizon Wireless, AT&T Wireless, and GTE Wireless. The expanded strategy gives E*TRADE the widest potential wireless reach of any financial services provider.

Worth magazine describes the company's future this way:

"E*TRADE is coming of age just as its core client group enters the period of life when financial decisions multiply. Young paycheck investors are turning into stock traders, 401(k) investors, bank account holders, insurance shoppers, and mortgage holders. E*TRADE is in a position to play a leading role in all those choices and to serve us as we sit in front of our PCs and Internet appliances at home and work, as we take our PDAs and Web phones on the road, and as we move through the day, at kiosks and storefronts and corporate compounds. If it can keep its new customers as loyal as its existing ones have been, the company's strategy will pay off richly."

PROMOTION
E*TRADE's marketing has been a driving force in the evolution of company goals from building awareness of the online investing industry to generating brand preference to its present position as a provider of a wide range of personalized products and services.

The advertising campaign launched in 1996 with the theme "Some day we'll all invest this way," educated consumers to the then-revolutionary notion of self-directed brokerage accounts. In 1999, the message was "It's time for E*TRADE. The #1 place to invest online," which built mainstream brand awareness and leadership. That campaign was geared to investor self-reliance and was part of an integrated marketing program that used a bold, creative style backed by a wide media reach to appeal to the changing profile of millions of U.S. investors.

It recognized the dramatic demographic change taking place as online investing shifted from a niche category to a major consumer lifestyle phenomenon.

The positioning of the current campaign is "E*TRADE. It's Your Money," which reflects the evolution into an integrated financial services company for empowered investors with multiple investment needs.

Says Michael Sievert, chief sales and marketing officer of E*TRADE Group, Inc., "E*TRADE is extending its value proposition to consumers beyond just that of online investing. Through the introduction of new products and features in banking, wealth management, and brokerage, E*TRADE is delivering a comprehensive and personalized approach to online financial services. This approach reflects today's consumers' unique voice, values, and needs. E*TRADE is striving to put power and choice back into the hands of individuals by giving them the tools they need to succeed and enabling individual investors to realize their financial potential."

BRAND VALUES
E*TRADE helped establish online investing and has moved from the role of pioneer to asserting its rightful position as the brand of choice. The E*TRADE brand is one of the world's most powerful, blue-chip, e-commerce brands existing today.

The brand resonates with individual investors because it reflects their unique voice and values and emphasizes the importance of giving power and choice to its customers.

Brand awareness reached 96 percent in February of 2000, compared with 80 percent just five months earlier.

FARMERS

THE MARKET

The mission of Farmers Insurance Group of Los Angeles, Calif., is to "become first choice in protecting and in building peoples' assets in our chosen markets." Farmers operates across a wide spectrum of the insurance and financial services field. Members of the Farmers Insurance Group include the third-largest provider of passenger automobile and homeowner insurance. Farmers is also a major presence in the financial services industry, offering a wide range of products that include home and vehicle financing, life insurance, investments, retirement planning, mortgage assistance, and education loans.

ACHIEVEMENTS

Efficiency and innovation have been the keys to success for Farmers since its founding as a small regional company more than 70 years ago. Farmers instituted direct billing. It issued six-month policies with automatic continuation upon payment of each renewal premium, eliminating the need for issuing policies annually or semi-annually. The company founded the Truck Insurance Exchange with trucking industry leaders serving as advisors on development of a safety-engineering program to reduce the frequency of commercial-vehicle accidents. As a result of continuing expansion that enabled it to provide a broad range of coverage, Farmers' agents were able to fill nearly all of a customer's insurance needs. The establishment of Prematic Insurance Corporation in 1961 allowed customers to make just one monthly payment on an account that includes auto, home, business, and life insurance. Now called Farmers EasyPay℠, the plan is not a finance arrangement. The customer pays a small monthly service charge, not interest.

Farmers was one of the first insurers to automate all auto and home coverage and its Agency Computer Network makes policies and client files available in agents' and district managers' offices as well as in the headquarters. The network, the first and most comprehensive in the industry, also links the home office with branch claims offices.

In 1998, the company introduced after-hours claims service, which allows customers to report a claim at any hour of the day or night.

The Farmers Friendly Review program enables review of a customer's entire insurance coverage to eliminate unnecessary and costly duplications and guard against gaps in protection.

The company, which installed the first IBM mainframe computers in California, has extended its technological capabilities to the point where it now processes 98 percent of all policies electronically and mails policy information to customers in less than 48 hours, compared with several days just a few years ago.

HISTORY

On March 28, 1928, the Board of Governors of the Farmers Automobile Inter-Insurance Company met for the first time. That meeting marked the beginning of the organization. Cofounders John C. Tyler and Thomas E. Leavey became president and vice president, respectively. The company opened for business the following month as Farmers Automobile Inter-Insurance Exchange in small rented offices in Los Angeles to serve the Southern California market. Its original strategy was selling auto-insurance to residents of rural areas at lower rates than those being paid by drivers in urban areas, where risks were higher.

The first policy was sold just two weeks after the first board meeting. Within two years, the new company had issued more than 40,000 policies. The staff expanded from four to 46 over that period, and some 700 agents were working out of 44 district offices.

By the end of 1931, Farmers was licensed to sell automobile insurance in eight states. A Midwestern branch was opened in 1935 with a teletype connection to the home office. While the country was in the grip of the worst economic depression in its history, Farmers premium income continued increasing throughout the early and middle 1930s, reaching $5 million in 1937, an unprecedented rate of growth for the insurance industry.

The addition of the Fire Insurance Exchange in 1942 enabled account selling, and by 1943 the Group was writing insurance in 19 states.

When it reached its 20th year in 1948, Farmers had nearly 700,000 policies in force and assets of $30 million, compared to its original $50,000. Life insurance was added to the Group offerings in the 1950s and a major step forward was the organization of Mid-Century Insurance Company as a multi-line carrier supplementing the coverage of the auto, truck, and fire exchanges.

THE PRODUCT

The Farmers Insurance Group offers a comprehensive portfolio of insurance products—

In late 1999, Farmers purchased the Foremost Insurance Group, the leading insurer of manufactured homes and other specialty lines.

PROMOTION

The organization's promotion centers on its basic promise to customers: Farmers. Gets you back where you belong®.

That pledge is based on the recognition that the ultimate test of any insurer's efficiency and service is the way it handles claims. Recovering from the loss leading to the claim is why individuals and businesses buy insurance in the first place, and Farmers sales efforts are keyed to that reality.

Television, radio, and print campaigns, geared to support of the fundamental mission, have been honored with a substantial number of awards testifying to the ads' creative excellence.

In June of 2000 alone, the company won seven awards at the Insurance Marketing Communication Association's annual meeting and Showcase Awards in Hilton Head, S.C. Earlier in the year, Farmers received six Mobius Awards, which recognize outstanding broadcast and print commercials and package designs, in the radio and print categories. And in 1999, Farmers' advertising was recognized with such prestigious awards as the ADDY and The Caddy, among the top honors in the field.

Jeff Beyer, Vice President of Corporate communications explains: "Our campaigns use humor to illustrate the mishaps that happen to each and every one of us and creative production to show how insurance can make your world right again."

BRAND VALUES

Farmers' guiding philosophy combines the best aspects of tradition and change and applies to the company as a whole and to individual agents. The tradition is the commitment to professional service delivered promptly and fairly. And Farmers also recognizes that change and modernization are crucial to keeping pace with customers' needs.

property/casualty with both commercial and business lines, life coverage for individuals, families, and businesses, and specialized coverage for hospitals, automobile dealers, franchises, restaurants, apartment houses, and all types of small businesses.

Martin D. Feinstein, chairman of the board, president, and chief executive officer of Farmers Group, Inc., points out that, in addition to insurance, company agents "can help customers plan for their financial futures with a variety of annuity

and IRA products, long-term care policies, and even education loans. We are quickly becoming a one-stop shop for all of our customers' risk-management and asset-accumulation needs."

RECENT DEVELOPMENTS

The implementation of Farmers' ideals created a company that drew attention and admiration from many other sectors of the business world and in 1988 B.A.T. Industries of Great Britain purchased the Farmers organization. The impressive growth of Farmers has continued since then with continuing expansion of cus-

tomer services. In 1998, B.A.T. Industries merged its financial group of companies, including Farmers, with Swiss-based Zurich Insurance Company as Zurich Financial Services Group. This group, says Farmers Chairman Feinstein, "is a truly global entity with some 66,000 employees in 53 countries and annual sales of more than $40 billion."

The merger brought the Zurich Personal Insurance organization based in Baltimore, Md., into Farmers, and set the stage for the expansion of Farmers into the eastern United States. The company now operates in 41 states.

THE MARKET

FedEx changes the way the world works.

In the rapidly expanding marketplace of dot-coms and traditional businesses, one company anticipated the "bricks and clicks" economy. FedEx was born in the spirit of the new economy nearly 30 years ahead of its time. FedEx envisioned the future – a marketplace fueled by dependable, affordable express delivery – and then led the industry.

With its own global transportation network, FedEx uses technology, logistics and Internet resources to deliver packages, information and solutions to its customers. Around the world, FedEx is recognized as the global symbol for fast, reliable, inventive delivery and logistics solutions.

ACHIEVEMENTS

FedEx is a company of firsts. FedEx® Express was the first company dedicated to express package delivery, the first in the industry to offer a money-back guarantee and the first to offer free proof of performance.

FedEx Express became the first company to win the Malcolm Baldrige National Quality Award in the service category. The company also received ISO 9001 registration for all of its worldwide operations in 1994, making it the first global express transportation company to receive simultaneous system-wide certification.

HISTORY

The FedEx story is virtually business legend. In 1965, while a student at Yale University, company founder Frederick Smith envisioned a new way to move packages from here to there. He wrote a paper proposing an air-freight system that would transport time-sensitive shipments such as medicines, computer parts and electronics. That idea would become the cornerstone of a worldwide industry.

In 1971, after a stint in the Marines, Smith bought controlling interest in Arkansas Aviation Sales in Little Rock, Arkansas. While operating his new firm, Smith experienced difficulty getting one and two-day packages and airfreight delivered on time. This motivated him to return to the distribution concepts he had developed at Yale and apply them to his current distribution system. This work changed his company – and eventually changed the world.

His new company, called Federal Express, officially began in 1973 with the launch of 14 small aircraft from Memphis International Airport. During its first day of business, the company delivered 186 packages to 25 U.S. cities, from Rochester, New York, to Miami, Florida.

Though the company didn't show a profit until 1975, it soon became the premier carrier of

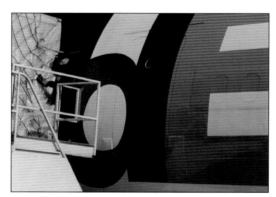

high-priority goods. The company's growth took off after air cargo deregulation in 1977, which allowed FedEx to use larger aircraft such as Boeing 727s and McDonnell-Douglas DC-10s.

In 1984, the company began service to Europe and Asia, and five years later acquired Tiger International. By integrating the Flying Tigers network and receiving carrier aviation rights to China, the company became the world's largest full-service all-cargo airline.

In 1994, Federal Express formally adopted FedEx as its primary corporate identity and in 1998, the company acquired Caliber System, Inc.

THE PRODUCT

As an $18-billion market leader in transportation, information and logistics solutions, FedEx Corporation provides strategic direction for its operating companies. Each one operates independently, focused on its market segment, but also competes collectively under the powerful FedEx brand.

It was the first company to offer its customers a PC-based automated shipping system. Through its Web site, fedex.com, FedEx Express was the first to offer online package status tracking so that customers could conduct business via

the Internet. FedEx® Ground was the first to introduce bar-code labeling to the ground transportation industry. FedEx became the first company to allow customers to process their own shipments through the Internet.

RECENT DEVELOPMENTS

In 2000, the FedEx Corporation extended its reputation to a broader range of companies and services. Now the FedEx name, as well as the value and trust associated with it, represents five operating companies:
- FedEx Express, the original company offering time-definite global express delivery
- FedEx Ground, offering small-package ground service, including FedEx® Home Delivery
- FedEx® Freight, offering comprehensive logistics and transportation management
- FedEx® Custom Critical, offering time-definite critical delivery and special handling
- FedEx® Trade Networks, offering high-tech customs clearance and trade facilitation

BRAND VALUES

From the beginning, the FedEx brand has succeeded because it is motivated not just by profits or the desire to compete, but by values. When people see the familiar logo on a vehicle or package, whether in Iowa or Italy, they know it stands for a company committed to deliver on time – and committed to principle. Today, FedEx is building on this tradition, championing brand values that change the way the world works. Those values are:

SIMPLIFYING

As life gets more complex, FedEx makes it easier. This means not just solving problems efficiently, but simplifying how people work: forms that are easy to fill out, procedures that

are practical and straightforward, one company for all delivery and logistics needs. By making things simpler, FedEx requires less of people's precious time, allowing them to devote more time to their own lives and work.

OPTIMIZING
FedEx knows that success is not always measured by minutes. Some FedEx customers need speed; others need economy, and some need both. By constantly optimizing, FedEx creates efficiencies for its customers and for itself. What's most important is that FedEx customers get what they need, when they need it, at the right price.

CERTAIN
In an uncertain world, FedEx reliability is one thing FedEx customers can count on. That

trust, that certainty, is one of the company's greatest achievements. It's also one of its greatest challenges. After all, reliability is the hardest reputation in the world to maintain. It has to be earned anew each day, with each job.

PERSONAL
Each FedEx customer is unique. People want to be listened to and understood. At FedEx, this means knowing its customers well enough to understand their unique needs and circumstances. The FedEx personal style is accessible, direct and professional.

INVENTIVENESS
At FedEx, the best way to solve a problem is to keep solving it. By constantly asking how to do things better, FedEx calls on the inventiveness of the entire company.

To deliver millions of packages and solutions every day requires inventiveness every day. FedEx relies on the unique creative approach of every employee. It's an attitude, a way of thinking that's essential to remaining competitive, and to inventing new solutions for tomorrow.

CONNECTING
FedEx touches the world – your world – by connecting people, products and information, in every combination, on every continent. As FedEx expands its range of services, it makes the benefits of a connected world accessible to even more people. By connecting the world, FedEx is helping it grow smaller.

As FedEx Corporation moves into the 21st century, it will invent new ways to serve its customers. It will be known by the services it offers, for changing business. But above all, FedEx will be known by the values it lives up to every day.

THINGS YOU DIDN'T KNOW ABOUT FEDEX

○ Through their physical networks, the five FedEx companies deliver nearly 5 million shipments every business day.

○ In a 24-hour period, FedEx Express planes travel nearly a half a million miles.

○ Through the corporation's virtual networks, FedEx handles more than 100 million electronic transactions a day.

○ Through the FedEx companies, more than 200,000 employees and contractors deliver more than packages: They deliver integrated business solutions.

THE MARKET

For 100 years, people the world over have demonstrated an insatiable appetite for the freedom, utility and innovation that the automobile has come to represent. Which is precisely why there is no more intensely competitive category than automobile manufacturing. Today, Ford Motor Company stands at the forefront of a host of global manufacturers offering vehicles in virtually all shapes and sizes to fill the driving needs of a world on wheels. It is one of the largest makers of cars and trucks on the planet, selling in 200 markets around the world products that are manufactured in facilities in 40 countries.

In order to remain competitive, large auto manufacturers are becoming larger as well as leaner, creating efficiencies through growth and strategic acquisition. Ford Motor Company is a leader in this arena with a diverse portfolio of automotive brands. The result is a dazzling array of consumer choice in vehicles for virtually every taste and every need. Ford Motor Company is transforming itself from a vehicle manufacturer into a full-line automotive services company. Ford's focus today is on identifying and anticipating consumer needs and providing the vehicles, brands and services to satisfy them.

ACHIEVEMENTS

Chairman Bill Ford has said: "A good company delivers excellent products and services; a great one delivers excellent products and services and strives to make the world a better place." On any measure, by any criteria, Ford Motor Company has accomplished much.

Ford Motor Company is ranked fourth on the Fortune 500 list of the largest U.S. industrial corporations based on sales. In 1999, worldwide sales and revenues totaled $163 billion. In 1999, Fortune Magazine named founder Henry Ford Businessman of the Century, and the Model T was voted Car of the Century by 126 automotive journalists and experts.

Ford was the first automotive company to certify all manufacturing plants globally to ISO14001 and the first to standardize dual airbags.

Ford voluntarily made all of its 1999 model year SUVs and Windstar minivans

"A good company delivers excellent products and services; a great one delivers excellent products and services and strives to make the world a better place."

BILL FORD – CHAIRMAN, FORD MOTOR COMPANY

Ford Motor Company
BETTER IDEAS.™

www.ford.com

comply with stringent Low Emission Vehicle standards years ahead of regulation and at no extra cost to the customer. This is the equivalent of eliminating the smog-forming emissions of 350,000 full-size trucks annually.

HISTORY

Henry Ford didn't invent the automobile. He invented the automobile industry. And, arguably, the process of sophisticated production that remains in place today. His guiding philosophy, stated in his own words, was elegantly simple: "I will build a motor car for the great multitude...it will be so low in price that no man will be unable to own one." Ford Motor Company was born in a small converted wagon factory in Detroit on June 16, 1903.

Between 1903 and 1908, Henry Ford and his engineers went through 19 letters of the alphabet from Model A to Model S, building, improving, experimenting, and testing ideas. The automobile in Henry Ford's time had been "a rich man's toy." Ford was committed to building a reliable means of transportation anyone could afford. The result of Ford's work and experimentation was the Model T. The process of its manufacture, combining standardized parts with the moving assembly line, revolutionized mass production. The first Model T sold for $260.

By the end of 1913, Ford Motor Company was producing half of all the automobiles in the United States.

A Model T rolled off the assembly line at the rate of one every ten seconds of every working day. Henry Ford startled the

world in 1914 by announcing a minimum wage for workers of $5 per day—double the existing rate of the time. His reasoning was that by paying workers higher wages he was also creating customers for his car.

The Model T and Ford Motor Company created a social revolution as well as an industrial one. Now, a broader world was opened to the average family by means of a machine that allowed travel over farther distances.

Starting from its earliest years, Ford Motor Company pioneered the use of recycled and alternative materials including soybean and other natural components.

Throughout its storied past, Ford cars have filled a niche in the American psyche with names that have become cultural icons, from the Model T to the T-bird. As Ford approaches its own centennial in 2003, Henry Ford's remarkable achievement of a company built on better ideas is alive and well. It has grown, thrived and prospered through years of prosperity and hard times, through war and peace.

THE PRODUCT

From its historical core to recent acquisitions, Ford Motor Company today offers eight unique, differentiating automotive brands including Ford, Mercury, and Mazda as well as Lincoln, Jaguar, Aston Martin, Volvo, and Land Rover. The latter grouping was organized under the Premier Automotive Group, established in 1999.

Ford's acquisition strategy, as articulated by CEO Jacques Nasser, involves "acquiring not just brand leaders but leading brands. Leading brands are the best in their category and also the ones defining the very direction of the category." A few examples of the diversity of the portfolio include:

- Ford Ikon, designed for the driving conditions, weather and traffic patterns of India.
- Aston Martin DB7 Vantage, delivering a sophisticated blend of luxury and exhilaration through a 6.0-liter 420-horsepower V12.
- Ford Focus, the first car to win both North American and European Car of the Year and the best-selling small car.
- Volvo V70 Sport Wagon, offering a range of family-oriented wagons ranging from all-wheel drive to turbocharged, each advancing a long-standing reputation for safety.

In addition to automotive brands, Ford Motor Company's portfolio of services includes automotive aftermarket specialties such as Ford Credit, a leader in automotive financing; Quality Care automotive services at Ford and Lincoln Mercury Dealers; Kwik-Fit maintenance and light repair service in Europe; and Hertz—a leader in airport car rentals.

RECENT DEVELOPMENTS

Ford Motor Company, under President/CEO Jacques Nasser, has re-focused its mission from being the world's leading automotive manufacturing company to being the world's leading consumer company for automotive products and services. At Ford, The Customer is Job 1 and customer satisfaction has become the top priority. Accelerated efforts in corporate citizenship and environmental responsibility have taken a more prominent role in Ford's engi-neering and manufacturing philosophy as well.

Ford Motor Company spends $700 million annually on research and development, yielding 700 patents every year and a continuous stream of new vehicle launches worldwide. In fact, over 50 percent of the research conducted at the Ford Research Laboratory has an environmental focus.

Ford recently introduced the lightweight, plastic-bodied, zero-emission TH!NK City, an all-electric vehicle launched in Europe designed to provide commuters with an environmentally responsible small car with a range of 50 miles and a top speed of 60 mph.

Ford has an aggressive and robust internet strategy interconnected with its core business of personal mobility. The internet is being used to revolutionize Ford's supply chain to reduce waste. It allows instant connections to customers for relationship management and loyalty through Ford.com and OwnerConnection.com, which average 162 million hits per month. Ford's recent association with Microsoft and CarPoint will allow consumers to find the car they want and energize the retail experience. And through PeoplePC, Ford is providing internet access to its employees.

PROMOTION

Ford Motor Company's corporate, or "Trustmark," campaign reflects an ongoing effort to highlight a set of core values and business principles. The "Better Ideas" campaign presents the brand's beliefs and values in the areas of safety, environmental responsibility, and global citizenship. These messages are presented by some of the 340,000 employees of Ford Motor Company around the world.

At the end of 1999, the Global Anthem television commercial was aired on a worldwide media roadblock celebrating the end of one millennium and the beginning of the next. Guinness World Records recognized this airing as the largest simultaneous television-advertising premiere.

BRAND VALUES

Ford Motor Company is dedicated to providing ingenious automotive products and services. Its actions reflect the company's concern for the environment, education, and a re-evaluation of the role a corporation can play in society through initiatives and partnerships to make the world a better place. Ford believes its responsibility to its customers and shareholders extends to the larger world to include conservation, environmental engineering, and sustainable manufacturing processes.

THINGS YOU DIDN'T KNOW ABOUT THE FORD MOTOR COMPANY

- ○ Ford recycles more than 50 million 2-liter plastic bottles each year to use in grille reinforcements and vent damper doors.
- ○ Ford sells 11 models of cars and trucks powered by alternative fuels including bi-fuel natural gas, bi-fuel propane and dedicated electric.
- ○ In Valencia, Spain, a Ford plant recycles its used water, cleans it, and re-uses it to irrigate nearby orange groves.

THE MARKET

The snack food and wholesale bakery industry in the U.S. is a $90 billion business. Within this universe, the world of salty snacks represents $20 billion in sales. Of the salty snack world, the corn chip category accounts for approximately four percent of that consumption. This translated to nearly $700 million of retail corn chips sales in 2000. FRITOS® is far and away the largest player in the category and the brand drives category growth. It is the only national corn chip brand, and, with a 93 percent share of the market, as FRITOS® goes, so goes the category.

Corn chips provide consumers with a snacking alternative to the larger potato chip and tortilla chip categories. Frito-Lay sister products such as Lays®, Doritos®, and Tostitos® dominate the potato and tortilla chip categories.

ACHIEVEMENTS

In 1954, the brand celebrated its 25th anniversary by achieving $28 million in sales. Since then it has grown into a global powerhouse brand with over $600 million in sales. FRITOS® is the 5th largest brand in the Frito-Lay portfolio behind Lays, Doritos, Tostitos, and Ruffles®, but FRITOS® is arguably the brand with the most storied history with its close ties to mainstream America. Year after year, FRITOS® continues to be one of the most recognizable of all consumer packaged goods brands. When compared to other food brands, FRITOS® achieves high scores because of its product quality, differentiated nature, and reputation as a product that delivers exceptional value.

HISTORY

FRITOS® was the first brand of what is now an $11 billion food company, Frito-Lay, Inc. At the very height of the Great Depression in 1932, a young Texan named C.E. Doolin launched a venture that resulted in the establishment of an entirely new and typically American industry. While operating a confectionery in San Antonio, Doolin first envisioned merchandising food products from display racks rather from

the huge glass jars then utilized. At the same time, he discovered a product known as a corn chip. It was of similar consistency to the present FRITOS®, but had the taste of a toasted tortilla. Doolin recognized this crudely packaged snack as a product that would lend itself to merchandising from the display racks he previously envisioned. For $100, Doolin acquired the recipe, the crude equipment for the making the product and the 19 retail accounts in the San Antonio area. Thus, the Frito Company was born.

Production soon moved from the family kitchen to production plants in Houston, Dallas, and Tulsa, and the company headquarters were moved to Dallas. In 1945, the Frito Company granted to the H.W. Lay Company exclusive franchise rights to manufacture and to distribute FRITOS® Brand Corn Chips in the Southeast. The following chronology of events best reflects the evolution of the brand from its hum-

ble beginning to its present day prosperity:
—In 1949 the words "FRITOS®, Golden Chips of Corn" were printed on bags of FRITOS®.
—In 1953 the Frito Kid was introduced and three years later, he appeared on the Today Show with Dave Garroway. At the same time, the Frito Company became the first Texas company to advertise on the NBC Television network. The Frito Kid represented the brand until his retirement in 1967.
—In 1958 FRITOS® adopted a new theme, "Munch a Bunch! of FRITOS® Brand Corn Chips" and a year later, Vice President Richard Nixon took a bag of FRITOS® to Nikita

Krushchev as a symbol of Americana.
—1961 became a landmark year when the Frito Company merged with the H.W. Lay Company to form Frito-Lay, Inc.
—In 1971 W.C. FRITOS®, a caricature of the popular actor W.C. Fields, was introduced as the new mascot for the brand. At this point in its evolution, the FRITOS® brand eclipsed $200 million in sales and continued to build momentum through the 1980s.

THE PRODUCT

FRITOS® Brand Corn Chips are made with fresh, whole kernels of corn and it is this freshness that helps create the hearty corn taste for which FRITOS® is famous. The corn arrives at the production facilities via railcar before being stored and dried to exact moisture requirements. Ultimately, the corn is cooked to soften the kernels before they are ground into a thick corn dough called "masa."

The masa is then put through an extruder that presses the dough at high pressure through narrow slits, creating ribbons of FRITOS® product. The ribbons are then cut to the correct length to produce the classic FRITOS® shape. The strips of raw masa are then dropped directly into hot oil and fried at precise temperatures and duration. Once removed from the oil, the fried chips are allowed to cool before salt or one of nine other flavors is applied. The seasoned chips are then quickly sealed into packages for shipment to stores nationwide.

A typical FRITOS® line produces over 1,000 pounds of FRITOS® every hour, or over 5 million pounds per year! Manufacturing plants are located throughout the country to minimize the time it takes to get the product to market. Over the course of a year, over 80 million pounds of oil and 170 million pounds of corn are used in the production of FRITOS®— enough corn to cover the turf of 1,000 football fields.

RECENT DEVELOPMENTS

The "Munch a Bunch! of FRITOS® campaign was modified and re-introduced in 1991 and for the first time in 58 years, FRITOS® Brand Corn Chips packaging was redesigned with brighter colors and an updated logo. The year 1993 saw the launch of the "I Know What I Like and I Like FRITOS®" campaign and a year later, FRITOS® brand SCOOPS!® was introduced to the marketplace. SCOOPS! was introduced to meet consumers' desires for a FRITOS® corn chip that was

conducive to dipping. Since then, SCOOPS! has grown to a healthy $140 million business.

In 2000 FRITOS® adopted the tagline, "Nothing Satisfies Like FRITOS®" to communicate the hearty, filling, and satisfying nature that defines the product's attributes. Today, the FRITOS® Brand supports nine flavored products and three unflavored (Original, SCOOPS! and King Size FRITOS® Brand Corn Chips). The Original FRITOS® Brand Corn Chip continues to be the volume leader and is responsible for nearly half of the overall brand's sales.

FRITOS® is continually striving to innovate in meaningful ways. All of the brand's innovation is driven by the desire to provide the consumers with a consistent product that delivers uncompromising quality and value with each and every bag.

PROMOTION

One of the many strengths of the Frito-Lay Company and the FRITOS® Brand in particular has been the meaningful way in which advertising and merchandising have been married. The FRITOS® Brand engages consumers both in their homes and on their shopping trips through impactful advertising, promotion and perhaps most importantly, through its impressive shelf presence. Frito-Lay sells over 1.2 billion bags of FRITOS® in a typical year. This volume pro-

vides over a billion shelf impressions that serve as miniature billboards. In the complex and crowded snack food world, FRITOS® and the other Frito-Lay brands have a retail presence that is unequaled.

The FRITOS® Brand has utilized celebrity spokespeople throughout its history. From W.C. Fields through country singers Mark Chesnutt and Reba McEntire, the FRITOS® Brand has delivered a consistent product even though the faces have changed. Today, the FRITOS® Brand is represented by NASCAR superstar Jeff Gordon and his #24 Racing Team. From 1998 to 2000, FRITOS® was an associate sponsor of Gordon's Busch Series PEPSI Racing Team. In 2001, FRITOS® and its sister company, PEPSI, became associate sponsors on Jeff Gordon's Winston Cup Racing Team. This valuable partnership allows the FRITOS® Brand to market its product to racing fans, that as a group, are becoming an increasingly larger segment of mainstream America.

BRAND VALUES

Nothing but FRITOS® gives you the satisfaction you need when you're hungry. The classic corn taste and the hearty crunch fill you up and hold you over. Nothing Satisfies Like FRITOS®. The essence of the Brand can be captured in one statement, "FRITOS® is the simple, hearty snack I can always count on to satisfy my hunger."

The brand identity is characterized as "classic, dependable, reliable, substantial, and satisfying." These are unique product truths and values for which the brand stands. FRITOS® is truly a symbol of Americana and the American dream as illustrated by the Frito Company's roots in the Doolin family kitchen and its evolution as the #1 snack company in the world.

THINGS YOU DIDN'T KNOW ABOUT FRITOS®

❍ The Frito Company's Mexican restaurant, Casa de FRITOS®, opened in 1955 in Disneyland. The photo on the previous page is of Frito Founder Elmer Doolin and Walt Disney with the Frito Kid.

❍ The first FRITOS® recipe book was printed in 1935.

❍ During its Silver Anniversary Year in 1957, FRITOS® sponsored the ABC Radio Network Program, "Don McNeill's Breakfast Club."

❍ The popularity of FRITOS® is evident in its widespread availability: it can be found just about everywhere, including 98 percent of the supermarkets and convenience stores in the U.S.

❍ Over 250 million pounds of FRITOS® were produced in 2000—it would take about 100,000 automobiles to equal that weight.

❍ The "Family-Size" bag of FRITOS® in 1937 cost 15 cents in the supermarket.

THE MARKET

Whether it's a wedding, holiday, anniversary or simply to tell someone they are special, sending flowers to commemorate an important occasion has become an American tradition. So much so, that the floral industry is estimated to be a $19 billion business. But to Florists' Transworld Delivery, Inc. (FTD®), it's more than a business; it's a family of the best florists in the world.

The FTD Brand is one of the most recognizable in the world. Simply put, FTD has become synonymous with flowers and has proven for more than 90 years to be the leader in the floral industry.

FTD promotes the FTD Brand both nationally and locally through co-marketing efforts with leading retail floral stores worldwide. FTD is the symbol of quality and reliability to floral consumers. FTD provides the premier services and support in the industry, including advanced business system technologies, credit card reconciliation/clearinghouse, floral containers and shop supplies.

ACHIEVEMENTS

As the pioneer in the global floral industry, FTD rides on the cusp of rapidly changing technology—from the early days of the telegraph to current hardware and software solutions. The FTD® Mercury® Network, a computerized network created to send and receive orders for 52,000 FTD Florists worldwide, has logged more than 750 million transactions since its debut in 1979.

Even with today's advancements in technology, FTD's Mercury® Network receives the highest volume of orders and is considered to be the most reliable computerized network in the floral industry. The Mercury® Network functions smoothly and efficiently because FTD built the technology around the needs of florists, in turn, helping them meet the demands of their customers.

The Mercury Network is the primary automated wire service used by FTD Florists to transmit floral and gift orders and messages. The system connects FTD Florists with around-the-clock support and offers unparalleled dependability. Mercury® Technology, including Mercury Wings™ and Mercury Advantage™, simplify the order process and have specific

floral-business capabilities to help keep costs down and service up.

The company continually strives to strengthen FTD's leadership position in the industry, which is proven every day through the great work of quality FTD Florists.

HISTORY

On August 18, 1910, a small group of florists met during a recess at the Society of American Florists' convention and formed the country's first continuing flowers-by-wire service, the Florists' Telegraph Delivery Association. Since that auspicious beginning more than 90 years ago, today's Florists' Transworld Delivery, Inc. is the most recognized symbol of the floral industry.

THE PRODUCT

FTD meets the demands of its customers by providing the freshest, most beautiful flowers available. To continue to reach these high expectations, FTD implemented the FTD Florists' 100% Satisfaction Guarantee.

FTD guarantees that every order sent through FTD for delivery in the United States and Canada and on all FTD Branded products purchased from an FTD Florist will fully meet the demands of every customer. If, for any reason, a customer is not satisfied with the purchased FTD product, the company will send a replacement or refund the full purchase price.

In an effort to support FTD's commitment to quality, a strong emphasis is placed on ensuring that all FTD Florists understand and utilize the FTD Florists' 100% Satisfaction Guarantee. The Satisfaction Guarantee provides the following benefits:

- Improves consumer confidence in FTD Florists and FTD products.
- Builds the value of the FTD Brand.
  - Differentiates FTD from other wire services.

RECENT DEVELOPMENTS

FTD has embraced the Internet wholeheartedly. FTD.COM, a business-to-consumer company, was founded in 1994 when it took the strong, trusted FTD Brand to the Internet. Today, FTD.COM is a leading Internet marketer of fresh flowers and specialty gifts that sells products directly to consumers. FTD's foray into the online arena affords the company the opportunity to continue building the FTD Brand by offering floral customers a choice when purchasing flowers. Consumers may buy FTD flowers and gifts by visiting their local FTD Florist, by dialing 1-800-SEND-FTD, or by shopping online at www.ftd.com.

PROMOTION

FTD looks for as many opportunities as possible to strengthen the FTD Brand through national advertising, sponsorships, and promotions.

National advertising has been one of the most important ways FTD helps to build the businesses of FTD Florists and add value to the FTD Brand. Over the years, FTD's advertising campaigns have focused on the emotions behind flowers—"Send your thoughts with special care," "Some of life's best moments come FTD" and "Be a Hero." These dynamic campaigns have been dedicated to selling flowers and bringing orders to FTD Florists.

FTD also is committed to seeking out national sponsorship opportunities that offer high-profile media and marketing opportunities to highlight FTD and the family of FTD Florists.

Since 1953 FTD has sponsored a floral float and advertised prominently during the popular Rose Parade®, which takes place annually on January 1st. To support FTD Florists and promote the Brand, FTD also has hosted consumer promotions that coordinate with the themes of the floats.

Each year since 1994, FTD also has hosted

FTD® Good Neighbor Day® throughout the United States and Canada. This grass-roots event combines the efforts of participating FTD Florists with their local communities to help promote the idea of friendship and goodwill. On FTD Good Neighbor Day, consumers are invited to visit their local participating FTD Florists to receive a dozen flowers free! In return, they agree to keep only one flower for themselves and give the other 11 flowers away to friends and family.

FTD's national sponsorship participation has included some very high-profile events. Numbered among these events was a multi-year title sponsorship of a national ice skating tour, FTD® Champions on Ice®, and a floral partnership with the primetime Emmy Awards show.

In addition to national sponsorships FTD and FTD Florists have continued the efforts in the cause-related marketing arena. Committed to making a difference in their community, Children's Miracle Network continues to be FTD's major philanthropy.

BRAND VALUES

For over 90 years, FTD Florists continue to reliably deliver quality floral products and gifts, gaining the trust and loyalty of consumers around the world.

Your thought well sent.
Almost anywhere in the world through your FTD Florist.

THINGS YOU DIDN'T KNOW ABOUT FTD

❍ FTD has 96 percent brand awareness— the strongest in the floral industry.

❍ Merlin Olsen, actor and Hall of Fame football player, began appearing in FTD advertising in 1983.

❍ The FTD® Pick-Me-Up® Bouquet was introduced in May of 1984 and was an instant success.

❍ The 1972 FTD Rose Parade float "Aquarius" was awarded a grand prize. The group Three Dog Night rode atop the winning float.

❍ In 1970 Rocky Graziano went on the road for FTD to present the "Hard Hitting Facts" campaign to florists at trade fair shows across the country.

❍ FTD presented a bouquet described as a "Liberty Bell made with flowers" to President Calvin Coolidge on his birthday, July 4, 1924.

FUJIFILM

THE MARKET

Imaging. It's the convergence of photography and printing with data and network communications, and it's one of the most exciting new frontiers of technology. As one of the leading manufacturers and marketers of imaging and information products, Fujifilm has helped drive this worldwide revolution in how pictures are taken, processed, stored and shared. The world's second largest producer of photosensitized materials, Fujifilm is a Fortune Global 500 company, with sales of $13.2 billion in its most recent fiscal year. The company's U.S. marketing subsidiary, Fuji Photo Film U.S.A., Inc. celebrated its 35th anniversary in 2000.

While its green boxes are familiar throughout the world, Fujifilm is much more than film. Fujifilm has more expertise in more imaging and information arenas than any other company. Its innovations in technology and commitment to quality and choice have enabled it to provide consumer, professional, and commercial photography and imaging products, and video and audio products; professional film for motion pictures, television and other produced film-based applications, and computer media, graphic arts, micrographics, and medical systems products.

Fujifilm's heritage as an imaging company and its complete product offerings give the company a unique perspective and singular ability to serve all of its customers—consumers, retailers, professionals, and businesses.

ACHIEVEMENTS

Fujifilm has a long history of imaging and information industry "firsts."

The company has twice introduced the world's fastest color print still film, an accomplishment it also achieved with color motion picture film.

Fujicolor Reala, the first film to reproduce colors as the human eye sees them, was introduced in 1989.

Fujifilm introduced the world's first one-time-use camera—QuickSnap—in 1986, creating what is now the photography industry's most robust growth category. This was followed in 1987 by the world's first 35mm one-time-use camera. In 1988, Fujifilm introduced the QuickSnap Flash, the first 35mm one-time-use camera with a built-in flash.

Fujifilm developed the world's first digital camera in 1988 and has maintained its leadership in digital imaging with a continuous flow

of revolutionary new products, including the first digital camera with a built-in printer.

In addition, the company's long heritage in film technology innovation has led to the development of a broad array of leading edge technologies for the industrial market.

In 1992, Fujifilm announced its exclusive ATOMM precision thin-layer coating technology (Advanced super Thin-layer and high-Output Metal Media), which has enabled the manufacture of high-density magnetic recording media for the computer industry.

Fujifilm created the unique 4th Color Layer Technology found in its 35mm Superia and 24mm Nexia film lines. This additional cyan layer actually helps the film to "see" like the human eye.

Fujifilm also developed the exclusive solid state laser technology found in its Digital Minilab Frontier photoprocessing equipment. The solid state lasers guarantee sharp, vivid prints with accurate color reproduction.

Fujifilm pioneered leading technologies in digital printing and led the development of digital minilabs for photoprocessing.

Fujifilm's technological advances have led to numerous citations and awards, including the 1982 Academy Award (the "Oscar") and two

Emmys for Technical Merit—in 1982 for Fujicolor A-250 high-speed color negative motion picture film and in 1990 for developments in metal particle tape technology. In 1991, Fujifilm received the Scientific and Engineering Award for its F-series of color negative motion picture film from the National Academy of Motion Picture Arts and Sciences.

HISTORY

The company entered the North American market in 1955 and culminated a decade of growth with the establishment of its subsidiary, Fuji Photo Film U.S.A., Inc., in 1965.

In 1989, the company opened a facility in Greenwood, South Carolina, to manufacture pre-sensitized plates and related products used in offset printing. Today, that facility represents an investment of more than $1.3 billion. A second factory opened in 1991 in Greenwood to manufacture videotapes. In 1995, the company opened a factory for QuickSnap cameras and, in 1996, a fourth factory began manufacturing color photographic paper. In addition, the company opened its 35mm color film finishing and packaging facility and its graphic arts film finishing factory in 1997. Fujifilm began fully integrated manufacturing of 35mm color film at the end of 1997—the first time that Fujifilm produced 35mm film in the U.S.

In 1999, Fujifilm began coating DLTtape™ IV data storage media, with final manufacture of U.S.-made DLTtape™ IV cartridges at Fujifilm Microdisks U.S.A., Inc., in Bedford, Massachusetts. This marked the first time an ATOMM-based computer storage product was fully manufactured in the U.S. Also in 1999, the Greenwood Research Laboratories opened for the research and development of photographic products.

THE PRODUCT

Fuji Photo Film U.S.A., Inc., offers a complete line of imaging and information products, systems and services to consumers and businesses. These include:

- Amateur and professional color photographic film; 35mm, APS, QuickSnap one-time-use cameras, 35mm and APS cameras, consumer and professional digital cameras and a range of medium-format cameras for professionals; photographic paper; black-and-white film; and minilab photofinishing equipment
- Digital Imaging products, such as digital printers and products for the capture and transfer of digital images
- Professional audio and video tape for broad-

online service, fujifilm.net.

In the business-to-business marketplace, the company has just introduced the next generation of computer storage media, LTO Ultrium and Super DLTtape, new motion picture film, digital plates for the graphic arts industry, and liquid crystal display materials.

PROMOTION

Fuji Photo Film U.S.A.'s current "Get the Picture" communication strategy underscores Fujifilm's heightened effort to delivering a full line of fun, easy-to-use products that encourage consumers everywhere to take pictures every day. As a result, Fujifilm has aligned itself with sponsorships and events that would support that strategy.

Clearly, Fujifilm is at the leading edge of the "Imaging & Information" industry, but also takes pride in its role in corporate social responsibility. To highlight its commitment to support the environment, Fujifilm is partnering with the Smithsonian's National Zoo in Washington, D.C., to provide an environmental educational focus on the giant panda, one of the most endangered species in the world. This joint venture will encourage children and adults to value our natural world and inspire them to save it. Fujifilm's partnership with Busch Entertainment Corporation's Adventure Parks also demonstrates a commitment to the preservation of animals.

These partnerships, while educating children and adults on the importance of the conservation of animals, also encourages families to take more pictures while visiting animals in the zoos or parks.

In addition, Fujifilm plays a significant role in the sponsorship of sporting events as well. As the "Official Film," Fujifilm sponsored the 1984 Los Angeles Olympics and has been a sponsor of World Cup soccer since 1982. Fujifilm currently sponsors the U.S.A. Track and Field Team, has been an official sponsor of the World Figure Skating Championships since 1995, and was a sponsor of the 1997 World Junior Figure Skating Championships.

Fujifilm is the "Official Film, Magnetic Tape and Computer Media" of the U.S. Open Tennis Championships and is the "Official Videotape and Audiotape" of the National Football League.

cast, production, duplication and industrial applications; consumer audio and video tape for analog and digital home recordings
- Consumer and high-capacity computer storage media, such as floppy disks, cartridge tapes and optical discs
- Professional film for motion pictures, television and other produced film-based applications
- Microfilm, chemicals and digital retrieval hardware for document storage
- Graphic arts film; conventional and digital plates, equipment and chemistry; analog and digital color proofing systems; drum and flatbed scanners; imagesetters; and computer-to-plate systems
- Wholesale photofinishing across the U.S.

RECENT DEVELOPMENTS

Because consumers care about the picture—not the technology or format—Fujifilm offers a choice of ways to capture images. These include 35mm, Advanced Photo System, and QuickSnap one-time-use cameras and digital cameras. Fujifilm's portfolio of films for professionals and consumers has been lauded for quality, consistency, color accuracy, and color enhancement. The company's awareness of consumer needs has resulted in the development of such new products as the new QuickSnap Golf and Colors, which are one-time-use cameras for golfers and teens, respectively.

Because consumers want processing, storage, and distribution options, the company's Digital Minilab Frontier enables traditional film and images stored on digital media to be produced as prints, stored as digital images on CD-ROMs, or up-loaded to the Internet. Fujifilm also supports photofinishing services offered by retail shops or through the Internet and offers its own

BRAND VALUES

As one of the best known and most instantly recognizable global brands, Fujifilm is a leader in the technological innovation of high quality products that meet the critical standards for businesses and professionals, while providing consumers with the same high quality products making the imaging and information experience easy and satisfying.

(Linear Tape-Open, LTO and Ultrium are U.S. trademarks of Hewlett-Packard, IBM and Seagate. DLTtape and Super DLTtape are trademarks of Quantum Corporation. Zip is a trademark of Iomega Corporation.)

THINGS YOU DIDN'T KNOW ABOUT FUJIFILM

○ Fujifilm holds the patent for one-time-use cameras – today's most popular camera.

○ The Empire State Building in New York City was Fujifilm's first U.S. corporate home— for all six employees. Today, the company employs more than 8,000 U.S. associates in its 45 facilities in 24 states.

○ Launched in 1984, the colorful red, white and green Fujifilm Blimp is one of the largest airships flying today. Close to 200 feet long, 67 feet high and weighing approximately eight tons, its envelope (or "gas bag") is a mere 17/1000 of an inch thick. When fully inflated, it holds 247,500 cubic feet of helium.

○ Fujifilm currently sponsors the U.S.A. Track and Field Team and is the "Official Film, Magnetic Tape and Computer Media" of the US Open Tennis Championships. Fujifilm is also the "Official Videotape and Audiotape" of the National Football League.

Gateway™

THE MARKET

Originally viewed as the South Dakota home PC company, Gateway has come to stand for much more. From front porches to loading docks, Gateway's cow-spotted boxes are a familiar, welcome symbol of trust in an intensely competitive, converging industry. Entertainment, electronics, computing, digital information, and communications are blurring into a single, connected world. Gateway foresaw that market shift and has evolved its brand into non-hardware avenues such as financing, training, and Internet service. By extending its brand beyond its traditional core PC product base, Gateway grew its nonsystem income to 40 percent by the end of 2000.

ACHIEVEMENTS

In just 15 years, Gateway has built a global technology brand with a vision to Humanize the Digital Revolution. In a time when the tech industry was tech-talking incomprehensible speeds and feeds, Gateway's friendly, approachable persona showed the public a better way to buy a better PC: personal service, good value, and fresh technology from someone you know and trust.

Gateway's powerful brand touches more consumers and businesses on a daily basis than any of its competitors. Gateway was rated among the top 10 corporations with the best reputations in America in a survey conducted in August 1999 and published in *The Wall Street Journal*. Gateway ranked as the most admired American company in the Computers and Office Equipment industry in a *Fortune* magazine survey ("America's Most Admired Companies," February 19, 2001). Gateway is also the top brand in customer loyalty and for first-time home computer purchases of Wintel-based PCs, according to the Harris Interactive Consumer TechPoll℠ study of 140,000 PC owners who use the Internet, released March 5, 2001.

HISTORY

Gateway was born September 1985 when friends Ted Waitt and Mike Hammond set up shop on the Waitt Family Cattle Farm in Sioux City, Iowa. IBM had the lion's share of PC sales at the time and Computerland had stopped selling Texas Instruments PCs, leaving TI customers stranded for parts and service, so Ted and Mike seized the opportunity by selling software and hardware upgrades for TI computers.

Ted and Mike shipped hardware and software during the day and often helped Ted's dad unload cattle during the night. After almost seven months, the operation outgrew the farmhouse, so they moved to the Livestock Exchange building at the Sioux City Stockyards, marking five generations of Waitt family business in the historic Exchange built in 1894. By 1987, Gateway was a $1.5 million business and had developed the "direct channel" business philosophy still in place today. The direct channel brought strong advantages. First, it put Gateway in direct contact with clients, on the telephone, at Gateway Country stores and through Gateway.com. Second, Gateway can build systems to order, personalizing each for every client with no costly inventory of finished systems sitting on shelves. Third, going direct cuts costly intermediaries, savings that Gateway passes on to clients.

Gateway moved to North Sioux City, South Dakota, in 1990 and has maintained its manufacturing facility in the sprawling cow-spotted, corrugated metal building there. Since then, the company has moved its headquarters to San Diego, Calif., and established locations in other U.S. sites, as well as in Europe, the Middle East, Africa and the Pacific Rim with more than 21,000 employees. Gateway had total global revenue of $9.6 billion in 2000.

THE PRODUCT

Gateway began and still excels in high-end, performance desktop computers targeting computer enthusiasts. Having developed a cult-like following early on among the tech experts, Gateway broadened its appeal to the mass audience through strong

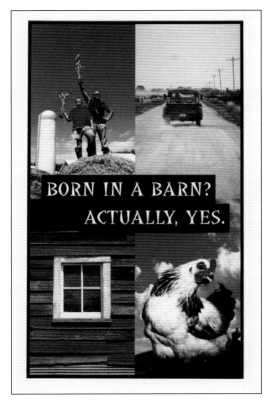

word-of-mouth recommendations from those enthusiasts to their less knowledgeable friends, neighbors, and colleagues. Today, Gateway's robust line of award-winning portables, servers, workstations, and desktop PCs provide home and business customers with cutting-edge technology, value and performance.

The Gateway Performance™ home desktop line delivers the latest technology and highest performance to PC enthusiasts. Gateway Essential™ desktop PCs provide traditional value, maximizing the features most important

to most people: processor speed, RAM amount and hard drive size. The sleek Gateway Profile™ all-in-one desktop system packs an entire computer into a slim LCD monitor for the smallest possible footprint in space-constrained environments.

In the business sector, the E-Series provides a stable desktop platform that companies need to manage and outfit entire networks. With the acquisition of Advance Logic Research in 1997, Gateway gained a server brand known for its innovative design and reliability. The Gateway ALR® series offers potent server capabilities for networked workgroups or an entire enterprise, while the E-5000 series workstations provide power users the tools for CAD/CAM/CAE and other graphics and data-intensive applications.

Gateway launched the industry's first sub-notebook, the HandBook, in 1992. Three years later Gateway introduced the award-winning line of Solo® notebooks, developing a broad range of models to meet diverse mobile computing scenarios, including a basic value portable, a stylish ultra-thin model, a rugged road machine, and a portable desktop.

RECENT DEVELOPMENTS
Gateway put a face on its direct business model when it opened its first Gateway Country® store in 1996. This revolutionary concept brought the strengths and efficiencies of the direct model to a retail setting, now around 300 stores.

Gateway was the first major computer company to become an Internet service provider, when it launched Gateway.net® internet service in 1997. By the end of 2000, Gateway.net was the fastest growing fee-based Internet service in the U.S.

In 1998, Gateway introduced the Your:)Ware℠ program, a whole new approach to technology ownership. Your:)Ware connects people with the right hardware and software, offers them Internet access, financing options, and training, and lets them trade their old computer toward the purchase of a new one.

PROMOTION
Gateway's first national magazine ad in 1988 featured the family cattle farm under the headline, "Computers from Iowa?". The juxtaposition of technology and American heartland was a far cry from other companies' ads and is credited with the sales explosion of 1988, which closed with $11.7 million in sales, a 1,100 per-

cent increase from the previous year.

Gateway's zany, quirky advertising used elaborate sets and employee models to tell stories in multi-page ad inserts that conveyed the company's "RobinHoodliness" message of technology power for the people. That message also gave rise to the long-lived "You've got a friend in the business"® slogan.

Perhaps the most compelling promotional step Gateway ever took was adding cow spots to its shipping boxes. A tribute to the company's Midwestern roots, the original cow-spotted box concept was created by a local advertising agency artist. When it was discovered how inexpensive the black-and-white pattern would be to produce, one of the world's most recognizable brands was born.

Gateway further increased its visibility with its first national TV commercial in 1994, and with shrewd product placement of computers and cow-spotted merchandise on such popular shows as "Seinfeld," "ER," "Wheel of Fortune," and "Oprah."

BRAND VALUES
Gateway's eight corporate values are the backbone of the company and guided Gateway from start-up success to global player. Those values are: caring, respect, teamwork, common sense, aggressiveness, honesty, efficiency, and fun. Living the values is an inherent part of the culture at Gateway and is manifested in how the company works toward its mission to Humanize the Digital Revolution. Rooted in its corporate values, the brand promises to put people first by showing individuals and businesses how to get the most out of technology and by staying with them every step of the way with the tools, advice, and support needed for the duration of the relationship. Gateway also practices its values by being a good corporate citizen. Formed in 1994, the Gateway Foundation has made hundreds of gifts to non-profit organizations in Gateway's home communities.

THINGS YOU DIDN'T KNOW ABOUT GATEWAY

○ The first digital signatures by two world leaders on an official document occurred on a Gateway laptop computer. U.S. President Bill Clinton and Ireland's Prime Minister Bertie Ahern signed the international electronic commerce agreement using digital signatures captured on a Gateway Solo 3100 laptop in September 1998.

○ Gateway was the first company to combine television and computer capabilities in one product, called the Destination PC/TV, launched in April 1996. The Destination system was hailed as one of the best new products of that year by Popular Science and Business Week magazines.

○ The first computer sale to outer space happened in November 1997 when Mir-24 cosmonauts ordered two 233 MHz multimedia PCs over the Internet from Gateway for $1,999 each. Gateway provided free shipping—to Russia.

THE MARKET

For nearly a century, Hanes has been clothing America. Since Hanes Underwear was first introduced in 1901, Hanes has evolved from a basic line of men's underwear to the leader in men's, women's, and children's clothing from socks and shoes to underwear and casual apparel. Today, more people buy Hanes and Hanes Her Way than any other brand of apparel.

The growth and popularity of Hanes is directly related to the changing retail landscape and the emerging popularity of mass merchandisers. Hanes products were initially sold through distributors to department stores nationwide. However, as discount retailers entered the market in the early 1980s, Hanes transitioned to its own regional sales force selling to retailers directly. By the early 1990s, more basic apparel — underwear and casualwear — was sold through mass merchandisers than through any other channel.

Today, the dominance of mass merchandisers in apparel retailing continues with the addition of new categories, retailer-owned brands and on-line shopping.

Hanes has played a key role in the evolution and growth of the discount channel. As new categories emerged, the brand expanded to develop products within those new segments and the Hanes megabrand was born. As the larger mass merchandisers looked to further reduce costs through economies of scale, they looked to brands like Hanes as a resource for multiple products from basic briefs and socks to tops and bottoms. Over time, Hanes grew beyond its underwear heritage to represent comfortable, quality clothing for the entire family.

ACHIEVEMENTS

Hanes and Hanes Her Way are widely recognized as the leaders in basic apparel. Across every segment, from casual apparel and underwear to intimate apparel and socks, Hanes and Hanes Her Way lead almost every consumer survey in brand recognition and reputation. In the Discount Store News Power Brand Survey, last published in 1997, Hanes was the only apparel brand to appear in the top 20.

In a new survey published in 2000 by Discount Store News/Retailing Today, Hanes maintains its position as most preferred discount apparel brand.

Across its major segments, from casual apparel and underwear to intimate apparel and socks, Hanes and Hanes Her Way have been recognized throughout the apparel industry as leadership brands. Every year, retailers across the country recognize key vendors for their contributions to the business landscape through Vendor of the Quarter and Vendor of the Year awards.

Hanes and Hanes Her Way also have won the prestigious SPARC Award *(Supplier Performance Awards by Retail Category)* in nearly every year it has been given. SPARC Awards is a national program organized by the industry's prime trade publication, *DSN/ Retailing Today*, and recognition is awarded to vendors based on retailer's evaluations against 10 key criteria.

Hanes Her Way also has been recognized for several years in a biennial survey on brand awareness called the Fairchild 100, conducted by Fairchild Publications. In the 2000 survey, Hanes Her Way ranked fourth among all women's fashion brands behind Timex, L'eggs and Hanes Hosiery. Both L'eggs and Hanes Hosiery are owned by sister divisions of Sara Lee Branded Apparel.

HISTORY

In 1901, Pleasant (P.H.) Hanes formed P.H. Hanes Knitting Co. to produce underwear for men. As an extension of the one-piece wool underwear that was the standard, Hanes introduced new two-piece underwear, a radical departure from the traditional style for that time. The same year, brother J. Wesley Hanes formed Shamrock Mills Co. to produce men's hosiery. By 1920, both companies had expanded and refocused — P.H. Hanes into undershirts, briefs, sleepwear, and knitted shorts, and Hanes Hosiery, as it was renamed, into the new market of women's hosiery.

Even through the struggles of the Great Depression, both the Hanes Knitting Company and Hanes Hosiery grew into strong and prosperous companies. In the 1940s, both companies contributed greatly to the WWII War effort, supplying underwear for servicemen and shutting down hosiery production to supply the military with nylon. In 1965, the two Hanes companies merged to form Hanes Corporation, the first time two companies with the same name merged.

©1999 Hanes

DO YOU BELIEV

PLATINUM SPONSOR OF THE 1999 SPE

In 1979, after several more years of strong growth, the hosiery and knit products businesses were once again separated when Hanes Corporation was acquired by Sara Lee Corporation, then known as Consolidated Foods Corporation. From this time through today, the hosiery business and the knit products business, both strong branded businesses, have maintained two visibly different brand identities. The familiar red logo is associated with the knit products business.

In 1986, Hanes introduced the Hanes Her Way brand for women and girls, launching with women's panties, expanding into other intimate apparel, and later adding casualwear and socks. The Hanes Her Way identity was closely tied to its successful Hanes heritage through advertising and packaging.

THE PRODUCT

The Hanes brand has several core product lines —underwear, intimate apparel, casualwear, and socks. Almost all originated in knit cotton fabrications, but have evolved into a variety of today's more advanced textiles. For example, Hanes Her Way Intimate Apparel has incorporated spandex and micro fiber yarns into many of their products for even greater comfort, and a smoother fit.

Hanes has an extensive line of product for the whole family including:
• Underwear
• Intimate Apparel
• Casualwear/Activewear
• Socks
• Babywear
• Sleepwear
• Casual Shoes
• Sheets and Towels

In recent years, product-related highlights for Hanes include its introduction of the men's boxer brief and the launch of the first successful cotton bra, called Cotton Curves, in the mass channel, both in 1996. Since then, many new products, as well as categories, have been successfully launched under the Hanes brand umbrella.

RECENT DEVELOPMENTS

Just in time for the new millennium, Hanes and Hanes Her Way have made some significant changes to both product and packaging with emphasis on style. In the men's and women's underwear categories, Hanes and Hanes Her Way have successfully increased their focus on delivering higher-end products, such as boxers and boxer briefs for men and stretch products

for women, with contemporary styling and new fabrics, in addition to their core basics.

Within the Hanes and Hanes Her Way casualwear segments, there is renewed emphasis on updated colors and styles that reflect today's trend toward casual dressing all the time. Hanes and Hanes Her Way socks have set the industry on its heel with new socks that included the Hanes and Hanes Her Way name knit into the toe. Great branding but even better for sorting laundry!

This emphasis on style is apparent in the new Hanes ad campaign, which focuses not only on the clothing, but also on the attitude of the people who wear it.

PROMOTION

Most consumers can remember with fondness the TV campaigns from the '80s and '90s. Past campaigns include Inspector 12 with her trademark *"They don't say Hanes until I say they say Hanes,"* the After-the-Game series featuring athletes such as Boomer Esiason, Lyle Alizado, Steve Largent, and Mike Ditka, the Hanes Her Way commercials featuring Carol Alt and Phylicia Rashad, and numerous appearances by Hanes spokespersons Joe Montana and Michael Jordan. *"Just Wait'll We Get Our Hanes on you,"* which ran for eight years, always brought a smile to viewers' faces.

In 1999, Hanes changed its tune, literally. The latest television campaign, called "Be You," features everyday people as well as celebrities in a variety of playful vignettes featuring Hanes and Hanes Her Way products emphasizing the importance of being comfortable and being ourselves. Energizing music by Perry Como, Muddy Waters and Cheryl Lynn set an upbeat tone for a very contemporary campaign. The commercials are as diverse as the Hanes and Hanes Her Way consumer, but they maintain the focused message on the breadth and depth of Hanes and Hanes Her Way products.

BRAND VALUES

Today and always, Hanes represents core values of comfort, quality and value. As Hanes has evolved into categories beyond underwear, and brought many new styles to market, consumers describe Hanes as *"for everyone," "stylish," "fun," "real,"* and *"honest."* This *"free to be me"* consumer sentiment directly influenced the tone and message of the Hanes *"Be You"* campaign.

THINGS YOU DIDN'T KNOW ABOUT HANES

❍ Hanes is 100 years old.

❍ Hanes makes everything from underwear to sheets.

❍ Hanes signed superstar Michael Jordan as its spokesperson in 1989, shortly after his move from North Carolina to Chicago, where he would become a sports legend.

❍ Hanes outfitted all 35,000 volunteers for the 1999 Special Olympics and 70,000 volunteers for the 1996 Olympic games in Atlanta.

THE MARKET

Despite the fact that it is a mature industry, the floor care business has experienced dramatic growth in recent years. In fact, floor care products represent the largest industry in the electric housewares category, with the exception of clocks, hair dryers and fans. Approximately 98 percent of American households own *at least* one full-size vacuum cleaner.

For the last decade, consumers have come to rely on *multiple* floor care products in their homes to meet a variety of cleaning needs. The floor care market is no longer a replacement market, but one driven by a continuous, ever-quickening flow of products with new features to add convenience to consumers' lives and meet their desire for "something new." Prolific advertising raises awareness of the latest offerings.

Another reason for the industry's continued growth is the fact that it has an ever-increasing, broad range of distribution channels. The Hoover Company sells its products through mass mer-

chandisers, department stores, catalog show-rooms, appliance stores, do-it-yourself stores, and vacuum cleaner specialty shops, to name a few. It sells through its own network of Company-owned service centers and retail outlets. Television home shopping networks and Hoover's Web site, www.hoover.com, are other avenues of opportunity.

ACHIEVEMENTS

Today, Hoover is the floor care market leader in North America. It takes great pride in its commitment to innovation, quality and customer service, striving to give customers not just what they want, but far more than they expect! Those efforts have not gone unrecognized. The company has been awarded the prestigious SPARC Award (Supplier Performance Awards by Retail Category) five years in a row by key merchandising executives in the mass-market retailing industry for excellence in new product innovation, quality control, advertising support and on-time delivery.

In recent years, Hoover has received vendor-of-the-year awards from Sears, Kmart, Wal-Mart and a host of other key retailers. The Hoover® WindTunnel™ upright was the first vacuum cleaner ever to win *Good Housekeeping* magazine's Good Buy Award, given annually to fewer than a dozen manufacturers for products that provide "exceptional performance and ingenious problem-solving features."

Hoover is also among a small number of select enterprises that have been awarded the Ohio Governor's Award for Outstanding Achievement in recognition of its ongoing efforts to develop and maintain environmentally safe manufacturing practices.

In its community, Hoover is well-known for its civic leadership and social responsibility.

HISTORY

Innovation has been the hallmark of The Hoover Company since it began business in 1908, in North Canton, Ohio, introducing a product that would become the first commercially successful portable electric vacuum cleaner.

The product was born from need: James Murray Spangler, a department store janitor, had difficulty sweeping the floor because the dust he raised aggravated his asthma. An inven-

tive man who had received patents on farming implements in the past, he created a "contraption" from a tin soap box, sewing machine motor, broom handle and pillowcase. It managed to pick up dirt, channeling it into the pillowcase and away from the air he breathed.

Spangler received a patent for the "suction sweeper," but did not have the funds to market it. He contacted a family acquaintance, William Henry Hoover, a leather goods entrepreneur, who saw the potential of the machine. He bought the patent, retained Spangler as his factory superintendent, and built a company that would

become the leader in floor care and a name recognized around the world for many subsequent decades.

Even early on, The Hoover Company was a leader in its industry with a series of developments in-house, including the spiral beater bar for deep-down cleaning, vacuum cleaner headlight, disposable paper bag, side-mounted hose configuration and self-propelled feature, to name a few.

THE PRODUCT

Hoover offers a wide array of floor care products at a wide range of price points to accommodate the budgets and diverse cleaning needs of every consumer. These products include: full-size uprights, canisters and stick cleaners; hot-water extractors; compact canisters, stick cleaners and extractors; hand-held cleaners, central vacuum systems; and a line of commercial products.

A far cry from their bulky predecessors produced during the industry's infancy, today's Hoover cleaners are lightweight but sturdy, thanks to durable plastic casings. They come in decorator colors such as forest green and deep wine, and some are the essence of the future, cloaked in transparent, gemlike tones of emerald green and sapphire blue.

Hoover products are built to be energy efficient and to offer convenience features that save time and effort for busy households. Designed for efficient manufacturing, they have fewer

parts, so are easier to assemble and service.

And, of course, Hoover products are built for superior cleaning effectiveness. Market research has revealed that one thing has not changed in the more than 92-year history of Hoover product development: The consumer wants a product that gets the dirt out of their carpets!

The company develops its products in keeping with its philosophy of Intelligent Innovation. That means it doesn't just create new products, but rather blends technology with intense consumer research to create *breakthrough* products. These products provide features that satisfy the consumer in ways superior to the competition and "wow" the consumer by coming to market even before the consumer realizes the need for them. Here are just two examples:

• WindTunnel™ technology — a patented enhancement to the agitator cavity of certain uprights which helps keep dirt from scattering back on the carpet.

• Embedded Dirt FINDER™ — a feature which actually communicates with the user, indicating via red and green lights when the carpet needs more vacuuming to remove embedded dirt and when the carpet is clean.

RECENT DEVELOPMENTS

Hoover has developed technology for bagless uprights that represents a giant step forward for the industry's bagless category. It's called the Twin Chamber System™, and it delivers excellent cleaning effectiveness, as proven when tested according to the American Society For Testing and Materials (ASTM) Standard Test Method F608 – the only industry-wide accepted cleaning effectiveness standard.

The Twin Chamber System helps the unit maintain cleaning effectiveness capability even after continued use. That's because it's designed to reduce build-up of dirt on the HEPA filter which can clog and restrict airflow.

A recent combination of this breakthrough technology with Hoover-developed Wind-

Tunnel technology has resulted in the creation of the WindTunnel Bagless, the best-cleaning bagless upright in America. The top model in this revolutionary line also features a powered hand tool — ideal for cleaning stairs and upholstery — which incorporates WindTunnel technology.

PROMOTION

William Henry Hoover realized as early as 1908 that advertising was necessary to tell the country about his suction sweeper, so he placed his first national advertising in the *Saturday Evening Post*. It offered a free, 10-day cleaner trial at home and generated hundreds of inquiries.

Today, Hoover invests millions of dollars annually in promoting its products through memorable television and print advertising campaigns to capture the attention of potential customers and to build brand name recognition. In so doing, it offers dealers invaluable publicity for their Hoover products and helps Hoover sales professionals by "pre-selling" to the consumer.

Hoover TV and print advertising typically features "slice of life" scenarios revolving around busy families or singles whose lives are

made easier and surroundings cleaner with the help of trusty Hoover products. A distinctive musical sound track with the popular "Nobody does it like you" melody and lyrics has significantly enhanced Hoover brand recognition. The Company's advertising slogan — "Deep down, you want Hoover" — underscores the brand's emphasis on getting out the dirt and subtly reinforces the consumer's emotional connection to the brand.

Other Hoover promotional efforts include carefully tailored dealer programs and promotions, trade show participation, editorial placements and TV and radio endorsements.

BRAND VALUES

Hoover is the North American market leader in floor care, with many decades of brand equity behind a name that is the best known in the industry. The HOOVER® brand, is, in fact, an American icon, virtually a household word, judged by *BrandWeek* magazine to be among the top "One Hundred Brands That Changed America." Both the name and its widely-recognized red-and-white circular emblem evoke images of trust, longevity, quality, reliability and innovation. For generations of consumers whose loyalty is legendary, Hoover has been considered a helpmate in the home, its products akin to trustworthy family members. Learn more about Hoover at www.hoover.com

HOOVER®

THINGS YOU DIDN'T KNOW ABOUT HOOVER

❍ The first Hoover vacuum cleaner weighed 40 pounds!

❍ The boyhood home of Hoover Company founder William Henry Hoover flourishes today as the Hoover Historical Center. This museum houses an intriguing collection of pre-electric carpet cleaners, milestone Hoover models, company memorabilia and Victorian-period furnishings and is open to the public free of charge.

❍ During World War II, Hoover ceased production of vacuum cleaners and aided the war effort by manufacturing helmet liners, parachutes for fragmentation bombs and the proximity fuze for missiles. As a result, the Company and its employees earned every possible government award.

❍ Hoover tests products from a consumer's point of view in its Human Engineering Lab, a one-of-a-kind facility right inside its headquarters building which duplicates in-home conditions.

HUSH PUPPIES®

THE MARKET
The shoes on your feet are a big business in the United States. Americans bought nearly 1.2 billion pairs of footwear in 1999, spending almost $39 billion, according to Footwear Market Insights, a footwear industry marketing intelligence service. Casual shoes and sandals represent 30 percent of all footwear sold — a 5 percent increase from 1996.

Casual is booming and that's really no surprise. Since the mid-1990s, America has been the center of a worldwide casual boom. Khaki trousers and comfortable knit shirts have replaced more tailored European fashions. Businesses established "Casual Friday" dress codes that soon extended to the rest of the week. "Uniform" business attire has given way to a relaxed, more individual style of dress. And Hush Puppies–the footwear brand that "invented casual"–has kept pace with appropriate, relevant product and styling that support its brand values of Fun, Comfort, and Genuine Style.

ACHIEVEMENTS
Since its introduction in 1958, Hush Puppies has become the world's best-loved shoe brand. Sold in 85 countries around the world, Hush Puppies enjoys a brand recognition of over 90 percent in the U.S. and nearly that high in most countries in which the brand is sold. Somewhere in the world, more than 30 pairs of Hush Puppies are sold every minute of the day!

HISTORY
The history of Wolverine World Wide, the parent company of Hush Puppies, dates back to 1888, when a leather-tanning operation began on the Rogue River in Rockford, a small community north of Grand Rapids, Mich. By 1904 the first shoe factory was open, making ladies dress boots and men's rugged work boots for farmers.

In the early 1950s the United States government approached Wolverine, asking them to devise an effective way to tan and use pigskin leather. Pigskin is one of the world's most durable leathers, but tanning it was not economical. Wolverine's chairman, Victor Krause, took a leave of absence to work on the project and invented the processes used around the world to this day.

Mr. Krause realized he needed a venue to showcase the now abundant supply of this new leather. He looked at the country and saw the post-war boom. Servicemen returning from the war were building homes and starting families. The original baby boom was underway.

Families were leaving cities and expanding into newly created suburbs, to homes on lots with lawns and driveways.

But what would this new generation of Americans wear on their feet? At the time, there were no true "casual" shoes. Men wore wing tips to work and once they were old, bought a new pair for work and used the old pair to mow the lawn. Women wore heels or canvas sneakers. Mr. Krause believed that this new consumer was ready for a new type of footwear. He took his new pigskin — naturally durable, treated in the tanning process to be water and stain resistant-and attached it to a lightweight crepe sole. The world's first "casual shoes" were born!

The history of the Hush Puppies name is also a slice of Americana. Jim Muir, the company's first sales manager, was traveling in Tennessee with this new-yet-unnamed line of men's and women's comfortable suede casual shoes. He stopped for dinner at a friend's house for a fried catfish dinner. His friend served hush puppies — fried cornmeal dough balls — with the catfish. When he asked where they got their name, he was told that farmers "use them to quiet their barking dogs." Jim laughed, because in the 1950s "barking dogs" was another name for tired, sore feet.

The result? Jim had an interesting idea...and that very day the comfortable shoes that soothe aching feet became "Hush Puppies." The Hush Puppies brand and famous Basset Hound logo soon became a part of American folklore.

That original Hush Puppies' style has been an example of classic, American style for over 40 years. Footwear News, a trade magazine, named it one of the best-selling shoe styles of all time. In 1996, the Council of Fashion Designers in America gave Hush Puppies their "Best Accessory" award, which put the brand in the company of such fashion icons as Ralph Lauren, Calvin Klein, and Tom Ford from Gucci.

THE PRODUCT
Today, there is a lot more to Hush Puppies than the original suede shoe that made them famous. Hush Puppies produces full lines of casual, tailored casual, and business casual footwear for men and women. These styles are appropriate for work, for play, or for leisure activity.

Hush Puppies is also a major maker of children's footwear with dress and play styles for infants as well as boys and girls up to 9 years old. You can also find the Hush Puppies brand name on your favorite accessories, from handbags to watches, eyewear, socks, and even plush toys.

While styles may look different, one thing remains the same with today's Hush Puppies — their comfort. Hush Puppies are known as "the world's most comfortable shoes™" and designers and technicians continually work to insure comfort is a top priority. Wolverine World Wide has received over 120 proprietary design patents over the course of its history.

RECENT DEVELOPMENTS
Today, Hush Puppies offers a wide range of comfort technologies, from "Zero G"—lightweight footwear built to athletic specifications to "HPO2 Flex"—a unique cushioning system designed to give incredible flexibility through

Form meets fun.

www.hushpuppies.com/2001

multi-directional flex grooves placed throughout the cushioning. For Fall 2001, Hush Puppies will introduce its new Float FX cushioning—a nitrogen/oxygen filled heel bubble, ABS stabilizer, and non-liquid forefoot gel pad to customize the entire walking motion from heel strike through toe-off.

PROMOTION

The Hush Puppies Basset Hound remains one of the world's great icons. It is as well known as "the Hush Puppies dog" as it is by its breed. Basset hounds were first introduced in many countries around the world with the introduction of the Hush Puppies shoe brand.

The Hush Puppies brand was one of the first nationally advertised shoe brands, appearing on the "Tonight Show with Johnny Carson" and the "Today" show with Hugh Downs. There

have been many memorable Hush Puppies moments in advertising — from shoes that "make the sidewalk softer" in the 1960s to "We Invented Casual" in the nineties. In 1988 Hush Puppies won the prestigious Gold Lion at the Cannes Festival for a commercial showing the Basset Hound on a subway grate with its ears flapping in the air as a train passed below. The ad was later named one of the top 100 television commercials of all time by *Entertainment Weekly* magazine.

Today, Hush Puppies advertising reflects the relevant, contemporary outlook of the brand. The tagline "Form meets Fun" suggests you can be comfortable with yourself and style-appropriate in the way you dress. The campaign targets Hush Puppies core consumers who know the benefit of looking good without being slaves to fashion.

BRAND VALUES

The Hush Puppies brand stands for Fun, Comfort, and Genuine Style. Fun — a light-hearted approach to life — can be expressed by friends, events, or simply a smile. Comfortable is a state-of-mind as well as a product attribute. When your feet feel good, you feel good, and when you feel good about yourself, you exhibit a sense of personal confidence and style. Genuine Style is the confidence to be an original, yet to be appropriate in all that you do.

THINGS YOU DIDN'T KNOW ABOUT HUSH PUPPIES

○ Hush Puppies is the original casual shoe company; it celebrates its 43rd birthday in September 2001.

○ Over 30,000 pairs of Hush Puppies are sold every day around the world, translating into about 1,800 pairs per hour.

○ It takes over 200 operations to make a single pair of Hush Puppies shoes.

○ Hush Puppies is the largest maker of comfort footwear for the entire family. A total of 85 foreign countries sell Hush Puppies, from as far away as Singapore to as close as Canada.

○ A Hush Puppies magazine campaign was once shot by celebrity photographer Richard Avedon.

○ Hush Puppies parent company Wolverine World Wide, Inc., holds over 120 proprietary patents in shoe design and comfort technology

Form meets fun.

www.hushpuppies.com/2001

THE MARKET

Hailed as "The Best Brand of the Internet Economy," IBM is at the center of today's extraordinary demand for 'e-business.' In 1997 IBM coined the term to convey the various ways that the Internet could transform business and society. Beyond browsing, IBM believed that every single interaction in the world would be affected, from buying and selling to government services, healthcare, and education.

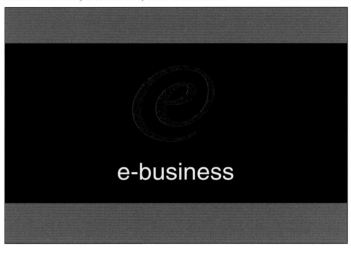

e-business

Since then, e-business has become a widely adopted industry and business term, and according to International Data Corporation demand is so great that worldwide information technology (IT) spending reached $908 billion in 2000. Moreover, e-business has galvanized the IBM brand, asserting the company's position at the core of the IT industry.

ACHIEVEMENTS

IBM Research, the largest private research organization in the world, is credited with making many scientific breakthroughs fueling today's information technology industry. Recent breakthroughs include chip-manufacturing technologies that improve performance and efficiency in a whole new generation of semiconductors and the creation of the most powerful super-computers in the world.

IBM's most significant contributions have historically been the application of technology to improve how businesses operate and people live. Today, IBM continues that legacy by helping customers become e-businesses, finding the most advantageous uses of Internet technologies to create business advantage.

As a corporate leader, IBM has extended the role of employer, enriching lives of employees through a well-developed corporate culture and extensive employee benefits. One of the first companies to provide group life insurance, survivor benefits and paid vacations to its employees, IBM continues to lead in this area by

recently offering domestic-partner benefits. The company is also frequently at the top of lists recognizing the best places to work for minorities, women, and working mothers.

HISTORY

IBM's origins can be traced to 1896, when Herman Hollerith formed the Tabulating Machine Company. It merged in 1911 with two other firms to form the Computing-Tabulating-Recording Company, or C-T-R, which manufactured products including scales, time recorders, and tabulators and punch cards.

In 1914, rapidly growing C-T-R turned to the former No. 2 executive at the National Cash Register Company, Thomas J. Watson, as General Manager. Watson, who would become president and chairman of the board, instilled more effective business tactics and fervent company pride and loyalty in every worker. Watson also stressed the importance of the customer, a lasting IBM tenet.

To reflect C-T-R's growing worldwide presence and focus on tabulators, its name was changed to International Business Machines, or IBM, in 1924. In what was called "the biggest accounting operation of all time," IBM fulfilled a government contract during the Great Depression and performed so well that other U.S. government orders quickly followed.

By the 1950s powerful computers could handle business applications such as billing and inventory control. In 1959, IBM unveiled the 7090, which used transistors rather than vacuum tubes. The computer could perform 229,000 calculations per second and would be used to run American Airlines' SABRE reservations system.

This period of rapid technology change also featured a new generation of IBM leadership. In 1952 Thomas Watson passed the title of president on to his son, Thomas Watson Jr. Watson Jr. foresaw the role computers would play in business and pushed IBM to meet the challenge.

In 1964, IBM introduced the System/360, the first large "family" of computers to use interchangeable software and peripheral equipment, a move that transformed IBM into an industrial giant with 1972 revenues of more than $9 billion. The number of employees rose

to over 260,000.

A new era of computing began in 1981 with the birth of the IBM Personal Computer, or PC. The PC put the most desirable features of a computer into one small machine. In 1985 IBM introduced networking technology which permitted computer users to exchange information and share printers and files. These advances laid the foundation for today's network-based computing, yet would throw IBM into turmoil.

The PC and networking technology unleashed the client/server revolution, developments that emphasized personal productivity and the desktop and moved business-purchasing decisions to departments and individuals. These were not places where IBM had traditional customer relationships and by the early 1990's IBM fell on hard times.

The arrival of Louis V. Gerstner Jr. in April of 1993 began a turnaround that would restore IBM as one of the greatest brands in the world. Despite pressures to break the corporation into many companies, Gerstner kept it as one entity, recognizing IBM's strength was its ability to provide integrated solutions.

The growth of the Internet again put IBM at the center of dramatic change, but this time it

was better prepared. IBM's combined strengths in services, products, and technologies enabled it to offer integrated business solutions to customers.

In the fall of 1995, Gerstner articulated IBM's new vision — that network computing would drive the next phase of industry growth and would be the company's overarching strategy. Two years later, IBM was the first to articulate the remarkable potential of the Internet, the ultimate network, with the phrase "e-business." Today, IBM is building e-businesses and creating the underlying technologies worldwide.

THE PRODUCT

IBM is the world's largest consultancy and business and technology services provider.

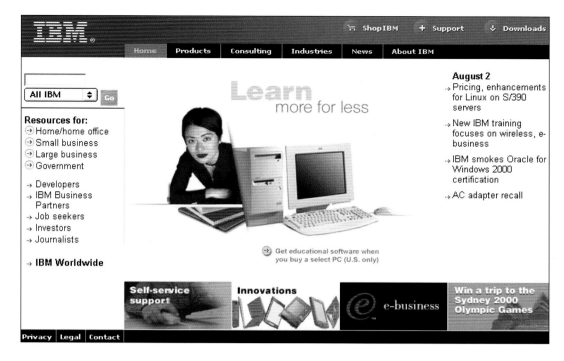

Focused on helping companies of all sizes manage IT operations and resources as well as e-business transformation, IBM's services range from strategy consulting and Web integration to infrastructure services and Web hosting.

IBM is the top producer of infrastructure software for the Internet. These technologies, also known as middleware help companies at every step of e-business transformation: creating and managing a Web presence; sharing information and knowledge; storing and leveraging data; managing complex networks; and handling the high-volume transactions of today's emerging e-markets.

IBM, of course, continues to develop and manufacture a wide variety of hardware. These include computer systems ranging from desktop PCs and laptops to the world's most powerful servers. IBM also produces component technologies including processor and memory microchips, displays and hard disk drives.

RECENT DEVELOPMENTS

IBM continues to focus on fundamental technologies, industry-leading products and, of course, applying technology. IBM is the top producer of super-computers, including the world's fastest, dubbed "ASCI White." Capable of 12 trillion calculations per second, it will be used by the Department of Energy to analyze and protect the nation's nuclear weapons stockpile. The company's rapidly expanding services arm is helping develop new growth areas, such as e-marketplaces, which are bringing traditional business applications to the Internet.

One keystone of the Internet is open standards, or common ways for computers to interact. IBM supports and develops open standards including Java and XML. Recently, the company launched an ambitious strategy embracing Linux. This popular open-source version of the Unix operating system has the potential to act in the manner of an open standard allowing myriad devices to interact seamlessly. Already, much IBM hardware and software works with Linux.

The company's focus on e-business transformation includes fashioning itself as a premier example. In 1999 IBM saw its e-commerce revenues more than triple to nearly $15 billion. The company also used the Web to generate remarkable savings: 42 million customer service transactions were conducted over the Internet for savings of $750 million. The company used the Web for $13 billion in procurement purchases saving more than $270 million.

PROMOTION

IBM maintains a broad range of traditional advertising, sponsorship and marketing activities.

In the spring of 1998, the company launched the e-business campaign, one of the highest profile and most successful for IBM. Featuring TV spots with business owners puzzling over how to use Internet technology, the ads introduced the now-ubiquitous red "e" logo and the often-copied blue letterbox effect.

The e-business campaign, still running today, embodies a strategy for the entire company to speak with one voice. Moreover, the ads explain the importance of the Internet, helping to make IBM one of the companies most identified with the Internet.

Extending IBM's embrace of e-business has been its trend-setting online advertising strategy. The company, one of the first to recognize the advertising opportunities presented by the Internet, sponsored the HotWired Web site in 1994. IBM has leveraged its Internet site and online investments with online events such as coverage of the famous chess match featuring the

I FEEL PRETTY.

IBM
the new NetVista x40 available at ibm.com

company's supercomputer Deep Blue, the first computer to defeat a sitting world champion. IBM also capitalizes on its e-business expertise through Web sites created in support of marketing sponsorships of events like Wimbledon and the U.S. Open.

BRAND VALUES

IBM's e-business leadership has effectively extended the IBM brand with the company acknowledged for its unique industry leadership. The company is considered the first to understand and articulate changes in business caused by technology.

In the competitive technology marketplace, this leadership is an especially powerful brand association. IBM's relentless focus on e-business and all its potential demonstrates, reinforces and adds to the company's legacy of integrity, experience and, of course, great technology.

Today IBM continues a strong forward momentum, helping customers develop and apply e-business capabilities to create new advantages and seize emerging opportunities.

THINGS YOU DIDN'T KNOW ABOUT IBM

○ IBM research has produced five Nobel prizes, four U.S. National Medals of Technology, and three National Medals of Science.

○ In 1999 IBM received 2,756 patents marking the seventh consecutive year in which the company was awarded the most patents in the U.S.

○ IBM has long benefited from collaborations with some of the world's greatest leaders in design, architecture and art. Graphic designer Paul Rand created the classic 8-bar IBM logo as well as much of the IBM design aesthetic. Charles Eames developed a variety of IBM World's Fair, Museum and Film exhibitions, and architects Mies van der Rohe, Eero Saarinen and I.M. Pei designed various IBM work sites.

○ IBM is today one of largest purchasers of online advertising.

THE MARKET

The men's underwear and women's intimate apparel categories are multi-billion dollar retail businesses. Status designers, mainstream brands, and store labels all compete for a share of this lucrative business. The demand for comfortable, high-quality fashionable undergarments continues to grow each year. In recent years "unmentionables" have generated widespread interest from the fashion and mainstream press. Underwear has evolved from basic white product, still the number-one seller, to a category featuring the latest in fabrics and styling innovation.

ACHIEVEMENTS

The Jockey brand is a remarkable success story. In its history, the company has not just influenced the underwear market but actually created parts of it and shaped other parts as well. The entire underwear industry literally changed its underwear to keep up with revolutionary Jockey inventions, including the brief, the bikini brief, the torso mannequin, transparent underwear packaging and the underwear fashion show.

Unlike many other firms in the apparel industry, Jockey has not gone public, merged with other firms or diversified into unrelated areas.

Today, Jockey is the number-one-selling brand of men's underwear and women's panties in department stores in the United States. The brand has over 95% consumer awareness and is one of the top apparel brands in the United States. Internationally the brand is sold in over 120 countries.

HISTORY

In 1876 Samuel T. Cooper's dedication to serving and helping others gave birth to the company now internationally recognized as Jockey International. Cooper, a retired minister with no textile experience whatsoever, was concerned about lumberjacks in the American Midwest whom he had learned were suffering from blisters and infections caused by their poor quality hosiery. Their socks, crudely shaped and made mostly from shoddy wool, wore prematurely and erratically.

When Cooper could not buy better socks for the lumberjacks anywhere in the region, he turned a livery stable into a tiny sock factory, S.T. Cooper and Sons. While others were primarily in business to make money, Samuel Thrall Cooper and his sons were in business to

Five Alarm Jockey

Let 'em know you're
JOCKEY
POUCH

Firefighters
Dallas, TX
November 20, 1998

serve others first, which would in turn earn them the right to make a profit.

For the Jockey brand, it all started in 1934, when a senior vice president at Coopers, Arthur Kneibler, happened to see a postcard from the French Riviera which showed a man wearing a swimsuit which ran just from the waist to the upper thigh. He was immediately inspired with an idea for a men's undergarment, which would provide the same support as an athletic supporter, known colloquially as a "jock strap."

In subsequent strategy sessions, it was decided that the new garment would need a clever name which would somehow connote this function, yet would be discrete enough for sensitive lady shoppers. After much brainstorming, the only name that appeared on everyone's list was JOCKEY, and the more they thought about it, the more they liked it. The JOCKEY brief was born.

The brief's public debut was as unusual as the garment itself. On January 19, 1935, Chicago's Marshall Field & Co. set up a department store window display to introduce the strange new JOCKEY underwear. But when the city was hit with one of the worst blizzards of the year, the store's management was afraid that the brief would be an absurd contrast to the biting winds, freezing temperatures and drifting

snow. It was decided that the window display would be pulled and the promotion canceled. However, the display men were delayed, and the window remained as it was. The entire stock of JOCKEY briefs was sold out before noon, in the midst of the snowstorm, economic hardships of the era notwithstanding.

That same year, Kneibler refined his invention further by developing the Y-FRONT opening, so named for the design of fabric panels, which offered consumers a buttonless fly.

In 1959, the Company created a briefer brief that was to cause almost as much of a sensa-

tion as the original Jockey brief did in 1935—bikini underwear, marketed under the trademark SKANTS. Although profitable in 1959, consumer demand for SKANTS bikinis exploded in the 1970s.

The Company became so famous internationally for the Jockey brand and its attendant innovations that in 1972 the company was christened Jockey International, Inc. In 1978, Donna Wolf Steigerwaldt assumed the chairmanship. Under Mrs. Steigerwaldt's leadership, the Company made a bold venture into a new frontier: women's intimate apparel. Perhaps the most lucrative move since the creation of the brief, the company developed a ladies' counterpart to what had been known only as a men's brand for nearly half a century. The company introduced JOCKEY FOR HER panties and tops in 1982, meeting with immediate success; sales surpassed even the most optimistic expectations.

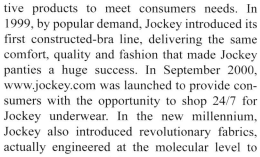

THE PRODUCT
Jockey products are designed with a commitment to comfort, fashion, quality and innovation. Jockey markets and distributes underwear and underwear related products through department stores, chains and specialty stores.

Jockey markets underwear for men, women, boys and girls. For men, Jockey produces a full range of classic cotton underwear and fashion underwear in a variety of styles and fabrics. For women, Jockey makes panties in a variety of styles, patterns and fabrics including cotton and microfiber.

Jockey has entered a number of underwear-related categories through licensing agreements, including activewear, thermalwear, sleepwear, hosiery, socks, and clothing for infants and toddlers.

RECENT DEVELOPMENTS
Throughout the '90s and into 2000, Jockey has continued to lead the market, offering innovative products to meet consumers needs. In 1999, by popular demand, Jockey introduced its first constructed-bra line, delivering the same comfort, quality and fashion that made Jockey panties a huge success. In September 2000, www.jockey.com was launched to provide consumers with the opportunity to shop 24/7 for Jockey underwear. In the new millennium, Jockey also introduced revolutionary fabrics, actually engineered at the molecular level to wick moisture, hastening evaporation and thereby maximizing comfort.

PROMOTION
Jockey has always been an innovator in underwear advertising. Jockey advertising has always reflected the values of comfort, performance, fun and quality. In a revolutionary move for its time, Jockey commissioned the *Saturday Evening Post's* legendary

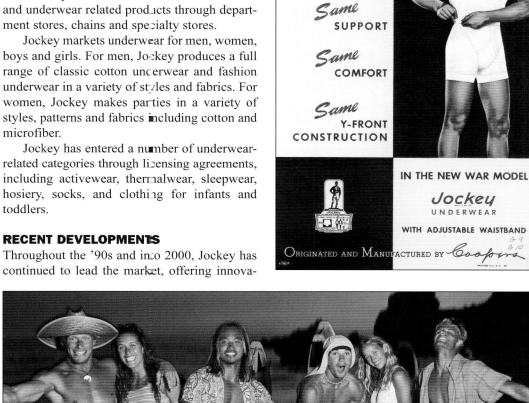

artist, J.C. Leyendecker, to produce a series of color illustrations of underwear, which would be used in the company's advertising program. The first ad appeared in the *Saturday Evening Post* in 1911.

Throughout its history, Jockey has featured a number of "Real People" promoting the brand. In the '30s and '40s, sports celebrities such as Babe Ruth, Tommie Armour, and Sammy Baugh endorsed Jockey underwear.

Jockey was the first to advertise underwear on television on NBC's "Home Show" with Hugh Downs and Arlene Francis. In the '70s, football stars Paul Hornung and Bart Starr were featured in television spots. In the 1980s, Hall Of Fame pitcher Jim Palmer and Bart Conner, the two-time Olympic Gold Medalist in gymnastics, were spokesmen. In 1992 Nadia Comaneci, the 1976 Olympics "Perfect 10," became the spokesperson for Jockey's women's products.

In 1998 the brand returned to its "Real People" roots with the introduction of the "Let 'em Know You're Jockey" campaign. This innovative fun campaign featured interesting groups of people tastefully showing off their Jockey underwear. Ten print ads featuring groups such as doctors, firemen, surfers, and snowboarders spurred strong consumer response and generated widespread publicity.

BRAND VALUES
To millions in the United States, Jockey stands for comfort, quality and value. Jockey's leadership in basic and fashion underwear has firmly established it as the classic American underwear brand.

The Jockey brand enjoys an international reputation for providing comfortable and high quality undergarments. The Jockey brand positioning is comfort. Jockey brand products provide both physical comfort through a great-fitting product and emotional comfort through a relaxed and enjoyable wearing experience. The core values of the brand include youthfulness, fun, quality, value, confidence, and innovation.

JOHN DEERE

THE MARKET

John Deere is a world-renowned equipment manufacturer that helps make those who work on the farmsite, worksite and homesite more productive. Increasing world populations, industrialization of other countries, and the desire for better lawn and turf care provide strong demand for John Deere equipment.

John Deere is the world's largest producer of agricultural equipment with preeminence in North America and expanding opportunities on other continents. John Deere agricultural equipment is needed worldwide due to the exodus of laborers in other countries from farms to cities. Meanwhile, large construction companies, governments, and other businesses now turn to John Deere for a full line of construction equipment and John Deere has expanded its presence on the forest harvesting worksite through the Timberjack brand—the world leader in this line.

Additionally, John Deere is now a leader in premium lawn and turf care equipment and utility vehicles. Homeowners, municipalities, park districts, golf course superintendents and others

use John Deere products to improve the care of landscapes. Another component of the company, John Deere Credit, has opened a variety of markets worldwide for financing the purchase of various equipment and products, including John Deere equipment.

While John Deere machines do the heavy lifting to improve productivity, John Deere equipment is also becoming more intelligent because of the recently established special technologies group. The group expands the use of computerization, global positioning and

other technology in equipment manufactured by John Deere and other companies.

ACHIEVEMENTS

John Deere migrated to Grand Detour, Ill., from his native Vermont in 1836 at the age of 33. A blacksmith by trade and innovator by nature, John Deere soon learned that Midwestern farmers faced a major problem—soil would cling to their cast-iron plows. Farmers stopped every

few steps to remove the clinging dirt. Needless to say, this made farming, the economic engine of the age, a slow and labor-intensive process. Using steel from a broken saw blade, John Deere created a plow with a highly polished surface that cut through the earth cleanly.

John Deere was the first to successfully sell others on this innovation, creating the foundation of a powerhouse company that still bears his name today. John Deere's spirit and creativity lives on in succeeding generations of John Deere employees with innovation as a hallmark of this most American brand. John Deere insisted his products should be reliable and of high quality. The company slogan—"Nothing Runs Like a Deere"—is a brand positioning statement meant to describe the commitment and integrity of John Deere products and people.

Innovation only began with the self-scouring plow. Later, John Deere patented the Gilpin riding plow—a product one historian said was the company's most important 19th century patent. In the 20th century, John Deere introduced the wire-tie baler; the self-propelled combine harvester; the self-propelled cotton picker; and the combine corn head, all which enhanced the productivity of farm producers and placed the advancement of farm equipment among the most significant engineering accomplishments of the 20th century.

John Deere also established a precision farming system and later the special technologies group—both of which deliver technological solutions for farming needs. As well, the Smithsonian Institution includes John Deere in the permanent collection of information technol-

ogy for using genetic algorithms in manufacturing, and John Deere products have received numerous design awards.

Today, Deere & Company is a global corporation with revenues in excess of $1 billion that does business on six continents and employs more than 40,000 people worldwide.

HISTORY

John Deere manufactured his self-cleaning steel plows in Grand Detour for 11 years before moving his company 70 miles south to Moline, Ill., in 1848, to take advantage of the Mississippi River. The river made it easier to bring in raw materials and to transport finished plows to market.

Charles Deere succeeded his father as president in 1869 and 17 years later John Deere died at age 82. Charles Deere established marketing centers called "branch houses" to serve the network of independent retail dealers. By the time Charles Deere died (1907), the company was making steel plows and implements.

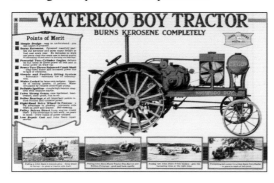

William Butterworth, a grandson-in-law of John Deere, was the third company president and established John Deere as a full-line manufacturer of farm equipment, largely through acquisitions. In 1918, John Deere moved from plows to tractors and began a new era with the purchase of the Waterloo Traction Engine Company.

In 1928, Charles Deere Wiman, a great-

78

In July 2000 John Deere updated its well-known leaping deer trademark with a more dynamic look and a greater emphasis on the John Deere name. In the updated design, the deer is leaping forward instead of landing as it had in all previous renditions. The new shape indicates an eagerness and energy toward future challenges.

PROMOTION

The company engages in several activities to extend the public respect for the brand. Prominent is the company's designation as official golf-course equipment supplier to the PGA TOUR and its title sponsorship of the John Deere Classic, a professional golf tournament televised live across the U.S. and Europe, with tape delay versions distributed in Asia, Australia, and South Africa. Additionally, John Deere was named the preferred golf and turf equipment supplier of the 2001 Ryder Cup.

grandson of John Deere, took over the company and guided it through the Great Depression and World War II. John Deere won the loyalty of farmers by refusing to repossess products from those who, due to hard times, were unable to make payments.

William A. Hewitt, Wiman's son-in-law and a great-great-grandson-in-law of the founder, led the company for 27 years, presiding from 1955-82. During Hewitt's era, the company became the world leader in farm machinery (1963) and developed a sizable presence in construction and grounds-care equipment. In the 1970s, sales grew five-fold, a period of unprecedented growth and investment.

The agricultural recession of the 1980s was one of the company's most difficult economic periods. However, under the leadership of Robert A. Hanson, John Deere emerged from this period as a more dynamic and flexible organization better able to react to growing worldwide competition. The company experienced record financial returns during the 1990s under the leadership of Chairman Hans Becherer, who was in charge from 1989-2000. Robert Lane assumed the company's top leadership position in 2000.

When John Deere began his company, he based his operations on four core values: quality, innovation, integrity, and commitment. Those values have guided the company and continue to do so today.

THE PRODUCT

John Deere is best known for its trademark

green and yellow farm equipment, which it manufactures and distributes throughout the world. The company also is a leader in construction and forestry equipment; commercial and consumer equipment for lawn and turf care; technology applications in large equipment and financing through John Deere Credit — one of the 25 largest non-bank sources of retail and lease financing in the United States.

RECENT DEVELOPMENTS

The decade of the 1990s saw John Deere expand its worldwide presence in agriculture and construction and more fully develop its commercial and consumer equipment group.

In agriculture, sales outside North America reached a full third of total sales. John Deere purchased Brazilian farm equipment maker SLC-John Deere; formed joint ventures to produce tractors in Turkey and India; entered a joint venture to produce combines in China; and acquired Cameco, the world's top manufacturer of sugarcane harvesting and handling equipment.

In construction, John Deere acquired equity interests in Bell Equipment, a South African manufacturer of articulated dump trucks; and purchased Timberjack, the world leader in forest harvesting equipment.

Meanwhile, John Deere expanded the commercial and consumer equipment product line by acquiring handheld power equipment maker Homelite; developing the "Sabre by John Deere" line; and finalizing an important distribution plan with the large Home Depot retail chain. Among newer initiatives, John Deere's golf and turf equipment—only manufactured since 1987—is already the market leader.

Licensed suppliers market products such as clothing, home goods, boots and other gear marked with the John Deere name or trademark to expand brand recognition. As well, the company published a coffee-table book in 2000 that includes both historical and contemporary photos to tell the company story.

BRAND VALUES

The name John Deere represents more than a farm machinery company. Over the company's history, John Deere has symbolized a set of genuine values — quality, integrity, innovation, and commitment. Today, the cumulative effect of dedication to these values by generations of employees has made the values become part of the company psyche, making John Deere not only a symbol of those values but their embodiment.

THINGS YOU DIDN'T KNOW ABOUT JOHN DEERE

○ The famous slogan "Nothing Runs Like a Deere" was first discarded and only chosen after an advertising copywriter had discarded one hundred other ideas in a brainstorming session with John Deere in the 1970s.

○ John Deere once made bicycles and snowmobiles.

○ The well known leaping deer in the company's symbol had always been shown in the passive landing position until the recent update of the trademark.

JVC

Excite your senses.™

THE MARKET

The digital century is upon us—a new era that is filled with opportunities for JVC. Based on JVC's management principle of enhancing people's lives through the culture of audio and video, the company has continually been a leader in the audiovisual field in the 20th century.

JVC continues to create superior products based on advanced technology and is developing the networking and system integration possibilities of digital products as a major area of business.

With the 21st century comes a lifestyle in which various types of "information," in the form of images, sound, and data, become a more integral part of people's everyday lives. Soon everybody will be able to access the information he or she wants, whenever, and wherever it is wanted. But for this to become a reality, the digitization of information and the networking of households become a necessity.

As Mr. Takeo Shuzui, President of Victor Company of Japan (JVC) said, "At JVC, we call this new environment the "home network", and we will strive to make it a reality based on the high-capacity digital media D-VHS, high-speed wireless optical networks, the D-ILA large-screen imaging device, as well as new mobile PCs that will network the user even if he's away from home, as the core technologies."

Although it is important to create a networked environment in which people can access information whenever and wherever they wish to, JVC also understands that it is equally important that people be able to access the specific information they need, in terms of content and services. JVC plans to be there to provide exactly such information.

ACHIEVEMENTS

JVC is one of the world's leading developers and manufacturers of sophisticated audio, video, and related software products. Building upon a wealth of technologies, exemplified by the JVC-developed VHS videocassette recorder in 1976 (see photo at right), the Company is moving decisively to offer appropriate solutions for the multimedia age. JVC's technological milestones in video include the development of the Hi-Fi VHS system in 1983; HQ (High Quality) VHS System in 1985; development of Super VHS format in 1987; development of D-VHS, Digital S, and the world's smallest digital video camera in 1995, and the development of the DVD player in 1996.

Audio technological developments include Japan's first LP (long-playing) records in 1953 and Japan's first EP (extended-playing) records

in 1954; Japan's first electronic organ in 1957, as well as the marketing of Japan's first stereo system—45/45-groove system for stereo records in 1958; the world's first quartz-servo turntable in 1973; development of Biphonic—the world's first binaural system using speakers in 1976; world's first metal-tap-compatible cassette deck in 1978; developed K2 Interface and CD-G (CD plus Graphics) in 1989, and the development of Dolby Pro-Logic 3D-Phonic technology in 1995. All these advances have radically impacted our entertainment standards, spawning new industry around the world.

HISTORY

JVC was born in 1927, not as a Japanese company, but as the Far East subsidiary of a great American company, the Victor Talking Machine Co. (which would become RCA Victor) of Camden, New Jersey.

The unique spirit of independence that has pervaded JVC for more than 70 years took root in our first four years of existence, largely through the influence of Ben Gardner, an American.

By 1930 Victor Talking Machine of Japan had already established an identity all its own. The influence of Mr. Gardner and the parent company in America had waned. The turning point came with the completion of a modern factory complex in Yokohama for the manufacture of records and phonographs.

With the construction of the manufacturing facilities in Yokohama, JVC was able to tap the insatiable appetite of the Japanese people for recorded music. Though the Victor Talking Machine Co. of Japan, through much of the 1930s, was almost alone in the Japanese market as a manufacture of phonographs, its popular image was in "software," in the marketing and distribution of records.

Besides making records and phonographs, JVC expanded into the recording business, with its own studios and recording artists under contract. In 1935, JVC entered radio, too, with a high-quality line of products. After World War II, JVC hired Mr. Kenjiro Takayanagi, who, in 1926 created a primitive "television" image, and his team of twenty engineers, in turn, led the company to technological leadership in television. In 1953, when Japanese stations began the first postwar television broadcasts, JVC had television sets on the market and by 1960 had a separate color television manufacturing facility.

The story of Video Home System (VHS) is the story of the 70s for JVC. That success has been chronicled in books and articles published throughout the world.

JVC takes pride in its history of innovation

and in the technologies that have contributed to the world. From birth in 1927 to achieving international status, JVC is building the foundation for new technologies in the 21st century.

THE PRODUCT

JVC is currently marketing a broad range of consumer products. JVC's video line proudly offers Digital Video Camcorders; Palm-Sized Compact VHS, and Super VHS Camcorders; LCD Monitor VHS-C and Super VHS-C Camcorders; Digital Still Camera; Video Printers; VHS and Super VHS VCRs; DVD Video Players; Satellite TV Systems, and A/V Selectors.

JVC's impressive color television line includes a 61" D'Ahlia 16:9 D-ILA™ Hologram Projection Television and 50 and 60" Dual Tuner Stereo Rear Projection TVs; Color TV/VCR Combos in 13 and 20" models; 27-inch, 32", and 36" color monitor/receivers.

JVC's Consumer Audio line is unsurpassed in quality, featuring Audio/Video Control Receivers; CD Players/Changers; MD Recorder/CD Changer; CD Recorder/Changer; Stereo Cassette Decks/Turntable; Home Theater Systems; Rack Systems; Mini-Systems; Micro-Systems; FS Systems; Micro-Component System; Executive Home Theater System; "Home Theater In A Box"; "Kaboom" CD Fashion Series; Portable CD/MP3 Players; Personal CD Players and "Attitude" Headphones.

JVC's Mobile Entertainment Products dominate the market with Changer Control CD Receivers featuring "El Kameleon"; Changer Control Cassette Receivers; Road Theater Packages; A/V Control CD Receivers; CD

sional and presentation equipment, including cameras, VTRs, editing equipment, D-ILA and LCD projectors, visual presenters, monitors and computer products.

RECENT DEVELOPMENTS

As the prime developer of D-VHS, the latest evolution in the VHS format, JVC was among the first to launch D-VHS recorders into the market in the U.S., Europe and Japan. The large data storage capacity of tape give D-VHS an advantage among new digital media for use in the large volume data recording required for full scale digital high-definition video, broad bandwidth audio and multimedia data. For high definition recording, JVC has developed a high-speed HS-Mode, which delivers the digital bandwidth necessary to record feature-length high definition programs. The development of D-VHS HS-Mode represents the next logical step, solidly positioning D-VHS as the recording method of choice for receivers of HDTV broadcast signals.

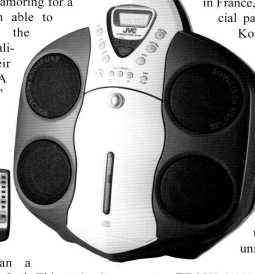

With digital broadcasting already underway in the United States, viewers will be clamoring for a television system able to fully reproduce the higher picture quality coming their way. The "D-ILA hologram device" is JVC's own innovation and was designed with breakthrough imaging technology achieved by using a "reflective" rather than a "transmissive" method. This technology, used in JVC's D'Ahlia Hologram Projection Television boasts the highest picture quality available in the industry.

cer supporter since 1982, celebrated its sponsorship during the World Cup '98 tournament in France, and continues its role as an official partner of 2002 FIFA World Cup Korea/Japan™. In 1997, JVC made headlines as the first-ever corporate partner of the Kennedy Space Center Visitor Complex. JVC has recently forged another elite corporate partnership with The ESPNZone, strengthening its leadership position in the consumer electronics arena. Spanning the senses, and reaching beyond international borders, these events contribute to culture in their own unique ways.

BRAND VALUES

At home, at the office, on the go, or on the road, JVC's leadership in the industry has fine-tuned its ability to connect technical innovation with consumer needs. For over 70 years, JVC's history has been one of continual quality and reliability, and the company continues to move ahead, interpreting the needs of the present and anticipating the desires of the future. JVC, Excite Your Senses…www.jvc.com

Receivers; Changer Control CD Receivers; 12-Disc CD Changer Package; Amps and Speakers.

JVC's Recording Media arena has flourished with an array of Blank Video (VHS/S-VHS/D-VHS/8MM tape) and Audio Tapes; Full-Size/Mini Digital Video Cassettes; Recordable Audio Mini Discs; CD-RW (Rewritable) for Audio and CD-R for Data.

JVC Professional Products Company distributes a complete line of broadcast, profes-

PROMOTION

Throughout more than seventy years, the JVC brand name has been associated with the very best in entertainment, music, and sporting events. Annual sponsorships of the world-renown JVC Jazz Festival and the Tokyo Video Festival have helped attract the attention of millions of customers.

In addition, JVC has been a worldwide soc-

JVC
Official Partner

2002
FIFA WORLD CUP
KOREA JAPAN

THINGS YOU DIDN'T KNOW ABOUT JVC

❍ JVC was established in 1927 as Victor Talking Machine Company.

❍ The dog "Nipper" was the mascot for Victor Talking Machine Company.

❍ The "Father of Television", JVC's own Mr. Takayanagi, was the first scientist in the world to successfully transmit and receive an image on a cathode-ray tube.

❍ JVC invented the VHS system in 1976 and has successfully contributed to over 600 million VCRs sold worldwide.

Kellogg's ®

THE MARKET

Grain-based products are at the heart of a healthy American diet. Six to eleven servings a day of products made from grain are recommended by the U.S. Department of Agriculture's food pyramid.

As Americans build grain-based foods into their diets, ready-to-eat cereal plays a most important role. The average U.S. resident consumes nearly 11 pounds of ready-to-eat cereal a year, providing both the goodness of grain and the added value of vitamin fortification.

Kellogg Company, the world's leading producer of cereal, manufactures more than 45 cereal products for the U.S. market. Kellogg also produces a wide-range of other convenient, nutritious, grain and vegetable-based products, including toaster pastries, cereal bars, frozen waffles, cookies, and veggie foods. Kellogg Company's name is found in the pantries of almost 90 percent of American homes.

Even as *Kellogg's*® great-tasting convenience foods respond to the growing number of consumers who eat "on the run," the company also serves the approximate 70 percent of children and adults who continue to eat breakfast at home.

ACHIEVEMENTS

Headquartered in Battle Creek, Michigan, Kellogg Company has a 95-year heritage of excellence and a reputation for products that provide value and contribute to a healthy diet.

With projected annual sales of more than $9 billion, Kellogg Company is the world's leading producer of cereal and a leading producer of convenience foods, including cookies, crackers, toaster pastries, cereal bars, frozen waffles, meat alternatives, pie crusts, and cones.The company's brands include *Kellogg's, Keebler, Pop Tarts, Eggo, Cheez-It, Nutri-Grain, Rice Krispies, Murray, Austin, Morningstar Farms, Famous Amos, Carr's, Planation, Ready Crust,* and *Kashi.* Kellogg icons such as *Tony the Tiger* and *Snap! Crackle! Pop!* are among the most recognized characters in advertising. These characters are recognized by 97 percent of American children.

Over the years, *Kellogg's* products have won

professional as well as consumer acclaim. For example, in 1999, *Kellogg's Raisin Bran Crunch* cereal became the only U.S. cereal ever to win advertising's prestigious Gold Lion Award.

Kellogg Company has compiled a long record of food industry leadership and global business growth. Kellogg products are manufactured in 19 countries and marketed in more than 160 countries around the world.

Kellogg Company also has a substantial record of social and environmental responsibility. The company has often been recognized for its social responsibility and responsiveness to employees. In addition, Kellogg Company's largest share owner, the W. K. Kellogg Foundation, is one of the world's leading philanthropic organizations.

Always committed to environmental stewardship, Kellogg Company is proud of its nearly century-long record of being one of the world's largest users of recycled paperboard. In fact, the very first cartons that came off the Kellogg production line in 1906 were made of recycled fibers.

HISTORY

Kellogg Company's worldwide leadership of its industry stems from the invention of flaked cereal—by accident—at the Battle Creek Sanitarium. The "San" was an internationally famous Seventh Day Adventist hospital and health spa. Its elite patients were offered a regimen of exercise and fresh air, plus a strict diet that prohibited caffeine, alcohol, tobacco, and meat.

Sanitarium Superintendent Dr. John Harvey Kellogg and Will Keith (W.K.) Kellogg, his younger brother and business manager, experimented to find good-tasting substitutes for the hard and tasteless bread on the San's menu. Wheat was cooked, forced through granola rollers, then rolled into long sheets of dough. One day, after cooking the wheat, the two men were called away. Although the wheat was rather stale when they returned, the brothers decided to see what would happen when the tempered grain was forced through the rollers.

Instead of the usual long sheets of dough, each wheat berry was flattened into a small, thin flake. When baked, the flakes tasted crisp and light. The San's patients loved the new food.

Seeing the commercial opportunity of ready-to-eat cereal, W.K. Kellogg left the San in 1906 and formed the Battle Creek Toasted Corn Flake Company, later renamed Kellogg Company.

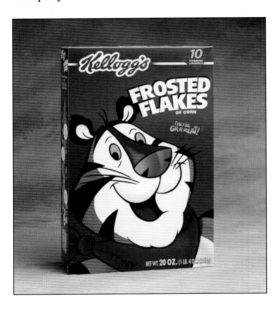

Mr. Kellogg boldly advertised his new product. He spent much of his working capital to buy a full-page ad in the July 1906 issue of *The Ladies Home Journal.* The results astonished him. Sales burgeoned from 33 cases to 2,900 cases per day. With more widespread ads and promotions to tell the public about *"The Original and Best" Kellogg's Corn Flakes,* the small company's annual sales surpassed a million cases by 1909.

W. K. Kellogg quickly expanded into international markets. He also expanded his product line, introducing *Bran Flakes* (1923), *All-Bran* (1916), *Rice Krispies* (1928), *Kellogg's Frosted Flakes* (1952), and *Special K* (1955) cereals. *Pop-Tarts* toaster pastries, launched in 1964, became an American institution of its own and, not surprisingly, the company's top-selling convenience food.

Kellogg Company also led the way in communicating good health. In the 1930s, Kellogg Company became the first company to print nutrition messages and recipes on cereal package side and back panels.

In the second half of the 20th Century, Kellogg Company's commitment to nutrition evolved into active support of scientific studies that have underscored the value of grain-based foods in a healthy diet.

In the 1990s, even as worldwide consumption of cereal continued to increase, Kellogg Company built an increasingly strong convenience foods portfolio that now accounts for 43 percent of the company's global sales, after recently acquiring Keebler Foods.

THE PRODUCT

Kellogg's products are a perfect fit for a healthy lifestyle. Many are low in fat and often help provide the dietary fiber that is lacking in the diets of many Americans. They also provide nutrition, great taste and convenience.

The appeal of *Kellogg's* products also encourages consumers to eat what nutritionists agree is the most important

meal of the day—breakfast. Research shows that people who eat breakfast tend to have less anxiety and improved memory. Children who go to school without breakfast have more trouble concentrating and their schoolwork can suffer as a result. Regular breakfast eaters have better diets and generally enjoy better overall health than breakfast skippers.

Kellogg's products also have a long-standing reputation for consistently delivering the highest level of quality to consumers around the world.

RECENT DEVELOPMENTS

With its world-class research and development resources at the W.K. Kellogg Institute for Food and Nutrition Research, Kellogg Company continues to be a global leader in food innovation. Just a sampling of Kellogg Company's innovation since 1990 includes:

- *Kellogg's Rice Krispies Treats squares,* a family of wholesome snack bars delivering the great home-made taste of a favorite *Kellogg's* recipe.
- Award-winning *Kellogg's Raisin Bran Crunch* cereal, a 1999 launch which has gained more than a 1 share of the U.S. market.
- *Kellogg's Pop-Tarts Pastry Swirls,* a great-tasting, great-selling extension of the company's powerful Pop-Tarts family.
- Kellogg has also developed a high-potential natural and frozen foods division that includes the acquisitions of Worthington Foods Inc. in 1999 and Kashi Co. in 2000.
- Acquistion of Keebler Foods Company, March 2001.

PROMOTION

W. K. Kellogg was a master of creative advertising and promotion.

In the company's early years, "Give the Grocer a Wink" won shoppers free samples of *Kellogg's Toasted Corn Flakes.* The Funny Jungleland Moving Pictures book in 1910 became the first of thousands of premiums offered to consumers who bought *Kellogg's* cereal. From the world's largest electric sign at Times Square in New York City to small grocery store windows, the Kellogg name, written in W. K. Kellogg's distinctive script— *Kellogg's* —reminded the public that "None Genuine Without This Signature."

Kellogg Company's marketing leadership continued through the decades as consumers sent their box tops to Battle Creek for Kellogg premiums, and as Kellogg became a leader in creative radio and television advertising. Kellogg sponsored early family shows on TV, including "Superman" and "Wild Bill Hickock."

The tradition of marketing leadership continues today as Kellogg has launched the cereal

industry's first frequent flyer promotion, with American AAdvantage Miles as well as exciting new promotions based on the popular Pokemon, Disney, and Cartoon Network characters. Kellogg also leverages sponsorships such as NASCAR, the Olympics, Susan G. Komen Breast Cancer Foundation Race for the Cure, to bring value added promotions to its consumers.

BRAND VALUES

Nearly a century after Kellogg Company was founded, Kellogg remains one of the best known and most popular brand names in America and all around the world.

There is tremendous consumer loyalty to *Kellogg's* brands. For example, more than 40 percent of the millions of Americans who eat *Kellogg's Frosted Flakes* have been doing so for more than 20 years, and it remains America's favorite cereal.

Kellogg Company's commitment is to continue to build its brands and to deliver superior value to consumers in the new century.

Consistent with the words of founder W. K. Kellogg, "We are a company of dedicated people making quality products for a healthier world."

For More Information
For more information, visit Kellogg's web site at http://www.kelloggs.com or Keebler's web site at http://www.keebler.com.

THINGS YOU DIDN'T KNOW ABOUT KELLOGG'S

- *Kellogg's Pop-Tarts* toaster pastries are incredibly popular with American consumers. If all the *Pop-Tarts* produced each year were laid end to end, they would circle the earth more than six times.

- With powerful brands such as *Kellogg's Raisin Bran* and *Kellogg's Raisin Bran Crunch* cereals, Kellogg Company *is the* largest purchaser of raisins in the United States—about 60 million pounds a year.

- *Tony the Tiger* is as well liked by young American children as Mickey Mouse.

- The Kellogg product providing the most dietary fiber is *Kellogg's All-Bran* with Extra Fiber cereal, which provides 13 grams of fiber per serving. This is about half the daily amount of fiber recommended for adults.

- Twenty percent of *Kellogg's Rice Krispies* cereal is used to make marshmallow squares at home

THE MARKET

The U. S. appliance market is a multi-billion dollar a year industry that has evolved dramatically over the past 75 years. Appliances make life easier, bringing time-saving and labor-saving devices into the home.

At the turn of the 20th century, women were the main caretakers of the home. Such mundane activities as washing clothes, ironing, cooking, baking and cleaning dominated the homemaker's life. With the introduction of electricity, life began to change. Washing machines became "electrified," and an activity as simple as wringing water from clothes—now automated—changed the way American women lived. Soon other appliances were introduced: ovens that could maintain an even temperature and refrigerators that needed no ice. Vacuum sweepers replaced rug beaters.

Today, as was true in the beginning, Kenmore® is the number one player in the appliance industry. More people buy Kenmore than any other brand. Kenmore's market share is extraordinary—50 percent higher than its closest competitor. Kenmore knows today's homeowners want convenience along with style, ergonomic design and ease of use: stainless steel refrigerators that provide ice and filtered water through-the-door, ranges with sensors that control the cleaning process, dishwashers with anti-bacterial cycles, microwave ovens that cook with waves of radio frequency and washing machines that fluff clothes at the end of the cycle.

Sears, Roebuck and Co. is America's largest and best-known retailer of home appliances. Kenmore appliances are available exclusively through Sears' 860 full-line department stores, 2,100 specialized retail outlets, and a variety of online offerings accessible at the company's Web site, www.sears.com.

ACHIEVEMENTS

Kenmore is the best known name in appliances. It is ranked number one or two in every major appliance category.

Category	Rank
Washers	#1
Dryers	#1
Gas Ranges	#1
Electric Ranges	#2
Refrigerators	#1
Dishwashers	#1
Compactors	#1
Freezers	#1

Throughout its long history, Kenmore

has been at the leading edge of product development and has sold more innovations in appliances than any other brand. For example, Kenmore was the first to market a frost-free refrigerator. Today, Kenmore leads the way in energy efficient appliances that save consumers water, energy and money.

HISTORY

The Kenmore brand was introduced in 1927. It was the name of a new washing machine, the sales of which were to dwarf the then popular Water Witch washing machine also sold at Sears.

The boom time that was the 1920s led manufacturers and retailers to offer a plethora of work-saving devices to free women from the hard work of keeping a home. Kenmore was positioned at the right time and right place to become an American icon.

Kenmore is intrinsically tied to Sears. The company was founded in 1886 by Richard Sears. An industrious lad, who at the age of 15 began selling watches to supplement the family income, he turned a simple idea into a $40 billion-a-year retail giant that is Sears today.

Through its annual catalogs, Sears could reach both urban and rural America. The idea was straight-forward: Provide customers with items that they need and want, produced of the highest quality, at the most reasonable price.

From the beginning, every item sold through the Sears catalog was backed by the now famous Sears promise: Satisfaction Guaranteed or Your Money Back.

The Kenmore brand remained on the washing machine line through various models and years including the Kenmore Gyrator, the Kenmore Hydro-Swirl Washer and the Kenmore Cycla-Fabric Washer. Customers soon learned they could trust the quality of Kenmore, and the name was rolled out to other appliances: vacuums, stoves, sewing machines, irons and finally refrigerators and dishwashers.

In 1946, the Sears catalog proclaimed, "Kenmore—the right way to say electrical appliances."

THE PRODUCT

2002 marks the 75th anniversary of the Kenmore brand. It has been shown in consumer research that customers trust Kenmore. In a 1998 Equitrend survey, consumers ranked Kenmore

Why did Jane Wyatt, who could afford any washer in the world, choose a Kenmore from Sears?

Sears | Kenmore Washer
for women who want the best even if it does cost less

higher on overall product quality than other leading brands such as Nike, Goodyear, Visa, Coca-Cola or Kellogg.

Kenmore's line is broad and deep providing a variety of products in every appliance category: refrigeration, dishwashers, ranges, cooktops, ovens, washers, dryers, microwaves, freezers and floor care products. This allows customers to match features and benefits to their particular lifestyle, budgets and tastes.

The Kenmore line has also been expanded to offer consumers a full range of products that help them manage their home environment, including Central HVAC units, window air conditioners, humidifiers and dehumidifiers, air cleaners, water heaters and water softeners.

In addition the Kenmore name can be found on a full line of small appliances such as water purifiers, disposals, blenders, mixers, irons, waffle irons, toasters, toaster ovens and coffee makers. In short, almost any task that needs to be done inside the home can be done with a Kenmore product.

Always wanting to give customers what they want, the brand is continuously updating product features and developing new products. Recent examples include water-conserving washing machines, and refrigerators that run on the same amount of electricity it takes to run a 75-watt light bulb.

Kenmore appliances are known for their high quality and guaranteed performance. While sturdy and dependable, the brand is also sleek, stylish and up-to-date.

No longer is a refrigerator simply a large white box. Instead, as the Kenmore Elite™ ad says, it's a stainless steel "grand ballroom where French vanilla ice cream and long, luscious crab legs have 20 percent more room to waltz."

RECENT DEVELOPMENTS
Kenmore has taken great strides in developing and selling products that are good for people and good for the environment. Ergonomic concerns such as ease-of-use and noise reduction are constantly addressed by product engineers. Kenmore now includes refrigerators which

have America's Quietest™ sound reduction system, dishwashers with QuietGuard™ Elite Plus sound insulation and washers and dryers carrying the Ultra Quiet Pak™.

The line includes many industry firsts, such as the 2000 Kenmore America's Best range line that features a child-lockout safety feature for the gas cooktop and breakaway racks for convenient loading.

For water and energy savings, Kenmore carries four different washer models that carry the U.S. Department of Energy's ENERGY STAR® rating. The U.S. Department of Energy and the U.S. Environmental Protection Agency named Sears the ENERGY STAR Retail Partner of the Year for 2000 and again in 2001.

In 1999, Kenmore rolled out a brand new line of premium products called Kenmore Elite™. This fully featured line offers unique styling and leading edge innovation, at a price that provides outstanding value. The new line was wildly accepted by the American public.

The styling of the line, dressed in stainless steel, or new colors such as graphite and Bisque, allows the new appliances to blend with any kitchen decor.

Introducing industry-first features such as the Kenmore Elite dishwasher with a giant-sized tub and the ability to wash over-sized dishes or picnic coolers, keeps Kenmore on the cutting-edge of technology.

In 2000, the introduction of the Kenmore Elite washer with Calypso™ Wash Motion literally redefined the term high-efficiency washer. It is a top-loading washer that utilizes a wash plate at the bottom of the wash basket, instead of a central agitator, to bounce clothes clean in a shower of clean filtered water. This new washer cleans better than any other full-size high efficiency washer, while saving 50% in energy and 68% in water vs. the average conventional washer.

PROMOTION
Historically, getting the word out on Kenmore was as easy as delivering the Sears, Roebuck and Co. catalog. Today, the brand has adopted an aggressive multi-million dollar advertising and

marketing campaign directed through media as diverse as advertising in and marketing partnerships

with women's and home magazines, newspapers, national television campaigns, the Internet at www.sears.com and www.kenmore.com and even the NASCAR Racing circuit.

BRAND VALUES
The name Kenmore stands for high quality, outstanding value, and innovative products. Kenmore continuously expands and develops new products to meet a wide variety of budgets and styles, and seeks to bring innovative products to the marketplace to make customers' lives easier. These values are backed by an assurance of satisfaction that customers have come to expect. The Sears promise: Satisfaction Guaranteed or Your Money Back, means just that. If any customer is not satisfied, they get a full refund.

THINGS YOU DIDN'T KNOW ABOUT KENMORE

○ Kenmore was introduced in 1927, the same year the first "talking" motion picture, The Jazz Singer, was released.

○ One out of two homes in America owns a Kenmore appliance.

○ Kenmore holds the highest repurchasing rate of any appliance brand — 42 percent.

○ Kenmore refrigerates more food than any other appliance brand.

○ More clothes are washed and dried in Kenmore washers and dryers than any other brand.

○ More trash is compacted, more rooms are cooled, more dishes are washed with Kenmore than any other brand.

○ Kenmore was the first appliance brand to introduce color to the kitchen with the introduction of its blue porcelain kitchen stove in 1932.

○ The American Association of Textile Chemists and Colorists (AATCC) which tests fabrics for sturdiness and color fastness, uses a Kenmore washer and dryer in its laboratory testing.

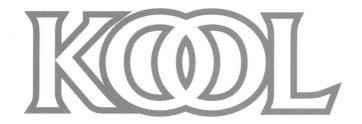

THE MARKET

Brown & Williamson Tobacco Corporation competes in one of America's most competitive and highly restricted industries: the U.S. cigarette market.

There are over 2,000 cigarette brands currently being marketed in the U.S. alone. Despite a declining overall market that peaked in 1982, approximately 1 in 5 adult Americans continue to enjoy cigarettes and other tobacco products. That's nearly 45 million people. Directly and indirectly, the industry provides approximately three percent of the country's Gross Domestic Product and a foreign trade surplus of more than $4 billion a year.

However, since the federal ban on broadcast advertising first took effect in January 1971, cigarette manufacturers have come under increasing pressure to limit the ways in which they market their products. Most recently, a Master Settlement Agreement (MSA) was reached between the states' attorneys general and the tobacco industry in November, 1998. As a result, companies like Brown & Williamson have been challenged to find alternative methods to market their products in more innovative ways.

ACHIEVEMENTS

KOOL was the first menthol brand to achieve national distribution. Its appeal helped create an entire category. Today, over 10 million people enjoy smoking menthol cigarettes thanks to the early product innovators at Brown & Williamson.

In 1973, KOOL achieved #3 U.S. brand status and sales volume establishing it as America's #1 menthol.

At its peak in 1975, KOOL commanded a 10.5% share of the total U.S. Market.

KOOL led the way for the menthol category by introducing KOOL Milds in 1972 — the first menthol cigarette with reduced tar and nicotine between full flavor and lights styles.

KOOL continued its innovative ways by introducing four new KOOL Natural Full Flavor and Lights styles in the fall of 1998. The product's use of natural menthol flavor makes it a unique offering in the category.

HISTORY

In February 1933, the year that prohibition was repealed and Congress passed the New Deal, B&W introduced KOOL to the world with a penguin symbol to reinforce the brand's unique menthol attributes.

Originally launched as a premium priced

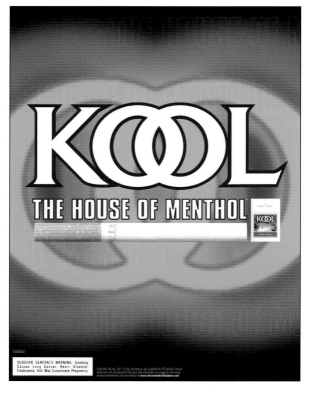

product to appeal to a small niche in the market, it would grow to become one of the world's most popular menthol brands.

In 1940, the price of KOOL was lowered to the then popular price of 15 cents per pack, but the brand remained a niche product until later in the decade when a new marketing effort featuring an updated Willie the Penguin proved highly successful in generating awareness among smokers who preferred menthol.

KOOL's remarkable climb throughout the '50s and '60s was largely the result of the collaboration of two men: John Braggard, head of marketing at B&W for decades, and Rosser Reeves, the Bates agency's guru of USP advertising. Together, they created one of the most powerful problem/solution campaigns in history:

"Tired of hot, harsh taste? Come up to KOOL."

Their unwavering commitment to this cam-

paign built the brand to menthol leadership. Why? KOOL was the solution to a very real problem: the harsh, strong taste of most non-menthol smokes. Starting in the era when most cigarettes had no filter and were five times as strong as today's cigarettes, "hot, harsh taste" was a real issue. Menthol was the answer, and KOOL defined the category.

From the mid '70s through early '80s, lower tar and nicotine cigarettes became the choice for a growing number of smokers. Manufacturers responded with a variety of new "light" and "ultra light" cigarettes, as well as line extensions of existing brands. Again, KOOL led the way for the menthol category by introducing KOOL Milds, the first menthol cigarette with reduced tar and nicotine, between full flavor and lights styles.

Over the last two decades, a more focused advertising and marketing approach was developed for the KOOL brand, concentrating resources in urban markets with high opportunities. This approach has been steadily expanded. Other strategies were also put in motion to invigorate the brand, including further updates to product packaging, zealous point of sale and direct marketing programs, bar promotions, and advertising campaigns.

THE PRODUCT

From its introduction nearly 70 years ago, the KOOL brand has been a leader and innovator in the menthol cigarette category. It has endured the test of time and is now enjoying a resurgence in popularity based on its heritage as an originator of the menthol cigarette.

With the 1998 introduction of KOOL Naturals in Filter Kings and Lights, the KOOL brand family has grown to include 17 product styles. It's the broadest portfolio of any U.S. menthol brand. Each has its own appeal, but all fulfill the brand promise of rich taste and smooth smoking pleasure.

KOOL is distinctive among menthol cigarettes in that it achieves a perfect fusion of rich tobacco taste and fresh menthol flavor. The fine tobaccos used in KOOL are not masked but rather enhanced by the addition of menthol. This masterful balance is symbolized by the interlocking Os within the KOOL logo which are still present today in much the same form as on the original product packaging in 1932.

RECENT DEVELOPMENTS

KOOL introduced its current "Waterfall" imagery packaging for 12 of the 13 "parent" styles in the first quarter of 1998. Prior to that, the packaging had remained virtually unchanged for decades.

And in June of 2000, KOOL launched a new media and point-of-sale advertising campaign, "The House of Menthol." The new campaign revitalizes the KOOL heritage and positions the brand as the menthol authority that all others follow. It stands on the breaking copyline, "We Built The House of Menthol."

The intensity and commitment of both the product and today's urban energy are captured with relevant lifestyle graphics, borrowing from contemporary music and modern technology.

PROMOTION

Bringing a brand to life in a highly restricted marketplace takes more than a great advertising campaign.

Like its competitors, KOOL must find ways to capture attention and make the brand relevant to its intended audience.

Even in its earliest days, the brand was an innovator in terms of its approach to sales promotion.

In the 1940s, Brown & Williamson used radio programs to promote the KOOL brand. The company not only sponsored these programs, but actually produced them as well. The primary sales promo-

tion vehicle during this period was a premium coupon program in which customers collected coupons found in KOOL packs and redeemed them for brand-name merchandise.

With the 1960s came the age of television marketing of cigarettes. Advertising for KOOL was designed to emphasize the brand's distinctive and refreshing menthol taste. Early commercials featured an animated Willie the Penguin. Later spots showcased "slice-of-life" ads with adult smokers switching to KOOL.

KOOL brand marketing continued to break new ground in the 1970s. Unusual promotions, such as a KOOL sailboat offer, were employed as techniques to increase advertising readership. Consumer response to the sailboat offer resulted in 18,000 boat orders in 1971. But the brand did more than attack by land and sea. KOOL took to the air as well, being among the first brands to promote in the skies with a hot air balloon tour.

This was also the era of the legendary KOOL Jazz Festivals, one of the largest corporate sponsorships of an art form in U.S. history. These and other KOOL music programs would be regarded among the most successful promotions of the times, solidly positioning KOOL with music in the minds of many consumers.

KOOL music promotions continued to grow and evolve in the form of KOOL Country On Tour, KOOL Latino Festival, KOOL Super Nights, and KOOL City Jams. Even today, the music tradition continues with KOOL MIXX.

During the 1990s, KOOL shifted its promotion into high gear with the sponsorship of the Team KOOL Green CART (Championship Auto Racing Teams). Team KOOL Green entered the 2000 FedEx Championship Series season following a spectacular 1999 campaign which saw its drivers, Dario Franchitti and Paul Tracy, finish 2nd and 3rd, respectively, in the FedEx Championship Series.

BRAND VALUES

As the cornerstone of the menthol category, KOOL is truly the menthol authority. The KOOL brand essence draws its energy and inspiration from the intensity of urban life. It is pure vitality.

KOOL captures that sense of freedom, energy, and exhilaration and combines it into a single, vivid experience. These are other major aspects of KOOL's brand values:

—KOOL has authenticity and genuine quality, is straightforward, and has substance. KOOL

is proud of its heritage and stature as the leader of the menthol category (the menthol authority).

—KOOL is a high quality, popular, premium brand providing the perfect blend of tobacco taste and menthol refreshment.

—KOOL is contemporary, dynamic and energetic while it embodies classic, tried and true values.

—KOOL is up with the times, engaged, committed and intense. It is a brand with integrity and self-assurance.

—KOOL has enjoyed a strong, enduring relationship with young adult (adult smokers under the age of 30), multicultural, urban smokers.

THINGS YOU DIDN'T KNOW ABOUT KOOL

○ The trademark application for KOOL cigarettes was filed on December 15, 1931, and the KOOL "O's" have been interlocked ever since.

○ Quantitative research was conducted among 4,000 magazine subscribers for their opinion on eight KOOL advertisements to deliver the KOOL proposition. Result: a landslide vote for Penguins!

○ Willie, the KOOL penguin, had a female friend named Millie.

○ KOOL was among the first nationally distributed brands to cast white collar African-Americans as the product "expert" and focal character in television commercials.

○ The KOOL brand name is among the few that actually capture a description of the key product characteristic in just four letters.

THE MARKET

In the year 2000 the Non-Chocolate Candy category had sales of over 4 billion dollars. LifeSavers had a 5.3 percent share of the category as well as being a leader in the hard candy segment with a 20 percent share.

The non-chocolate confection market is extremely competitive and highly complex. It is an extensive category with an enormous variety of choices. Confections consumers are looking for extreme variety and are very impulse-driven when it comes to purchasing candy. The primary brand drivers are news and top-of-mind awareness. New products, new packaging, strong branded promotions, and a consistent media presence are all crucial elements to driving awareness and interest as well as building brand value. On average, new products account for 23% of total non-chocolate candy sales.

ACHIEVEMENTS

Life Savers candy has existed for nearly 90 years and remains the nations top selling Non-Chocolate Candy. The LifeSavers name has been licensed for products ranging from Ice Pops to Barbie Dolls. Recent awards include Candy Manufacturer of the Year (1999), Silver Anvil Award (2000), and Promo Gold Award (2000).

HISTORY

Edward John Noble was selling advertising space on New York City street cars in 1913 when he happened to visit a candy store and noticed some tubular packages of mints called Crane's LifeSavers. He was so impressed with the taste, shape, and name of the candy, that he went to Cleveland, Ohio, to urge the manufacturer to advertise the product.

But Clarence Crane was not interested. He explained the mints were just a summertime replacement for his principal product, chocolates, whose sales fell in hot weather. Crane had hired a pill maker to turn out a hard candy that he wanted to be different from the square, pillow-shaped products then generally available. He specified that his mints have a hole in the middle and in 1912 registered the trade mark LifeSavers because the finished product

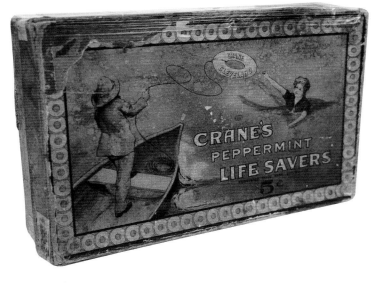

looked like a life preserver.

When Noble continued to argue to Crane that LifeSavers could become a strong seller with proper promotion, the manufacturer offered to sell him the manufacturing rights.

Noble did not have the $5,000 that Crane wanted, and he asked a boyhood friend, Roy Allen, to join him in the venture. They could only raise $3,800 but negotiated a final sale price of $2,900, leaving them with $900 in working capital.

Noble quickly discovered that the product he had liked so much had just arrived at the candy store. Thousands of older rolls of LifeSavers had turned stale on retailers' shelves because their cardboard tubular package had absorbed the volatile, peppermint flavor.

He began using tinfoil to protect the mint flavor. While retailers would not buy, they agreed to exchange their worthless inventories for new stock.

Noble visited saloons, cigar stores, barber shops, restaurants, and drug stores and persuaded mangers to take a few boxes. He suggested that they put them next to the cash register with a five-cent price card and give all customers a nickel as part of their change.

Noble kept his day job, paying his employees from his salary, but within a few years his Mint Products Company's sales rose to $250,000 annually. The manufacturing facilities were moved from Cleveland to New York City in 1915.

Sugar shortages and Noble's own military

service slowed production of the mints drastically during World War I, but sales shot up 200 percent in the post-war years and have been increasing ever since. The company shifted manufacturing to Port Chester, N.Y., in 1919.

Life Savers Corporation was acquired in 1926 by Drug Inc., a company that had extensive medical-product and drug-store holdings. Drug, Inc., spun off Life Savers Corporation in 1933, and Edward J. Noble once again directed it. In 1956 the Life Savers Corporation merged with Beech-Nut, Inc., forming Beech-Nut Life Savers, Inc., which in 1968 merged with E. R. Squibb & Sons. Nabisco Brands bought LifeSavers, Inc., in 1981, and in 1985 Nabisco Brands merged with R. J. Reynolds Industries to form what would become RJR Nabisco, Inc.

THE PRODUCT

LifeSavers drops were introduced in 1924, and in 1929 the technology for production of boiled drops with a hole was developed. Since that date, all roll candies sold under the LifeSavers name have had a hole.

The original LifeSavers flavor was Pep-O-Mint, and Noble's first flavor addition came in 1920 with Wint-O-Green. Later additions were Wild Cherry in 1934, Spear-O-Mint and Five Flavors in 1936, Butter Rum in 1939, Tropical Fruits in 1966, LifeSavers Pops in 1974, and LifeSavers Delites in 1995,

LifeSavers also offers a variety of seasonal

products for Valentine's Day, Easter, Halloween, and Christmas. They include the extremely popular Sweet Storybook, which contains eight rolls of LifeSavers Candy and fun games. It is the oldest multi-pack of LifeSavers, having originated in the early 1930s as a gift to shareholders.

RECENT DEVELOPMENTS

In 2000 Philip Morris Companies, Inc. acquired Nabisco and incorporated it into Kraft Foods. Today, LifeSavers candies are marketed by the Kraft Confections Division.

The 1990s brought a flurry of new products to the Life Saver Company's portfolio. LifeSavers Gummies, a soft chewy candy with the classic hole, was introduced nationally in 1993. In 1994 LifeSavers Candies were introduced in peg bags, followed by laydown bags in 1999. Peg and laydown bags contain individually wrapped pieces that are 50 percent larger than their roll counterparts.

The LifeSavers Company entered the growing, multi-million-dollar sugar-free candy category with the introduction of LifeSavers Delites in an assortment of fruit-based and dairy-based flavors. Delites dairy-based candies are the first of their kind ever to reach the national marketplace.

Creme Savers were introduced in 1998 and have enjoyed huge success. It is a hard candy that uniquely combines real cream and fruit. Creme Savers truly is "the Creamiest, Dreamiest, Life Saver Yet."

The newest addition to the LifeSavers brand is Jellybeans. These are a premium jellybean with flavor-packed centers that were launched in time for Easter 2001.

PROMOTION

Life Savers advertising began when the original manufacturer, Clarence Crane, packaged Life Savers mints with a printed label showing an old seaman dressed in a yellow oil skin slicker tossing a life preserver to a young woman swimmer in distress. The copy read; "Crane's Peppermint Life Savers...5c...For That Stormy Breath."

Edward J. Noble was working in the advertising field when he bought the brand, and the continuity and development of its advertising over the years reflect the confidence that he and his successors have had in effective promotion.

LifeSavers used the services of an advertising agency as early as 1916. The agency carried out his strategy of promoting LifeSavers through use of the bright, poster-type streetcar-card advertising he had been selling.

The brand's print advertising has always been outstanding for its simplicity, good humor, and appetite appeal. Simple and refreshing artwork and copy presented LifeSavers as a simple

Give "A Sweet Story"
(to a sweet someone!)

and refreshing product. Simple compositions, life-like color, and brief catchy slogans were characteristics of the print campaigns.

The 1990s brought a series of campaigns called Celebration. The campaign consisted of 3 television spots showcasing the "Refreshing Flavors of Life," Five Flavor, Tropical Fruits, and Mints.

LifeSavers recently held two hugely successful promotions. The "Refresh the Roll" promotion in 1999 asked consumers to vote on whether to replace the Pineapple flavor in the Five Flavor roll with Strawberry or Watermelon. Pineapple was the winner and the Pineapple Treasure Hunt promotion began. To celebrate Pineapple's victory LifeSavers produced special Five Flavor rolls and bags filled with all Pineapple candies. Whoever found these special packs could instantly win its weight in gold. These promotions created news and drove sales adding 10 percent to the brand's annual volume.

LifeSavers' internet site is www.candystand.com. This interactive site offers a broad range of product information, games, contests, and other activities designed to reach out to consumers.

BRAND VALUES

High quality, outstanding taste, a wide variety of genuine fruit and mint flavors, bright colors, and a fun-to-eat shape have been the hallmarks of the LifeSaver brand for generations of Americans. "LifeSavers" is one of the most familiar of all brand names, not only in the United States but throughout the world. Since 1912, consumers have been responding enthusiastically to the friendly invitation to "have a LifeSaver."

THINGS YOU DIDN'T KNOW ABOUT LIFESAVERS

○ During World War II the LifeSaver Company supplied U.S. military forces with more than 23 million boxes of Five Flavor Candy, each with 20 individual pieces of candy that went into troops ration kits.

○ On an average day, the LifeSavers plant in Holland, Mich., where all LifeSaver hard candies are made, will turn out 54 miles of roll candy using over 225,000 pounds of sugar!

○ When you bite into a Wint-O-Green LifeSaver, a phenomenon called Triboluminescence occurs. It is a spark that is the result of fractured sugar crystals reacting with the wintergreen flavor.

○ LifeSavers hard candy production in 2000 totaled 284 million rolls and 89 million bags for a total of 57.5 million pounds of candy.

○ Consumers constantly share with the company the innovative uses they have found for Life Saver candies. They have used the candy to flavor tea, to "cure" seasickness, as Christmas ornaments, candle holders on birthday cakes, and golf tees, and to make necklaces and bracelets.

THE MARKET

Brown & Williamson Tobacco Corporation competes in a highly restricted industry. Opportunities depend largely on developing effective and engaging marketing programs that encourage adult smokers to select Luckies rather than competitive brands.

Lucky Strike appeals to an adult smoker who's looking for a brand with a mind of its own. Contemporary urban smokers who value a brand of unparalleled history and a fresh view of the world find something unique, even intriguing, in the brand that started it all.

What does "started it all" really mean? Simply put, Lucky Strike is the first cigarette manufactured in the United States. It has a history and tradition that date back almost 130 years, years filled with marketing innovation, an unshakable commitment to product quality, and unsurpassed smoking pleasure.

Lucky Strike is more than living history, it is also one of the most unique and non-traditional marks in American business today.

Its current advertising and promotions are created with a certain playful intelligence that separates the brand and its consumer from the well-defined mainstream of the US tobacco market.

In every market, there are consumers driven by the search for new ideas and experiences. They expect the brands they select to offer the unexpected and original. Curious by nature, these consumers are experimental, and enjoy the new, the different and the out-of-the-ordinary. They are willing to go against traditional thoughts and values. They are individuals who go their own way.

In short, they look for brands like Lucky Strike.

ACHIEVEMENTS

Throughout its history, Lucky Strike has been an innovator. Beyond its icon pack design and well-known theme lines, "LS/MFT" and "It's Toasted," Lucky pioneered many of the marketing tools that are now part of our culture.

Starting in the 1930s, Lucky sponsored the long-running radio show, "Your Hit Parade," which kept America up to the minute with popular music and introduced the country to the talent of its rising young star, Frank Sinatra.

Lucky became so much a part of the American cultural landscape that it even became the center of classic skits such as Humphrey Bogart's famous turn on the Jack Benny Show and the subject of one of Keith Herring's most recognized works.

It is even considered one of the first brands to recognize the power of public relations

when it retained Edward Berneys to create events around the brand such as the famous women's march to proclaim their equal right to enjoy the pleasures of the brand.

Since the Second World War, Lucky Strike has become one of the American brands that have spread around the world.

From the C rations of GIs liberating Europe to the Army of Occupation in post-war Japan, Lucky came to represent America on a global scale. Even today, Lucky has a strong and growing presence in Japan and Germany and is continuing to attract the attention of smokers

from Latin America to Central and Eastern Europe.

More recently, in the United States, Lucky has been once more receiving focused marketing support from Brown & Williamson, the current brand owner.

Working to build its business in the market where it began, B&W has developed unique and innovative methods to reach prospective adult consumers, specifically to give smokers a clear alternative to that ubiquitous guy on the horse.

In 1999 Lucky drew the attention of smokers with innovative attention to the smallest elements of the marketing mix. The brand, for example, printed a toll-free number on the side of every pack to help consumers locate their nearest Lucky Strike retailer. Due to legal restrictions, the Lucky Strike brand name was not mentioned, yet the number's voice recording reflected a smart, intriguing, and unexpected message—the voice and attitude that is consistent with Lucky Strike's traditions and core character. It delivered the message that became one of the most circulated e-mails for the year. It was mentioned on numerous news programs, such as CNN, and was listed in Esquire magazine's "Top 100 Things a Man Must Do Before He Dies" list. Brown & Williamson was soon flooded with up to 40,000 calls a day.

HISTORY

Lucky Strike is one of the greatest trademarks in history, cigarette or otherwise. It has a rich tradition of doing things differently, of taking the lead and creating its own path.

Lucky Strike began in 1871, the first manufactured cigarette in America. The name, "Lucky Strike," was inspired by the fabled California Gold Rush.

By the end of the first decade of the 20th Century, Lucky had become the cornerstone of the American Tobacco Company, the firm that would dominate the market for the first six decades of the century.

Luckies were sold in a green pack until 1940. Then, in a stroke of marketing genius, American changed the color of the pack to white in 1942 to support the war effort, as green dye was in short supply painting tanks and other military equipment. This inspired the copy line, "Lucky Strike green has gone to war."

In 1944, as the war was ending, American launched one of the most memorable campaigns

in American marketing history, "Lucky Strike Means Fine Tobacco." "L.S./M.F.T." was added to every pack. This slogan was so popular, it is still on the Lucky Strike cigarette packs sold today.

That unique and enduring pack design has almost become part of our cultural landscape. Its designer, Raymond Loewy, is one of America's most famous industrial designers. Life Magazine recently selected Loewy as one of the 100 most influential Americans of the 20th century. His other design icons include the Coca-Cola bottle, Air Force One, and the Greyhound Bus.

THE PRODUCT

Great product has always been the foundation of Lucky's success. As far back as 1917, "It's Toasted" appeared on every pack, describing the way extra flavor is extracted from every leaf of fine tobacco.

RECENT DEVELOPMENTS

Currently, Lucky Strike remains committed to the values that built the brand, updated and re-expressed in the context of the current market.

In the context of current marketing restrictions, it takes real imagination and care to establish a meaningful connection with demanding adult smokers.

PROMOTION

Being a smoker in an urban environment presents daily challenges. Smokers today tend to feel ostracized, often being forced to smoke in the cold, near garbage cans, or in generally unpleasant environments.

In 1999 Lucky Strike launched what Brandweek Magazine named "guerilla Marketing Campaign of the Year." Launching a series of unique marketing initiatives through an awareness-building program called the Lucky Strike Force, street teams spread the message that Lucky Strike understands what it means to be a smoker in an urban environment. Each initiative was developed and

executed to enhance consumers' smoking moments. The Strike Force offered free coffee to smokers freezing outside their office buildings and use of a cell phone in crowded, flight-delayed airports at holidays. The Force members also offered smoking consumers a rose on Valentine's Day. Each smoker approached by the Force received a card that read "Lucky Loves You," including a 1-800 number that lets consumers learn more about Lucky Strike.

Lucky store promotions are as unique as its street teams. Instead of traditional price discounting, Lucky Strike offered a free black-and-white camera with purchase. The program was an enormous success because Lucky Strike offered a promotion relevant to the prime prospects' personal creativity, not just their wallets.

BRAND VALUES

Every point of consumer contact presents an opportunity to strengthen brand values.

Lucky Strike respects its customers' intelligence and never takes itself too, too seriously.

While Lucky Strike certainly carries a retro appeal to some, the values and identity created by and for Lucky Strike are timeless. Just like many of today's leading edge consumers, Lucky Strike remains unaffected by short-term fad or fashions, always challenging convention.

Lucky stays closely tied to city life. Lucky Strike taps this urban energy in everything related to the brand. In designs, advertising, and especially events and promotions.

Making an impression on consumers, particularly without access to many traditional commercial media, is no easy task. Smokers don't often change brands, and it takes a lot to get them to consider an alternative to their established choice.

Creative, original and self-expressive, young adult urban smokers demand much from the brands they choose in any category.

To gain their consideration, Lucky is committed to the originality, creativity, and unexpected insight that were the foundation of its historical success and remain the key to its future.

THE MARKET

Chocolate continues to be America's favorite flavor when it comes to confectionery products. Americans ranked 8th worldwide in the consumption of chocolate, with England having the highest rate of consumption. In a recent poll, 52 percent of American men and women voted for chocolate as their favorite flavor in confectionery products and desserts. Within that group, 65 percent chose milk chocolate and 27 percent voted for dark chocolate. The remaining 8 percent did not have a preference.

Chocolate sales have been increasing during the past year, possibly due to the news of antioxidants found in chocolate and the health benefits provided by their consumption. Halloween is the number one candy-consuming holiday in the U.S., followed by Christmas, Easter and Valentine's Day. Retail candy sales in America were an estimated $23.3 billion last year. Retail chocolate sales alone were worth 12.9 billion. (Sources: National Confectionery Association, U.S. Department of Commerce).

ACHIEVEMENTS

Today, the "M&M's"® Brand is sold in over 70 countries and is the largest, most popular confectionery brand in the world. In North America, "M&M's"® is the #1 Brand and is 50 percent

become the mainstay of the confectionery category, continually driving growth for over 50 years. In a time of the five-cent candy bar, "M&M's"® led the trend from impulse candy buying to in-home future consumption. The Brand also led the way into mass merchandising in the 60s and more recently into online ordering. Whether driven by being the first confectionery product to advertise on TV in 1954, or the Brand's constant commitment to innovative promotions like the 1995 "Color Vote," or its imaginative novelty packaging, "M&M's"® has clearly set the industry standard. In short, an innovative product format, coupled with a steadfast positioning, elevated "M&M's"® to the position of confectionery leader. Today the "M&M's"® Brand has established itself as an American icon brand.

HISTORY

Following the path of nearly every other great American dream, "M&M's"® Chocolate Candies came about as an idea garnered from a faraway land, gained great popularity and found success across the world and even in space. As the story goes, Forrest Mars, Sr., visited Spain during the Spanish Civil War and encountered soldiers who were eating pellets of chocolate in a hard, sugary coating. The coating kept the

problem, and, after its introduction in 1941, Americans could enjoy chocolate in the form of brown, yellow, orange, red, green and violet "M&M's"® Plain Chocolate Candies all year.

During the 1950s "M&M's"® Chocolate Candies were quickly becoming a staple in the American household. Advertising helped increase the popularity of these irresistible candies, using the famous slogan "The Milk Chocolate Melts in Your Mouth—Not in Your Hand"®.

Since their creation, "M&M's"® had served America's military, so it was only natural that the candies were officially made part of the American space program as well. They became part of the first space shuttle astronauts' food supply in 1981. In 1984, "M&M's"® made their first trip into space on the shuttle and have been a part of shuttle missions ever since. Aside from venturing into space, "M&M's"® Chocolate Candies also began venturing out of the United States and began to be sold internationally. It was also in the 1980s that "M&M's"® made an appearance at the Olympic Games, as the "Official Snack Food" of the 1984 Games in Los Angeles.

As the 20th century came to an end, the "M&M's"® Brand Characters proclaimed themselves the "Official Candy of the New Millennium"®.

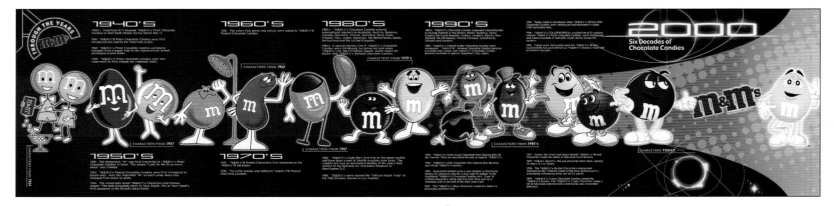

larger than the #2 brand. Over the last 20 years, sales have grown by more than 1,000 percent, rocketing the Brand to approximately $2 billion in retail sales, while growing at twice the rate of the category and achieving nearly double-digit compound growth since 1995. "M&M's"® has maintained its leadership in the category by its commitment to making its essence of colorful chocolate fun fresh and relevant to its millions of loyal and new consumers.

In 1941, "M&M's"® transformed chocolate from a dark or light brown product into a colorful, bite-sized chocolate treat. Even today, nearly 60 years since its launch, no one has been able to encroach upon this truly unique product platform or positioning. In fact, the unrivaled format of "M&M's"® has enabled the brand to

chocolate from melting. Inspired by the idea, Mr. Mars brought his dream back to America, went back to his kitchen, and invented the recipe for "M&M's"® Plain Chocolate Candies.

Originally sold to the public in 1941, "M&M's"® Plain Chocolate Candies earned a solid reputation from American GIs serving in World War II who first enjoyed the candies in their food rations. Chocolate candy that could survive in hot weather was unheard of during that time. The colorful candy shell on the "M&M's"® candies solved that

THE PRODUCT

"M&M's"® Chocolate Candies are a unique blend of the highest quality milk chocolate with a strong taste that is not too sweet and not satiating. Individual candies are covered with a thin, crisp, colorful sugar shell that imparts the unique "M&M's"® texture. The shell colors are bright, shiny, and lustrous. It is the milk chocolate inside and the crisp outside sugar shells that provide all the taste—the color has no taste.

"M&M's"® are made in nine varieties: Milk Chocolate

Candies (the original "M&M's"®), Peanut Chocolate Candies, Peanut Butter Chocolate Candies, Almond Chocolate Candies, Crispy Chocolate Candies, Mint Chocolate Candies, MINIs Milk Chocolate Candies, Milk Chocolate and Semi-Sweet Chocolate Mini Baking Bits and COLORWORKS® Custom Candies.

"M&M's"® COLORWORKS® are a collection of 21 vibrant-colored Milk Chocolate Candies that can be selected in any combination to create personal color choices. They can be used in a colorful blend to add innovative touches to parties, conferences, events, and as gifts.

RECENT DEVELOPMENTS
Over the years, the "M&M's"® Brand and the "M&M's"® Brand Characters have evolved into true American icons. They were "C" rations in World War II (MRE's today) and, since 1984, space food for U.S. astronauts, which earned them a permanent display at the Smithsonian Institute. They are popular costumes for Halloween and in recent years the "M" Characters have participated in the Macy's Thanksgiving Day Parade. In Las Vegas, "M&M's WORLD"® occupies a 28,000 square foot "retail-tainment" store on the Strip. In fact, "M&M's"® is so much a part of the lives of Americans that during the brand's 1995 "Color Vote", over 10 million consumers voted for the new color of "M&M's"® Chocolate Candies.

To young and old alike, the Brand is a special part of our everyday lives, either as a delicious snack or as a tool to teach children counting and colors. The consumers' relationship with the Brand is further manifested through the immense popularity of the "M&M's"® Spokecandies. After 37 years they are more popular than ever, allowing the Brand to successfully expand into the world of licensed merchandise. Simply, while many mature brands begin to lose rele-vance, the "M&M's"® Brand has proven its appeal to be evergreen.

PROMOTION
Historically, the "M&M's"® Brand has had one of the most memorable taglines: "The Milk Chocolate Melts in Your Mouth—Not in Your Hand."® Along with that slogan, "M&M's"® promotion has been distinguished by the presence of the Brand's famed "Spokescandies." In 1995, along with the legendary "Color Vote" promotion when Blue joined the characters Red and Yellow in life, the spokescandies transformed from cartoon characters to real-time animation, bringing the characters to a more celebrity-like status.

In 1996 USA Today rated the advertising campaign featuring the characters No. 1 among more than 60 campaigns. The characters' popularity with consumers reached new heights, surpassing that of Mickey Mouse and Bart Simpson, according to Marketing Evaluation, Inc.

That same year, the characters went "virtual Hollywood" on the internet with the opening of the "M&M's"® Studios (*http://www.m-ms.com*). Visitors to the site find themselves within the star studded, glamorous world of the "M&M's"® Brand Spokescandies. The site employs Shockwave and RealAudio technology for the characters' lifelike animation and sound.

Not only were the characters having fun on the internet, they were speeding around the NASCAR® Winston Cup series as the title sponsor of the #36 "M&M's"® Racing Team. The car was driven by Ernie Irvan in the early years, followed by Kenny Schrader after Irvan's retirement.

A highlight of 1997 was the debut of Green, who was not only the first female among the characters, but was also a talented author. She starred in a number of popular commercials and "toured" the country promoting her biography "I Melt For No One."

And in 2000, a major event changed the ever famed "M&M's"® Plain Chocolate Candies. M&M/MARS decided that the candies were just too good to be called "Plain", and their name was changed to "M&M's"® Milk Chocolate Candies.

BRAND VALUES
The "M&M's"® Brand has represented superior quality and enjoyment to consumers since Mr. Mars developed the Brand in 1940. The appeal of "M&M's"® Chocolate Candies is universal, crossing age, gender and nationality boundaries, bringing colorful chocolate fun to everyone.

THINGS YOU DIDN'T KNOW ABOUT M&M'S CHOCOLATE CANDIES

❍ More than 146 billion "M&M's"® Chocolate Candies are produced annually.

❍ A line of all the "M&M's"® Chocolate Candies produced each year would encircle the globe 56 times, go to the moon and back 5.9 times, and travel from New York City to Los Angeles 586 times.

❍ The "M" is put on each "M&M's"® candy with a machine designed for that specific operation. It is calibrated to apply the letter without breaking the candy shell. The process is similar to offset printing.

❍ It takes four to eight hours to make one "M&M's"® Chocolate Candy, depending on the variety of the candy—milk, peanut, almond, peanut butter or crispy.

❍ The original "M&M's"® Chocolate Candies were somewhat larger than the present product and sold in a tube for five cents.

MAIL BOXES ETC.®

THE MARKET

Since its founding in 1980, Mail Boxes Etc. (MBE), a UPS company, has become one of the greatest success stories in the world of franchising. Today, MBE is the world's largest franchisor of retail business, communication, and postal-service centers. There are more than 4,400 locations operating worldwide, and agreements are in place for the development of the MBE business in more than 80 countries.

With the mission of making business easier worldwide, MBE locations are now operating in countries such as Canada, Italy, Singapore, United Kingdom, Venezuela, Australia, Saudi Arabia, Japan, Korea and Austria, among others. On average, one new MBE location opens somewhere in the world each business day.

In addition to servicing general consumers, the MBE system supports the burgeoning small office/home office (SOHO) market. "Each of our franchisees understands the needs of small business," MBE explains, "because each of them is a small-business owner."

Through its extensive brick-and-mortar network, the company has become a fulfillment provider in the rapidly growing world of e-commerce by providing a physical link to the virtual world. MBE serves as the "returns desk" for consumers to return merchandise to online retailers or catalog companies.

ACHIEVEMENTS

System sales rose to $1.5 billion a year (FY00), with the company enjoying double-digit growth in same-store sales for nine consecutive years. MBE is the largest non-food retail storefront franchise and one of the fastest growing franchises in the world. Far outpacing its imitators, MBE is over seven times larger than its largest competitor, and nearly three times larger than its five largest competitors combined.

Over the years, MBE has received numerous accolades. For 2001, *Entrepreneur* magazine ranked MBE as the number-one postal and business services franchise for the eleventh consecutive year. Additionally, MBE was ranked second in *Entrepreneur's* "Franchise 500," a comprehensive ranking of all franchises worldwide.

The power of the MBE brand has brought it opportunities to work with some of the most well-known names in the business world, including UPS, FedEx, United States Postal Service, DHL, Xerox, Konica, IBM, and eBay, among many others.

HISTORY

Founded in 1980 by Herb Goffstein and Pat and Mimi Senn, the first MBE center opened in Carlsbad, Calif., as a convenient alternative to the post office. MBE began franchising that same year, and to this day, all MBE locations are independently owned and operated.

Since its inception, MBE has grown in quantum leaps. Within the company's first 10 years, the number of franchises surpassed 1,000. Three years later, that number increased two-fold, and today there are more than 4,400 MBE locations operating worldwide.

THE PRODUCT

MBE franchisees offer a full range of packing, shipping, postal, copying and other business services that continue to expand significantly as a result of increasing demand for MBE's traditional services and its growing role as a major fulfillment support system for e-commerce. The company explains: "MBE provides solutions to the challenges facing small offices and home-based businesses. With MBE, small businesses have the ability to operate like big businesses, regardless of where they are located in the world."

RECENT DEVELOPMENTS

A New Parent Company—In 2001, MBE was purchased by UPS, taking the twenty-year relationship between the two companies to a new level. Through shared vision and strategy, MBE and UPS will continue to excel in meeting the needs of small businesses, Internet consumers, and retail customers around the world.

A New Look—As the new millennium approached, MBE saw the need to redefine its concept to keep it relevant in the ever-changing world of global commerce and to further set it apart from its competition. A major strategy was a complete redesign of the MBE retail center concept.

The new design, dubbed "MBE 2000," employs a softer palette of beige, gray and black with high-impact graphics to create a professional, business-like atmosphere. The redesign also creates better traffic patterns for added convenience and a more customer-intimate setting. The early response from customers and franchisees alike is overwhelmingly positive.

Technology—The rapidly developing world of e-commerce brought a new opportunity to MBE. MBE's Internet strategy is to provide a bridge between the physical and virtual worlds. To realize this goal, the company deployed state-of-the-art technology, making MBE the largest networked franchise system in retail business-support services. This technology helps MBE franchisees improve customer service, streamline accounting functions, and deliver products and services to Internet customers.

Says James H. Amos, Jr., president and chief executive officer, "MBE's unrivaled brick-and-mortar network, combined with these technology initiatives, uniquely positions MBE to be the physical pipeline for service and distribution that runs alongside the virtual superhighway. MBE brings high-trust and high-touch to the world of high-tech. It's a platform no one else can claim."

The system is also designed to enhance services for corporate account customers who are looking to provide greater convenience and consolidated services for their sales forces and "road warriors." MBE's corporate accounts program enables the company to offer preferred pricing throughout its network and to provide consolidated billing for participating companies. Among the well-known companies utilizing these services are: Agilent Technologies Amway, Hewlett-Packard, Konica, Motorola, Ricoh, Samsung, Thomson Electronics, Qwest and Xerox.

Non-Traditional Locations—In addition to expanding its network of conveniently located MBE centers, the company has programs for nontraditional site locations. An MBE center is operating at the nation's busiest airport, Chicago's O'Hare, to help business travelers get the job done while on the road. Centers are also opening in college campuses, military bases, convention centers, hotels, gas station/convenience stores, and in urban renewal areas.

In addition to providing the company with the opportunity to expand its brand presence, these nontraditional sites enable MBE to bring its services to consumers and small-business people, regardless of where they live, work, or travel.

GMBE—The worldwide growth of e-commerce and catalog companies has provided MBE with an opportunity to bring these services to a broader international market. Through its proprietary Global MailBox Express (GMBE) service, MBE enables customers in other countries to order and receive merchandise from U.S.-based e-tailers and catalog companies by offering them a U.S.-based mailing address.

PROMOTION

Mail Boxes Etc. conducts multi-million dollar national marketing and advertising campaigns designed to support and promote the MBE brand. The advertising mix includes network and cable television, radio, print and Internet marketing.

Other elements of the MBE marketing mix include a company Web site (mbe.com), online marketing and public relations materials, a toll-free phone number for customers to locate its centers, in-center merchandising, and regional advertising co-ops. In recent years, MBE has joined forces with alliance partners, such as American Express, VISA and eBay, for joint national promotions.

BRAND VALUES

MBE offers its franchisees an established brand name as a worldwide leader in business, communication, and postal services, the world's largest network of franchised business-support centers, and widespread consumer recognition.

To ensure that MBE's vision is shared throughout its worldwide network, the company regularly hosts a "family reunion," a gathering of MBE franchisees from around the world. The weeklong event features motivational speakers, informative workshops, award programs, and opportunities to experience the collective strength of the MBE global brand.

The MBE mission statement reads: "Making business easier worldwide through our service and distribution network; delivering personalized and convenient business solutions with world-class customer service."

MBE's core values are: Caring, Honesty, Fairness, Integrity, Trust, Respect, Commitment, and Accountability. Together, the mission statement and core values form the foundation by which MBE manages its day-to-day operations.

MBE franchisees have a long and distinguished history of giving back to their communities. In addition to providing direct support to numerous community-based organizations, such as schools, hospitals, shelters, etc., many franchisees serve on boards and provide professional expertise.

In 1998, MBE took social responsibility to a new level with the formation of the MBE We Deliver Dreams Foundation. By fulfilling the dreams of individual children at risk, this non-profit organization strives to counteract the cycles of abuse, neglect, violence, poverty and illness that compromise a child's ability to grow and flourish physically, mentally and emotionally.

THINGS YOU DIDN'T KNOW ABOUT MAIL BOXES ETC.

○ There are nearly 3,500 MBE locations in the United States, and more than 900 international locations in 31 countries.

○ MBE rents mailboxes to nearly half-a-million customers.

○ Each year, roughly 40 million packages are shipped through MBE locations.

○ MBE is over seven times larger than its largest competitor, and nearly three times larger than its five largest competitors combined.

○ MBE locations serve as recycling centers for polystyrene plastic "peanuts" used to protect products in shipping packages. Participating locations accept clean and reusable peanuts, thereby keeping them out of landfills and helping to protect the environment.

MANPOWER®

THE MARKET

The major labor and skill shortages of recent years have put workforce management in the forefront of business strategy for the 21st century. Behind every great product, brand, or service stand skilled and quality-conscious employees. The increasing competition for talent worldwide means that effective ways of developing and retaining a workforce are more important than ever before.

Manpower, a world leader in the staffing industry, excels at providing innovative workforce management services and solutions to customers all over the world. For decades, the company built its reputation on the timely provision of skilled workers who were meticulously matched to customer requirements; today, the company does that and much more.

Manpower's customer companies require assistance not just in filling positions, but with their overall workforce design and resource management strategies. Through its broad and growing array of services, Manpower has kept one step ahead of the escalation in workforce and productivity needs for more than 400,000 customers worldwide.

The company draws on its global resources and local service network to fill even the most specialized jobs and solve the most complex staffing challenges.

ACHIEVEMENTS

Since its earliest days, Manpower has consistently been a staffing industry innovator and pioneer.

With a philosophy that there is no such thing as an unskilled job—or an unskilled worker—Manpower developed groundbreaking assessment tools that identify the skills, whether proven or latent, that each worker has to offer. In anticipation of the widespread computerization of office work during the early 1980s, the company developed software training programs that expanded into the tremendous variety of skills training programs it offers today. These assessment and training tools form the basis of Manpower's proprietary system for matching workers with customer needs, which has been the foundation of its quality service for more than 50 years.

Manpower also anticipated the labor and skill shortages of the 1990s with workforce development programs that reach out to traditionally underemployed populations, including participants in welfare-to-work programs and workers with disabilities.

The company has broadened the scope of its services to match customer needs, including the expansion of its specialty staffing function into Manpower Professional. It is a major operating unit that provides skilled professionals in information technology, engineering, telecommunications, accounting, scientific, human resources, marketing, and other fields.

Manpower was one of the first global service firms to achieve registration to ISO 9002, the international standard for quality. The company has earned ISO 9002 certification for nearly all of its offices throughout North America, Europe, and the Asia/Pacific region.

In addition, Manpower has earned many prestigious awards and recognitions for business and service excellence, including:

- Xerox Certified Quality Supplier
- Texas Instruments' Supplier Excellence Award
- IBM Key Supplier and Assist Awards
- Eastman Kodak Quality First Award
- Honeywell IAC Division Supplier of the Year
- Ford Motor Company Q1 Award
- Best Practice, Harvard Business Review
- "100 of America's Best," *Fortune* magazine
- "400 Best Companies," *Forbes* magazine
- United Kingdom's Investors in People Award

HISTORY

The labor shortages of the prosperous era that followed World War II created an opportunity for two law partners and entrepreneurs named Elmer Winter and Aaron Scheinfeld. One night, while working late to finish a legal brief, they needed clerical assistance but quickly found that no company could provide that service. As a result, they established Manpower in 1948 with offices in Chicago, Ill. and Milwaukee, Wis., where the company's international headquarters is still located. Manpower's standard of high-quality supplemental staffing spread quickly throughout the U.S. and went international in the mid-1950s, when the company opened offices in Canada, the United Kingdom, and France. Today, Manpower continues to grow and operates more than 3,700 offices in 59 countries, with annual sales of $12.4 billion worldwide in 2000.

THE PRODUCT

During Manpower's early years, the company focused on providing workers to fill temporary

or unexpected openings in customers' clerical and light manufacturing operations. Today, while Manpower still carefully matches worker skills

to customer job requirements, those staffing requirements have grown more sophisticated. It is not unusual for customers to ask Manpower to staff and manage entire departments or business functions.

Manpower meets and exceeds those requirements through the continual pursuit of its vision: To be the best worldwide provider of higher-value staffing services and the center for quality employment opportunities. The company's services and solutions include:

- Professional, technical, and traditional staffing resources, from engineers and information technology specialists to accountants, receptionists, and assembly workers.
- Quality assessment, testing, and training processes for virtually any type of job or skill requirement.
- On-site management of supplemental and contract staffing.
- Flexible staffing to match fluctuations in business cycles.
- Global and multi-national service contracts.
- Staffing and management of start-up operations.
- Re-engineering of employee skill sets.

- Outplacement programs to ensure a positive transition for outgoing employees.
- Transitional staffing and management during major events, such as mergers and acquisitions.
- Master vendor services, in which Manpower manages the services of multiple staffing providers.
- Total outsourcing of human resources and other business functions.

RECENT DEVELOPMENTS

To better serve the continuous skill development needs of its workforce and its customers, Manpower has made its extensive library of training programs accessible via its own online university. The company's Global Learning Center (GLC) Web site (manpowernet.com) makes training, skills assessment and career management services available 24 hours a day. Online training offerings include more than 1,700 software and information technology training modules, as well as more than 100 business skills courses that cover topics such as finance, marketing, business law, human resource management, and accounting. The GLC's Community Center enables Manpower's employees to connect with fellow students and mentors, participate in live, expert-led seminars and access online skills-certification programs.

While the GLC is one way that Manpower utilizes the Internet to enhance the employment process for the benefit of its workers and customers, the company continuously "e-thinks" every aspect of its business. For example, Manpower offers e-procurement tools that enable small and medium-sized enterprises to order its staffing services via the Internet; for global enterprises, Manpower provides Web-based order management tools that track and manage the fulfillment of every staffing request.

For years, Manpower has provided consulting services to customers to help them develop and implement effective strategies in the areas of corporate staffing and organizational performance. That capability was recently enhanced through the formation of a new operating division, The Empower Group, which provides organizational performance consulting services to major corporations worldwide. Key services include consulting support on strategic human resource initiatives; organizational, design and development; internal branding and communication strategy. The Empower Group can help companies assess and maximize competence, develop leaders, and enhance individual performance and growth.

PROMOTION

As a global firm, Manpower promotes its brand in the ways that are most appropriate and effective for each service location. However, the company enjoys worldwide visibility at major events such as the World Cup soccer championship, which Manpower sponsored in 1998, and at the Millennium Dome in Greenwich, England, where Manpower sponsored the Work Zone portion of the Dome's New Millennium Experience.

Manpower's Chairman, President and Chief Executive Officer, Jeffrey Joerres, also contributes to Manpower's high profile with his membership on various boards and CEO councils. He is a frequent guest speaker at such events as the American Productivity and Quality Center's Knowledge Symposium and the World Congress on Human Resources Management.

BRAND VALUES

Manpower believes that work can make an essential contribution to the development, self-esteem, fulfillment, companionship, reward, and well being of every human being. Manpower's approach to employment and service are guided by these global values:

People
We care about people and the role of work in their lives.

Knowledge
We learn and grow by sharing knowledge and resources.

Innovation
We dare to innovate and be pioneers.

THINGS YOU DIDN'T KNOW ABOUT MANPOWER

- ❍ Manpower annually provides employment to more than two million people worldwide.
- ❍ Manpower operates more than 3,700 offices in 59 countries around the world.
- ❍ Manpower ranks 174th on the 2000 list of *Fortune* 500 companies.
- ❍ Manpower serves 96 percent of the *Fortune* 500 Companies.
- ❍ France is Manpower's largest market, closely followed by the United States and the United Kingdom.
- ❍ Manpower Professional addresses specialty markets through its sub-brands, including Manpower Engineering, Manpower Finance, Manpower IT, Manpower Science, Manpower Telecom, and Manpower Professional.

MAXWELL HOUSE®

THE MARKET

America loves coffee, and for more than 100 years, Maxwell House has been "America's coffee." Nearly four-fifths of Americans drink coffee daily or occasionally, and the vibrant American retail coffee market, which last year reached $18.5 billion, has experienced especially strong growth in the last decade.

While coffee remains a staple in the American home and a mainstay at the family breakfast table, a new generation of coffee drinkers has burst open the doors to the world beyond the home, creating a new gourmet coffee market segment to complement the market's traditional segment. With premium blends, varieties, and an ever-expanding menu of coffee beverages, consumers are experiencing a heightened awareness and interest in making nearly every moment and nearly every social environment a potential coffee opportunity.

In other words, the new two-tiered coffee market has further enabled American consumers to enjoy coffee that is "good to the last drop." Maxwell House is bringing premium coffee to the whole landscape of coffee lovers, from traditional coffee drinkers who rely on their daily brew to others who enjoy sampling different flavors and blends. While Maxwell House continues to be a leader in the traditional retail coffee segment, the company is also offering the premium choices that today's newest coffee drinkers demand—priced to be enjoyed every day.

ACHIEVEMENTS

Providing Americans with more coffee choices has been a long tradition at Maxwell House. Among the many coffee innovations the brand can claim, two stand out: the development of decaffeinated coffee and instant coffee.

Maxwell House's Sanka® was the world's first decaffeinated coffee, introduced in 1906 in Germany and France, and then in 1923 in the United States. In the 1930s Maxwell House experimented to invent another new coffee product—

one that would not need brewing, but instead could be made just by adding water. The advent of World War II and the demand for coffee from troops stationed around the globe speeded up the development of soluble, or "instant," coffee. Maxwell House began shipping its brand of instant coffee overseas to supply American troops in 1942, and in 1946 Maxwell House introduced the first all-coffee instant.

Perhaps the brand's greatest achievement is its near-universal recognition. The traditional blue can and the cup-and-drop logo are known around the country, and the brand's famous slogan, "Good to the Last Drop®," is recognized by an astounding 98% of Americans.

HISTORY

The Maxwell House Coffee Company had its beginnings following the Civil War. In 1873, a Kentucky farm boy named Joel Cheek moved to Nashville, Tennessee, and found a job as a traveling salesman for a

Maxwell House Division–General Foods Corporation

wholesale grocery firm. A coffee lover himself, he was displeased with the quality of the coffee blends he was offering, and so on his own time he began to experiment, seeking to concoct the perfect blend of different coffees. After years of effort, he convinced Nashville's newest and most exclusive hotel, the Maxwell House, to try his new blend. Soon customers were praising its rich flavor, and in 1892, the hotel agreed to lend its name to Mr. Cheek's coffee.

From that point on, the business grew rapidly. Spurred by the continued popularity of Maxwell House, Cheek joined forces with grocer John Neal to form the Cheek & Neal Coffee and Manufacturing Company in 1901, and in 1903 they constructed the first Maxwell House plant in Nashville.

In 1907, legend has it that President Theodore Roosevelt proclaimed Maxwell House coffee "good to the last drop," and this casual comment soon became the brand's trademark slogan.

Throughout the following decades, Maxwell House has produced coffee products for the way Americans really live. When electric percolators became widely used, Maxwell House accommodated coffee drinkers with its

1966 product Electra-Perk, the first coffee designed specifically for this use. More recently, coffee connoisseurs have appreciated the rich tastes of premium products, such as

Maxwell House Italian Espresso Roast, Colombian Supreme, Rich French Roast, Lite, 1892 and Slow Roast.

THE PRODUCT

Although it started with a single blend that became synonymous with a landmark hotel, the brand now boasts a rich variety of blends and specialty coffees. Rooted in its rich heritage, the "blue can" Maxwell House regular coffee and the company's Master Blend® coffee form the backbone of the traditional product line and continue to satisfy coffee lovers who crave smooth, fresh taste at affordable prices.

Sanka®—with its familiar orange label—also remains a strong element in the brand's product line, and Maxwell House continued its innovative leadership in the decaffeinated market with the introduction in 1991 of Maxwell House Lite™ —blended choice regular and naturally decaffeinated coffee beans that bring consumers a rich, aromatic coffee with half the caffeine of Maxwell House regular coffee.

Today, the Maxwell House brand means not only the orange Sanka label and the blue Maxwell House can; it also means a rich variety of specialty coffees available at everyday prices.

Those who crave rich roasts can now choose from among Maxwell House 1892®, a slow roasted coffee; Maxwell House Rich French Roast, which is available in regular (ground and instant) and decaffeinated (ground and instant) versions; and Maxwell House Italian Espresso Roast—the first nationally available espresso-roast coffee, which offers consumers the deep, full-flavored taste of espresso-roast coffee without the harsh, bitter aftertaste. For those seeking a single-origin variety, Maxwell House offers Colombian Supreme, made from 100 percent Colombian coffee beans, "The Richest Coffee in the World."™

RECENT DEVELOPMENTS

In the past few years, Maxwell House has continued its expansion into the specialty coffee market, offering gourmet coffees at everyday prices. In 1999, the company introduced Slow Roast premium ground, a special blend of beans slowly roasted to perfection, resulting in a mellow, well-balanced, not bitter yet full flavored coffee.

The newest addition to Maxwell House's stable of gourmet coffees is its new Premium Cup Collection, a line of 100% Arabica beans available in eight different ground or whole bean varieties, including Columbian Select, Supreme French Roast and Hazelnut.

PROMOTION

With spokespersons ranging from Danny Thomas to Willard Scott, and programs ranging from the 1930s radio hit "Maxwell House Show Boat" to its award-winning Build A Home America™ partnership with Habitat for Humanity, Maxwell House has built its promotional campaigns on the foundation of its rich heritage and the emotional value of its product as a way of bringing families, friends and communities together.

Few commercials have captured the imagination of viewers like the "perking pot" television ad, launched in 1959. The ad's catchy signature tune was on the lips of millions of coffee drinkers for years to come, and it is still well known today. In the 1980s, commercials featuring the music of Ray Charles captured the attention of a new generation. One constant has been the enduring trademark promise, "Good to the Last Drop®," a slogan so popular that it has been featured on numerous game shows, including "Jeopardy," "Wheel of Fortune," and "Who Wants to Be a Millionaire."

At its essence, the slogan speaks to the dream of savoring the very best moments in life. Today's promotional campaigns unleash this potential, encouraging consumers to enjoy coffee that is "good to the last drop." From a new advertising campaign to a fully integrated marketing and communication platform across all media using TV, print, radio, and other media vehicles, Maxwell House shows people of all ages getting the most out of ordinary moments.

One of the most successful ways of showing that Maxwell House is a caring brand has been

Build A Home America™, a program with Habitat for Humanity in which Maxwell House built 100 homes for 100 families in 100 weeks. Twenty-six mayors proclaimed Build A Home America Day, and the campaign received wide national media coverage, even inspiring Oprah Winfrey to award Maxwell House's president an Oprah Angel Award. Maxwell House has been a supporter of Habitat for Humanity since 1994.

BRAND VALUES

One of the reasons the brand's famous slogan, "Good to the Last Drop," has been so enduring is that it encapsulates values that have characterized American culture from the dawn of the jazz age to today. These are values that also characterize America's coffee. Maxwell House embodies the confidence that comes from forming an active and emotional connection to more than five generations of Americans.

THINGS YOU DIDN'T KNOW ABOUT MAXWELL HOUSE

○ Since 1934, millions of Jewish families have celebrated traditional Seder dinners with "Maxwell House Passover Haggadahs."

○ In 1983, years before he gained TV fame, Jerry Seinfeld appeared in a Maxwell House commercial as a young, stand-up comic.

○ The "perking pot" music from Maxwell House commercials inspired a 1960 RCA instrumental recording, called "Perky," featuring famed trumpeter Al Hirt and guitarist Chet Atkins.

○ The name of the world's first decaffeinated coffee, Sanka, was derived from the French words "sans caffeine," which mean "without caffeine."

○ The common practice of using the color orange to differentiate decaffeinated coffee from regular coffee owes its origin to the distinctive orange label of Maxwell House's Sanka.

THE MARKET

Maytag Corporation competes in several markets offering household and commercial appliances and equipment. Principal products include major home appliances, floor care, vending machines, and food-service equipment.

ACHIEVEMENTS

Maytag made its name synonymous with quality and dependability from its earliest days. It was a pioneer in the home-appliance business with the introduction of a machine for washing clothes, which replaced the washboards and scrub brushes that women had used for generations. The company made a major breakthrough in the appliance industry in 1949, when it introduced the Maytag AMP—for automatic Maytag pump—which replaced the wringer washer and marked the beginning of a new era in washing machines.

Continuing improvements in its washing machines, new products that included an automatic clothes dryer, a substantial presence in the commercial laundry business, and major acquisitions that made it a highly diversified company were other milestones in the evolution of today's Maytag Corporation.

HISTORY

Frederick Louis Maytag, known as "F.L.", had built a highly successful business manufacturing farming machinery early in the 20th Century, but that particular line had an off-season. Seeking a way to utilize the company's employees and facilities during the down time, he decided on a product that was in the forefront of a revolution that would change drastically the

way that American women maintained their homes.

In 1907 The Maytag Company brought out the Pastime, a hand-operated machine for washing clothes. The tub was made of the best cedar available to give it a long operating life. In insisting on quality in all aspects of the machine, F.L. Maytag was taking the same approach that had made him highly successful in the farm-machinery business.

The washing machine was an instant hit because of its labor- and time-saving capability.

In 1911 the company introduced the first electrically powered washer and also offered the first "swinging wringer," which allowed the user to position the wringer over a sink for drainage.

The year 1915 was a particularly significant one for the company. It produced a gasoline-powered washer, making sales of the new washing machines possible in the many areas of the country still lacking electricity.

Within six months of the introduction of that model, sales of washing machines had doubled and that division outperformed Maytag's farm machinery production for the first time.

After a number of years of research, the company in 1920 replaced its wooden tubs with cast-aluminum tubs that were both rugged and attractive. The resulting sales boom eventually led to a decision to drop the farm-implement business to concentrate on the appliance line.

A 1922 innovation firmly established Maytag as a world leader in its industry. Up to

that point, washers utilized pegs to drag clothes through the water. Maytag introduced a new concept based on blades that forced the water through the clothes. The aluminum gyrofoam agitator was born. Orders hit record levels. By 1924 Maytag was making 20 percent of all the washers sold in this country.

With the outbreak of World War II, Maytag suspended production of washing machines to concentrate on critical parts and equipment for bombers, fighter planes, and tanks.

Production of washers resumed with the end of the war, and the demand was so great that production records fell repeatedly. Maytag made its five millionth wringer washer in 1947, just six years after it turned out its four millionth.

THE PRODUCT

Since 1980, Maytag has grown from a company with a limited line of major appliances and sales of around $350 million to a diversified enterprise with full lines of both home and commercial appliances and annual sales of more than $4 billion.

Its transition to a multi-billion-dollar corporation began in 1981 when Maytag launched a program of growth by acquisition of premier companies in the appliance field. It purchased Hardwick Stove Co. of Cleveland, Tenn. The following year, it acquired Jenn-Air Corporation of Indianapolis, Ind.

The Maytag Corporation was formed in 1986 with the merger of the expanded Maytag Company and Magic Chef, Inc., which also included several individual companies. In 1989 Maytag added a full line of refrigerators and floor care (Hoover) appliances through the acquisition of Chicago Pacific.

RECENT DEVELOPMENTS

In 1996 Maytag created a single business unit—Maytag Appliances—to manage all aspects of product design, manufacturing, marketing, and service for its four home appliance brands—Maytag, Jenn-Air, Magic Chef, and Admiral.

Married in 1932

Got Maytag in 1933

Both marriage and
Maytag still working

The Maytag in the picture at right is not the one that Mr. A.W. Bell of Vandergrift, Pa., bought for his wife back in 1933.

The Maytag Washer you see is similar to the one he gave Mrs. Bell in 1960, because she wanted the most modern automatic available.

Though her 27-year-old Maytag was still working, she felt it would be nice to have an automatic that has all the new features, plus the one that makes them work ... Maytag dependability.

She expects both marriage and Maytag to continue working just as before. The remarkably long

lives of so many of the 14,000,000 Maytags built since 1907 strongly suggest that Mrs. Bell has no reason to expect otherwise.

Today, Maytag offers you all these features right along with dependability: *Big-Load Capacity, Automatic Bleach Dispenser, Automatic Dispenser for fabric conditioner, Lint-Filter Agitator, a Safety Lid that stops action in seconds when opened, and a Zinc-Coated Steel Cabinet that protects against rust!* For a complete guide to all Maytag Washers and Dryers, send 10¢ to: The Maytag Company, Dept. 310LS, Newton, Iowa.

Get Maytag dependability during "Maytag Retail Rally Days. "See the values your Maytag dealer is offering on dependable Maytags!

Maytag set a new standard with its 1997 breakthrough—the high-efficiency Maytag Neptune® clothes washer.

PROMOTION

Maytag's legendary "Lonely Repairman" advertising campaign, now in its 34th year, has attracted so much attention that it has become a news-making event in itself. The retirement of Jesse White from the role and his replacement by Gordon Jump received widespread media coverage, as did the opening of the "Lonely Repairman Hall of Fame" featuring actors who had filled that role.

The highly successful campaign was another milestone in Maytag promotion efforts marked by creativity and effectiveness since the company first began advertising in 1916. Early ads featured the revolutionary aspect of the company's first product—the emancipation of women from the washboard by a mechanical device. Later ads focused on the product's dependability.

Company officials concluded in the 1950s that washing-machine advertising by all manufacturers had become virtually identical, and they launched a campaign to identify the "inherent drama" of its products.

The 1961 campaign drew on the thousands of unsolicited testimonials the company received every year. "Both marriage and Maytag still working," said a 1961 print ad that showed a bride on her wedding day in 1932 and noted her Maytag was bought the same year. The theme was also used in television ads but Maytag sought even greater promotional impact.

The company was already sponsoring a Canadian radio program in which a repairman sadly reported that the dependability of Maytag products left him with little to do. That repairman, the company recalls, "planted the seed for one of the most powerful advertising ideas ever created for television."

The goal set by ad agency head Leo Burnett was to make the character not only sad but also humorously frustrated. Over the years, the Lonely Repairman found himself filling his time teaching a parrot to talk, warning a fledging repairman that he'd do better to take up knitting, or simply snoring peacefully through an entire, 30-second television spot.

"With this campaign," the company says, "Maytag singularly reinforced its washer as the best in existence."

BRAND VALUES

Maytag Corporation offers many of the best-known brands in the home and commercial appliance fields.

The flagship Maytag delivers dependability, quality, and performance across a full line of home appliances.

The Hoover Company brand is the world's most recognized name in floor-care products and also offers a complete line of commercial products.

The Jenn-Air brand is synonymous with distinctive styling and innovation. A relative newcomer to the home appliance industry in the 1960s, Jenn-Air introduced the first range with a ventilation system that made grilling indoors a year-round activity. Today, the Jenn-Air brand offers a full line of cooktops, wall ovens, ranges, dishwashers, and refrigerators. Dixie-Narco is one of the oldest name brands in the industry and today is the leading producer of soft-drink vending equipment. Its vending machines meet the variety of beverage dispens-

ing options that soft-drink companies require in world markets.

Magic Chef's heritage dates back to the first gas stove produced in 1928—truly a "magic" chef in the kitchen. Today, the brand offers a full line of home appliances and is especially strong in the gas-range segment. RSD is the brand name of washing machines produced in China by the Maytag and Hefei Rongshida joint venture.

Blodgett Corporation dates to 1848 and today supplies commercial cooking equipment

to all major hotel and restaurant chains around the world. It is first or second in each product category in which it competes.

The Jade Range Company was acquired by Maytag Corporation in early 1999. Its Jade brand product line is focused on ultra-premium commercial ranges for the food service industry. The Dynasty brand focuses on commercial-style ranges and outdoor grills for the residential market.

THINGS YOU DIDN'T KNOW ABOUT MAYTAG

○ On Oct. 12, 1926, Maytag shipped five trainloads of aluminum washers, valued at nearly $2 million, from its Newton, Iowa, headquarters. At that point, it was the largest shipment of merchandise in industrial history.

○ Maytag's expertise in simplifying machine design resulted in a major contribution by the company to the U.S. military in World War II. Maytag made aluminum castings for bombers and fighter planes, track pins for tanks, and hydraulic devices that operated landing gears, bomb bay doors, and wing flaps. Company engineers made continuing improvements to the products and production processes.

○ Maytag was briefly in the auto-manufacturing business, producing the Maytag-Mason in Waterloo, Iowa, from 1909-11. But F.L. Maytag sold his interest to concentrate on his top priority—running the Maytag company, of which he had become sole owner, and developing its fast-growing washing-machine business.

○ In 1974, Maytag launched a search for the oldest still-working machine from the original 1949 production run of its first automatic washer model. It received 25,000 responses and identified the oldest as being in the home of the Hornbacher family in Story City, Iowa. It was the 12th automatic washer made when the company began production of the model in 1949.

McDonald's

THE MARKET

Dining out has always been a popular social activity. These days, it's part of everyday life that many of us take for granted. However, it's easy to forget that a meal in a restaurant was once an occasional indulgence enjoyed by a privileged few. The popular food service revolution of the last 50 years changed all that. Today, dining out is an activity enjoyed every day throughout the world by people of all ages and backgrounds. In fact, 16 percent of all meals in the United States are eaten away from home. For McDonald's, this translates into 20 million customers every day across the nation.

ACHIEVEMENTS

McDonald's is the world's leading and fastest-growing food service organization in 120 countries on six continents. McDonald's operates over 29,000 restaurants worldwide and generated over $40 billion in system-wide sales for the first time in the year 2000.

Few other brands can match McDonald's for the power and ubiquity embodied in the company's familiar Golden Arches. McDonald's was rated the world's greatest brand in a study published by leading international brand consultancy Interbrand. The study reviewed the performance of the world's leading brands and assessed each one for its strength as a marketing and financial asset. Interbrand concluded: "Nothing compares with McDonald's for the power of a branding idea, the skill of its execution, and the longevity and width of its appeal. McDonald's is the quintessential American brand which has traveled the world on the strength of two quite distinct phenomena - one cultural, the other commercial". Although McDonald's has its roots in the United States, it has become a citizen of the world.

And McDonald's is committed to being a

good corporate citizen. Ronald McDonald House Charities (RMHC) has awarded nearly $250 million in grants to children's programs worldwide since 1984. The cornerstone of RMHC is the Ronald McDonald House program, which provides "homes-away-from-home" for families of seriously ill children being treated at nearby hospitals. The first Ronald McDonald House opened in Philadelphia, Pa., in 1974, and there are now over 200 Houses around the world.

HISTORY

The McDonald's story began 46 years ago in San Bernadino, California. Ray Kroc was a salesman supplying milkshake multi-mixers to a drive-in restaurant run by two brothers, Dick and Mac McDonald. Kroc, calculating from his own figures that the restaurant must be selling over 2,000 milkshakes a month, was intrigued to know more about the secret behind the success of the brothers' thriving business. He visited the restaurant, which promised its customers "Speedee Service" and watched in awe as restaurant staff filled orders for fifteen cent hamburgers with fries and shakes every fifteen seconds. Kroc saw the massive potential and decided to get involved. The McDonald's brothers accepted Kroc's offer to become their first franchisee. On April 15, 1955, he opened his first McDonald's restaurant in Des Plaines, a suburb just north of Chicago.

Rapid growth followed. McDonald's served more than 100 million hamburgers within its first three years of trading and the 100th McDonald's restaurant opened in 1959. In 1961 Kroc paid $2.7 million to buy out the McDonald's brothers' interest and in 1963 the billionth McDonald's hamburger was served live on prime-time TV.

The brand proved equally popular outside the United States. McDonald's quickly established successful international markets in

Canada, Japan, Australia, and Germany. Today, more than 1.5 million people work for McDonald's around the globe. What started as an American phenomenon has become a truly international brand.

THE PRODUCT

From its early roots as a small, family-run hamburger restaurant, McDonald's has evolved into

a multi-billion dollar quick service restaurant industry. While hamburgers and fries remain the mainstay of McDonald's business, an instinctive ability to anticipate and fulfill real consumer needs has been central to McDonald's success. A prime example of this approach is the Filet-O-Fish sandwich, which was conceived by Lou Groen, a Cincinnati-based franchisee in a predominantly Catholic area. Groen noticed that his business was negatively impacted on Fridays, which was then a day of abstention from meat for many Catholics. He developed a fish-based product to meet the needs of the local

community. The Filet-O-Fish sandwich was launched in 1963 and went on to become a popular menu item in many of McDonald's international markets.

Another franchisee—Jim Deligatti from Pittsburgh—was responsible in 1968 for the creation of McDonald's most successful menu item ever, the Big Mac sandwich. Nine years later, the same franchisee was the driving force behind the development of McDonald's breakfast menu—a move that would change the breakfast habits of millions of Americans.

RECENT DEVELOPMENTS

Innovation has played an important part in McDonald's growth. The company has invested heavily in technology to continually improve the consumer experience at McDonald's. One of the biggest breakthroughs came in 1975 with the opening of the first drive-thru restaurant in Sierra Vista, Arizona. Once again, the idea sprang from the need to solve a local sales problem when servicemen from a nearby Army base were forbidden to get out of their cars in military fatigues. The drive-thru concept was an immediate success. Today, drive-thru

accounts for more than half of McDonald's business in many of its markets.

McDonald's serves its customers top-quality food. The best raw ingredients are purchased from long-time suppliers. Food is prepared to a consistently high standard in the restaurant. McDonald's menu is continually reviewed and enhanced to ensure that it meets—and wherever possible — exceeds customer expectations. In the U.S. McDonald's menu includes beef, chicken, fish, salads, and vegetarian products, as well as a full range of desserts, shakes, and hot and cold drinks for every taste.

McDonald's was the first quick-service

restaurant to make publicly available a complete ingredient listing and detailed nutritional analysis of all its products. In 2000, McDonald's introduced innovative McSalad Shaker and Fruit N' Yogurt Parfaits, making it easy to eat well on the go.

PROMOTION

From the earliest days, McDonald's recognized the key role of marketing in the brand-building process. As Ray Kroc put it: "There's something just as basic to our success as the hamburger. That something is marketing, McDonald's style. It's bigger than any person or product bearing the McDonald's name." Advertising is certainly not the only cause of McDonald's success. It is, however, inseparable from it. To this day, a fixed proportion of restaurant sales is reinvested back into advertising and sales promotion in every market in which McDonald's operates.

McDonald's displays a rare ability to act like a retailer while thinking like a brand; delivering sales for the immediate present while building and protecting its long-term brand reputation. Television advertising has been instrumental in transforming McDonald's brand image from that of a multi-national corporation to part of the fabric of society. Through high profile brand advertising, McDonald's has developed a powerful emotional relationship with its customers based on trust and a fundamental warmth and humanity unmatched by its competitors.

McDonald's is also involved in sports sponsorship. McDonald's uses its association with prestigious global sporting events such as the World Cup and Olympic Games to reinforce its international brand stature, while tailor-made sponsorship programs are used to address local market needs.

In addition to national advertising and promotional campaigns, McDonald's is strongly committed to Ray Kroc's passionate belief that McDonald's should contribute to the communities that it serves. Local activity takes many different forms, ranging from social mornings for senior citizens to fund-raising work with local schools, youth groups, and hospitals.

BRAND VALUES

Founder Ray Kroc developed his brand vision for McDonald's around a simple but effective consumer-driven premise of quality, service, cleanliness, and value. Kroc's winning formula was quickly shortened to QSC&V - an acronym that would become and remain an enduring cornerstone of the brand.

If QSC&V is the cornerstone of the

McDonald's brand, then trust is its bedrock. To its customers, McDonald's is a brand that can be trusted; placing the customer at the center of its world; knowing the right thing to do.

The key to McDonald's success has been its capacity to touch universal consumer needs with such consistency that the essence of the brand has somehow always been relevant to the local culture, no matter how different that culture might be from McDonald's origins. With one of the most powerful brands in the business, McDonald's looks set to enjoy healthy growth long into the future.

THINGS YOU DIDN'T KNOW ABOUT MCDONALD'S

- ❍ McDonald's serves 45 million people per day worldwide—more than 20 million in the U.S. and over 25 million outside the U.S.

- ❍ McDonald's opens a new restaurant somewhere in the world every eight hours.

- ❍ Eight percent of the American adult population visits McDonald's on an average day.

- ❍ The first "McSki" opened in Lindvallen, Sweden, in 1996. Customers can enjoy a Big Mac, hot chocolate or apple pie on the ski slopes without taking off their equipment.

- ❍ An investment of $2,250 of 100 shares in 1965 has grown to 74,360 shares worth over $3.2 million as of Sept. 30, 1999.

- ❍ Ronald McDonald speaks more than 25 languages, including Cantonese, Portuguese, Hindi, Tagalog, and Russian.

- ❍ Since 1984, Ronald McDonald House Charities (RMHC) national body and its global network of local charities has awarded nearly $250 million in grants to children's programs worldwide.

MONOPOLY

THE MARKET

It is heartening to know that traditional toys and especially games are holding their own against the avalanche of computer-based games. Not that The Monopoly® Game, the world's biggest-selling game, is falling behind in any way; there is a CD-ROM version of The Monopoly Game and even a hand-held electronic version! But even in its traditional form, The Monopoly Game continues to outsell all comers.

More than 200 million copies of the board game have been sold worldwide, and more than 500 million people have played the classic game. It is sold in 80 countries, and has been translated into 26 languages. In today's technology-driven society, there is something truly magical about the interaction that board games like The Monopoly Game provide, and that other types of games cannot. When friends and family members sit down to play The Monopoly Game together, they share a rich connection that transcends the generations.

ACHIEVEMENTS

Probably no other game has ever attracted the kind of devotion, and ingenuity, that The Monopoly Game has. That is shown very clearly by the lengths to which devotees will go to play a unique game; The Monopoly Game is not just the world's best-selling game, it is also one of the world's most inspiring ones.

Players have reached high. The record for the longest game played in a tree house is 240 hours, and the German Monopoly championship was once held on top of the Zugspitze, the tallest peak in the German Alps.

The game has had its ups and downs, too. A 16-day game has been played in a moving elevator, and the record for the longest inverted Monopoly game, played upside down, is 36 hours. The longest game in a bathtub lasted 99 hours.

The Monopoly Game had a strong following in Cuba until Fidel Castro took over and ordered all sets to be destroyed. But his former supporters in Russia were not so immune to the game's charms, and in 1989 the first Russian Monopoly game was produced.

HISTORY

It's ironic that it should have been a stock market crash that set the stage for the appearance of The Monopoly Game, the quintessential game of capitalism. Charles Darrow lost his job as a result of the great crash of 1929. He had been a successful salesman of heating and engineering equipment, and now he was reduced to doing odd jobs.

That was not enough to feed his growing family, so he made things. Some were for fun, but others were just amusements for his family; and one evening in 1930 he began drawing on the oilcloth that covered his kitchen table in Germantown, Pennsylvania. He sketched out a square, drew smaller squares inside it and began to fill in the names of some of the streets he remembered from happier days when the family was able to afford vacations in Atlantic City.

A local paint store gave Darrow free samples of several colors, and he used them to make his game brighter. He cut the houses and hotels he needed from scrap wooden moulding, found stray pieces of cardboard for the title cards, selected some colored buttons for the tokens (although some sources say that he raided his wife's charm bracelet) and "printed" up some play money.

Family and friends loved the game, and began to ask for sets of their own. Darrow went into very small scale manufacturing, making up to two and then six sets a day. Each set, selling for $4, brought him more customers. Eventually he decided to approach a games manufacturer with an offer to sell them the concept. Parker Brothers rejected him, with the now-famous explanation that the game had "fifty-two fundamental errors."

But that didn't stop Darrow's hand-made Monopoly sets from selling, and then a local department store caught on and began ordering wholesale quantities. Darrow went into full production with a printer friend, and then Parker Brothers came back to him. He sold. Later, he commented: "Taking the precepts of Monopoly to heart, I did not care to speculate." He never regretted his decision. In 1970, a few years after his death, Atlantic City erected a commemorative plaque in his honor.

The Monopoly Game is now marketed and distributed by Hasbro, Inc., one of the world's leading children's and family entertainment companies whose product portfolio includes famous brands such as Candy Land, Clue, and Mr. Potato Head, to name but a few. They receive 19,000 unsolicited games every year from hopeful inventors. It's doubtful that any of them will ever be able to emulate The Monopoly Game.

THE PRODUCT

The Monopoly Game is the most famous board game in the world. There cannot be many people who do not recognize that familiar command: "Go directly to jail. Do not pass Go. Do not collect $200."

The continued success of The Monopoly Game is testimony to its universal appeal. Few games have stood the test of time nearly as well. But of course even the most traditionally minded toy makers can find ways of using technology in an intriguing and effective fashion.

In the late 1990s, Hasbro launched a hand-held version of The Monopoly Game. Through advanced voice technology, players get to hear more than 400 words, sound effects and music as they take on up to three artificial intelligence opponents. There is now also a CD-ROM edition, which makes it possible to play on the Internet. And of course The Monopoly.com Edition, which allows players to buy today's hottest web sites, search engines and ISP providers as they travel the board.

Another electronic version of the game is the Monopoly Jackpot hand-held game, a version for adults based on the popular casino slot machine game. Players can sample the game at home before deciding whether playing for money in the casinos of Atlantic City or Las Vegas is for them.

There are many other Monopoly games available, some targeted at specific countries or sports and some aimed at different age groups. What they all have in common is the theme, and that famous brand.

© 2001 Hasbro

RECENT DEVELOPMENTS

After 40 years, a new game token was added to The Monopoly Game in early 1999. The sack of money bested fellow candidates the piggybank and the biplane in a vote that formed part of the Monopoly Game Token Campaign. This brought the total number of tokens to eleven. The last time tokens were added was in the early 1950s, when the dog, wheelbarrow and horse and rider joined the game.

The Monopoly Game is not only popular in its country of origin. In 2000, it was voted 'Game of the Century' by the British Association of Toy Retailers. Also in 2000, Hasbro launched The Monopoly Pokemon Edition featuring the most popular Pokemon characters.

There is now a dinosaur edition for children, Dig'n Dinos, as well as a number of Star Wars editions, which actually date back to 1996, and other special editions are constantly in preparation. One of the most recent is The Monopoly Millennium Edition featuring a collectible embossed game tin, a game board of silver-colored, holographic foil and eight specially redesigned Millennium tokens.

PROMOTION

The best and most effective advertisement for The Monopoly Game is the name and the reputation that carries with it. The

game is, however, periodically advertised on television to children of eight and over. Another important part of the promotional mix are public relations events such as the various Monopoly championships, right up to the World Championship. This is staged every four years; in 1996, Monte Carlo attracted elite players from 36 countries, and in 2000 Toronto saw more than 40 countries participating. The winner, and current Monopoly World Champion, is Yutaka Okada of Japan.

BRAND VALUES

In its 66th year of production, The Monopoly Game remains everyone's favorite board game. Edward P. Parker, former president of Parker Brothers, once suggested that it was about "clobbering your best friend without doing any damage." Its essence might be about making deals and taking risks with the ultimate goal of "owning it all," and success and status are the rewards. It caters to the fantasy of success and wealth that everyone likes to indulge in. Despite this, The Monopoly Game remains a game for family and friends, where children can compete on the same level as adults and nobody really loses.

THINGS YOU DIDN'T KNOW ABOUT THE MONOPOLY GAME

○ When Atlantic City tried to change some of the street names made famous by their appearance on the The Monopoly Game board, the resulting public outcry saw the proposal vetoed and the names Baltic and Mediterranean remain on the road map.

○ A special The Monopoly Game set was made for underwater Monopoly record attempts at a cost of $15,000. It disintegrated after the last record-breaking attempt, a 1,080-hour marathon played by the Buffalo Dive Club. Some 350 divers took turns to keep the game going. In 1978, the Neiman Marcus Christmas Catalogue offered a chocolate version of the game priced at $600.

○ Charles Darrow, the man who sold The Monopoly Game to Parker Brothers, retired a millionaire at the age of 46 and devoted his life to world travel and collecting orchids.

○ The Monopoly Game set made by Alfred Dunhill, with gold houses and silver hotels, sold for $25,000.

○ More than five billion of the game's little green houses have been 'built' since 1935.

○ Many famous people play The Monopoly Game, including the Queen of England, but Fidel Castro doesn't like it.

105

MR. C☕FFEE®

THE MARKET

Today, "coffee culture" is a bona fide social and commercial phenomenon. The evolution of this culture has included the expansion of coffeemaker manufacturing, which in 2000 constituted a $470 million consumer market—the largest category in the small appliance industry.

In addition to increased coffee consumption, the growth of the coffeemaker category (up 20 percent from 1997 to 2000) has been fueled by early product replacement, new features, and in no small part, by the performance of the Mr. Coffee brand as market share leader (33 percent of units).

But coffee making is just one area of expertise for the brand. It also competes in the iced tea maker category, which it created and still dominates, and other categories including espresso makers, the fast-growing coffee grinder category, and disposable coffee filters.

Despite dramatic proliferation of competitive brands in these categories over the years, today the Mr. Coffee brand remains the leader in beverage-making appliances by delivering quality, style and innovation to the marketplace.

ACHIEVEMENTS

Few brands can boast the kind of staying power exhibited by the Mr. Coffee brand, which has been the leader of the coffeemaker category for nearly three decades. In 1972, the Mr. Coffee brand introduced the first household automatic drip coffeemaker (ADC), creating the category that would revolutionize home coffee brewing.

Its debut model, the MC1A, brought ADC technology, previously seen only in restaurants and institutions, into millions of American homes. By 1991, nine out of ten readers of *Consumer*

Reports magazine were drinking coffee brewed with an ADC.

Before the introduction of the MC1A, home brewing was generally limited to percolated coffee, often burnt and laden with over-extracted grounds. These pitfalls were eliminated by ADC technology, and this advance made the Mr. Coffee brand a household name almost overnight. By 1975, it had become the best-selling brand of coffeemaker in the U.S.

Since then, high quality products, continuous innovation (both inside and outside the coffeemaker category) and consumer trust have earned the brand a reputation for outstanding value and quality service.

As a result, the Mr. Coffee brand has remained the number one brand of ADCs since its introduction. But the brand has proven it can do more than make a great cup of coffee. Today, it's the No. 1 player in iced tea makers, branded coffee filters and replacement decanters.

Mr. Coffee is also the #2 market share leader of espresso machines for the home, and successfully markets a range of other products such as coffee grinders, mug warmers, permanent filters and a hot cocoa maker called Cocomotion.

HISTORY

The Mr. Coffee brand of ADC for household-use was introduced in 1972 by North American Systems, Inc., founded in Cleveland, Ohio, by real estate developer Vincent G. Marotta, Sr. and his partner, Samuel Glazer.

Their success was significant and immediate, and by the late 1970s, the Mr. Coffee brand held more than 50 percent of the ADC market, with annual sales of over $150 million. It has remained the share leader since, despite increasing competition.

The brand's staying power can be attributed in large part to innovation. For instance, during the coffee shortage of 1977–78, the company maintained an edge over competition with an innovative coffee-saving feature built into the basket of its coffeemakers. This feature allowed consumers to use a minimum amount of coffee when brewing by making the water flow directly through the coffee grounds in the brew basket and not around the grounds. With this feature, the consumer was able to change the diameter of the brew basket in order to brew the same amount of coffee with less coffee grounds. While the device was no longer viable in the market after coffee prices settled, it was an effective product enhancement that served the brand (and consumers) well in difficult times.

When the coffee shortage ended, many new competitors, encouraged by the success of the Mr. Coffee brand, began descending on the ADC market. This emergence of competition in the marketplace prompted Mr. Marotta to sum up the brand's position in an April 1982 issue of *Forbes*: "There used to be only 4 or 5 companies making drip coffeemakers. Now there are around 25. [The competition] has been eroding our market share point by point. But we still have at least double the market share of each of

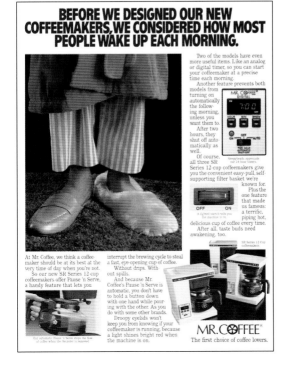

our nearest competitors in the field." This is a claim the brand can still make today.

In 1987, after a leveraged buyout led by John M. Eikenberg, the company name was changed from North American Systems, Inc. to Mr. Coffee, Inc. President and CEO Eikenberg set out to introduce Mr. Coffee-branded products

targeting a more upscale market segment. New competitors, among them European brands with cutting-edge designs popular among emerging Baby Boomers, sought a piece of the action.

Convinced that Mr. Coffee could not hold more than 40 percent of the ADC market, management's key strategy in the late 1980s and early 1990s was to further diversify the product line into small food appliances, Mr. Coffee-branded to aid consumer acceptance. Out of this strategy came a Mr. Coffee food dehydrator and the Mr. Coffee Iced Tea Pot™ product.

The Iced Tea Pot™ product, introduced in 1989, was the first automatic iced tea maker and could make up to two quarts of tea in ten minutes. Always attuned to the increasingly fast-paced lifestyle of consumers, the Mr. Coffee brand soon innovated the product to allow up to three quarts of tea to be brewed in still only ten minutes.

This and other measures succeeded, with total sales in 1989 increasing 24 percent from 1988. But the upswing was short-lived. In the early 1990s, competition became still more intense, with American appliance makers leveraging established brand equities in the coffeemaker category. This coincided with an American recession that slowed household appliance purchases.

In 1994, the Mr. Coffee brand extended its product line by merging with Health-O-Meter, a producer of medical goods and consumer weight scales. Then, in 1998, Sunbeam Corporation purchased Mr. Coffee, Inc. from then-owner Signature Brands. Seizing the latent power of the Mr. Coffee brand name, Sunbeam revived consumer marketing efforts in 1999, and in 2000, launched a national campaign boosting its newly designed coffee makers.

THE PRODUCT
Since the 1972 introduction of the MC1A, the Mr. Coffee line of coffeemakers has been innovated in numerous ways. While the 1972 introduction included a built-in warming plate and in 1977 the coffee-saver feature was introduced, other innovations have included Pause 'n Serve, adjustable warming plates, removable brew baskets and programmable timers. Later

models feature, among other things, a heater that shuts off automatically after two hours.

Unremarkable today, these were eye-popping, innovative gadgets when first introduced, and have since become absolute necessities in the minds of many consumers.

Innovations, however, were not limited to coffeemakers. In 1992, the brand introduced Mr. Coffee Water Filters, developed in response to reports of dangerous levels of lead in tap water and problems with bottled water. The Mr. Coffee Water Filter reportedly removed over 90 percent of the lead, chlorine and copper in household drinking water. The ad campaign for these innovations, which included the tag line, "Mr. Coffee—What'll he think of next?", relied on the image of a personified Mr. Coffee tinkering in the tool shop after brewing away in the kitchen.

RECENT DEVELOPMENTS
Sunbeam Corporation continues to enhance the Mr. Coffee line of coffeemakers. The innovations most recently brought by the brand are ones that continue to meet both the functional and style needs of consumers while not jeopardizing the superior quality and taste expected from the Mr. Coffee brand. A few innovations include: coffeemakers with thermal carafes so consumers can enjoy fresh, hot coffee for up to four hours; removable water reservoirs that allow consumers to fill the coffeemaker with water without all the mess and a steeping lever on the Iced Tea Pot (for adjusting the strength of the brew).

PROMOTION
The continuous innovations introduced by Sunbeam Corporation over the years have provided no shortage of "news" to report to consumers who are ever hungry to learn of products that enhance their living. As a result, the Mr. Coffee brand has leveraged an impressive and continuous array of advertising and consumer promotions to communicate its latest benefits.

With the purchase of the company by Sunbeam Corporation, the brand's promotional efforts, which had been dormant for several years, were revived in 1998. Most recently, the company re-launched the brand with print and television advertising touting the coffeemaker line's sleek re-design. The print ads played up the "seductive" new look of the brewers, while the television campaign created a "mock-umentary" about the coffeemaker's recent "facelift."

At the same time the new ads began running, the Mr. Coffee Web site (www.mrcoffee.com) was launched providing a comprehensive one-stop destination for coffee lovers seeking to enhance their enjoyment and entertainment of home-brewed coffee. The site provides brewing tips and techniques, various recipes for coffee and complementing treats and an entire section on entertaining with coffee.

In addition, the Mr. Coffee brand remains close to consumers with its 1-800 MR COFFEE consumer hotline. Consumers can receive brewing tips, replacement parts and accessories and have any product questions answered by speaking to a Consumer Service Representative at the hotline.

BRAND VALUES
Since the beginning, the Mr. Coffee brand has been dedicated to producing high quality products and continuous innovation to meet consumer needs. Starting with the revolutionary MC1A coffeemaker, Mr. Coffee appliances have helped millions of consumers save countless hours in the kitchen and more fully enjoy the foods and beverages they prepare. Continued adherence to these core values of quality and innovation will continue to support the reputation that has helped the Mr. Coffee brand remain the leader in beverage-making products for nearly three decades.

THINGS YOU DIDN'T KNOW ABOUT MR. COFFEE

- During production in 1972, approximately 1,000 Mr. Coffee brewers were manufactured per day. Within three years, over 18,000 coffeemakers were produced each day and that quantity could still not meet sales demand.
- Research shows that consumers prefer to drink their coffee at 168 degrees Fahrenheit.
- The Mr. Coffee brand was the first to introduce timers on its coffeemakers.
- The first set of coffeemakers produced by the brand could only make 10 cups of coffee. Today, the units have been designed to give consumers the option of making 2–12 cups.
- Americans drink more iced tea than do any other people in the world! More than 46 billion glasses of tea are consumed each year with 37 billion of those glasses served iced.
- Compared to today's feature laden high-tech products, the original Mr. Coffee product manufactured over 25 years ago would still be considered as one of the fastest brewing automatic drip coffeemakers available.

NYSE
New York Stock Exchange®

THE MARKET

The New York Stock Exchange is proud to be one of the world's most powerful and recognizable brands. Renowned as one of the most prestigious organizations in the global economy, the NYSE has been building upon the strength of its brand for more than 200 years and its reputation as the world's leading equities marketplace, home to the world's greatest companies. An association with the NYSE brand is a true reflection of the powerful company you keep as a member of the Exchange family.

The NYSE stands alone in providing today's public companies with the world's largest, most efficient and most equitable marketplace for the trading of their shares. At the same time, an Exchange listing gives shareholders the confidence of knowing that they own shares of the world's best companies and, when buying and selling shares, that their orders are being handled in the most efficient and fairest way possible. Because of this, issuers and investors have trusted the Exchange for the listing and trading of securities for more than two centuries. The NYSE will continue to

build on this trust, expanding its role as the center of global business for many more centuries to come.

ACHIEVEMENTS

A New York Stock Exchange listing has achieved status as a globally recognized signal of strength and leadership. The Exchange's stringent listing standards ensure this mark of merit holds true. Because the Exchange lists only the greatest companies in the world, the NYSE brand is built on the strength of its companies. With nearly 3,000 listed companies valued at more than $17 trillion globally, the NYSE is larger than the world's next five-largest markets combined. The NYSE's more than 400 non-U.S. listed companies from 51 countries alone have a market capitalization of more than $5.5 trillion.

The Exchange is proud to have among its listed-company family such world-class brands as AOL Time Warner, Sony, Coca-Cola, IBM and Disney. Listed companies range from such "blue chip" corporations and virtually all of the Fortune 500 companies, to many smaller and mid-market companies, to many of the world's leading technology and high-growth enterprises. These businesses have found that their NYSE listing enhances the marketability of not only their securities, but their products and services, and have developed broad shareholder constituencies through exposure to the widest possible range of individual and institutional investors. The unmatched quality of the NYSE auction market—access to the world's largest pool of capital and outstanding liquidity and transparency, the opportunity to significantly expand and diversify shareholder base, greater global visibility, extensive research coverage, and the

most efficient and cost-effective capital-raising process—are often cited as the most compelling reasons to list.

HISTORY

Since its inception in 1792 under a Buttonwood Tree, the NYSE has stood as one of the world's best brands and leading financial institutions. As business and commerce evolved on a global scale, so too has the Exchange, ever expanding its role at the center of global business. Perhaps no single entity represents the global economy better than the NYSE. Over the years, the NYSE has changed to support capital markets, and has continued to evolve to meet the needs of issuers and investors alike.

For example, more and more companies are raising capital on the NYSE through initial public offerings (IPOs). In fact, the NYSE lists about 90% of all qualified U.S. initial public offerings. In 1983 the Exchange developed special procedures that enable companies to list concurrent with their IPOs. Since then, more than 1,000 companies have listed their IPOs directly on the Exchange.

THE PRODUCT

A leader in innovative trading capabilities and systems, the NYSE employs the most advanced technology to deliver fast, efficient, reliable and cost-effective trade executions. The Exchange's integrated auction-market trading platform provides investors with unmatched liquidity and depth, the opportunity for price improvement and the option of high-speed, automatic executions. In fact, the NYSE is the world's most technologically advanced marketplace. And the strength of the NYSE brand is built upon its commitment to technology and innovation. The Exchange's $2.5 billion investment in technology over the past 10 years has meant rapid and continuous improvements in trading systems and capacity, unrivaled reliability, and continued deployment of new market-information products and order-execution services.

RECENT DEVELOPMENTS

Most recently, the Exchange launched several technology initiatives that are being rolled out under the Network NYSE umbrella. From NYSE MarkeTrac™, a data-rich online investor tool on nyse.com that gives investors a 3-D connection to the point of sale, to NYSE Direct+ ™, a high-speed electronic connection for immediate automatic execution of limit orders up to 1,099 shares, to e-Broker™, a

wireless handheld order-management tool for floor brokers, the NYSE is making markets more interactive and dynamic and further extending the benefits of the Exchange to all market participants.

Other recent developments include Global Equity Market, or "GEM", the proposed linkage of world exchanges that would allow for the sharing of liquidity and the creation of a mechanism for 24-hour trading of the world's global companies, the development of Global Shares that trade freely across borders, and the trading of exchange-traded funds (ETFs) on the basis of unlisted trading privileges. The NYSE began trading ETFs in December 2000 with the listing of the iShares S&P Global 100 Exchange Traded Fund (NYSE: IOO), which is based on the S&P Global 100 index. *To learn more about these and other developments at the NYSE, visit www.nyse.com.*

PROMOTION

The Exchange continues to position itself at the center of global business and as the world's first truly global marketplace. One of its most visible expressions is its logo, which was recently modified to incorporate the NYSE's strongest brand attributes. Launched in 2000, the new, contemporary logo (pictured), in keeping with the Exchange's business model, adopted a "portal," reflective of market transparency, openness to change, and access and connectivity for all market constituents. The Exchange's first logo (also pictured), in place from the 1860s through 1900, featured an elaborate coat of arms fashioned out of the intertwined letters N, Y, S, and E.

While the logo has evolved over time to reflect the evolution of the Exchange itself, the tag line that accompanies the logo, "The world puts its stock in us.™" has been in place for almost a decade. As one of the great thematic lines of all time, research shows how it reflects and supports the confidence and trust investors

and companies alike place in the New York Stock Exchange.

Working to build brand awareness for all its listed companies, the NYSE provides multiple visibility opportunities. Many companies have partnered with the Exchange to reach their most important audiences by using the NYSE facilities at 11 Wall Street in New York City to host street events, press conferences, employee-relations programs, analyst and board meetings,

product launches, branding campaigns, and more. Listed companies are also featured on nyse.com, which receives millions of hits each day, and in the pages of *The Exchange* monthly newsletter and quarterly *nyse magazine*.

Advertising is another way the Exchange reinforces and strengthens its brand. The NYSE's recent campaigns not only showcase the companies that make up its brand, but serve to educate the investing public and help bridge the gap between Wall Street and Main Street.

Helping to close that gap has been the media presence at the NYSE. The Exchange is the center of financial and business news. With well over a dozen domestic and international network broadcast bureaus on site and live programming from the trading floor every day, more people have access to the financial markets than ever. In fact, the opening and closing bells are the most-watched daily events in the world. Millions of global viewers each day tune in to see business leaders, government officials, world leaders, and celebrities—from Muhammad Ali to Ronald Reagan to Jack Welch—open and close the trading day.

And close to a million visitors of all ages and backgrounds descend upon the Exchange each year to see first hand the epicenter of the world financial markets, where more than $50 billion worth of trading takes place each day, and to learn more about the companies whose products and services affect their daily lives.

BRAND VALUES

As study after study shows, being listed on the NYSE is ultimately a mark of excellence, a symbol of success, and a sign of global leadership. The NYSE is frequently called "the place for tomorrow's business leaders", "truly innovative"

and "progressive", and is associated with "integrity" and "long-term stability". Companies that list on the New York Stock Exchange are considered "very established, well respected and important," "stable," "credible" and "global"; are looked upon as "solid companies with strong financial positions"; and are viewed as having "investors that are treated fairly".

Because of this, many companies use the NYSE-listed emblem, which marries a company's trading symbol or logo with the NYSE brand, to elevate public awareness of their status as a listed company. Analogous to the Good Housekeeping seal of approval, as studies reveal, the emblem is often used in corporate marketing materials, on product packaging, in annual reports and other financial documents, in print advertising, on corporate websites, and on business cards and stationery.

Another core attribute of the NYSE brand is its regulatory strength. As a self-regulatory organization, the Exchange oversees each and every trade. Every transaction that takes place on the NYSE is under constant surveillance. With more than one-third of its work-force dedicated to market oversight, the Exchange goes to great lengths to make sure investors are protected, and that every investor—from the small investor in Idaho to a large institution in Indonesia—is operating on a level playing field.

THINGS YOU DIDN'T KNOW ABOUT THE NEW YORK STOCK EXCHANGE

- ❍ The Exchange has invested more than $2.5 billion in technology over the past 10 years.

- ❍ Average daily trading volume on the NYSE is more than 1.2 billion shares.

- ❍ $50 billion worth of stocks change hands on the Exchange each day.

- ❍ nyse.com receives on average 12 million hits per day.

- ❍ The global market capitalization of the NYSE's near 3,000 listed companies from more than 50 countries is $17 trillion.

- ❍ 93% of all orders are delivered to the trading floor electronically.

- ❍ The Exchange's optical cable network stretches for 250 miles.

- ❍ The NYSE trading floor spans 45,000 square feet.

- ❍ An entire day's worth of trading on the NYSE 10 years ago is now handled in the first 15 minutes of the trading day.

Nikon

THE MARKET

A multi-billion dollar precision technology company with extensive manufacturing, research and marketing capabilities, Nikon was recently ranked among America's ten most-respected brands. Its cameras, lenses, and accessories are used by more professional photographers than all other 35mm brands combined. Its Coolpix cameras have received more awards and top rankings than any other consumer digital cameras. Its microscopes command the largest share of the U.S. life science market, both in research and diagnostic laboratories. And its ultra-high precision stepper products have been indispensable for the success of the semiconductor industry.

The majority of Nikon's revenues worldwide come from the sale of its semiconductor manufacturing equipment, which dominate chip fabrication facilities throughout the U.S., Europe and Asia. In addition to these and its legendary photographic products, Nikon offers many other precision optical systems. For instance, it markets instruments used by eye-care professionals, as well as prescription eye-

wear and sunglasses. Nikon construction and surveying equipment is used to help build and maintain the world's roads, bridges and buildings. And Nikon's binoculars and sport optics are used by outdoor enthusiasts the world over.

ACHIEVEMENTS

Nikon's performance and innovation provide inspiration to photographers at every level. Nikon has led in technical innovations for 35mm cameras for more than 50 years. Nikon cameras have been the choice of more Pulitzer Prize winning photographers than all other brands combined. The company has earned scores of Editor's Choice, Top Product of the

Year, and Best Design awards in the past year alone. Considered a "best buy" by well-known consumer testing and rating organizations, Nikon cameras are acknowledged for setting performance, reliability, and ease-of-use standards for professionals and general consumers.

Nikon microscopes also offer new optical systems to allow researchers to see minute features that could never before be viewed. Nikon instruments have been at the forefront of science in such areas as AIDS, Alzheimers, cancer, in vitro fertilization, and genetic research. Nikon also offers high quality photomicrography camera systems for researchers, with new technology for light metering, autofocus, speed and accuracy. Nikon most recently introduced the world's most advanced professional digital SLR.

HISTORY

Nikon's story began in 1917, an era when the greatest optical designers were based in Europe. The Japan Optical Company (known as Nippon

Kogaku K.K.) invited some of the most talented technicians in Germany to come to Japan and lead the fledgling company's optical development capability. Their presence marked the beginning of the world's greatest optical company – Nikon.

Nikon's first products weren't cameras. Instead, Nippon Kogaku K.K. began to produce binoculars, and later expanded to microscopes, telescopes, surveying equipment, measuring devices, and camera lenses. The first time the name Nikon was used was 1946, and by 1948, the first Nikon range-finder camera was introduced. Only a handful of these cameras made it to the US, but they became the hottest new technology for camera professionals. A 1950 New York Times article touted the superiority of Nikon cameras and lenses to the US public, and by the end of that decade, the first system-oriented SLR camera, the groundbreaking Nikon F, began its 15-year domination of the industry.

In the 1970s, NASA came to Nikon for a customized version of the then-famous Nikon F

professional 35mm SLR. Their collaborative effort resulted in the first Nikon to go into space. Since the Apollo 15 mission, Nikon cameras have been aboard every manned NASA space flight, including the space shuttle and space station projects. Nikon also began, at this time, to become involved with the electronics industry and created its first products for the production and inspection of integrated circuits.

By the 1980s, Nippon Kogaku K.K. decided to take its world-dominant Nikon brand as its corporate name, and became Nikon Corporation. The 1990s brought the introduction of the flagship F5 camera, the widest variety of lenses and speedlights ever available, the award-winning Coolpix line of compact digital cameras, the ground-breaking D1 professional digital SLR, the Eclipse line of high-resolution, long working distance microscopes, the first surveying field stations, and much more.

THE PRODUCT

Nikon offers a huge range of high-precision products, ranging from its world-renowned semiconductor manufacturing steppers to its highly visible digital and film camera systems, lenses and accessories, to its microscopes, measuring and inspection instruments, binoculars, surveying equipment, eyewear, scanners, underwater photography systems, ophthalmic instruments, and more. Virtually its entire product line is based upon its hallmark—Nikon glass, from which its precision optical lenses are crafted.

Nikon is the only major optical company in the world that still controls and manufactures every aspect of its glass-making, which gives it the ability to finely tune Nikon lens specifications, quality and performance. From the raw silicon to the final coatings, Nikon glass production is both a science and an art form.

RECENT DEVELOPMENTS

Nikon has long been seen as a technology innovator. In 1999, it introduced its first mega-pixel, pro-quality digital SLR camera—the Nikon D1.

N I K O N ' S   S M A L L   W O R L D   2 0 0 1

This camera has revolutionized the way sports, fashion and journalism pictures are captured, providing pictures that have appeared in thousands of newspaper articles, magazine stories and presentations.

Nikon's ultra-durable F5 camera offers the most advanced 3D color matrix metering, high-

precision ultra-fast auto-focus, and advanced, auto-balanced fill flash. The new F100, N80 and N65 cameras offer unmatched performance and ease of use. Nuvis Advanced Photo System compact cameras are fun and easy to use. Nikon's film scanners are the choice of thousands of graphic arts and design professionals. And Coolpix digital cameras are among the most lauded consumer electronics products of our generation.

In the realm of research, Nikon offers the new CFI60 optical system, allowing scientists using Nikon microscopes to view never-before-seen phenomena deep within living cells. CFI60 optics also allow them to work at extreme magnifications, with extraordinary brightness, resolution and contrast.

PROMOTION

Nikon's famous tag line, "We take the world's greatest pictures." was recently amended to add "Yours." This addition linked the company's heritage among pro photographers with today's consumers. Nikon's industrial, bioscience, and other products also employ trend-setting, provocative advertising and promotions. In addition, Nikon's extensive public relations and dealer-support programs help build the brand's reputation among the media, key industry influentials, and the public.

For more than 30 years, Nikon has helped people at all levels of experience learn how to take better pictures with its Nikon World magazine and the highly regarded Nikon School of Photography. Nikon School travels to nearly two dozen cities per year, teaching people how to capture memorable, beautiful SLR photos. And, through a special program just for registered professionals, Nikon Professional Services attends worldwide sporting events, space launches, presidential inaugurations, and other high-profile news events to provide equipment loans and free service to its members.

Nikon has also taken a key market position online. Its new www.nikonusa.com web site offers not only a look at Nikon products and an outlet store, but also creates a unique photo community experience. It offers photo sharing, a special on-line version of the Nikon School of Photography, help in selecting a pro photographer, and a new site, Microscopy, dedicated to the art of photomicrography, chat, contests, events, special dealer access, and much more.

Nikon also plays an active role in supporting many worthy organizations, events and workshops. These programs include the Eddie Adams photojournalism workshop, the Great American Photography Weekends, the W. Eugene Smith Grant in Humanistic Photography, the Nikon International Small World Photomicrography

Competition, the Nikon Photo Contest International, and To Make the World a Better Place, among many others.

BRAND VALUES

The Nikon name is equated with extraordinary performance, innovation, precision, and optical quality.

And, because images are so woven into the fabric of our lives, the Nikon brand's photo excellence carries an additional emotional impact. Photography is a tool to heal, educate and inspire. Nikon embodies the power of photography to document history, state opinions, stir emotions, create controversy, generate excitement, document breakthroughs, reflect beauty, ensure the quality of manufactured products, preserve our precious memories and record scientific findings.

THINGS YOU DIDN'T KNOW ABOUT NIKON

○ Nikon instruments have been part of some of the most famous life science developments in recent history. For instance, Nikon's Diaphot microscope was used for the country's first in vitro birth, and is still the predominant microscope for assisted reproduction. And a Nikon microscope was used to clone "Dolly" – the sheep that was the first successful cloning of a fully-grown mammal.

○ Many of the world's most memorable photographic images over the last four decades have been captured with Nikons – from John Kennedy Jr. saluting at his father's funeral, and the defiant Tienanmen Square student standing in front of a military tank, to young Elian Gonzales cowering in a closet as authorities closed in.

THE MARKET

Prior to the introduction of NutraSweet® brand sweetener, the market for diet products had languished for a decade. Far from mainstream, the diet category was perceived as being exclusively for the obese or individuals on restricted diets. In retail outlets, products were grouped together in a small, separate section of the store.

The lack of interest in the diet category was predominantly driven by the taste perception of the sweeteners available at the time, primarily saccharin. Consumers felt diet products tasted bitter and were less flavorful than products made with sugar.

The launch of NutraSweet created a revolutionary change in consumer perception and usage of low-calorie products. Now consumers could have the benefits they wanted—safe, great-tasting products with no calories or sugar!

ACHIEVEMENTS

A product whose logo is recognized by 9 out of 10 American adults hardly needs an introduction. Today, NutraSweet brand sweetener has won regulatory approval in more than 100 countries on six continents and is used in approximately 5,000 products by 250 million people regularly.

NutraSweet has been widely acknowledged as the product that enabled the meteoric rise of the diet category. By teaming up with soft drink giants and other food and beverage manufacturers, The NutraSweet Company built solid, long-term relationships with its customers on a global basis, offering them unrivaled technical, R&D and regulatory support, competitive pricing and an experienced management team.

In 1999, BrandMarketing magazine named NutraSweet brand sweetener one of the top 100 brands that changed America, and Newsweek magazine named it one of the top inventions of the century. NutraSweet has also been lauded by

the Harvard Business Review for its branded ingredient strategy. In addition, it was named Fortune magazine's Product of the Year in 1982.

HISTORY

America got its first taste of NutraSweet in 1981, when millions of gumballs were sent through the mail to consumers throughout the U.S.

However the story began 15 year earlier when James Schlatter, a research scientist for the pharmaceutical company G.D. Searle & Co. was experimenting with combinations of amino acids in his work developing ulcer medications. He happened to lick his finger as he picked up a piece of paper. In that moment, Schlatter discovered that the unique combination of amino acids on his finger tasted intensely sweet. This was the world's first taste of NutraSweet.

Schlatter's serendipitous discovery led to a comprehensive schedule of more than 100 scientific studies over more than 15 years, making

NutraSweet one of the most thoroughly studied food ingredients in U.S. history to receive FDA approval.

In order to create an enduring franchise for its ingredient and to motivate consumers to try and preferentially select products containing aspartame, Searle chose to brand its product and call it NutraSweet. The name was chosen because it emphasized both its natural origins and its purpose as a sweetener.

Following approval in the United States, submissions for use and subsequent approval of aspartame followed globally. Support for the NutraSweet brand worldwide mirrored that in the United States. As a result, NutraSweet brand sweetener is one of the best-known brands.

THE PRODUCT

Aspartame is made from the combination of two amino acids, the methyl ester of phenylalanine and aspartic acid, which are building blocks of protein. These amino acids are consumed every day in foods such as meats, dairy products, fruits, and vegetables. When kept separate, these amino acids have no sweetening power. But together, they are extremely sweet—approximately 200 times sweeter than sugar on a pound for pound basis.

Aspartame contains approximately 4 calories per gram, roughly the same as sugar. Because of aspartame's sweetening power, far less of it is needed to obtain the same sweet taste. For instance, a 12-ounce can of soda containing high fructose

corn syrup has about 160 calories; a can sweetened with aspartame has less than 1 calorie.

As a protein, aspartame avoids one of the drawbacks of sugar. The bacteria that cause tooth decay feed on carbohydrates like sugar. Aspartame does not promote tooth decay because proteins are not an energy source for the bacteria.

Everyone except those individuals who have a rare hereditary disease called phenylketonuria, or PKU, can consume aspartame safely. These people are diagnosed at birth by a blood test performed on all newborns. Those with PKU must limit all natural sources of phenylalanine. Aspartame is just one of the many foods that must be monitored for intake.

RECENT DEVELOPMENTS

In January 1986, The NutraSweet Company was sold by Searle and became a wholly owned independent subsidiary of Monsanto. Nearly a decade and half later Monsanto sold NutraSweet to J.W. Childs Equity Partners II L.P. The sale included the sweetener business, the NutraSweet® brand name and other sweeteners in development. On May 30, 2000, the new NutraSweet Company was born.

PROMOTION

The marketing behind NutraSweet® brand products has been instrumental in the success of the brand and the growth of the diet category.

Marketing occurred on many fronts. Manufacturers, health care professionals and even retailers received direct mail as well as targeted advertising and promotions to tease, inform, and excite them about NutraSweet and its great sweet taste. Manufacturers were encouraged to formulate with NutraSweet. Health care professionals were informed about the safety and efficacy of the product. Retailers were motivated to stock and display products featuring NutraSweet.

It was in the consumer arena that the branded ingredient strategy NutraSweet pioneered was most evident. During the first three years of NutraSweet's introduction, the company invested over $120 million in advertising and co-op

advertising to promote the NutraSweet brand name and what it represented. Campaigns such as "What it isn't" and "Bananas and Milk" conveyed to consumers in simple, fun ways what NutraSweet was and how safe it was. The series of commercials and print ads in the "Why Some Things Taste Better Than Others" campaign and the Mr. Magoo campaign encouraged consumers to look for products with NutraSweet and, in particular, the 100% NutraSweet logo. NutraSweet's sponsorship of ice-skating reinforced the image of health and vitality.

NutraSweet customers benefited from this now widely copied branded ingredient strategy. As a result of the consumer marketing effort, food and beverage manufacturers had a simpler advertising message for the new products they were introducing. By stating the sweetening ingredient was NutraSweet, consumers instantly understood that the product was sugar free, great tasting, contained no saccharin, and was safe.

BRAND VALUES

With global headquarters based in Chicago, The NutraSweet Company is considered the gold standard in aspartame manufacturing. As the market leader, The NutraSweet Company's focus is on producing the highest quality aspartame in the world while continually improving operational efficiencies to remain the lowest cost producer. In its tradition of innovation, work continues today at NutraSweet on new sweetener solutions that promise to revolutionize the sweetener industry once again.

Today, NutraSweet brand sweetener is the most widely recognized sweetener brand in the world. And 20 years later it continues to meet consumers' needs with its clean, great sweet taste.

THINGS YOU DIDN'T KNOW ABOUT NUTRASWEET®

- ○ NutraSweet is approved in over 100 countries.
- ○ Over 5,000 products are sweetened with NutraSweet.
- ○ Over 250 million people enjoy products sweetened with the great taste of NutraSweet.

THE MARKET

Snacking is one of the most important contemporary trends in the food industry today. As two-income families, time pressures, and other factors converge to reduce the number of sit-down meals, snacking has become a $48-billion market that is growing twice as fast as other packaged foods categories. The biscuit market—which includes cookies and crackers—is an $8-billion-plus segment that is growing 5.7 percent a year.

Americans now get some 30 percent of their calories from snacks. More than 40 percent of people eat on the run. Some 12 percent eat their lunch in the car. More than 45 percent of Americans say that convenience foods are important in their diet. And lunch hour? It's a thing of the past. For most people, the average is 20 minutes.

ACHIEVEMENTS

OREO cookies have reigned for the better part of a century as America's number one cookie, the title they hold today. The brand is so connected to consumers that it has been on the shelves since 1912. At an age when most products that old have long been relegated to the consumer products graveyard, OREO is not just surviving, it's thriving. This $700-million brand recorded double-digit growth in each of the past three years.

An important part of that success is OREO's global appeal. It has proven to be an excellent world traveler, with the potential to hit the billion-dollar sales mark. It is now made in 12 countries—including China—and sold in 74 markets. It has yet to go into a single country where it hasn't been a quick success, turning in yearly international growth close to 30 percent.

HISTORY

Going back to the brand's earliest days, this much is known for sure: The OREO cookie was developed to meet consumer demand for an English-style biscuit, which was popular in the early 1900s. The first OREO cookie was produced in late February of 1912 and sold March 16 to a Hoboken, N.J., shopkeeper named S.C. Thusen. The product was distributed in bulk tins—not packages—directly to grocers for 30 cents a pound.

But why the name OREO? Nobody really knows. Some say it came from the Greek word OREO—for hill or mountain—reflecting the mounded shape of some early test versions. Since the original label had considerable gold scroll work on a pale green background, some believe that the name comes from "or," French for gold. Others say that if you take the "re" out of the middle of cream, and put it between a double "O," the shape of the cookie, you have

OREO. And there are those who take a more direct approach: Nabisco founder Adolphous Green just liked the sound of "OREO."

THE PRODUCT

The basic design of the cookie has not changed since its introduction. In 1913, OREO became the official trademark, and in 1974 it received its full name: OREO Chocolate Sandwich Cookies. In 1974, the brand added the successful DOUBLE STUF, to the applause of the "twisters" who go straight for the filling. Then, in 1987, Nabisco targeted the "indulgence" segment of the market with a fudge-covered version. In the mid-1990s, at the height of the fitness boom, OREO introduced a reduced-fat version, so the counters of fat-grams would not have to give up their favorite cookie.

RECENT DEVELOPMENTS

OREO was always a major force in its market: It was big, it was stable, it generated cash. But it wasn't a growth brand, which wasn't much of a surprise, given its advanced years.

But a new chapter in the story of OREO began to take shape in the late 1990s. After virtually ruling the cookie and cracker industry for years, Nabisco stumbled. Core brands were losing share, the vaunted innovation machinery started to rattle and smoke, a reorganized delivery system failed to deliver, and costs were rising as productivity was declining. As problems mounted, more marketing money was being diverted to shore up the bottom line, which only accelerated the share loss.

Under new leadership, the company began its climb back in 1997. Its basic strategy was to ignite the growth of its core brands, with OREO as the global centerpiece. The company reasoned—correctly as it turned out—that icon brands like OREO could use their loyal base and brand awareness to market their way to regained share and renewed growth.

While much of the brand's recent success has come from growth of the core product, new products figure prominently in the future. Product variations like seasonal cookies in different colors and a cookie that turns milk blue when dunked—a major hit with kids—have been solid growth-drivers on the power of short-term promotions. But to meet its growth targets, it was clear that the brand needed a major new product hit. It found it in Mini OREO Bite Size!, the first permanent addition to the OREO family in a number of years and a

business with clear power-brand potential. The Mini OREO product figured prominently in another growth strategy—expanding distribution. One of the brand's key distribution strategies was to put OREO within easy reach of consumers everywhere—from stores to vending machines to cafeterias to a featured place on fast-food dessert menus. One of the most important distribution opportunities was convenience stores. The new Mini product and new single-serve packages of the regular cookies—along with a targeted line of Planters, LifeSavers and other convenience-packaged snacks—are being sold through a sales unit created specifically to bring Nabisco products to the $9.2-billion convenience store market.

PROMOTION

The resurgence of Nabisco was guided by a vision of Total Brand Value—defined simply as satisfying consumers and retail customers faster and more completely than the competition. It was a means to connect every business, every strategy, every resource to the cause of brand building. It made every person in the company a marketer, helping them redefine their roles around the health, growth, and future of the brands.

And no brand was more important than OREO. If the turnaround was a battle for renewal and growth, then OREO was the flagship.

The plan of attack was simple: never miss an opportunity. Nabisco dramatically increased market spending behind the brand, combining advertising, marketing, public relations, and channel promotions to rebuild the cookie's profile.

The ads aimed at reconnecting the OREO cookie to times in their lives that consumers associated with OREOs. The campaign was called "Only OREO Moments." Consumers were invited to send in their own moments, with the winning ideas turned into themes for commercials.

Nabisco also gave consumers new opportunities to enjoy OREO by offering special varieties—for example, colored fillings for Spring and the holidays and tie-ins with professional and college sports.

Consumer promotions became a big part of the growth story—with the brand launching at least one major event every quarter.

The major consumer promotion—and arguably one of the most successful product marketing events of all time—is the annual OREO Stacking Contest. The series of local contests to see who can stack the most OREO cookies in a given amount of time culminate in finals at a high-profile location, such as Universal Studios, Fla. The contest has grown into a must-cover event for print and television, attracting hundreds of millions of print impressions a year and wide television coverage, including virtually all of the morning talk shows.

The Stacking Contest, along with other promotions, such as Don't Eat the Winning OREO—which awarded prizes to those who find specially marked cookies in the package—earned OREO recognition from *Promotion Magazine* as one of the 50 best promoted brands.

BRAND VALUES

Sometimes a brand can be more than a product. It can be part of life. It can be intertwined with memories. It can cross generations. The OREO cookie is one of those products

It is ironic in these early days of the 21st century that a brand conceived in the early days of the 20th Century continues to be Nabisco's most powerful engine of growth. But that's the power of a brand like OREO, a product that people have welcomed not only into their homes but also into their lives.

The OREO brand creates a solid platform on which to add new markets, new products, and new channels.

THINGS YOU DIDN'T KNOW ABOUT OREO

○ Earning its title of "America's Favorite Cookie," OREO captured over 13% of the Cookie category in 2000—almost 3 points more than the next biggest cookie brand.

○ Over half of all U.S. households purchased a package of OREO cookies in 2000. OREO is sold in 74 countries around the world.

○ Consumers eat more than 20 million OREO cookies every day.

○ Double Stuf OREO is the most widely liked cookie among kids and teens.

○ Double Stuf is a popular evening snack: 43 percent of Double Stuf OREO cookies are eaten in the evening.

PALL MALL

FAMOUS CIGARETTES

·IN HOC SIGNO VINCES·

"WHEREVER PARTICULAR PEOPLE CONGREGATE"

THE MARKET

The tobacco industry in America has a rich heritage dating back to the discovery of the New World in 1492. The aromatic dried leaves that were held in such high value by native Americans intrigued early explorers, including Columbus. In later years, they would discover that tobacco use was an accepted custom long before the first ships set sail from Spain.

Revenues from trade in tobacco essentially formed the foundation of the United States economy in its early years. During the nineteenth century, use of chewing tobaccos, and later smoking tobaccos, would become extremely popular in the U.S.

Hand-rolled cigarettes, on the other hand,

commensurate with premium quality. PALL MALL was built on the fact that it delivers a smooth, less irritating smoking experience due to a unique product point of difference. Mildness has always been a significantly appealing attribute among cigarette smokers, particularly females. Most importantly, however, the PALL MALL brand has historically represented a significant value to consumers because it delivers "more puffs for the money."

PALL MALL is truly an elite brand. It is one of only five brands in the entire history of the U.S. cigarette industry to become the number one best-seller. In fact, over two trillion PALL MALL cigarettes have been sold in the U.S. since 1899.

In 1907, the American Tobacco Company purchased Butler & Butler and along with it, the PALL MALL brand. After the purchase, PALL MALL began to appear with a regal British crest on its packaging and became the first cigarette to actually advertise on the back of magazines. By 1920, PALL MALL became the absolute leader in what, at that point, was the "premium" 25-cent per pack price segment. This segment contained only the finest, most distinctive cigarettes at a time in history when most cigarettes were priced at just 15 cents a pack. PALL MALL advertising consistently featured the phrase, *"A Shilling in London, A Quarter Here."*

The brand did quite well during the 1920s,

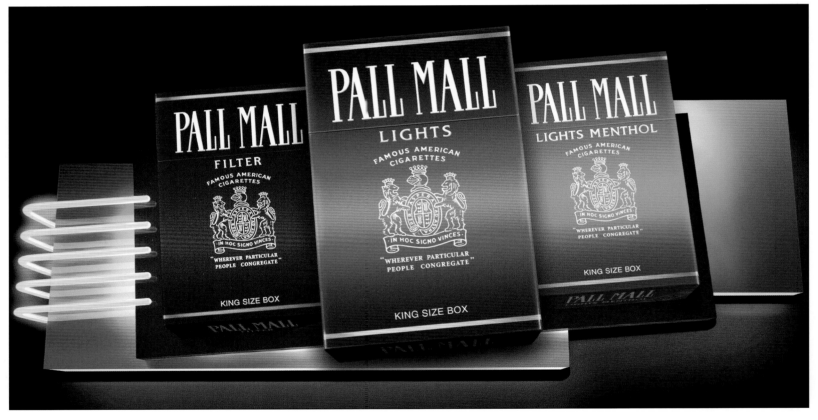

were generally considered a novelty in the New York society of the late 1800's. Not long thereafter, advances in technology would make mass production possible. PALL MALL, introduced in 1899, was one of the very first brands to be produced solely through the use of automated manufacturing. By the early 1920's, cigarettes became the largest-selling tobacco product in the U.S.

Today millions of people enjoy the custom of cigarette smoking. Tobacco remains one of the very largest contributors to the U.S. economy.

ACHIEVEMENTS

PALL MALL became a successful brand because it featured a name and package that are

HISTORY

In 1899, a small tobacco company in New York City called Butler & Butler introduced a premium brand of cigarettes with a special blend. At that time, it was felt that cigarettes with British-sounding names like Chesterfield, Parliament, and Marlboro implied higher "imported" quality and heritage. In order to give this new brand the same benefit, Butler & Butler named its new cigarette after a famous street in London— PALL MALL.

PALL MALL was one of America's first truly premium cigarette brands. It featured an all-Turkish tobacco blend and was state-of-the-art in that its manufacturing process helped to ensure uniform quality from one cigarette to the next.

but ran into trouble at the onset of the Great Depression. Obviously, this was a time when a third of Americans were out of work and every penny counted. Selling a pack of cigarettes for 25 cents had become extremely difficult. Not only were most brands priced at 15 cents a pack, but even lower-priced brands had started to appear—priced primarily at 10 cents a pack.

Between 1931 and 1936, American Tobacco's share of the U.S. cigarette market had dropped from 40.5 percent to just 22.8 percent. The company was struggling due to external economic factors, extremely aggressive competition from the industry leaders, and many of its consumers switching to lower-priced brands. Something needed to be done.

In 1936, the company decided to launch what it called the New PALL MALL. The New PALL MALL featured a completely different "modern blend" of American tobaccos. At the same time, the price of PALL MALL was reduced from 25 cents to 15 cents a pack. The New PALL MALL blend was smoother and less irritating than its predecessor was, and the packaging was changed from a box to a soft pack.

Interestingly, two Latin mottos were added to PALL MALL's packaging. The first motto read: "Ad astra per aspera" which means, "To The Stars Through Adversity." The second

sized cigarettes on the market. One of the things that certainly made this longer length relevant was PALL MALL's higher puff count. Some of the ad copy pointed to PALL MALL's modern design that actually "gentles" the smoke, making it a smoother, less irritating cigarette. By 1950, PALL MALL's share of market reached an astounding 6.2 percent.

In the mid-1950s, some dramatic changes occurred within the industry. This was the advent of what has subsequently been dubbed the Filter Derby. Winston was introduced in 1954. Marlboro was re-introduced a year later

Again, the aspect of additional value was an important part of the equation. PALL MALL could continue to rightfully boast that it delivered more puffs than any other cigarette on the market.

THE PRODUCT
The PALL MALL product has been developed to deliver smoothness, suitable strength, low irritation, pleasant aftertaste, and, above all else, a slow burn. Slow burn is the one attribute that consumers claim they are not getting from other brands — and this benefit rightfully belongs to PALL MALL, in light of its unique history.

PALL MALL burns slower than other leading brands in the cigarette industry.

RECENT DEVELOPMENTS
PALL MALL was re-launched nationally as the New Filtered PALL MALL in January, 2001. The New Filtered PALL MALL features six colorful box styles at a new, affordable price. Two older styles, Non-Filter and Gold 100's, remain on the market as well.

PROMOTION
The primary objective of PALL MALL's marketing plan is to increase consumer awareness of the brand proposition. Consumer research indicates that a significant percentage of cigarette smokers are willing to switch to PALL MALL once they are fully aware of the brand's product benefits and affordable price. The primary marketing tools employed consist of print advertising, direct mail, and in-store merchandising and promotion programs designed to increase consumer awareness of the brand, as well as inform consumers of the premium product benefits at the "not-so-premium" price.

BRAND VALUES
The brand positioning objective, how the company wants consumers to perceive the brand, is to establish PALL MALL as the premium, contemporary brand that delivers superior value due to its incomparable quality, slow burn, smooth smoke and affordable price.

PALL MALL motto read: "In hoc signo vinces", which translates to, "Under This Sign You Will Conquer." Both mottoes would prove to be prophetic.

In 1939, the head of American Tobacco, George W. Hill (whose first job in marketing years earlier was as the PALL MALL brand manager), discovered that a recently established government limit allowed for 17 percent more tobacco in cigarettes without the added burden of an increase in the federal excise tax. George Hill sought to take advantage of this opportunity by increasing the length of PALL MALL, thus providing additional value and a point-of-difference. As a result of the tobacco-content increase, PALL MALL became the world's first king-size cigarette, at 85 mm in length versus the industry standard of 70 mm. Further package modification also took place at this time. A new logo featured elongated letters, accentuating the fact that PALL MALL was now a longer cigarette. An added motto, "Wherever particular people congregate," lent an aspect of sociability to the brand.

In the 1940s, PALL MALL's advertising compared this new, longer cigarette to regular-

in 1955. These new product introductions provided the impetus for the tremendous growth of the filter segment. This dynamic also called for a change in tactics for marketing the PALL MALL brand. Television ads began to compare PALL MALL to filtered brands with such claims as "tobacco makes its own best filter," and "there's no flat, filtered-out flavor" when you smoke a PALL MALL. A final claim even boasted of the fact that "you could light either end" of the cigarette.

The brand continued to enjoy significant consumer appeal, particularly among females. As a product benefit, mildness was deemed to be a relevant claim due to the fact that PALL MALL was a longer cigarette. In 1960, PALL MALL surpassed Camel to become America's best-selling cigarette. The brand maintained this market leadership position until 1966, when the filtered segment, led by Winston, finally emerged as the industry standard.

Another first for PALL MALL occurred in 1965. At that time, the brand launched the first major 100 mm cigarette. Once again, PALL MALL emphasized additional length as the primary reason why it was a milder cigarette.

THINGS YOU DIDN'T KNOW ABOUT PALL MALL

○ The famous London street, PALL MALL, was named after a seventeenth century French croquet game called paille-maille, which used to be played on this street during the 1600s. A mallet and balls used in the game were found in 1845 and are now in the British Museum.

○ PALL MALL sponsored two TV shows—"The Tales of Wells Fargo," starring Dale Robertson, and "M Squad," starring Lee Marvin—during the late 1950s.

○ PALL MALL is now sold in over 60 countries around the world, including Germany, Russia, Italy, Indonesia, and Mexico. Once marketed by several different companies, PALL MALL is now solely owned and marketed by British American Tobacco p.l.c., which operates in 180 countries worldwide.

Panasonic®

THE MARKET

At the dawn of the digital century, Panasonic takes its place on the global stage as one of the largest and most diverse technology brands, offering a vast range of products from the world's smallest semi-conductors to the most advanced, networked systems for the home, office, and industry. Serving nearly every major market, and touching nearly every aspect of consumers' lives, the Matsushita Electric family of companies, best known worldwide as Panasonic, is poised to become the critical e-brand for the 21st century.

ACHIEVEMENTS

From the introduction of the Panasonic transistor radio in 1960 to the digitally networked systems of the new century, Panasonic has been at the forefront of technological innovation. Today, Panasonic is a world leader in digital technology, with enviable distinctions in audio/video products and systems, as well as optical disk, storage and networking technologies.

As a leading U.S. manufacturer of digital TVs and systems; the world's first digital TVs and set-top boxes, as well as the first High Definition Television (HDTV) tuner decoders were from Panasonic. Today, Panasonic engineers push the technological envelope, creating flat panel plasma and rear projection TVs with exceptional resolution, multi-task functionality and ultra-slim, ergonomic design. Behind the scenes, Panasonic also produces the optical disk products and systems that have revolutionized professional recording technology. Panasonic's DVC Pro High Definition (HD) camcorders are the platinum standard for the television, sports, news and entertainment industries, capturing the times of our lives, from major sporting events to the Millennium celebrations seen around the world. Not surprisingly, Panasonic has won more than a dozen Emmy Awards for its achievements in the broadcast and film industry. But

Panasonic's optical disk innovations aren't just for news and entertainment. They include breakthrough medical cameras so small they can fit on the tip of an endoscope, and security cameras that are so advanced they capture fast-moving images in the dark.

Seizing the digital moment, the Panasonic brand also leads the way in digital and networking storage technology. Panasonic was first with DVD recorder/players, as well as with portable DVD players, DVD audio systems, DVD-ROM and DVD-RAM drives. At the forefront of automotive electronics, the Panasonic rear seat DVD audio system is found in many of today's most popular cars and SUVs. A prime mover in networking storage technology, Panasonic's Secure Digital (SD) Memory Card, developed in conjunction with SanDisk and Toshiba, has become the essential e-accessory for a new generation. Allowing for secure Internet downloads and optimized data storage and security, it is positioned to become the universal storage medium for a wide range of portable, wireless and web-based applications.

HISTORY

Panasonic was the vision of Konosuke Matsushita, chairman of Japan's Matsushita Electric Industrial Co., Ltd., who saw the vast potential of the U.S. market. Begun in 1959 as a sales company with a three person staff, its U.S. operations went on to become a leading sales and manufacturing company with 25,000 employees, over 1,500 products, and 150 business locations throughout North America.

With a keen eye on the U.S. audio electronics market of 1960, corporate executives were quick to adopt the brand name Panasonic, meaning "wide ranging sound." Soon, Americans were twisting to Chubby Checker on Panasonic transistor radios and watching their favorite TV programs on Panasonic's popular black-and-white TVs. If Panasonic rocked in the 60s, it rolled through the 70s, developing an impressive line of entertainment, home, office and automotive electronics. Every day, Americans woke up to Panasonic's digital clock radios, used Panasonic pocket calculators, and cooked entire meals in Panasonic microwave ovens. The Panasonic brand would continue to grow, and in 1975, the company opened its expansive Secaucus, NJ headquarters.

It was in the 80s that Panasonic would come of age with the introduction of the "talking" chip, as well as CD players, camcorders, VCRs and sophisticated broadcast systems and establish itself as a key player in the consumer entertain-

ment and broadcast industry. As Panasonic entered its fourth decade in the U.S., new strategies emerged to target a power position and usher in the Digital Revolution. Key strategic alliances were formed, and R&D facilities were expanded to a network of 15 domestic research and development groups. By the end of the 90s, Panasonic would become one of America's most successful brands and an established global leader in digital and networking products.

Empowered by the legacy of founder Konosuke Matsushita "to enhance the lives of all people," Panasonic would also point the way in educational and environmental initiatives. Founded in 1984, the multi-million dollar Panasonic Foundation works with local school districts by providing valuable assistance for educational reform. Since 1989, Panasonic's Kid Witness News® program has helped children in over 200 schools across the country with its hands-on video education program. Pioneering the development of energy-saving technologies, Panasonic has also earned the U.S. government's coveted Energy Star Home Electronics Partner of the Year Award, and currently produces over 450 Energy Star labeled products, more than any other manufacturer.

THE PRODUCT

Panasonic is a developer and manufacturer of digital products and systems for nearly every customer market. Restructured in 2001 to serve these varied markets more efficiently, Panasonic's businesses are now organized into three key areas serving the consumer, systems and industry sectors.

Panasonic's Consumer Sector is home to many of Panasonic's flagship categories, including consumer entertainment products, cameras, telecommunications, home and personal care appliances. Leading the way are Panasonic's vast range of cutting-edge DVD products, hard disk recorders, plasma TVs and SD products. Panasonic's ShowStopper® hard disk recorder lets consumers control, pause and rewind live TV at the touch of a button. Designed for modern lifestyles, Panasonic's new flat panel plasma displays provide crystal clear reception, and are so thin they can even be hung on a wall.

Harnessing the power of the Internet, Panasonic has developed SD memory cards, SD audio products, as well as web-connectable wireless phones, and digital cameras and camcorders that connect to personal computers. In personal care and home appliances, Panasonic boasts the "world's fastest shavers", state-of-the-art complexion care, robotic pets and ultra-pampering electronic loungers.

Functioning as a "one stop shop", the Systems Sector coordinates product selection and purchasing to help build cost-efficient technology infrastructures for large organizations and institutions. A key systems provider to leading stadiums and sports organizations, Panasonic has brought the Olympic Games to billions of viewers worldwide since 1984, and recently outfitted San Francisco's Pacific Bell Park with a state-of-the-art giant Astrovision® screen. Panasonic also provides CCTV security systems, television and entertainment systems for luxury stadium suites and has even pioneered a revolutionary digital-based coaching system. In the area of security, Panasonic has employed the latest security technology for the Vatican, as well as several U.S. government buildings, leading hotels, and Las Vegas casinos. Panasonic also provides state-of-the-art products for the office such as the Workio™ copier. This modular document imaging system can be customized to not only copy, but fax, scan and e-mail data with the touch of a button. In the field of medicine, Panasonic paves the way for medical advances with sophisticated optical systems that are critical to today's breakthrough, non-invasive procedures.

In the Industry Sector, Panasonic companies provide many of the components and parts for several of today's brand name computers, cameras and

audio/video products. Panasonic also provides crucial micro-components, such as the new multi-functional LSI semi-conductors that allow manufacturers to literally shrink the total size of their product, while adding phenomenal multi-task efficiency.

RECENT DEVELOPMENTS

From streamlining business operations to creating advanced networking products to forging critical business alliances, Panasonic is positioning itself as a leading e-brand for customers worldwide.

Turning the digital dream house of tomorrow into tangible reality, Panasonic is currently developing home networking applications that are part of a broadband gateway system that links household appliances and utilities to the Internet, including a web-based homecare solution system that connects homebound patients with their doctors, and Bluetooth-supported wireless communications equipment.

Seizing today's challenge to develop increasingly efficient, multi-task products, Panasonic has been quick to develop an impressive network of mutually supportive business alliances. Working in partnership with SanDisk and Toshiba, Panasonic developed the new postage stamp size SD memory card that allows for secure, optimized data storage and are essential components in many Panasonic products and other brand name electronics. Marketed under the name of e-wear™, Panasonic's line of SD audio players are so slim and "wearable," they have become fashion essentials for a whole new generation. In partnership with AT&T, Panasonic has debuted two multi-network cellular phones, and in a new licensing agreement with Iridian Technologies, Inc., Panasonic will develop and manufacture Authenticam™, a security identification device using the fastest, most accurate, scalable, and stable biometric technology in the world. As the Internet gives rise to a new world economy, the Panasonic Internet Incubator will also continue to seek out and nurture lasting relationships with today's most innovative e-businesses and entrepreneurs such as the Women's Technology Cluster in San Francisco, California.

PROMOTION

If Panasonic is the "digital face" of America, the face Panasonic shows to American consumers is its advertising. Award-winning TV commercials introduced the revolutionary technologies of HDTV and DVD, and continue to celebrate the vast array of Panasonic marvels from digital

Palmcorder video cameras, to high-tech microwave ovens, to cutting-edge personal grooming shavers. Radio reinforces consistent, brand-focused print and outdoor campaigns for the newest state-of-the-art electronics like SD-based e-wear™ players; i-Palm™ digital still cameras; Shockwave® audio equipment, and plug-and-play home theatre and stereo components. In all advertising efforts, the same promise of excellence is applied equally to diverse everyday products such as laser fax machines, megahertz cordless phones, and efficient vacuum cleaners.

Supporting Panasonic's advertising is a wide artillery of other marketing tools, including Shadow Traffic radio reaching listeners daily in key markets nationwide, major sporting events and awards programs throughout the year and powerful corporate sponsorships such as the Olympic Games.

Along with exciting on-line web services, vivid signage in major stadiums and arenas across the nation, and of course, the signature NBC Astrovision® screen by Panasonic in Times Square, which has become virtually synonymous with New Year's Eve in America, Panasonic comes forward as a leader in this new age of communication. Marketing efforts will ensure that Panasonic emerges from the intensely competitive fray as the e-brand to know and to trust.

BRAND VALUES

From its introduction, Panasonic upholds the philosophy of Konosuke Matsushita to put the "Customer First". Understood in its most profound sense, it is a lifetime partnership with every customer; from idea generation to customer care to the continued development of newer, more innovative products. From components to complete, state-of-the-art systems, Panasonic strives to anticipate customers' needs and to provide the very best solutions to meet the demands of an ever-changing world. This has led to products of uncompromising quality, value and service that have come to define the Panasonic brand. The final, underlying objective is "to enhance and improve the lives of all people."

THINGS YOU DIDN'T KNOW ABOUT PANASONIC

- Grand Central Station in New York City shows off its refurbished beauty by illuminating it with Panasonic lighting.

- In 1999, 2000 and 2001 the U.S. Environmental Protection Agency named Panasonic "Partner of the Year" in recognition of the company's development of energy-saving products.

- The Panasonic Digital Concepts Center in Silicon Valley nurtures new companies and has teamed up with the Women's Technology Cluster.

- When you watch the ball drop at One Times Square on New Year's Eve the three-story-high NBC screen you see is an Astrovision® by Panasonic.

- Panasonic's rugged Toughbook® PCs are popular with U.S. government agencies to provide mobility combined with wireless capabilities.

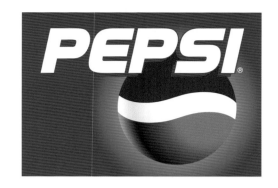

THE MARKET

Pepsi's popularity is stronger than ever. Today, nearly one out of every four soft drinks sold worldwide is a Pepsi product, totaling more than 200 million servings a day and growing.

Worldwide, consumers spend about $32 billion on Pepsi-Cola beverages. In the United States, consumers annually drink almost 55 gallons of carbonated soft drinks per capita, making soft drinks by far the country's most-consumed beverage.

In Europe, that number is closer to 12 gallons of soft drinks per person each year, but it's growing steadily as carbonated soft drinks become an increasingly important piece of the beverage industry.

ACHIEVEMENTS

Headquartered in Purchase, N.Y., Pepsi-Cola Company is the global beverage division of PepsiCo, Inc. Last year, PepsiCo achieved annual sales of more than $20 billion and was the number one contributor of sales growth and net profits to U.S. retailers.

Caleb Bradham, a pharmacist from New Bern, North Carolina, founded Pepsi at the turn of the 20th century. His soda fountain creation was an immediate hit and soon after the Pepsi-Cola Company was born.

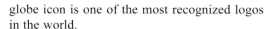

From its humble roots, Pepsi survived two bankruptcies to grow into the world's second-largest beverage company. Today, the Pepsi globe icon is one of the most recognized logos in the world.

Pepsi-Cola beverages can be found in every corner of the globe and in more than 195 countries.

HISTORY

In 1886, Bradham could not possibly have known the degree of Pepsi's future success when he developed a digestive aid made from carbonated water, sugar, vanilla and rare oils. It was sold locally as "Brad's Drink" but in 1898 Bradham renamed his refreshing, energizing beverage "Pepsi-Cola" and prepared to take it to a larger audience.

The brand fared well over the next two decades. But sugar, transportation, and other shortages of World War I forced the company into bankruptcy. New owners revived it, but the Great Depression pushed it back into bankruptcy in 1931.

At that point, Charles Guth, president of Loft Industries, a candy and soda-fountain store chain, purchased a majority stake in Pepsi and put the brand into his stores. To economize, he purchased used 12-ounce beer bottles as containers for Pepsi, which sold for 10 cents when the standard soft drink was a six-ounce size sold for a nickel. To boost sales, Guth cut his price to five cents but kept Pepsi in the 12-ounce bottles, setting the brand apart from competitors.

In 1938, Walter Mack was selected as the new president of Pepsi-Cola and soon introduced new advertising behind the 12-ounce package with the jingle, "Nickel, Nickel." The song became so popular that it was recorded in 55 languages. Renamed "Pepsi-Cola Hits the Spot," the tune was called "immortal" by LIFE magazine in 1940.

After World War II and into the 1950s, Alfred Steele presided over an extended period of growth. With the economics of the soft drink industry changing, Pepsi adopted standard pricing and a strategy of achieving a world-class, sophisticated image.

That's when Pepsi developed a distinctive "swirl" bottle and a new ad campaign, "Be Sociable, Have a Pepsi." Those initiatives launched the first Pepsi campaign to focus on young people.

The stage was set for another advertising breakthrough. The baby-boom generation was heading into the future with high optimism. Pepsi captured that spirit with a name that has stood the test of time—The Pepsi Generation.

For more than 30 years, that theme was the common thread running through much of the most popular advertising of the time. The Pepsi Generation also brought about a new offering—Diet Pepsi—in 1964. It had its own catchy ad jingle, "Girlwatchers," which hit the Top 40. Mountain Dew, a regional soft drink, was added that year and has since become one of the most popular soft drinks in the world.

As the '60s gave way to the '70s, Pepsi began to close the gap on its largest competitor with increasing success. Innovations under CEO Don Kendall included the development of the first two-liter bottle, along with lightweight plastic bottles that were lighter and stronger than glass. The company merged with Frito-Lay and moved its headquarters to Purchase, N.Y., a small suburban town north of New York City.

In the mid-'70s, the Pepsi Challenge was born. Consumer tests showed that more people preferred the taste of Pepsi over the largest brand of cola, and soon the Challenge made its way into television advertising. By 1976,

Pepsi-Cola became the single largest-selling soft drink brand in American supermarkets, and by the time the '80s dawned, Pepsi was the #1 brand in take-home sales.

Throughout the '80s and into the '90s, a long list of superstars lent their magic to Pepsi, including Michael Jackson, Tina Turner, Michael J. Fox, Ray Charles, and Cindy Crawford.

In 1998, Pepsi celebrated its 100th Anniversary and unveiled a new logo for the new millennium— a three-dimensional globe against an ice blue background which unifies the brand's graphic identification around the world.

THE PRODUCT

Pepsi-Cola's standing as a "total beverage company" is the single greatest reason for its success around the world.

Pepsi-Cola Company's brands in the United States include Pepsi, Diet Pepsi, Pepsi ONE, Mountain Dew, Sierra Mist, Slice, Mug, Wild Cherry Pepsi, Aquafina, All Sport Body Quencher and FruitWorks. The company also makes and markets ready-to-

drink iced teas and coffees, respectively, via joint ventures with Lipton and Starbucks. Major products sold internationally by Pepsi include Pepsi Max, Mirinda and Seven-Up.

What makes Pepsi so special? When that feeling of thirst hits, someone opens a Pepsi and the magic begins.

But how can the people at Pepsi be sure that every bottle and can of Pepsi-Cola is always great-tasting, sparkling and fresh? That process begins with the finest ingredients. Then, Pepsi uses the best technology available and all the care it can muster to blend those ingredients.

The process continues through Pepsi's own exacting production and quality standards and a local distribution system designed to make sure that the Pepsi opened at home is as fresh and delicious as it was when it was sealed at the plant.

Complicated? For sure. But there's no other way to be certain that the Pepsi-Cola products are the highest quality, best-value products possible.

RECENT DEVELOPMENTS

In 2000, Pepsi brought back the "Pepsi Challenge," its most compelling promotional campaign ever. The challenge is a blind, side-by-side taste test between Pepsi and its largest competitor. The Challenge takes place in hundreds of cities and towns across America in places like malls, fairs, amusements parks, beaches, ballparks and other high-traffic areas and events.

Many consumers remember when the Pepsi Challenge first grew into a national phenomenon in the mid-1970s and early 1980s. And what was true then is still true today— nationwide, more people prefer the taste of Pepsi. Those who can't make it to an actual Challenge are invited to log on to www.pepsi.com for details on how to conduct the challenge at home.

PROMOTION

Staying on the leading edge of advertising and consumer promotions is a hallmark of Pepsi-Cola Company. In fact, the company is recognized worldwide as a leader in advertising, marketing, sales and promotional support. Its advertising campaign, the "Joy of Pepsi," leverages Pepsi's key equities of humor, humanity and music and captures the passionate feelings only offered by the Pepsi experience.

First launched in 1999 as the "Joy of Cola," and since renamed the "Joy of Pepsi," the campaign was a runaway hit in USA TODAY's ongoing Ad Track survey, scoring the third-highest rating among the 50 commercial campaigns monitored by USA TODAY.

The company's most recent commercials include pop star Britney Spears singing her version of the "Joy of Pepsi" and former U.S. senator Bob Dole expressing his love for his "little blue friend," Pepsi-Cola.

BRAND VALUES

Pepsi is all about taste, choice and that feeling of optimism and youthful exuberance. These qualities come through in all Pepsi advertising, and led to the development of Pepsi's "Joy of

Cola" slogan in the states and its "Ask for More" overseas. Pepsi always has tried to be a little younger, a little hipper, and a little more relevant than its competitors. That's what has helped keep it what it is today—simple, joyful refreshment.

Pitney Bowes

THE MARKET

The information industry is the fastest-growing, most dynamic industry in the new digital economy. At its core are mission-critical business processes that enable companies to successfully create, organize, manage, disseminate and deliver information, products and services to billions of customers.

These processes—including business mail, document management, distributed print strategies, and business and financial services —are the engines that drive industry.

Pitney Bowes, a leader in designing and developing the most advanced mail, messaging, document, information and financial management solutions, has long served as a key architect at the hub of these processes.

At the turn of this century, Pitney Bowes helped businesses shift from a largely paper-based bricks-and-mortar landscape to one that now includes the rapid-paced e-commerce and digital environment of the Internet with integrated mail and document-management innovations. Whether the needs are business-to-business, business-to-consumer, or e-business, Pitney Bowes offers unparalleled end-to-end solutions.

ACHIEVEMENTS

At Pitney Bowes, achievements permeate our products and services, customer and employee relations, community involvement and corporate citizenship, and performance for our shareholders. Pitney Bowes' technologies and business applications, which are key in the new

economy, include mailing, encryption, laser printing, shipping, cellular telephones, and ticketing, to name a few.

The company is among the top 200 firms receiving U.S. patents, with more than 3,300 active patents worldwide. Pitney Bowes was cited by Killen & Associates as one of the companies in "the best position to seize electronic B2E opportunities, because it offers a multi-channel capability"—Pitney Bowes' docSense™ Digital Document Delivery platform, to create, deliver, and receive digital documents. Pitney Bowes also holds a record for awards—seven "Copier Pick of the Year" awards in one year (1997) and "Most Outstanding Copier Line of the Year" (1997 and 1998) from Buyers Laboratory Inc.

Pitney Bowes' customer relations achievements can be measured by its continuous sales growth and successful partnerships with over two million companies in more than 120 countries around the world. Customers respond with loyalty to Pitney Bowes' brand and products.

HISTORY

Founded in 1920 by the remarkable Arthur Pitney and the resourceful Walter Bowes, Pitney Bowes opened for business with a seemingly simple, yet immensely consequential idea: a better way to affix postage on a mailing envelope. They developed the world's

first U.S. Postal Department-approved postage meter, the Model M.

The tradition of innovation in mail and messaging processes has continued steadily for more than 80 years.

The company entered the new millennium as the leading messaging solutions provider, making history with attention to the customer, excellence in product and service design and development, and quick recognition of and response to changing market needs.

These are among the key developments in the Pitney Bowes success story:

April 23, 1920—The Universal Stamping Machine Company and American Postage Company merged to form the Pitney Bowes Postage Meter Company.

1922–23—First commercial installations. The government collected $4,339,070 in postage from more than 400 meters in service. Pitney Bowes began selling its products outside the U.S.

1930s—Pitney Bowes expanded the use of meters as cost-saving mail solutions for many Depression-era businesses.

1940s—The new "R" line, omni-denomination meters and mailing machines won broad acceptance. Company income topped $4 million and employees numbered 1,243.

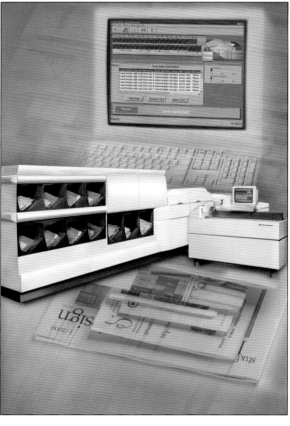

Pitney Bowes manufactured 28 different war products and received four Army/Navy "E" awards for war production excellence.

1950s and 60s—The company grew rapidly to meet the rising demand for meters, particularly the "DM" desk model C. New products included folders, Tickometers, and an electric mail opener.

1970s and 80s—Nearly 800,000 Pitney Bowes postage meters were in service; revenue exceeded $1 billion. Electronic POSTAGE By PHONE® resetting and full lines of facsimile, copier/printers and other computerized document and mail inserters, folders and related products were introduced. Pitney Bowes Management Services was created to provide outsourcing services that enable customers to focus on their core responsibilities.

1990s—The product line and services grew to meet the needs of the Information Age. Intellilink™, Pitney Bowes' state-of-the-art distributed architecture, transformed meters into

intelligent, networked terminals that communicate information between customers and postal services that enhance efficiency, build customer loyalty, grow revenue and provide convenience and cost-savings for customers. Internet messaging solutions were launched to help all market segments manage the secure production, routing, delivery, and tracking of documents. Pitney Bowes celebrated its one millionth customer in the U.S.

2000—New products and services offer electronic statement presentment and bill payment, automated incoming mail sorting systems, and software-based tools that track and manage documents and package flow.

THE PRODUCT
Today, Pitney Bowes' mail and document management and information and financial solutions are supported by more than 30,000 Pitney Bowes professionals worldwide.

The company's mission is to help customers find cost-effective solutions that support their

mission-critical activities—from managing their customer relationships and transactions, to fulfilling customer orders to managing their cash flow, costs, and productivity.

One key strategy is developing customized, direct mail that reaches the right people, gets noticed, opened, and read, and results in action. DocuMatch® Integrated Mail System, DirectNet™ Internet-based mailing and printing service, Mail Essentials™ database software, docSense™ 1:1 marketing software and AddressRight™ address systems help companies accomplish this goal.

On the transaction management front, Pitney Bowes delivers advanced solutions—both physical and electronic. docSense™ Digital Document Delivery software and services bridge Web-based electronic bill presentment and payment with electronic statement presentment communications. And, PitneyEscrow℠ services facilitate secure e-commerce growth with online escrow services that enable fast, reliable high-value Internet transactions.

Pitney Bowes' solutions for physical billing streams—like Paragon® II and DM 300™ Digital Mailing Systems—are highly effective. At the same time, our 5 Series™ Tabletop Inserting System significantly cuts the time and labor involved in collating, folding, and inserting mail pieces.

Pitney Bowes' solutions for order fulfillment include Conquest™ online logistics software and In Motion, a world-class fulfillment processing system. Both provide advanced multi-carrier shipping and transportation management that integrates data throughout the supply chain.

On the incoming side of the mail track, Pitney Bowes M3™ Mixed Mail Manager System takes in mixed mail, reads the address, locates the recipient in the employee database, and sorts the mail accordingly. Pitney Bowes Arrival® routing and tracking software expedites the receipt of accountable mail and packages. And, its Ascent™ shipping management software enables mid-sized businesses to keep every shipment "in sight" throughout the delivery process.

Pitney Bowes iSend® Online Document Delivery system reliably and securely sends and tracks messages over the Internet, while the Pitney Bowes Message Center seamlessly links the desktop document creation environment with varied distribution methods such as postal or overnight mail, fax, or secure online delivery. PitneyWorks Small Business Solutions ensures that the small and home office sectors benefit from Pitney Bowes' latest technology.

Pitney Bowes makes these products more affordable by offering a wide array of leasing, rental and credit programs.

The strength behind many of these work-enhancing products and services is Pitney Bowes' proprietary state-of-the-art encryption technology and other patented processes, the results of dedicated research that make Pitney Bowes the world leader in safe, secure Internet-based money transactions and information transmissions. As an example of Pitney Bowes' high level of dependability and reliability, Pitney Bowes' POSTAGE By PHONE® system has processed over $14 billion in postal funds in 2000 without missing a penny.

RECENT DEVELOPMENTS
Pitney Bowes is a firm believer in making great products and services even better. That's what is behind the development of new enterprise products designed to help businesses and individuals deliver their messages more efficiently and cost-effectively.

For example, ClickStamp® Enterprise, a Web-based solution for downloading and printing postage with a PC and printer, and ValueShip3™, a multi-carrier online shipping tool, both allow for multi-user environments and enterprisewide accounting and reporting. iSend® Messaging Solution, which enables secure online delivery of content, also offers secure desktop faxing.

These enterprise tools are integrated into applications and processes that businesses and individuals use on a daily basis providing a seamless, one-stop solution for their mail and messaging needs.

BRAND VALUES
Through an ever-changing technological and competitive landscape, Pitney Bowes continues to stay ahead of the curve, researching and developing innovative, real-market solutions to help its customers manage and grow their businesses.

Pitney Bowes enhances the work of over two million businesses and their customers worldwide with exceptional products, service, and support, making the Pitney Bowes brand a symbol of excellence in quality, reliability and dependability.

THINGS YOU DIDN'T KNOW ABOUT PITNEY BOWES

❍ The U.S. Postal Service derives more than $15 billion a year—61 percent of its annual metered postage revenue—from 1.4 million Pitney Bowes postage meters.

❍ Pitney Bowes' production mail machines process, fold, and insert 100 million pages of financial credit card statements a month.

❍ In facilities managed by Pitney Bowes Management Services, nearly 1.7 million copies are made every hour. That's over 28,000 every minute.

❍ If all Fortune 500 companies used Pitney Bowes StreamWeaver® software to automate and streamline the development, management, and distribution of transaction documents, they would save three million hours of MIS programming or approximately $115 million in costs.

❍ Purchase Power®—a revolving line of credit offered through the financial services group of Pitney Bowes—has helped more than 285,000 companies finance their postage costs.

❍ Pitney Bowes' cutting-edge employee contribution programs support the broad issues of education, economic development, diversity and youth initiatives, and the company promotes and financially supports employee volunteer efforts in communities around the world.

Prudential

THE MARKET

As much as the powerful forces of technology and internationalization have transformed the financial services marketplace in recent years, some things have remained the same. People still look for the same qualities in a financial services provider—financial strength and quality products and services that meet their needs. The Prudential Insurance Company of America has been the embodiment of these qualities, bringing together a wide range of financial products for people in the U.S., and increasingly, abroad.

ACHIEVEMENTS

As of Dec. 31, 1999, Prudential had more than $366 billion in assets under management and over $1 trillion of life insurance in force. The company serves millions of individual and institutional customers worldwide and offers a variety of products and services. Its many products and services include life insurance, property and casualty insurance, mutual funds, annuities, pension and retirement related services and administration, asset management, securities brokerage, real estate brokerage franchising and relocation services for companies.

HISTORY

The Prudential Insurance Company of America is the brainchild of John Fairfield Dryden, an insurance agent who saw the need to provide affordable life insurance to the working class, the largest segment of the American population in the late 19th century.

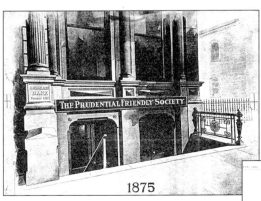

1875

It was also a time when life insurance was largely considered a luxury afforded by the wealthy—at least before Dryden. When the basement office doors to the Prudential Friendly Society opened for the first time at 812 Broad Street in downtown Newark, New Jersey, in 1875, so too did the opportunity for a greater spectrum of American society to protect their lives from financial hardship.

With the average annual income of breadwinners in 1874 just $424, Dryden's young insurance company sold "industrial" life insurance, or "insurance for the masses" in policies with a face value of $100 to $500 for a cost starting from three cents a week. These first-of-their-kind policies were tailored to the needs of laborers and their family members.

Dryden, who during his presidency at Prudential was elected to the U.S. Senate representing New Jersey, was to be a pioneer for the era. The 19th century was a time before the existence of most modern conveniences we know today. The telephone was not yet a household fixture. The most common means of transportation were the horse-drawn carriage and bicycle. The majority of individual dwellings had no electricity and were heated by nothing more than a cumbersome coal-fueled stove.

In an America where the majority of families were too poor to bury their dead, the opportunity the Prudential Friendly Society offered was an element of dignity in times of limited means. As the appeal of the Prudential Friendly Society grew, the company changed its name in 1877 to The Prudential Insurance

Prudential's first investment branch in Tokyo

Company of America and by 1885 had individual life insurance policies in force with a face value totaling more than $1 million.

By 1923, Prudential's assets reached $1 billion. Even as America struggled through the Great Depression in the 1930s, Prudential continued to grow, despite unprecedented levels of policy loans and mortgage delinquencies. It even expanded its offerings to provide major medical insurance, "sickness and accident insurance" and group credit life insurance.

Prudential arrived on Wall Street in 1981, with its purchase of Bache Halsey Stuart Shields, a well-respected brokerage firm, later named Prudential-Bache Securities and subsequently, Prudential Securities, as it is known today. The acquisition of Jennison Associates in 1985, a major stock and bond manager for pension funds, helped expand Prudential's role as an institutional money manager.

The 1987 introduction of the Prudential mutual fund family capitalized on an increasingly popular investment vehicle. Prudential continued to grow domestically with acquisitions of real estate brokerage franchising and relocation management services for companies.

Prudential's overseas expansion had already begun in the late '70s, with the formation of Sony Prudential Life Insurance Company, a joint venture with the Sony Corporation of Japan, which ended in 1987. But later that year, Prudential established Prudential of Japan, a very successful insurance business that the company has used as a model for other international insurance ventures

THE PRODUCT
In recent years, Prudential has made it easier for customers to access the products and services they need by offering an increasing number of Prudential products through third parties, as well as offering other companies' products through Prudential's distribution channels. This approach allows Prudential to offer customers

greater choice, gain greater exposure in the marketplace and strengthen the company's image as a provider of a wide range of financial services.

RECENT DEVELOPMENTS
By leveraging experience gained in ventures in the United States and beyond, Prudential continues to pursue new opportunities overseas in insurance and investment and asset management.

Prudential today continues to expand internationally through building on successful business models and developing and expanding local expertise.

For many years, Prudential has helped people achieve financial security as a mutual company. In light of changes

Midnight, New Year's 1997
Prudential comes to Times Square

occurring in the global financial services marketplace, Prudential is now considering whether conversion from a mutual insurance company to a stock insurance company would allow it to more effectively compete and provide value to its policyholders.

PROMOTION
Prudential's famous Rock of Gibraltar image first appeared in an August 20, 1896 advertisement. The Rock image has been central to Prudential's logo ever since, conveying the enduring characteristics of the

company's strength and reliability. More recently the distinct Gibraltar image shot to prominence in the U.S. in the 1970s, with the slogan, "Get a Piece of the Rock." The slogan holds its place as one of the more memorable pieces of advertising in U.S. history.

Throughout most of its 125-year history, Prudential has relied on print advertising as the primary means of communicating its important message to a mass audience. But it has also been adept at getting its message out to a broader audience, using a variety of prevailing media, be it radio or television programs, motion pictures or over the Internet.

Today, Prudential's in-house advertising agency, formed in 1996, produces ads for markets around the world, from South America to the Far East. Prudential's distinctive high-content advertising regularly appears in leading financial publications such as *Barron's* and *The Wall Street Journal*. In addition, Prudential uses a variety of advertising vehicles such as feature film brand placements, television commercials, highway billboards, Internet banners and marquee signs bearing the Prudential logo, such as the neon sign high above New York City's Times Square and a similar sign atop Tokyo's bustling Ginza district. The Prudential logo can also be found throughout suburban America, stamped on real estate "For Sale" signs in use by franchised agents.

BRAND VALUES
Prudential's distinctive Rock of Gibraltar logo and the Prudential name are among the most enduring brands in U.S. corporate history. Prudential today is recognized for the breadth of products and services it provides and continues to be a recognized company of quality financial services at home and abroad.

THINGS YOU DIDN'T KNOW ABOUT PRUDENTIAL

○ Several movies were filmed in Prudential offices, including *The Apartment* with Jack Lemmon and Shirley MacLaine in 1960 and *The Thomas Crown Affair* with Steve McQueen and Faye Dunaway in 1968.

○ Prudential once owned New York City's landmark Empire State Building.

○ When Prudential's headquarters building in Newark was razed in the late 1950s to make way for a new structure, more than 260 gargoyle statues that adorned the old building's exterior were sold to private citizens who wanted to own a piece of Prudential's history.

○ Home-run king Henry "Hank" Aaron was a Prudential agent during an off-season.

○ There is continued debate over the origins of the Prudential Rock of Gibraltar logo. According to the most popular version, a company executive traveling by train noticed a huge shelf of rock that impressed him as an object that could best convey a company's strength. The Rock of Gibraltar was later chosen as the right rock for the role.

PURINA®

THE MARKET

Pet ownership and thus, pet-product sales, are on the rise. People own pets for many reasons, primarily companionship. A recent poll shows seven of 10 consumers consider their pet part of their family. In the United States today, pet-owning households make up 61 percent of the total population. And while more households own dogs than cats, many own both.

Pet owners spend more per shopping trip and shop more frequently than non-pet owners. Every year, Americans lavish $25 billion on their pets. And dog and cat food purchases comprise 66 percent of all pet care dollars spent.

ACHIEVEMENTS

For nearly 100 years, the red-and-white checkerboard symbol has represented Ralston Purina® in the United States and around the world. A lot has changed since Purina's inception, when William H. Danforth mixed his company's first bags of mule feed by hand on the floor of a mill along the Mississippi River. Today, Purina nutrition scientists are at the forefront in identifying the unique nutritional needs of pets.

The result of nearly 75 years of pet food innovation is Ralston Purina's full line of nutritionally advanced dog and cat products as well

as one of the most well-recognized brands in the world – Purina® brand pet foods. With leading-edge approaches to business and state-of-the-art technology, Ralston Purina is an innovative leader in the pet-products industry.

HISTORY

It began in 1926, when Purina introduced Purina® Dog Chow® Checkers, the first dry dog food. In later years, Purina pioneered the extrusion process, which dramatically changed the pet food industry. Today, 85 percent of dog food is extruded and Purina® Dog Chow® is one of the most popular dry dog foods in America.

In 1962, Purina® Cat Chow® was introduced and became the leading dry cat food. One year later, Purina® Puppy Chow® was introduced and became the largest-selling puppy food. This was followed by Purina® Hi Pro and Purina® Kitten Chow® — the first dry cat food formulated to meet the unique nutritional needs of growing kittens. Later introductions include Purina® Fit & Trim®, Meow Mix®, Purina O.N.E.®, Purina Pro Plan® and Purina Cat Chow Special Care® — the first product to receive regulatory agency review to make claims regarding feline urinary tract health.

Ralston Purina is now the world's largest manufacturer of dry dog and dry and soft-moist cat foods, as well as the leading producer of cat box filler in the United States.

THE PRODUCT

Through intensive study and years of conversations with pet owners around the world, Purina has remained a leader in pet science and nutrition. With nine pet food manufacturing plants in the United States alone, Purina makes certain that Purina pet products consistently meet the highest standards of great taste, proper appearance and unsurpassed nutrition.

For more than 70 years, Purina has been dedicated to understanding the physical and emotional needs of pets. And because Purina also understands that every pet is as unique as the relationship he shares with his owner, a portfolio of Purina brands has been developed to help meet the evolving needs of pets around the world.

Introduced in 1926 as Purina Dog Chow Checkers, Purina Dog Chow has experienced steady growth over the years, remaining one of America's most popular dry dog foods. Today the Purina Dog Chow line-up consists of three products: Purina® Dog Chow® Nutritional Excellence Formula, Purina® Dog Chow® Little Bites, and Purina® Dog Chow® With Lamb & Rice. Every Purina Dog Chow Formula is formulated to help promote a

healthy immune system so every dog can reach his full potential.

Introduced in 1963, Purina Puppy Chow is the puppy food of choice for the majority of puppy owners. In fact, more puppy-owning households buy Purina Puppy Chow than any other dry puppy food. Available in three varieties, Purina Puppy Chow is made with highly digestible ingredients and a taste puppies love.

After over 25 years, Meow Mix® brand cat food is still the cat food that tastes so good cats ask for it by name. Introduced in 1974, Meow Mix is the #1 dry cat food brand in the United States. The original Meow Mix offers fun shapes and crunchy bites in a delicious blend of chicken, turkey, salmon and oceanfish flavors. And Meow Mix™ Seafood Middles combines mackerel and tuna with crunchy seafood-flavored middles.

Another highly familiar product, Purina Cat Chow, is more than just great nutrition. Cat Chow offers support to cat owners through a shared community of resources. Examples include the Purina Cat Chow "Way of Life" Tour which travels across the country providing cat lovers with free information and entertainment, and the Purina Cat Chow Mentor Panel which provides an accessible panel of feline experts offering free information and advice.

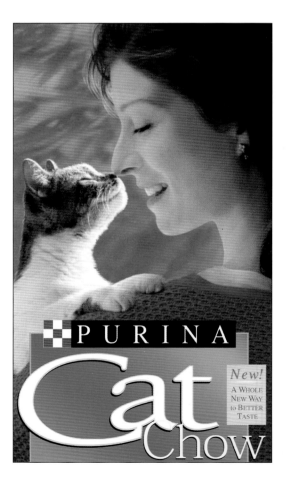

Distinguished on shelf by its brightly-colored foil packaging, Purina O.N.E. pet foods were launched in 1986. Purina's first super-premium pet food, Purina O.N.E. dog and cat foods are made with real meat, fish or poultry as a primary ingredient. Purina O.N.E. quickly became one of Purina's fastest-growing brands, with its unique foil packaging showcasing the brand's high-quality ingredients.

In 1987, Purina made its debut in pet specialty stores with Purina® Pro Plan®. Pro Plan dog and cat formulas are made with real meat, fish or poultry as primary ingredients. Pro Plan offers a wide variety of products scientifically formulated for every life stage. The nutrition in Pro Plan takes pets beyond good health – they're ready to live life to the fullest.

RECENT DEVELOPMENTS

Two of the most recent pet foods to be added to Purina's product portfolio are also two of the most innovative. Purina HA HypoAllergenic™ brand Canine Formula and Purina DM Diabetes Management™ brand Feline Formula, two of 13 products which comprise Purina Veterinary Diets™, show Purina's commitment to the health of every pet. This line of pet foods is available exclusively through veterinarians.

Purina HA HypoAllergenic Formula is a technologically advanced, patent-pending diet for dogs who suffer from food allergies. Protein is a key nutrient in dog foods, but the size and structure of the protein molecules cause allergic reactions in some dogs. In developing the HA HypoAllergenic Formula, Purina scientists incorporated modified protein, which actually changes the physical characteristics of the protein molecules so that an allergic dog's immune system will not elicit an allergic response. This technological advancement makes it possible to help manage a dog's food allergies and, in some severe cases, literally save his life.

Purina DM Diabetes Management Formula helps manage the symptoms of feline diabetes. Despite the differences between cats and dogs, the nutritional treatment for feline and canine diabetes has traditionally been the same. However, Purina scientists recognized that a cat's metabolism is unique and developed the

first and only diet which uses high-protein nutrition to effectively help manage glucose levels in diabetic cats.

PROMOTION

Innovative marketing has been a key driver of the Purina brand's impressive performance. One of the first and most successful brand marketing campaigns, launched in the 1960s, promoted Purina Dog Chow with the slogan, "Flavor so rich, nutrition so complete, all you add is love®."

Since then, Purina has benefited from some of the pet food industry's most memorable ad campaigns including Meow Mix commercials featuring Baxter the cat. Many cat owners can relate to the Meow Mix brand because of Baxter's mischievous, insistent nature. No matter if Baxter's owner is driving to work, vacationing or getting married, Baxter interrupts with a phone call reminding his owner to pick up a bag of great-tasting Meow Mix.

Today the Meow Mix brand is brought to life with the Meow Mix Mobile, a cargo van that has been customized to look like the cat depicted on Meow Mix product packaging. The Meow Mix Mobile comes complete with a tail, moving tongue and two full-time drivers who take the big cat all over the country promoting the "Give Us A Jingle" contest.

For many dog owners, "It's gotta be the Dog Chow™," a slogan which has grown in popularity as a result of television and print advertising. Ads depicting dogs performing incredible feats, thanks to the incredible nutrition in Purina Dog Chow, help increase Purina Dog Chow brand awareness, loyalty, and trial. And in a series of canine competitions showcasing incredible dogs, the Purina Dog Chow

Incredible Dog Challenge further strengthens the brand and its presence in the marketplace.

BRAND VALUES

The innovative nature inherent in the Purina brand helped make it an internationally recognized symbol. And today, the nutritional "firsts" continue with Purina pet foods. Every day Purina scientists are making breakthrough discoveries which lead to a better life for pets around the world. By creating innovative and nutritious pet foods, Purina is improving life for pets while continuing to strengthen the most well-recognized pet food brand in the world.

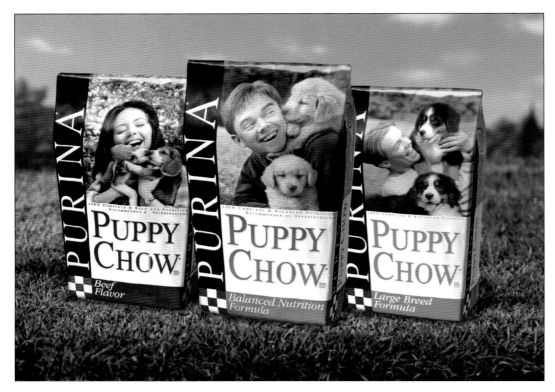

THINGS YOU DIDN'T KNOW ABOUT RALSTON PURINA

○ More breeders recommend Purina brands than any other pet food.

○ Since its inception 15 years ago, the Purina Pets for People Program has donated more than $14 million to participating humane shelters and matched more than 140,000 shelter pets with owners.

○ The Purina Pet Care Center constantly contributes new learning that leads to scientific advancements and new pet products. Most recently, the Pet Care Center contributed to the development of Secondnature® litter for dogs.

○ Purina recently created the Purina Pet Institute with the pioneering mission to improve the quality of life for all dogs and cats. Scientific innovation and enhancement of the relationship between owners and their pets are the cornerstones of the Institute.

○ Purina's Healthy Pets 21 Consortium is working to set the pet-health agenda for the next century by monitoring the most important health issues our pets are facing today.

THE
ROYAL DOULTON
COMPANY

MARKET

Pottery and ceramics are a strong indicator of the art and lifestyle of a given age. Indeed archaeologists rely on pottery fragments to establish the level of sophistication of past civilizations.

Today, consumers are more demanding and discerning than ever before.

The rise in home entertainment has been matched by the introduction of contemporary, functional tableware. At the other end of the spectrum, the decrease in traditional family meals and rise in solo eating, TV dinners and convenience foods have seen the companies extend their casual tableware ranges.

When it comes to gifts, despite many alternatives, the ceramic form is sought after as offering true qualities of heritage, traditional craftsmanship and real, long lasting value. In fact, ceramic giftware has enjoyed considerable growth—gift-giving, home decoration and investment being the main motivations.

The key markets worldwide for premium ceramic tableware and giftware are the UK and Continental Europe, North America, Asia

Doulton, the company, is a thriving global business, with around $280 million in annual sales, employing about 6,000 people across its UK production houses and numerous distribution operations worldwide. Approximately half of its sales are generated outside of the UK.

The company's Hotel and Airline division is also the world's largest supplier of bone china to the international airlines industry. Indicative of its position, the division holds major contracts with British Airways, Emirates and South African Airlines as well as other leading airlines. All three are noted for their high quality in-flight service, and Royal Doulton – aware of the need for brand differentiation – prides itself on creating

a small pottery in Lambeth, south London, in the UK.

His son, Henry, built the business, relocating it 60 years later to Stoke-on-Trent in Staffordshire, England known around the world as "The Potteries." By 1901 the quality of Doulton's tableware had caught the eye of King Edward VII, who permitted the company to prefix its name with 'Royal' and the company was awarded the Royal Warrant.

The company expanded its production facilities and by the 1930s was involved in the manufacture of figurines and giftware.

Royal Doulton was awarded the Queen's Award for Technical Achievement in 1966, for its contribution to china manufacture – the first china manufacturer to be honored with this award.

During the 1960s and 1970s Royal Doulton discarded its drainpipe production interests and acquired Minton, which had begun china production in 1793, and crystal manufacturer Webb Corbett.

In 1972, Royal Doulton was bought by conglomerate Pearson and merged with Allied English Potteries adding a number of key brands, including Royal Albert.

In 1993, Royal Doulton was demerged from its parent and became a public company listed on the London Stock Exchange.

THE PRODUCT

Each of Royal Doulton's principal brands – Royal Doulton, Minton and Royal Albert – enjoys a long association of royal patronage, and holds at least one Royal warrant. They are also trademark registered.

When drawing up new product design, Royal Doulton designers study the market, analyze consumer research and often refer to their own archives for inspiration.

The Royal Doulton Archives, located at the Sir Henry Doulton Gallery in Burslem, Stoke-on-Trent, house a variety of material dating from 1815 to the present day. The Royal Doulton Pattern Books contain over 10,000 hand-painted water-colors illustrating the talent of artists over the years. Apart from providing an invaluable historical record of decorative ceramic styles – from the exquisitely gilded and delicately hand-painted cabinet and tableware of the Victorian and Edwardian era to the bright bold angular design of 1930s Art Deco – this collection is inspirational for today's Design Studio.

Pacific and Australasia. In total the global market is estimated to be worth over $2.1 billion.

ACHIEVEMENTS

Royal Doulton plc is one of the world's leading manufacturers and distributors of premium ceramic tableware and giftware. Its illustrious brand names include Minton, Royal Albert and the core Royal Doulton brand.

With almost 200 years of heritage, Royal

uniquely distinctive ranges for each client.

In total, Royal Doulton produces around 30,000 different items across a broad range of product groups.

HISTORY

Royal Doulton has been producing ceramic items for almost 200 years. As far back as 1815 the company founder, John Doulton, began producing practical and decorative stoneware from

As well as a wide range of tableware, Royal Doulton today lists among its products an extensive giftware collection. This includes character jugs, china flowers and an array of collectable figurines and sculptures. Some of the figurines are inspired by history and literature, for example the figures of Heathcliffe and Cathy

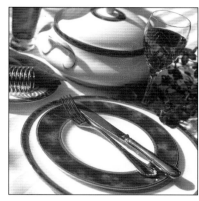

from *'Wuthering Heights'* and Shakespeare's tragic lovers Romeo and Juliet.

For junior members of the household, Royal Doulton produces nurseryware, although many of these ranges are of interest to adult collectors. The most popular collection is 'Bunnykins,' while 'Brambly Hedge' giftware and the Disney collections such as 'Winnie the Pooh' have also excited and sustained much interest.

Royal Albert, which traces its origins back to 1896, has become an internationally recognized brand, offering domestic tableware and gift items. Royal Albert's *'Old Country Roses'* is the world's best selling bone china pattern, with over 150 million pieces having been sold since its introduction in 1962.

Equally famous, with an illustrious heritage, dating back to 1793, is the Minton brand, currently best known for its popular Haddon Hall pattern, a particular favorite of the Japanese market. Minton is also renowned for its intricate gold decoration, where one plate can cost $7,000. Many of these unique works of art are purchased as heirlooms.

Royal Doulton has a manufacturing capacity of around 500,000 pieces per week. Its tableware production factories are considered among the most advanced in the world – a tribute to the research and development department based in Stoke-on-Trent. The company is noted for its high standard of working practices and technology which is heralded as being among the most developed and professional in the entire international china industry.

As the corporate ambition is to generate 50 percent of its sales outside of the UK, an extensive distribution chain is required to oversee global sales and marketing. The company currently operates in over 80 different markets with its own distribution companies in key markets – in New Jersey in the USA, and in Canada, Australia and Japan.

RECENT DEVELOPMENTS

Royal Doulton is in an important period of change in its history, currently implementing a brand master-vision as a first step in repositioning the company's brands. Clarity for the position of the Royal Doulton and Royal Albert brands within the tableware and collectables marketplace has been key to the review.

The Royal Doulton brand has been segmented into five categories – Classics, Archives, FUSiON, Studio and Café – and identities have been created for each, together with a new Royal Doulton brand logo. New global merchandising systems, in-store environments, point of sale and trade and exhibition design have all been identified as key to the repositioning.

Of course, despite significant changes in direction, Royal Doulton has continued to do what it does best – produce top quality chinaware collections. The new ranges of casual diningware are stylish, functional and user friendly, suited to all modern appliances.

The Licensing Division, created in the mid 1990s to propel the Royal Doulton brand into new product sectors, has achieved considerable success, not least the launch of 'Doulton' luxury perfume, created by Patricia Bilodeau, Senior Perfumer at Dragoco.

Other categories inspired by the company's rich heritage and design include an extensive collection of decorative fabrics and furniture sold in the USA as well as teas, textiles and ties in Japan. In the UK, licensed products include kitchen textiles, Flemish tapestries and throws, stationery, children/baby gifts and accessories.

PROMOTION

Central to Royal Doulton's promotional and marketing activity has been the re-positioning of the brand. The introduction of everything from new logos to in-store point of sale and branded fixtures has demanded that the focus of activity be centered on the communication and effective introduction of the recent significant changes.

Royal Doulton's immediate goal is to become more global, offering greater consumer relevance through a diversity of products and an extension of its offering in contemporary creations.

At grass roots, Royal Doulton continues to

employ a variety of traditional promotional techniques ranging from trade fairs, in-store promotions, and selected magazine and press advertising, backed by strong, effective public relations campaigns.

Added to this, the visitor center at the main Royal Doulton factory, in Stoke on Trent, is very popular. Open seven days a week, it features the world's largest public display of Royal Doulton figures, numbering over 1,500. Visitors can tour the factory during the week, although bookings have to be made in advance.

BRAND VALUES

Around the globe, Royal Doulton is valued for its sense of heritage and Englishness. As one of the oldest and best-recognized chinaware brands in the world, Royal Doulton has earned itself a reputation for excellence, quality and distinctiveness of design – values which it intends to build on to take the brand forward in the new millennium.

Prized by collectors the world over, Royal Doulton has an international reach extending way beyond its English roots and product. To sustain its position, Royal Doulton's emphasis for future brand growth centers on its ability to focus on people, to understand its consumer base fully and then to produce products which suit individual tastes and needs.

THINGS YOU DIDN'T KNOW ABOUT ROYAL DOULTON

❍ The largest and most expensive figure made by Royal Doulton takes more than 160 hours to hand paint and costs over $20,000.

❍ Royal Doulton was the first china to enter space. China plates were carried on the inaugural flight of the space shuttle 'Discovery' in 1984.

❍ Royal Doulton ceramics are included in a time capsule inside the base of Cleopatra's Needle on the Thames Embankment in London, UK.

THE MARKET

The Scotts Company is the world's leading supplier of consumer products for lawn and garden care, with a full-range of products for professional horticulture as well. The company owns what are by far the industry's most recognized brands. In the U.S., consumer awareness of the company's Scotts®, Miracle-Gro®, and Ortho® brands outscores the nearest competitors in their categories by several times, as does awareness of the consumer Roundup® brand which is owned by Monsanto and marketed exclusively by Scotts to consumers worldwide.

ACHIEVEMENTS

Since its founding in 1868, The Scotts Company has nurtured a reputation for quality—and for helping consumers and professionals obtain the best results possible. Studies show that consumers acknowledge the company's commitment: in a survey of discount store shoppers, Scotts and Miracle-Gro brands were rated as the top two preferred lawn and garden brands!

Scotts research has resulted in innovations such as the first lawn spreader, the first selective control for broadleaf weeds in lawns, the first crabgrass preventer, the first patented Kentucky bluegrass and many more.

HISTORY

The company known today as The Scotts Company began as O.M. Scott & Sons. Orlando McLean Scott managed a seed elevator in Marysville, Ohio, and in 1868 he purchased a hardware store and seed business. After the turn of the century, the company began to focus on grass seed and sold 5,000 pounds of Kentucky bluegrass seed to a New York real estate firm that was building one of the nation's first golf courses. Within five years, one out of every five golf courses in America was being seeded with Scotts grass seed.

In 1928, Scotts created a product that would begin an entirely new industry in the United States. Up until that time, people who wanted to improve their lawns used farm fertilizers. Then Scotts discovered a readily available nutrient source with

a high concentration of nitrogen. Turf Builder® lawn fertilizer was born.

Miracle-Gro was founded by Horace Hagedorn in 1951, along with his partner Otto Stern. Horace realized a greater opportunity existed in marketing a consumable product—rather than just selling plants and trees. Horace and Otto began shipping a small packet of water-soluble fertilizer with each plant. Customers were soon asking for more plant food. That same year, a full-page Miracle-Gro ad in a New York City newspaper produced $22,000 in cash orders, and the company was on its way to success. Today's awareness tests show an astounding 99 percent of gardeners recognize the Miracle-Gro brand. In 1999, Scotts entered the control industry through agreements with the Monsanto Company for exclusive U.S., Canada, UK, France, Germany and Australia agency and marketing rights to Monsanto's consumer Roundup herbicide products; and for the purchase of the Ortho and related lawn and garden business. The Ortho business group was established and relocated to Marysville.

More consumers use Roundup than all other weed control products combined! Roundup quickly eliminates virtually every weed—more than 125 varieties in gardens and yards.

THE PRODUCT

Miracle-Gro, and the powerful advertising behind it, has played a major role in the growth of the entire lawn and garden industry. Before Miracle-Gro was introduced in 1951, gardeners had to buy large bags of agricultural fertilizers for their plants and shrubs without knowing how much to use.

But then came Miracle-Gro, a water-soluble plant food that was easy to use and guaranteed results. Suddenly, growing beautiful plants and flowers was easy.

Scotts makes control of bugs and weeds in lawns and gardens a simple matter of product selection. Ortho's popular "B-Gon" is the perfect name for a product: it instantly tells consumers exactly what it does. If you have weeds in your yard, use Weed-B-Gon®. If bugs are the problem, there's Bug-B-Gon®. There's also Brush-B-Gon® and Flea-B-Gon®.

RECENT DEVELOPMENTS

In 1998, Scotts began research in the field of biotechnology, which could lead to commercial development of genetically transformed turfgrasses, flower and woody ornamentals.

In 2000, Scotts introduced Miracle-Gro Garden Soils®—a pre-mixed rich organic product made of manure, sphagnum and peatmoss. It quickly became a hit and one of Scotts' most successful product launches. Scotts has plans to introduce yet another new product, a line of Miracle-Gro Select Plants.

The Scotts Company has become the world's leading producer and marketer of products for consumer do-it-yourself lawn care and gardening, professional turf care and horticulture.

lishes its Problem Solver book, also available on CD-ROM.

Scotts' web site (www.scotts.com) provides one of the Internet's largest libraries of lawn and garden content. In 2000, the Scotts web sites generated more than three million visits. A recent survey of Scotts' Internet visitors found that 70 percent have "bookmarked" the Scotts site indicating that they find it helpful and plan to return to it.

BRAND VALUES

The Scotts Company's goal is to plant, protect and nurture. The company is working to secure its leadership position by continuing to produce quality, environmentally-sound products that meet the consumer's needs.

The Scotts Company believes that it is important to be involved in the community— to support community initiatives, to participate, and to give back. The Scotts Company's corporate caring program is called Give Back to Grow™ and focuses on causes such as feeding the hungry, taking abandoned lots and turning them into flower gardens, introducing children to the wonder of gardening and encouraging teenagers to consider a career in agriculture or horticulture.

It is Scotts' constant mission to strengthen its position as the world's foremost marketer of branded products and services for lawn and garden, while meeting challenging profit and return–on–investment growth goals. For more information on The Scotts Company and its individual business units, visit the Scotts web site at www.scotts.com.

Scotts is also branching out into other territories by introducing Scotts LawnService®. Roughly 15 percent of homeowners use professional lawn care services. Scotts has staked out the premium end of this market, leveraging brand power with Scotts LawnService and Miracle-Gro Tree & Shrub Care Service.

PROMOTION

Mention a brand like Scotts Turf Builder or Miracle-Gro and many people think of the extensive advertising Scotts uses to support them.

Investing money in advertising has been a major factor in the success of Scotts and Roundup brands. But the company brings much more than advertising to the equation.

A product has to deliver results. Scotts, with its "strong roots" ranging from the industry's largest research and development organization with the most advanced production technology, makes sure its products deliver these results. The scale of the company's operations and its use of patented technologies in key areas not only enables Scotts to deliver superior results, but it creates important competitive advantages in the marketplace.

In 1972, Scotts introduced the toll-free Consumer Hotline to provide homeowners with a reliable source for helpful lawn care advice. It has proven so popular that Scotts lawn consultants now receive more than 850,000 calls per year.

To further help gardeners figure out just what those weeds and bugs in their gardens are, and how to control them, the Ortho group pub-

SNICKERS

THE MARKET
SNICKERS® competes in the 80 billion dollar U.S. snack food market.

ACHIEVEMENTS
SNICKERS® has become a global brand and is available in over 35 countries around the world. According to independent research, Americans name SNICKERS® as their favorite candy brand. This preference for the brand is reflected in the fact that 45% of the U.S. population eats a SNICKERS® every month.

HISTORY
The global company that is now Mars, Incorporated, traces its origins to the kitchen of a modest home in Tacoma, Washington, where Frank C. Mars, Sr. and his wife, Ethel, began making a variety of buttercream candies in 1911. Their first candy bar product was introduced in 1923 and was called Milky Way®. The bar was an instant success and the first advertisement was "A Chocolate Malted Milk in a Candy Bar." The second offering, introduced in 1930, was even more popular. It was called SNICKERS® and sold for five cents.

From 1933 to 1935, the SNICKERS® Bar was sold in a two-piece package labeled "Double SNICKERS®" Bar, but was returned to the single format in 1936. In 1939 the slogan, "Have you tried SNICKERS® Frozen?", was introduced.

The SNICKERS® Bar went on sale in the United Kingdom as the MARATHON® Bar in 1968. The name "SNICKERS®" was not initially chosen because of the obvious similarity to the word "knickers," which refers to women's undergarments.

In 1979 the SNICKERS® FUN SIZE® Bar was introduced nationally and is the top selling candy at Halloween. It takes four months to produce enough SNICKERS® FUN SIZE® Bars to meet the demand of consumers for the Halloween season.

The introduction of the SNICKERS® Ice Cream Bar in 1989 translated the confectionery experience to ice cream by substituting vanilla ice cream for nougat. Today, the SNICKERS® Ice Cream Bar THE BIG ONE® is a top selling ice cream novelty product. In 1996 the SNICKERS® Ice Cream Cone brought America's favorite brand again to the frozen food aisle as a one-of a-kind frozen treat.

A step in the development of a global brand took place in 1990, the brand's 60th anniversary year, when the MARATHON® Bar was renamed the SNICKERS® Bar in the United Kingdom.

THE PRODUCT
The SNICKERS® Bar is made of peanut butter nougat topped with caramel and roasted peanuts and covered with milk chocolate. The nougat center is first formed into very large slabs that are cut to size after the caramel and peanuts have been added. After the centers are formed, they are coated with thick, rich, milk chocolate. The crisp-textured peanuts have an excellent flavor and keep very well. Nougat is made by whipping egg whites until they are light and frothy. Sugar syrup is then added, stabilizing the foam and creating a "frappe." This recipe results in the delicious taste of SNICKERS® Bar that has been enjoyed by Americans for over 70 years.

Consumers can select the SNICKERS® Ice Cream Bar or the SNICKERS® Ice Cream Cone. Another choice in the frozen category is SNICKERS® Ice Cream, which is produced by Dreyer's Grand Ice Cream, Inc. under a joint venture.

The SNICKERS® Brand is sold in a variety of sizes to accommodate each snacking desire—Miniatures, FUN SIZE®, Single Size, King Size and with special packaging for seasonal holidays.

RECENT DEVELOPMENTS

The newest addition to the SNICKERS® Brand is SNICKERS CRUNCHER™, which was introduced in December 2000. The SNICKERS CRUNCHER™ is a new crisped-rice version of the popular SNICKERS® Bar.

PROMOTION

In 1939 the first advertising campaign for the SNICKERS® Bar was launched on the Dr. I.Q.

campaign—"Hungry? Why Wait?" The Clio Award was given to the SNICKERS® Brand during 1997 and 1998 for the creative advertising campaign around sports celebrities, including former Buffalo Bills head coach Marv Levy.

A television advertising campaign was launched in October 2000 that was focused on the close U.S. presidential election. The ad was set in a voting booth where a young man was debating his choices. The undecided citizen

radio program. Today, the brand continues to produce memorable and award winning advertising. The SNICKERS® Brand has won many awards for its innovative advertising. The Grand Effie Award was won in 1997 for the advertising

pondered his decision while animated characters in the form of a Republican Elephant and a Democratic Donkey perched on his shoulders and argued the merits of their respective candidates. The SNICKERS® slogan—"Not Going

Anywhere For Awhile? Grab a SNICKERS"— resulted in much media attention and the commercial received national broadcast coverage for its relevance and humor.

During Super Bowl 2001, SNICKERS® ran its first interactive television commercial to support its SNICKERS CRUNCHER™ product launch. Americans were asked to vote on the pop culture phrase that they would most like to crunch. Over 10,000 Americans exercised their voting rights through the SNICKERS® website during an eight-day period in January 2001, with "What's Up" garnering the majority of the votes. The phrase became part of the commercial that aired during the 2001 Super Bowl. This was the first time that consumers had the opportunity to determine the content of a Super Bowl commercial.

The SNICKERS® Brand has taken an active role in sponsoring sporting events throughout the world. The SNICKERS® Brand has served as a sponsor of soccer's World Cup, NASCAR® Winston Cup racing and the Olympics. The brand provides the quick energy needed by sporting enthusiasts everywhere.

The brand home page, www.snickers.com, also offers assistance in using SNICKERS® and other M&M/MARS products for fund-raising projects and a consumer affairs center that provides nutritional information on SNICKERS®.

The ties that the SNICKERS® Brand has to the Olympics, World Cup Soccer, and the NASCAR® Winston Cup Circuit, as well as the current agreement with Youth Soccer, reflect the brand's commitment to athletic competition. SNICKERS® was an Official Snack Food sponsor for the 1984 Olympics in Los Angeles, a primary sponsor for a car in NASCAR® racing in 1990, and a sponsor of World Cup soccer in 1994 and 1998.

BRAND VALUES

The brand value of SNICKERS® consists of its overwhelming popularity, recognition as a top-quality product and the respect and admiration that its manufacturer, Mars, Incorporated, has gained as a world leader in the snack food category.

THINGS YOU DIDN'T KNOW ABOUT SNICKERS® BAR

❍ The SNICKERS® Candy Bar was named after a favorite horse owned by the Mars family.

❍ Introduced in 1930, SNICKERS® Bar was still offering the traditional "five-cent candy bar" as late as 1967.

❍ SNICKERS® FUN SIZE® Bars are the top-selling fun-size product for Halloween treats.

SONY®

THE MARKET

Sony Corporation is a leading manufacturer of audio, video, communications and information technology products for the consumer and professional markets. Additionally, the company's music, motion picture, television-production, game, and online businesses make Sony one of the most comprehensive entertainment companies in the world.

ACHIEVEMENTS

Today, Sony employs almost 190,000 people worldwide, with some 26,000 working in the United States. For fiscal year 2000, Sony Corporation had total sales of more than $58 billion, with the electronics segment providing more than two-thirds of the revenues.

Sony Electronics Inc. (SEL), formerly known as Sony Corporation of America, was established in 1960 to oversee Sony's sales and marketing activities in the U.S. Today, Sony's U.S. operations include research and development, design, engineering, sales, marketing, distribution, and customer service.

Sony has become not just the market leader in consumer electronics but through research and development it has made considerable inroads in the areas of professional broadcasting, mobile communications, PCs, storage and media, and now, the Internet.

Sony is a corporation with convergence at its very heart. Driven by an integrated business model, the company has positioned itself to bring new benefits to consumers by combining hardware, software, content, and services.

HISTORY

Sony founders Masaru Ibuka and Akio Morita complemented each other with a unique blend of product innovation and marketing savvy.

In 1950 in post-war Japan, Ibuka and Morita created Sony's first hardware device, a tape player/recorder called the G-TYPE recorder. Materials were so scarce that the first tapes were made of paper with hand-painted magnetic material.

Ibuka was a practical visionary who could foretell what products and technologies could be applied to everyday life. He inspired a spirit of innovation in his engineers and fostered an exciting working atmosphere and an open corporate culture.

Through Ibuka's persistence, the magnetic tape recorder evolved into the Model P (for "Portable"), which became the company's first profitable product.

When the company obtained licensing rights to the transistor from Western Electric in 1953, Ibuka urged his engineers to improve production methods with the goal of creating a transistor radio. The introduction of the TR-55, Japan's first transistor radio, in 1955 led to Sony's 1957 launch of the world's first pocket transistor radio, establishing a market leadership position for the company.

Akio Morita was a true marketing pioneer who was instrumental not only in making Sony a global brand but also in creating the name itself. With the firm establishing itself in the U.S. and other foreign markets, he suggested to Ibuka that the original name of Tokyo Tsushin Kogyo be changed to one that was easily pronounceable and recognizable. "Sony" was created by combining the Latin "sonus," the root of such words as "sound" and "sonic," and "sonny," meaning little son. The combination conveyed the reality of Sony as a very small group of young people with the energy and passion for unlimited creation.

In the video area, Sony's Trinitron® has set the world standard for high quality since its introduction in 1968.

As a proponent of global operations based on a local presence, Morita set up manufacturing plants all over the world. Its Trinitron® color television assembly plant in San Diego, Calif., built in 1972, was the first consumer electronics manufacturing facility built in the United States by a Japan-based company.

Morita's deep confidence in another legendary Sony product, the Walkman® personal stereo, was the key factor in its ultimate success. While retailers were initially resistant, the Walkman's compact size and excellent sound quality attracted consumers and, ultimately, ignited the personal audio revolution.

Kazuo Iwama was a detail-oriented person, admired for his scientific knowledge and discipline. He was made president of Sony in 1976, and became thoroughly involved in developing the "charge coupled device," or CCD, which paved the way for the camcorder and digital still camera. While he was president, Sony launched the Betamax® video cassette recorder and the compact disc player, another Sony innovation that changed the way people listened to music.

THE PRODUCT

Throughout its history, Sony has demonstrated an ability to capture peoples' imaginations and enhance their lives. The company has been at the cutting edge of technology for more than 50 years, positively impacting the way we live. Further, few companies are as well positioned to drive the digital age into homes and businesses around the world for the next 50 years and beyond.

Sony innovations have become part of mainstream culture.

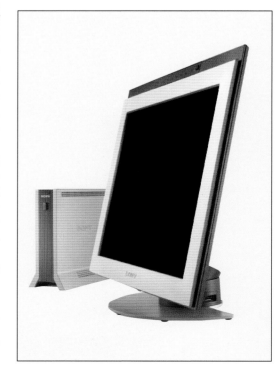

ing. During his tenure as president from 1982 to 1995, Sony was transformed from an electronics company into a total entertainment company through the establishment of the music, pictures, and gaming businesses.

Sony acquired CBS Records in 1988 and Columbia Pictures in 1989, which today are Sony Music Entertainment (SME) and Sony Pictures Entertainment (SPE), two of the world's largest content producers.

Today, Sony continues to fuel industry growth with the sales of innovative Sony products, as well as with the company's convergence strategy.

Sony's approach is to make it possible for consumers to enjoy various forms of content on both "home networks" consisting of connected electronic devices, and "mobile networks" that are accessible through mobile terminals.

Sony's vision is to give consumers easy, ubiquitous access to entertainment and information anytime, anywhere.

In the company's view, the Internet is an "e.Playground" where consumers can collect, share and manage everything from data and text information, to digital images, movie clips and music. The result: New ways to enjoy Sony products.

In the future, look for Sony to create entirely new forms of entertainment, blending movies, computer generated worlds, games and music. Sony has the vision, technology, and content to forge a direction in consumer entertainment that no other company can match.

RECENT DEVELOPMENTS

Norio Ohga was responsible for bringing Sony into the modern age and injecting it with a unique sense of style through product planning, stylish product design, and innovative market-

Through Ohga's persistence, the Sony PlayStation® game console was launched in Japan in 1994 and worldwide in 1995 in a market then dominated by Nintendo and Sega. With PlayStation and, most recently, PlayStation2, Sony has become the most successful game manufacturer ever.

Nobuyuki Idei, current chairman and CEO, played a key role in moving Sony into the digital network era by emphasizing the integration of audio-visual and information technology. He was responsible for Sony's image campaign, "Do you dream in Sony?" and helped coin the term "digital dream kids". The premise of the campaign was to provide shareholders, customers, employees, and business partners who come into contact with Sony with the opportunities to create and fulfill their dreams.

Sony has also given consumers new reasons to visit the Internet, including the recent launch of SonyStyle.com, a new information rich, e-commerce site for everything Sony.

PROMOTION

Sony, whose Walkman personal stereo changed the way the world listens to music, again set its sights on transforming the portable music landscape when it kicked off a comprehensive marketing campaign to relaunch the Walkman brand in June 2000.

Titled "The Walkman Has Landed," the marketing campaign, which included broadcast, print, and online advertising, Internet and dealer events/promotions, and grassroots consumer and public relations components, strategically communicated the lifestyle attributes of the Sony Walkman line to generation Y, its primary target market.

Additionally, the campaign brought together an entirely new product lineup comprised of CD Walkman, MD Walkman and Network Walkman personal digital audio players.

Sony promoted a new Walkman ideology based on personal freedom, independence, imagination, and creativity in a way that appealed to new techno-savvy, style-conscious consumers who favor digital downloading and ripping CDs.

The MiniDisc did not become a success in the U.S. until it was marketed as a digital music player that could record from the Internet. MD has become a Gen Y favorite and U.S. sales have increased by more than 40 percent.

BRAND VALUES

In the company's annual welcoming ceremony for new employees, Chairman of the Board Norio Ohga cites Sony's strengths in these words: "We have many marvelous assets here. The most valuable asset of all are the four letters, S, O, N, Y. Make sure the basis of your actions is increasing the value of these four letters. In other words, when you consider doing something, you must consider whether your action will increase the value of SONY, or lower its value."

Sony's brand equity is rooted in product innovations. To ensure the future of that brand, the company recently launched an extensive, company-wide initiative in the U.S. designed to foster a common understanding of the Sony

brand among employees, customers, and consumers. The project, dubbed "Being Sony," was necessitated by expansive company growth, an influx of new employees, and converging business opportunities.

The company's desire is to establish a new Sony – a customer-centric entity centered around broadband entertainment, yet driven by the venture spirit of Sony's founding days.

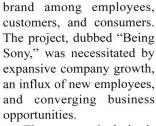

THINGS YOU DIDN'T KNOW ABOUT SONY

❍ Sony's first product was a rice cooker.

❍ Sony established its first major overseas operation in New York City (514 Broadway) in 1960 with a capital investment of $500,000.

❍ Sony became the first Japanese company in the United States to make a public offering—two million shares of common stock in the form of American Depository Receipts (ADRs) in 1961.

❍ In 1986, the name "Walkman" was included in the *Oxford English Dictionary*.

❍ Before the Walkman personal stereo became a worldwide brand name, it was introduced under a variety of names, including the Soundabout in the U.S., the Stowaway in the UK, and the Freestyle in Australia.

THE MARKET

In 2000, the telecommunications industry was a major driver for the U.S. economy with revenues of about $335 billion. By 2003, a conservative forecast puts revenues at about $449 billion. And it's not just about long-distance anymore. Internet and wireless technologies are fundamentally changing the way people and businesses communicate—and this means unprecedented opportunities for the traditional "telecommunications" companies.

Sprint's market consists of individuals, families, small business owners, Fortune 500 companies, the U.S. government—every individual and business customer that needs workable communications solutions. Today, these customers confidently throw around phrases like bandwidth, mobility and seamless integration, and they're demanding faster, better, easier results. Sprint has responded by transforming itself into a high-growth, data-driven company committed to offering total, on-demand access to communications.

ACHIEVEMENTS

Sprint's reputation for high-tech quality and customer care has made the brand a powerful leader in the telecommunications industry. Sprint views the market in terms of total access solutions - all distance, wireline and wireless, voice and data. Having built strong positions in consumer long distance, local services, wireless service, the Internet and business services with a myriad of voice, video and data capabilities,

Sprint will concentrate its resources to deliver service to the most attractive customers in key geographic and demographic markets.

Industry accolades attest to Sprint's success. Fortune's 1999 list of America's "Most Admired Companies" ranks Sprint first in the telecom category for all eight attributes of corporate reputation: innovation, quality of management, employee talent, quality of products and services, long-term investment value, financial soundness, social responsibility and use of corporate assets. Sprint was also chosen as one of the top five brands that most consistently meet consumer expectations by a Brand Keys study of 146 brands. (Brandweek, May 28, 2001).

HISTORY

Sprint began in 1899, as the Brown Telephone Company, a local carrier determined to bring the citizens of Abilene, Kansas an alternative to the phone monopoly of the day. After decades of expansion, a diversified "United Telecommunications" served more than 3.5 million local telephone lines coast to coast. In 1984, plans were announced for the first nationwide 100% digital fiber-optic network, which was completed in 1987. In 1992, United Telecom adopted the nationally recognized identity of its long distance unit, changing its name to Sprint Corporation.

Sprint won the rights to PCS wireless licenses in 29 major trading areas in 1995, and Sprint branded PCS service now covers nearly

260 million people across the United States, Puerto Rico and the U.S. Virgin Islands. In 1998 Sprint announced Sprint ION® Integrated On-Demand Network, a new telecommunications capability that can provide homes and businesses with virtually unlimited bandwidth over a single existing telephone line for simultaneous voice, video and data services.

From building the first 100% digital, fiber optic network to the development of Sprint ION®, Sprint's legacy has been built on innovations that make communicating easier for real people.

THE PRODUCT

Sprint is leveraging its existing assets by investing in growth areas such as:

Internet—Sprint operates a Tier 1 Internet backbone, carrying high volumes of traffic for many thousands of businesses, web sites and Internet Service Providers. Sprint will also deploy its Internet backbone in 35 cities in Europe and Asia. Sprint is creating data centers with several thousand sellable square feet, targeting the web hosting market. For those always on the go, Sprint PCS allows customers to browse the Internet, get news, entertainment and information and make purchases on their Internet-ready PCS phones.

Wireless—Sprint operates one of the fastest growing all-digital PCS wireless network. Sprint's wireless network technology and existing capacity make it better positioned to move to third generation (3G) high-speed data services. Beginning in 2001, third generation technology (3G) will double network capacity and increase data transmission speeds 10-fold, allowing Sprint PCS to provide higher capacity for voice and data to customers. Sprint's MMDS (Multipoint Multichannel Distribution System) fixed wireless service opens up the "wireless cable" market. Sprint's MMDS footprint will reach up to 30 million households in 90 key markets. Utilizing sophisticated technology, Sprint's broadband fixed wireless capabilities have a range of 30 miles and deliver high-speed data to homes and small businesses via a third portal.

Local Broadband—Sprint provides local service in 18 states, and has targeted DSL (Digital Subscriber Line) expansion in its local markets. By the end of 2001, Sprint will have provided last-mile network infrastructure for more than 2000 sites in 115 markets in support of Sprint ION and for Sprint FastConnect DSL®. Additionally, Sprint expects to have built out nearly 100 network element nodes for metropolitan networks in 6 markets by yearend 2001.

The technologies are cutting-edge, but they're not vaporware—shiny new products that dazzle but don't solve real-world problems.

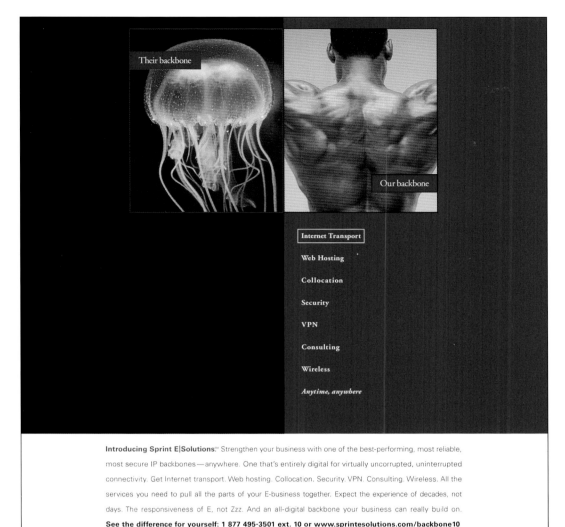

Their backbone

Our backbone

Internet Transport

Web Hosting

Collocation

Security

VPN

Consulting

Wireless

Anytime, anywhere

Introducing Sprint E|Solutions. Strengthen your business with one of the best-performing, most reliable, most secure IP backbones—anywhere. One that's entirely digital for virtually uncorrupted, uninterrupted connectivity. Get Internet transport. Web hosting. Collocation. Security. VPN. Consulting. Wireless. All the services you need to pull all the parts of your E-business together. Expect the experience of decades, not days. The responsiveness of E, not Zzz. And an all-digital backbone your business can really build on.

See the difference for yourself: 1 877 495-3501 ext. 10 or www.sprintesolutions.com/backbone10

Sprint.

Sprint E|Solutions

Sprint products and services are built to provide complete, integrated solutions. This commitment to total solutions extends to the way Sprint products and services are packaged. Customers prefer bundling their communications services, so Sprint offers packages of local service, network features, long distance, local broadband and wireless. In the near future, Sprint will be able to offer customers a single voicemail account for their standard and wireless phones and a single e-mail account for all access points.

Sprint's premier integrated offering is Sprint ION Integrated On-Demand Network, a service that enables customers to use the Internet at speeds up to 100 times faster than today's modems, while using their phones and fax lines at the same time. It's a way of "networking" the home or business that's never before been possible.

RECENT DEVELOPMENTS

The demand for broadband services is virtually insatiable. Sprint expects fiber to remain the main conduit for serving large and medium business customers. However, looking three to five years down the road, consumers and small businesses will increasingly get broadband services via wireless, mainly because of the inherent cost advantages and convenience. Sprint's multiple platforms for broadband delivery—including traditional "wireline" networks, the MMDS network, and the PCS network with 3G—allow Sprint to offer broadband and high-speed data services directly to customers in the way that best works for them.

PROMOTION

Sprint's famous pin drop broadcast advertising is just part of the picture. Extensive print advertising, a growing retail presence, and a strong sponsorship program round out Sprint's promotional strategy.

Sprint's aggressive sponsorship strategy has brought it together with some of the top sports

properties in the nation—Petty Enterprises, the US Ski Team, American Skiing Company (ASC), Vail Resorts, and PGA of America. By choosing events and sponsorships that can be leveraged to bring the Sprint brand to selected growth markets, Sprint advances and reinforces its business and marketing objectives. Partnerships are also a key part of Sprint's retail approach, bringing the Sprint Brand inside RadioShack, Best Buy, Circuit City and Staples stores.

BRAND VALUES

According to the New York Times (Oct. 5, 1999) "One reason the Sprint corporate identity is perceived as so strong is because the brand's variegated advertising and marketing campaigns have resonated deeply with the consumers. The image perhaps most familiar is the 'pin drop,' initially included in commercials to convey that a Sprint long distance call was quiet and thus high-quality."

Sprint has always been different—not a faceless corporate bureaucracy, but an independent-minded, slightly irreverent company that talks to its customers in plain English. The now-famous Sprint pin drop, introduced in 1986, represents more than just a clear connection. It signifies a commitment to making the whole world of communications clear, simple and accessible to real people—every day.

THINGS YOU DIDN'T KNOW ABOUT SPRINT

❍ It has nothing to do with the 100-yard dash…

The Sprint name was actually created in 1978 by the Southern Pacific Communications Company, which created a service called, "Switched PRIvate Network Telecommunications," or Sprint, which was later acquired by GTE. In 1984, United Telecom and its U.S. Telecom long distance unit formed a 50/50 partnership with GTE and its GTE Sprint unit to form US Sprint. United Telecom purchased an additional 30.1 percent of U.S. Sprint in 1986, gaining control of the company, and bought the remaining share in 1990. Shortly after the acquisition, the parent company changed its name from United Telecom to Sprint Corporation, a first step toward enabling all the company's business units to benefit from the widely recognized Sprint brand.

❍ Waterfalls at work?

Sprint marked the beginning of a new era on October 1, 1999, when it dedicated its new World Headquarters in Overland Park, Kansas, the largest building project in the history of the Midwest (6,532,351 bricks will be needed to complete the 22 buildings on the 200 acre campus). Sixty percent of the grounds are dedicated to "green space"—featuring 4,000 trees, a 7-acre lake, two outdoor athletic fields, and yes, waterfalls. The gradual transition of more than 14,500 employees to the Sprint Campus will continue through 2002.

THE MARKET

Sprite is America's and the world's most popular lemon-lime soft drink and the third best-selling carbonated soft drink after Coca-Cola and Pepsi.

Sprite has been one of the fastest-growing carbonated soft drinks in the world for some years now. Other top markets for the beverage outside the U.S. include such diverse countries as China, Mexico, the Philippines, and Germany. The brand clearly has outstanding appeal to claim this kind of popularity in very different environments, and this indicates a highly successful future for it.

ACHIEVEMENTS

Sprite is the second-best selling soft drink of The Coca-Cola Company. It was the third brand to be introduced by the company.

In 1994, the brand made the leap from competing with other lemon-lime sodas to the soft drink mainstream after interviews with Sprite drinkers gave the brand's promotional style a new direction. Interviewers learned that drinkers liked Sprite not only for its lemon-lime flavor but also for its irreverent, unconventional attitude. The new Sprite slogan became, "Follow your instincts. Obey your thirst." and this, along with the relationship with the National Basketball Association, made it the fastest-growing brand of the day.

As a result of the repositioning, Sprite took the lead in the non-cola segment of the soft-drink market in the same year, incidentally also passing the one billion unit case mark worldwide, and it has not relinquished it since. Sprite is now sold in 188 countries worldwide.

HISTORY

There can't be many brands in the world where the name and the mascot pre-date the product itself by far. Sprite is such a brand. The name "Sprite" actually originated through the charac-

ter of the "Sprite Boy," an elfin imp drawn by Haddon Sundblom that symbolized the life and sparkle of Coca-Cola and helped to convey the message that "Coke" means "Coca-Cola" and nothing else.

The first advertisement featuring the silver-haired Sprite Boy appeared in 1942, and he was used in magazine advertising and on signs, posters, cartons, clocks, napkins, and even toys. The Sprite Boy continued to be used until the late 1950s, around the time that The Coca-Cola Company began developing a light, tart, carbonated drink to compete with other non-cola products. Once the drink had been formulated, it was natural to choose the short, sharp, and memorable sound of "Sprite," and the name was bestowed on the new brand that

would eventually become one of the world's leading soft drinks.

Once the Company purchased rights to the name, test marketing of the product began in August, 1960, in seven-ounce and 12-ounce bottles in Lansing, Michigan, and Sandusky, Ohio. The test marketing was a success, and in 1961 U.S. consumers were invited to taste the tingling tartness of this new soft drink called Sprite.

The lemon-lime beverage was introduced by the Fanta Beverage Company, then a division of The Coca-Cola Company. Up to that time, the only brands offered had been Coca-Cola itself and Fanta, an orange-flavored drink. Sprite was made available to all bottlers in 1961 in four bottle sizes ranging to 16 ounces, and in cans.

By October of the first sales year, Sprite was being produced by 214 bottlers and available in 40 states.

THE PRODUCT

Sprite is a tart, light, carbonated lemon-lime soft drink. The Sprite bottle design, bright green with refreshing bubbles decorating its surface,

Here's **Sprite**

Taste its Tingling Tartness!

... FROM THE SAME COMPANY THAT BOTTLES COCA-COLA

is still considered one of the most distinctive in the soft-drink industry.

RECENT DEVELOPMENTS

Helping Sprite's popularity with teens is a ground-breaking Internet promotion launched in late 2000. Sprite has joined forces with RocketCash, a leading online gateway featuring more than 100 e-tailers, to create Sprite.com, a portal dedicated to enabling teens to shop online and buy what they want without a credit card.

Teens are able to collect and redeem RocketCash codes found under the caps of 20-ounce, one liter and 500 milliliter bottles of Sprite. The codes represent the online currency that enables them to make purchases at Sprite.com. The brand is distributing more than a billion Sprite bottles marked with the special codes, or with an instant-win message for a free Sprite.

PROMOTION

The first ad campaign for Sprite was geared to the slogan, "Taste Its Tingling Tartness", but after a ground-breaking re-launch in 1994 the brand's marketing has switched to a more youth-oriented approach.

The current Sprite advertising campaign, which is based on the slogan, "Obey Your Thirst," employs a globally relevant concept that has a dual meaning, youth relevance, and a message that speaks to the core essence of what Sprite and young people are all about. It encourages teenagers to be self-reliant and to drink what tastes good when they are thirsty.

The ads use a straightforward approach, often incorporating irreverent humor, to reinforce the Sprite brand personality and encourage teenagers to trust their instincts.

The Sprite name is also kept highly visible in the United States through its role as the official soft drink of the National Basketball Association and the brand's association with snowboarding and skateboarding. The brand is also linked with Hip Hop music and its culture.

Similarly, the Sprite "Trust Your Instincts" campaign highlights moments of creativity in the player's game and encourages teens to express their individual styles. NBA stars like Kobe Bryant of the Los Angeles Lakers and Grant Hill of the Detroit Pistons have been featured in Sprite advertising and promotions.

The essence of both snowboarding and skateboarding also closely fits the Sprite brand architecture. Each of those activities requires participants to trust their instincts, be true to themselves, have such qualities as self-confidence, individualism, freedom, a personal style, and an ability to express themselves.

BRAND VALUES

While Sprite has seen outstanding success as a brand among a diverse range of age groups and ethnicities, it has found its place primarily among teens. What makes it stand out for teenagers is only partly the taste; the brand's attitude, its irreverence and unconventionality have turned out to be equally distinguishing for

the brand. Sprite's latest packaging reinforces this attitude with bold green and blue design highlighted by silver bubbles.

THINGS YOU DIDN'T KNOW ABOUT SPRITE

❍ The Sprite Boy, the character that embodies the soft drink, has strong links with two other brand names, Coca-Cola and Coke. His original mission was to introduce the name "Coke" as synonymous with "Coca-Cola."

❍ The Sprite Boy was drawn by Haddon Sundblom, the man who also created the modern image of Santa Claus for The Coca-Cola Company.

❍ There are 450 different soft drinks available on the U.S. market; Sprite is the third-best seller, and the best selling non-cola drink.

❍ Diet Sprite has been advertised by model Paulina Porizkova.

❍ It is interesting that Sprite has found its followers in the ranks of teenagers, considering that back in 1965, Sprite was promoted with the slogan, "Naturally tart for adult tastes."

❍ Market research has indicated that its drinkers like Sprite primarily for its irreverent, unconventional attitude. The taste comes second!

THE MARKET

Whose life has not been touched in some way by a product bearing the Stanley® name? From the hammer housed in your toolbox, to the hinges used on your microwave, to the level and plane employed to make your kitchen table, to the tools that assembled your car, to the automatic doors that you walk through at the grocery store, to the mirror doors you see as you enter many hotels... Stanley touches more people on a daily basis than can ever be imagined.

The name Stanley is synonymous with quality and reliability. Stanley is a worldwide producer of over 50,000 tool, hardware, and door products for professional, industrial and consumer use. The company is known globally and receives nearly 20 percent of its revenue from Europe, where the Stanley brand is stronger than anywhere else in the world.

ACHIEVEMENTS

As one of the oldest tool manufacturers in America, Stanley believes in the power of a strong brand.

Since the brand was introduced over 155 years ago, Stanley ingenuity and excellence have led to numerous firsts, from patents for new products, to design improvements on existing products, to what may have been the first patent issued for ergonomic tools in the industry. Stanley's solid heritage has not only gained the loyalty and trust of consumers but it has also won the praise of many industry leaders for advertising creativity and the innovation and design of its products.

From engineering research to design excellence to new product innovation, Stanley has received awards and recognition across all of its product categories for its distinctive and quality items. Add to this one of the greatest awards of all— the fact that antique Stanley tools have become valuable collectors' items. That recognition is a testament to both the superior quality of the products and the long, impressive history of the company.

HISTORY

In 1843, an enterprising businessman named Frederick Trent Stanley established a little shop in New Britain, Connecticut to manufacture door bolts and other hardware made from wrought iron. Stanley's Bolt Manufactory was only one of dozens of small foundries and other backyard industries in a town struggling to succeed by producing metal products.

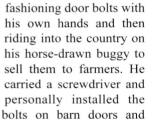

While the manufacturing shop epitomized the storied Yankee virtues of enterprise and craftsmanship, Stanley also possessed a special innovative spirit and an uncommon passion for doing things right. Although he employed a few skilled craftsmen, Stanley often made the products himself, fashioning door bolts with his own hands and then riding into the country on his horse-drawn buggy to sell them to farmers. He carried a screwdriver and personally installed the bolts on barn doors and farmhouses, thereby establishing customer service as a company hallmark.

In less than ten years after starting his small bolt business, Stanley had built a strong reputation for quality and received sufficient product demand to warrant the opening of a second shop to make hinges and other hardware. He joined with his brother and five other investors to incorporate The Stanley Works with a workforce of 19 men.

The Stanley Works flourished under the leadership of several great presidents, and a diverse group of products were produced under the Stanley name. With the acquisition of the Stanley Rule & Level Company, another New Britain-based business which had been cofounded by a distant cousin of Frederick T. Stanley, The Stanley Works boasted a broad line of rules, levels, and planes, as well as hammers, carpenter squares and other hand tools.

Emerging new American markets allowed for new territory for Stanley's products. Capitalizing on the advent of the automobile age, Stanley introduced hardware sets for home garage doors in 1914. To counter the Great Depression, which practically paralyzed the building industry, the company created new markets with products such as portable electric tools and the "Magic Door®", which, to the astonishment and convenience of those who passed through it, opened automatically in response to a signal from its photoelectric cell.

Today, over 155 years after the founding of the company, The Stanley Works continues to be an innovative developer, manufacturer and marketer of tools, hardware and specialty hardware products for home improvement, consumer, industrial and professional use. The Company still bears not only Frederick Stanley's name but also the spirit and passion that drove him to succeed in a business where others had not.

THE PRODUCT

The Stanley Works provides a comprehensive line of world-class, professional-grade, industry-specific products. These products fall into eight product groups, which are in turn housed under two business segments: Tools and Doors.

The Tools segment includes carpenters, mechanics, pneumatic and hydraulic tools as well as tool sets. The Doors segment includes commercial and residential doors, both automatic and manual, as well as closet doors and systems, home décor and door and consumer hardware.

RECENT DEVELOPMENTS

A "great brand" is a brand that shows performance improvement year after year and is built through consistent excellence in products, people, customer service and financial returns.

Stanley's brand vision and strategy is comprised of three elements: Growth, Positioning and Competitiveness.

GROWTH—Stanley's commitment to continuous innovation has created a steady stream of new products and business opportunities worldwide. Innovative new products have been developed to make the professional's job easier and more productive, and a push into new or previously untapped market segments has created additional needs and demand for Stanley products, both old and new.

POSITIONING—Stanley has realized that the key to winning a strong retail position is to merchandise stores effectively with innovative products. Targeting the professional user, they complemented this strategy by repositioning the brand with one look and feel, which was achieved through consistency of both colors and packaging.

COMPETITIVENESS—Stanley believes that the key enablers of growth are competitiveness and exceptional customer service, both of which depend upon simplicity, standardization and systemization.

In 1997 and 1998, the company began the introduction of electronic technology to Stanley tools: the IntelliTools® product line is comprised of 18 models of electronic sensors, laser levels and electronic measuring tools, offering a technically advanced array of electronic builder's tools.

The recent introduction of the FatMax™ product line included the FatMax™ tape rule, which features a standout of 11 feet, the longest standout in the industry, and has gathered praise and press coverage for its original design.

Continuously diversifying, Stanley also created AccuScape® Garden Tools, a line of over 60 products designed for both the landscape professional and the avid home gardener, from shear and hand pruners to hedge clippers and loppers.

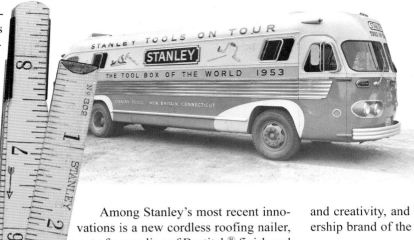

Among Stanley's most recent innovations is a new cordless roofing nailer, part of a new line of Bostitch® finish and framing nailers.

More than 300 new products have been introduced over the past three years, and 36 licensing agreements have been signed for products adjacent to the current lines, such as work gloves and power tool accessories. Appropriately representing this exciting period of new product innovation, Stanley unveiled a bold new brand campaign and the tagline: "Stanley. Make Something Great.", defining the end result from using Stanley products.

PROMOTION

The slogan "Stanley. Make Something Great." also defines what Stanley does all over the world. One of the world's most trusted names, Stanley's commitment to its customers goes well beyond providing a wide range of products: through continuous product innovation and strong product support, the company encourages and enables every professional to do his or her very best on every job.

Stanley's commitment to people is expressed in its long-time support of Habitat for Humanity. Stanley volunteers have helped to build thousands of homes for the needy. The company has also sponsored the TeamBuild® Competition at the SkillsUSA Championships, an event that teaches students the importance of team-building skills in business and tests their technical skills in the masonry, carpentry, electrical and plumbing trades.

BRAND VALUES

Stanley's strength lies in its heritage of quality, innovation, knowledge and integrity. The world-class brands that Stanley has built have been designed for professionals and for those who think like professionals. Stanley's brand vision is to inspire and motivate consumers to fully realize their skills, vision and creativity, and by doing so, to be the leadership brand of the hard-goods industry.

THINGS YOU DIDN'T KNOW ABOUT STANLEY

- ❍ Stanley® Hardware is used in some of the most prestigious buildings in the world, including the White House, the Empire State Building, Buckingham Palace, Windsor Castle, and the Petronas Towers in Malaysia, the tallest building in the world.

- ❍ Stanley® Air Tools are used to build nearly every car and truck made in North America.

- ❍ Stanley® tools have been used to build nearly every home, school, church and hospital in America.

- ❍ The U.S. government is using Stanley® Hydraulic Tools to demolish the nation's MinuteMan III nuclear silos.

- ❍ Eight out of 10 wood manufacturing plants use Stanley® Bostitch® Pneumatic Tools.

- ❍ Millions of people worldwide pass through Stanley® Automatic Doors every day.

- ❍ Stanley® is a leader in residential Steel Entry Doors sold through retail outlets.

- ❍ Stanley® Jensen® is the leading tool supplier to electronics technicians.

Sunkist

THE MARKET

Sunkist Growers, Inc. is a major sales contributor to the U.S. retail grocery industry, a marketplace with annual sales of $472 billion. Fresh produce typically contributes $40 billion in total sales, and fresh oranges are among the top six fresh fruits sold in America. As testament to the power of the Sunkist brand, nearly two percent of all fresh produce sold in the U.S. is Sunkist branded citrus. Which makes Sunkist a key driver for grocery retailers, because the fresh produce department delivers the highest percentage of profit contribution to the store, and is the second highest contributor to weekly sales totals.

The domestic grocery retail landscape is rapidly changing, as traditional grocery retail sales channels are being challenged by national discount chains which have added groceries, including fresh produce and perishables, to their product offerings. Having strategically built the only national brand of fresh citrus, Sunkist is poised to continue to be an essential sales contributor in this growing, brand-centric arena of discount store grocery retailing, while retaining its stronghold in traditional grocery channels.

Beyond American shores, Sunkist enjoys the position of the world leader in fresh citrus, with roughly one third of annual Sunkist crop production being sold into overseas markets.

Another factor that helps sustain Sunkist brand recognition is a well-established trademark licensing program, which keeps the Sunkist name constantly on display around the world on package goods in a wide variety of categories, including fruit juices, fruit drinks, carbonated beverages, jellies, jams and marmalades, healthful snacks, confections, and vitamins. Sales of Sunkist's licensed products in the U.S. and abroad total more than a billion dollars a year.

ACHIEVEMENTS

Sunkist oranges were the first perishable food products ever advertised. In 1907, Sunkist Growers, then known as the Southern California Fruit Exchange, asked its advertising agency to develop a major advertising campaign. The next year, Lord & Thomas launched a $7,000 advertising effort in Iowa. These ads were so effective that orange sales increased by 50 percent.

Convinced that its advertising worked, the Exchange increased its advertising budget to $25,000. Lord & Thomas proposed using the name "Sunkissed" in the ads and that name was quickly shortened to "Sunkist."

In April 1908, the board adopted the word "Sunkist" as its trademark for its highest quality oranges. And in February 1952, the California Fruit Growers Exchange officially changed its name to Sunkist Growers, Inc. to more closely associate itself with the brand name that had become so famous.

For the past 94 years, Sunkist has worked closely with its advertising agency, now known as FCB Worldwide. This makes their client/agency partnership the second longest lasting in the business of advertising.

Sunkist Growers, Inc., remains one of the most successful fresh produce marketing co-op organizations in the U.S., with over 6,500 grower-members committed to sustaining the consistent product quality that the Sunkist brand has come to represent here and around the world.

HISTORY

During the 1840s, thousands of prospectors rushed to California in search of gold. Many fell victim to scurvy. But soon word spread that eating citrus could prevent the disease. Demand skyrocketed, and lemons sold for as much as a dollar a piece. From this humble beginning sprang California's citrus industry.

Although early farmers found Southern California's climate favorable for growing citrus, it wasn't until the completion of the transcontinental railroad in the 1870s that they had a way to deliver their bountiful crops to consumers back east.

But agents shipped fruit with no knowledge of demand or supply in local markets. They handled citrus on consignment. Payment was made only if there was a sale. The growers bore full financial responsibility for the fruit. The next few years were difficult, and many growers faced financial ruin.

Growers throughout Southern California began to band together to market their fruit for themselves. In 1893, some 100 prominent orange growers met in Los Angeles to discuss formation of a general cooperative, organized by and for the growers. Within a few months, the Southern California

No One Can Resist A Sunkist® Orange.

Fruit Exchange, now known as Sunkist Growers, was born.

One of the first issues tackled by the Exchange was quality control, and both growers and their packinghouses were required to meet the highest grading standards for their fruit. During its first season, the Exchange shipped six million cartons of the state's seven million total cartons at a net price of about $1 per box—an estimated 75 cents more than the growers would have received selling on their own.

Over the years, Sunkist has met its share of challenges, not the least of which is Mother Nature herself. Sunkist has helped its grower-members prosper amid crop freezes, political battles, and market swings, and will continue to support its growers by aggressively pursuing new opportunities in the ever-expanding global marketplace.

THE PRODUCT

Consumers know from experience that they can depend on the quality of fresh citrus that bears the Sunkist name. In an agricultural industry, maintaining consistent quality is no small feat. Citrus crops are always at the mercy of the sun, the rain, and countless other uncontrollable variables. For Sunkist's grower-members, quality control is therefore a matter of sorting crops according to written regulations. Inspectors make daily visits to the packinghouses to ensure that the rules are followed. This system of self-policing is one of the strongest elements in Sunkist's success. And it has helped develop enviably strong consumer confidence and brand preference.

With favorable weather and conditions, a single year can bring in over 90 million cartons

of citrus and a billion dollars in revenue. Sunkist's grower-members produce navel oranges, lemons, valencia oranges, grapefruit, and tangerines, and other exotic varieties, such as minneola tangelos and blood oranges.

RECENT DEVELOPMENTS

The biggest opportunities and challenges for Sunkist currently lie in international trade. Market barriers are falling. Quotas are being phased out. Tariffs are being reduced. And foreign economies are becoming more stable. It's an exciting time for Sunkist, but it brings new challenges as well. Global production is rapidly increasing, and that increase in volume is looking for a home. Now more than ever, Sunkist must maintain its position as the category leader in domestic and foreign markets.

Sunkist is strongly positioned to prosper in the global marketplace, having created a Strategic Planning Committee and a special Global Task Force, to formulate action plans to speed success in the shifting marketplace abroad while defending the Sunkist market position domestically.

PROMOTION

From the beginning, Sunkist has made history with its innovative promotional programs.

The highly collectible Sunkist crate labels are an early example of the effectiveness of branding through point-of-sale efforts. Today, packaging and in-store materials remain an important part of Sunkist's marketing program, along with sampling and consumer promotions.

Sunkist has also worked to increase demand through extensive public relations activities and

advertising. Its efforts introduced serving ideas that are almost universal today. Sunkist was first to promote the idea of drinking orange juice. The board also popularized the idea of serving a wedge of lemon with fish and seafood, adding a slice of lemon to water glasses, and garnishing restaurant plates with an orange slice.

Sunkist also has a long tradition of leadership in nutritional education. It was the first national advertiser to discuss the value of Vitamin C. And many early Sunkist ads emphasized the importance of ensuring that children receive proper nutrition. Today, advertising efforts include print advertising targeted to trade and consumers, as well as a television advertising campaign. In a recent television commercial entitled "Classroom," a young boy is unable to resist the scent and flavor of the Sunkist orange in his lunch bag. He quietly shares it with classmates, but the tantalizing aroma gives him away. The teacher discovers the culprit, but rather than scolding her student she smiles, revealing an orange slice in her mouth.

BRAND VALUES

Consumers have come to trust that an orange bearing the Sunkist name will be sweet, juicy and delicious. For years, Sunkist's tagline boldly promised "You have our word on it." As the brand evolved, the emphasis moved to the incredible pleasure of the eating experience, as reflected in the more recent tagline, "Can't resist a Sunkist orange."

Also key to the Sunkist brand is the amazing nutritional value of fresh citrus, which is as relevant today as it was over 100 years ago.

THINGS YOU DIDN'T KNOW ABOUT SUNKIST

○ Sunkist Growers, Inc. is the oldest agricultural marketing cooperative in the world.

○ Riverside, California, is home to an orange tree that's 128 years old. Most of the millions of navel orange trees in California can be traced directly to this tree or two sister trees that were planted at the same time.

○ In 1908, Sunkist oranges became the first perishable food product ever advertised.

○ Sunkist once offered silverware in exchange for the tissues that wrapped their fruit. The promotion was so popular that the cooperative became the largest purchaser of flatware in the world.

○ Japan is Sunkist's largest export market.

○ In 1998, Sunkist sold over 90 million cartons of citrus and brought in over a billion dollars in revenue.

THE MARKET

Pepper sauces are hot, and not just to the taste buds. As the popularity of flavor-packed cuisines from Mexico, Thailand, Indonesia, the Caribbean, and, of course, from America's Louisiana bayou country, has spread across the nation, so has the demand for pepper sauces. Americans are looking for ways to heighten the flavor in all of their meals—from early morning scrambled eggs to late night sushi. The appetite for spicy, well-seasoned food is greater than ever.

Today, pepper sauce is in over half of all U.S. households, according to a 1999 study by McIlhenny Company, maker of world-famous Tabasco® brand pepper sauce. Tabasco sauce is a favorite brand of pepper sauce users, who splash it on their favorite foods both at home, and when eating out.

Tabasco sauce has the highest awareness of any pepper sauce and is used by hot sauce aficionados nationwide. Primary reasons are for its piquant flavor, level of heat and premium brand status.

ACHIEVEMENTS

Louisiana's best-known product and a staple in American cuisine for over 130 years, Tabasco sauce is selling better than ever. As the hot sauce industry continues to grow, Tabasco remains the market leader and standard for this condiment category.

Now labeled in 20 languages and marketed in over 100 countries and territories, Tabasco sauce is known and loved throughout the world.

International sales have climbed in the last five years, fueled by increased worldwide consumption of bold and flavorful foods and new distribution in Eastern Europe.

Next to the U.S., Japan is the second largest market for Tabasco sauce. Seventy percent of total consumption of Tabasco sauce in Japan takes place at the food-service level, primarily on pizza and pasta. Other leading international markets include Canada, Germany, Hong Kong, England, Mexico, and France.

Now Tabasco sauce has established a truly global presence. The familiar red bottle can be bought almost anywhere in the world, from Belgium to Thailand, and Israel to Australia. It was even airlifted by NASA to *Skylab* when astronauts complained about their bland rations and is presently being used on the International Space Station.

HISTORY

Tabasco sauce was created in the mid- to late 1860s by Edmund McIlhenny, a New Orleans banker and gourmet who, after fleeing Union attacks, returned to Avery Island in south Louisiana at the close of the Civil War.

Realizing that his banking business was ruined, McIlhenny sought work in New Orleans. There he was given seeds of Capsicum frutescens peppers from Mexico or Central America that he then took back to Avery Island and planted. He created a pepper sauce to relieve the monotony of the post-war food of the Reconstruction South. He crushed the ripest, reddest peppers, mixed them with local salt, and aged the mixture for 30 days in crockery jars or barrels. McIlhenny then blended the mash with French white wine vinegar and aged the mixture for at least another 30 days before straining and bottling, regularly hand-stirring it to blend flavors. After straining, he transferred the sauce to small cologne-type bottles, which he then corked and sealed in green wax.

"That Famous Sauce Mr. McIlhenny Makes" proved so popular with family and friends that McIlhenny decided to market it, growing his first commercial pepper crop in 1868. The next year he sent out 658 bottles of sauce at one dollar apiece wholesale to grocers around the Gulf Coast, particularly in New Orleans. He labeled it "Tabasco," a word of Mexican Indian origin believed to mean "place where the soil is humid" or "place of the coral or oyster shell." McIlhenny secured a patent in 1870.

His northeastern agent helped McIlhenny forge an alliance with one of the nation's largest food distributors, E.C. Hazard and Company of New York City. Hazard successfully introduced Tabasco sauce to consumers nationally and by the end of the decade McIlhenny was exporting the hot sauce to Europe.

Twenty years after its creation, upon McIlhenny's passing, his oldest son, John Avery McIlhenny, assumed control of the business. When he enlisted in Theodore Roosevelt's "Rough Riders" volunteer cavalry regiment in 1898, brother Ned took over.

In 1949, Walter Stauffer McIlhenny succeeded his uncle as head of the company, and expanded sales around the world. A brigadier general in the Marine Corps Reserve, McIlhenny was inspired by letters from U.S. soldiers in Vietnam to publish *The Charlie Ration Cookbook* of C-ration recipes and to produce camouflaged Tabasco sauce bottle holsters. Mini bottles of Tabasco sauce are now packed in every military MRE packet (Meals Ready to Eat). It was also during this time that a new factory was built to meet the growing demand for Tabasco sauce.

Two of E. McIlhenny's great-grandsons have followed in his footsteps to become leaders of McIlhenny Company. Edward "Ned" McIlhenny Simmons succeeded

Movies and television programs have provided Tabasco sauce with endless opportunities to leverage brand awareness. McIlhenny Company has also realized continued success with its humorous Super Bowl commercials that market the product memorably—award-winning "Mosquito" in 1997 and "Comet" in 2000.

In addition to utilizing various entertainment outlets, Tabasco sauce has also established an ongoing presence at various food shows, such as the International Association of Culinary Professionals, and it can most always be found on any tabletop.

On January 1, 2000, Tabasco sauce greeted Y2K with the Millennium Mary™, a 10-foot-tall glass containing over 1,000 gallons of Bloody Mary, in Latrobe Park in New Orleans' French Quarter. Spiced up with 12 gallons of Tabasco sauce, the enormous cocktail provided over 15,000 drinks to ease revelers into the "morning after."

The Tabasco trademark diamond logo is an important marketing tool, inspiring recognition wherever it is positioned, whether it is on a bottle, T-shirt or commercial.

BRAND VALUES

Tabasco sauce is about a unique heritage and culture, and enormous dedication.

McIlhenny Company prides itself on a reputation of prestige and excellence for maintaining superior quality in its product, while never losing sight of the old-fashioned values and family traditions that are the essence of this world-famous brand.

Walter in 1985 and is now chairman of the board. Paul C.P. McIlhenny, also a 4th-generation family member, is the president and chief executive officer.

Several members of the McIlhenny family personally inspect the fresh pepper mash transported from Latin America as well as the barrels of three-year-old oak-aged pepper mash for aroma and color before final processing.

Tabasco sauce is still produced much as it was in E. McIlhenny's time, over 130 years ago, except now the aging process is longer.

Every fall, a member of the McIlhenny family selects the seeds for future crops by walking the pepper fields row-by-row and draping twine over the best plants. Because peppers in various stages of ripeness grow on the same bush, only an experienced picker can determine which are ready for harvest.

Until the 1960s, all peppers were grown on the Island. Most of the pepper crop is now grown in Latin American countries, but all of the pepper sauce is still manufactured on Avery Island.

THE PRODUCT

Frequently used as a flavor enhancer, the distinctive piquant flavor of the world's favorite pepper sauce has also established it as a staple ingredient in contemporary cooking.

In the 1990s, McIlhenny Company added a line of new pepper sauces under the Tabasco brand label. Offering consumers a broad spectrum of tastes and heat levels, the line includes the original Tabasco sauce, a milder Tabasco® green pepper sauce, a zestier Tabasco® garlic pepper sauce, and an even hotter Tabasco® habanero pepper sauce.

RECENT DEVELOPMENTS

A Visitors Center was opened in 1989 to serve the over 100,000 people who come to Avery Island each year from around the world.

The dramatic expansion of licensing, merchandising and co-branding initiatives for Tabasco sauce resulted in the opening of the Tabasco Country Store on Avery Island, with branches in New Orleans, Louisiana, San Antonio, Texas, and Kemah, Texas. Along with Tabasco apparel and gift items, the stores sell food products spiced with Tabasco sauce.

In 1996, McIlhenny Company launched the Tabasco PepperFest® web site, offering a virtual festival for everyone from the casual Tabasco sauce user to the professional chef.

THINGS YOU DIDN'T KNOW ABOUT TABASCO® BRAND PEPPER SAUCE

○ In June 1995, the world's largest stern-wheeler, *American Queen*, was christened with the world's largest bottle of Tabasco sauce. Measuring 44 inches tall and 16 inches in diameter at the base, the bottle held 21.3 gallons of pepper sauce—enough to flavor 392,602 servings of crawfish étouffée. It was crafted in three pieces because of its massive weight: about 50 pounds empty and 210 pounds when filled.

○ Tabasco sauce was present at the excavation of King Tut's tomb, and in the Himalayas climbers rewarded their Sherpa guides with bottles of the condiment.

○ Each year, several pounds of select seed are taken from the peppers grown on Avery Island and stored in a bank vault in New Iberia, Louisiana, to insure against possible crop losses. A large quantity of seed is stored on Avery Island and then shipped to numerous pepper growing countries in Central and South America throughout the year.

○ E. McIlhenny originally wanted to call his concoction Petite Anse Sauce, after Avery Island, which then was known as Petite Anse Island. However, when family members balked at the commercial use of the name of their island, McIlhenny opted for his second choice—Tabasco.

THE MARKET

Texaco Inc. is a fully integrated energy company engaged in exploring for and producing oil and natural gas; manufacturing and marketing high-quality fuels and lubricant products; operating trading, transportation and distribution facilities; and producing power. Directly and through affiliates, Texaco operates in more than 150 countries.

Growing worldwide energy demand, rapid advances in technology, geopolitical influences, environmental concerns and deregulation are among the factors reshaping the global energy industry. While oil currently represents a significant share of the global energy mix, energy companies like Texaco are researching and developing a range of energy solutions in this complex and dynamic business environment to help meet the world's energy needs.

Texaco has been a part of the global energy industry since 1902 and has one of the world's most recognizable and respected brands. During the past 100 years so many transforming changes have occurred that the industry bears little resemblance to the roughneck, oil boom days of the early 1900s.

The fundamental changes in the industry became more apparent than ever before in the year 2000. It was the year Texaco chose to take a dramatic step forward to ensure that, in this new world of energy, the company can continue to deliver superior value to shareholders, not just for one year but for many years to come. On October 16, 2000, Texaco Inc. and Chevron Corporation announced a merger to create a new company ChevronTexaco Corporation. This merger will join two leading energy companies and long-time partners to create a United States-based, global enterprise that is highly competitive across all energy sectors.

ACHIEVEMENTS

For almost a century, Texaco has built itself on its employee's abilities to anticipate the direction of the marketplace and to shape its business by leveraging current capabilities and recognizing new opportunities.

Oil and natural gas are produced from Texaco's global portfolio that increasingly concentrates on major high-impact projects. It has total production of 1.15 million barrels of oil equivalent per day. Net proven reserves stand at about 4.9 billion barrels of oil equivalent as of the end of 2000.

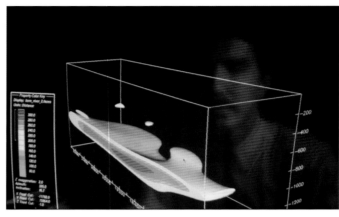

But, Texaco is about more than just numbers; it is about integrating its business goals with support to communities in which it does business. It is an industry leader in corporate philanthropy, has put in place a world-class program to nurture diversity in the workplace, and has made significant investments to protect and preserve the environment.

As a result of commitments made and met, Texaco has been included in the Dow Jones Sustainability Group Index, representing the top 10 percent of companies that are leaders in sustainability from more than 2000 stocks listed in the Dow Jones Group Index. In addition, Innovest, an investment advisory firm that evaluates companies on their response to environmental trends, ranked Texaco fifth out of 17 global integrated oil and gas companies in a July 2000 report.

According to the Roper/Fortune Corporate Reputation Index for the year 2000, the general public rated Texaco the #1 Petroleum Company with the highest quality products in the United States. This same group viewed Texaco as the most environmentally responsible company in comparison to its competitors. Roper's Influential American group ranked the company #1 overall and as the most innovative petroleum company in the industry.

HISTORY

Texaco Inc. was founded in 1902, shortly after the start of the Spindletop oil boom in Texas. Originally known as The Texas Company, this small maverick enterprise led by oilman Joseph "Buckskin Joe" Cullinan and New York investor Arnold Schlaet was founded upon the idea of buying Texas crude oil at low prices and selling it to northern refiners for a profit. Anticipating further oil discoveries, Cullinan and Schlaet formed The Texas Company with $3 million in capital and a handful of employ-

ees in Beaumont, Texas. This company, which would become a multi-billion-dollar corporation, survived and prospered because its founders possessed financial expertise, foresight and a thorough understanding of the ever-changing nature of the oil business. Skills which continue to differentiate the employees of Texaco today.

After seeing "TEXACO" in a cable address of The Texas Company's New York office, George M. Brown, an asphalt salesman in St. Louis, Missouri, used the term as a product name for the first time. In 1906, TEXACO became The Texas Company's first registered trademark and by 1907 was appearing on more than 40 different products.

Anticipating the potential for refining and marketing all useful components of a barrel of crude, The Texas Company distinguished itself by manufacturing products beyond the easily made and sold. This ingenuity paid off with the advent of the automobile when it become the first company to ever sell more motor fuel than kerosene. The Holmes-Manley Process, invented by two company researchers in 1918, became the first commercially successful continuous process for refining crude oil, allowing refiners to more than double the gasoline yield from a barrel of crude oil.

During the ensuing decades, The Texas Company grew into a worldwide enterprise through increased investments in exploration, producing, refining, transportation, research and marketing facilities. In doing so, The Texas Company established an early worldwide balance between all sectors in the industry, making

it one of the first truly integrated oil companies.

Texaco Inc. became the company's official corporate name in 1959—formally acknowledging that the public identified the company by the name they had seen for decades at Texaco service stations nationwide. The brand name and the company name had become synonymous in the public consciousness.

Today, Texaco Inc. operates, directly and through affiliates, in more than 150 countries. At year-end 2000, the company had nearly $31 billion in assets and generated more than $51 billion in revenues.

THE PRODUCT

Texaco produces a full range of products from advanced lubricants and coolants to high-octane gasolines.

Since the time when Texaco's unique motor oil was able to silence the noisy transmission of the Ford Model T, it has been at the forefront of marketing innovative products to meet the needs of consumers and businesses alike. Today, the company is producing technologically advanced gasolines like CleanSystem$3^®$ that provide top quality and help reduce deposits on fuel injectors and intake valves, resulting in improved performance.

The company became a leader in advanced lubricant technology when it acquired Indian Refining Company in 1931 and began producing Havoline Premium Motor Oil. Havoline is

still one of the most recognized and top-selling oil brands on the market.

Through a strategic alliance, Texaco is also a leading supplier of marine fuels and lubricants worldwide and has been servicing the aviation industry for almost 90 years. Today, Texaco serves 125 aviation customers at nearly 550 airports, in more than 50 countries.

Texaco is building on its core businesses by expanding its energy portfolio to provide effi-

cient solutions to meet changing market needs. These solutions range from established technologies such as gasification—a process that turns low-grade, "dirty fuels" into clean synthesis gas which then is used to generate power and chemical feedstocks—to "over-the-horizon" technologies, including fuel cells, hydrogen storage, photovoltaics (solar energy) and advanced batteries that present alternatives to traditional hydrocarbons.

PROMOTION

Throughout its history, Texaco has been responsible for some of the world's most recognizable advertising, sponsorships and philanthropic endeavors. To this day, people still associate the likes of Milton Berle, Ed Wynn, Fred Allen and Bob Hope with Texaco advertising. The tagline "You Can Trust Your Car to the Man Who Wears the Star" remains one the most recognizable and most recalled taglines in advertising history. Today, through a wide array of creative advertising and the "Texaco. A World of Energy" tagline, Texaco continues to be a leading advertiser within the industry.

Texaco distinguishes itself by supporting world-class teams, players and events through the company's sponsorship programs. These efforts are targeted at a wide range of cultural, social, educational and athletic sponsorships. For instance, the company has been supporting auto racing since 1917 and has been associated with some of the most legendary names in the sport, including Mario Andretti. Sixty-one years ago, Texaco began sponsoring live radio broadcasts from the Metropolitan Opera in New York City. Today, opera lovers in 35 countries around the world hear these Saturday afternoon broadcasts.

BRAND VALUES

Since Texaco was founded, hundreds of thousands of men and women have contributed their creativity and innovation to create the strategic and competitive company it is today. The vision, daring and determination of its employees have shaped the character of the company for nearly a century. Texaco's brand reflects these attributes, as well as the passionate, efficient and forward-thinking culture of the company.

RECENT DEVELOPMENTS

Market forces and rising environmental standards are driving the development of the next generation of energy products, and Texaco is positioning itself to be a leader in this technological future. In addition to focusing on its core oil and gas businesses, the company has developed strategic partnerships to advance the

development and commercialization of environmentally smart energy technologies such as fuel cells, photovoltaics, advanced batteries and hydrogen storage.

Texaco's proposed merger with Chevron offers the best opportunity to apply the traditional strengths of Texaco to the energy company of the future. ChevronTexaco will be among the world's largest, most competitive and successful energy companies, focused on delivering superior shareholder value while providing the marketplace with reliable energy solutions in a responsible manner. The company will build on the record of Texaco achievements over nearly 100 years, which stands as a testament to the abilities, talents and spirit of the Texaco family.

THINGS YOU DIDN'T KNOW ABOUT TEXACO

❍ In 1928, Texaco became the first, and, to date, only company to market under the same brand in all 48 states in the nation.

❍ Texaco's sponsorship of the Metropolitan Opera Radio Broadcast is the longest running radio sponsorship program in broadcast history.

❍ Texaco opened the first "service station" in 1917, providing its customers with new services such as customer restrooms and concessions for sale. Prior to this, stations were "filling stations" where motorists simply refueled.

❍ Texaco's aeronautical advisor Captain Frank Hawks set speed records in the *Texaco No. 13* to prove the viability of a "pony express" service of valuable documents between the East and West Coasts in 1930.

❍ In 1943, the *SS Ohio*, a Texaco tanker on lease to the British government, endured repeated attacks by German submarines and airplanes to deliver crucial fuel supplies to the besieged island of Malta. This voyage became one of the great epic stories of World War II.

❍ Universal Studios Florida chose a 1940s Texaco service station design to evoke a classic symbol of motor travel. This station is available to motorists as well as for use in films set during this period.

T-FAL®

THE MARKET

Housewares products are a huge business. An estimated 94 percent of American households own at least one fry pan. The market for cookware is at nearly $2 billion annually. Kitchen electrics, including steam irons, represent more than $3 billion.

The non-stick cookware segment now commands approximately 70 percent of the market, far surpassing stainless steel, enamel, aluminum, and coppper. T-Fal®, the inventor of non-stick cookware, is today the largest selling brand worldwide. And, in the U.S., T-Fal is the brand Americans think of first when it comes to cookware. In electrics, T-Fal is one of America's fastest growing manufacturers of small kitchen and household appliances, including deep fryers, indoor grills, toasters, kettles, multi-purpose electrics, and steam irons. As in cookware, T-Fal's hallmarks in electrics are innovation, quality, style and convenience.

One of only a few companies that bridge both cookware and small appliances categories, T-Fal is positioned to accelerate its growth in electrics while at the same time broadening its offerings in fine quality non-stick cookware.

ACHIEVEMENTS

T-Fal is unique among housewares manufacturers today. Its product development reflects the company's keen sense of the American marketplace and what it is looking for in kitchen products.

Historically, T-Fal has been about innovation, beginning with its invention of non-stick cookware in the 1950s, a development that enabled healthy cooking and much easier kitchen cleanups.

Over the past four decades, T-Fal has continued to research and develop non-stick coatings and technologies. Its breakthrough technologies include Ultrabase®, Resistal®, Armaral®, Integral®, and Thermospot™ cookware—all of which incorporate industry-leading non-stick surfaces with unique exterior engineering that significantly increases the performance and life of the cookware.

At the high-end, T-Fal recently introduced Culinaire and Restaurant Gourmet, all-new collections that bear the endorsement of Le Cordon Bleu, the world-renowned French cooking school for professional chefs.

In 2000, T-Fal introduced the first major new development in non-stick cookware since the invention of the non-stick category itself by T-Fal in the 1950s. This revolutionary line of

cookware, Thermospot, features a visual heat indicator, built into the non-stick coating, which signals when the pan is preheated to the optimum temperature.

T-Fal, which revolutionized pressure cooker safety with its invention of the seamless stamped pot, also has a large U.S. market for its stainless-steel Sensor 2 and other pressure cooker models.

T-Fal's many firsts in electric appliances include the development in the mid-1980s of the first steam iron with a patented Durilium™ coating on its soleplate. T-Fal's exclusive soleplate transformed ironing, thanks to its unmatched glideability and ease-of-use.

Today, T-Fal produces an impressive line of smartly designed steam irons, all featuring its patented Ultraglide™ soleplate and other advanced technology. In 1968, T-Fal introduced the first electric deep fryer with exterior controls for optimum safety, and an exclusive charcoal filter system for odor-free operation.

T-Fal also introduced the first wide-slot toaster, the Avanté line, featuring a Hi-Lift mechanism that raises smaller pieces of bread for safe removal.

The company also offers an extensive line of high-efficiency Multi-Grill indoor grills designed with channels to draw fats away from the food.

HISTORY

The T-Fal story began in France in the 1950s, when Colette Grégoire asked her husband, Marc, an aeronautics engineer and fishing enthusiast, if the non-stick coating that prevented fiberglass fishing line fragments from clinging to his aluminum fishing rod could also keep an omelet from sticking to a fry pan.

Within a year of his wife's inquiry, Marc Grégoire patented a process for applying a non-stick coating to aluminum.

When manufacturers showed little interest, he went directly to consumers, demonstrating his culinary miracle at trade shows and department stores.

With demand growing, Marc Grégoire formed the Société Tefal, later to be called Tefal S.A., on May 2, 1956. And before too long, cooks throughout France were buying these amazing non-stick pans.

The debut of Tefal non-stick cookware in America was a tremendous success.

In Europe, Tefal's market growth continued at a vigorous pace both in cookware and in electric appliances. Tefal was acquired by The SEB Groupe in 1968.

T-Fal embarked on a major marketing push in the U.S. and, in 1976, opened a U.S. manufacturing facility.

Innovations over the next 25 years have continuously improved the quality and performance of non-stick cookware, and have made it a staple part of our everyday lives, eliminating the once-dreaded chore of cleaning dirty pans

From an idea born out of a fishing rod, T-Fal's products today are present in hundreds of millions of households around the world.

THE PRODUCT

T-Fal is one of the leading cookware brands in the U.S. and also the largest worldwide. Its Ultrabase®, Resistal®, Armaral®, Integral™ and Thermospot™ cookware lines, as well as its pressure cookers, are marketed throughout the country.

In a recent unaided-recall market study*, consumers cited T-Fal as the number one brand in nearly every cookware category.

One of the few companies in the U.S. marketing both cookware and electrics, T-Fal is among the fastest growing kitchen appliance suppliers. Its range of products includes deep fryers, indoor grills, toasters, steamers, kettles, steam irons and multi-purpose appliances such as the Gourmet Grill 'N' Skillet.

The emphasis in all of the T-Fal food preparation products is healthy cooking.

With its unsurpassed non-stick coating technologies, T-Fal designs and engineers products that require little or no added fats, thus promoting more healthful cooking.

RECENT DEVELOPMENTS

In 1999, T-Fal introduced its top-of-the-line Integral, an all-new cookware collection designed and made in France for the serious cook, which combines elegant styling and superior performance. This state-of-the-art cookware, with its professional quality, heavy-gauge aluminum fabrication, embodies features found only in the most advanced cookware.

Highly engineered, the cookware's exterior base features an embedded stainless-steel anti-distortion disc, or ADD®, with a unique 7-beam star relief, that provides optimum heat diffusion and up to 40 times greater

*Source: research by Shapiro & Associates, May 2000

warp resistance than conventional pans. Inside is T-Fal's next-generation easy-care coating, a star-patterned T-Fal non-stick that is more resistant to scratching and abrasion than any previous coating.

In 2000, T-Fal debuted Thermospot, the most significant advance in non-stick cookware since they invented the category in the 1950's. This extraordinary innovation features a visual heat indicator built into the non-stick coating that signals when a pan is pre-heated to the optimum temperature.

T-Fal has extended the Thermospot concept to its newest indoor grill, the Multi-Grill StoreAway.

In another recent introduction, T-Fal unveiled the Gourmet Grill 'N' Skillet, a unique multi-purpose electrical appliance that functions as an indoor grill, an electric skillet, and a steamer or poacher.

PROMOTION

T-Fal is a rare example of a housewares company that supports the use of mass-market television advertising to generate brand awareness and communicate product benefits.

In 2000, T-Fal rolled out a national 30 second television advertising campaign promoting Thermospot (see below). The Thermospot campaign also encompassed print advertising in leading consumer publications throughout the nation.

Earlier, T-Fal had conducted a national television campaign for its Armaral cookware collection.

In recent years, T-Fal has also been a pioneer in using TV infomercials, developing large-scale productions for network and cable broadcast for both its cookware and appliances.

T-Fal regularly supports its cookware and

electrics products by advertising in leading consumer and bridal magazines.

In parallel, T-Fal also employs a variety of public relations strategies to capture the attention of consumers. There is an impressive plan targeting newspapers and magazines to publicize T-Fal products in editorial. The company's website, www.t-fal.com, is another promotional element for the brand. T-Fal also relies on television spokespersons for national media and satellite media tours to reach millions of Americans.

BRAND VALUES

"I love my T-Fal," is a recurring theme among consumers, including many original buyers of the first T-Fal pans introduced in the U.S. in 1960s. Nurturing and sustaining that emotional connection is a key objective of T-Fal, which prides itself on consumer loyalty and satisfaction.

T-Fal stands for quality, innovation and performance, and the company backs up its products with first class customer service.

Simply put, an American home isn't complete today without T-Fal.

The New York Times

THE MARKET

It is the core purpose of The New York Times "to enhance society by creating, collecting and distributing high quality news, information and entertainment." The Times is read nationwide by those seeking the most complete, compelling and thoughtful report on news and trends in a single package.

It is sought out by leaders in every profession, the intellectually curious and discerning.

In recent years, The Times has expanded both its home delivery and retail access to areas of the country where it had not been widely available before. It has extended its national availability in part by forming alliances with other companies: such as local papers (willing to offer delivery of The Times to readers who wish to purchase it) and retailers (such as Starbucks Coffee, which is making The New York Times available in more than 2,000 of its locations in 2001). Increased national circulation has led to increased national advertising in The Times, which now exceeds local advertising.

According to the leading marketing and media study of the U.S. adult population, Mediamark Research Inc. (MRI), The New York Times has nearly five million (4,977,000) (Source: MRI Spring 2000) readers of the weekday and Sunday newspaper.

And Times readers are known to have an exceptionally intense relationship with their newspaper.

"In over 25 years of researching loyalists in virtually every product or service category," says Bonnie Goebert, president and owner, The Bonnie Goebert Company, a marketing research firm, "I have rarely encountered such a dedicated group. Without The Times, there seems to be an absolute gap in their lives that no other paper, indeed no other medium, can fulfill."

ACHIEVEMENTS

The New York Times is one of the most honored names in journalism, the recipient of 79 Pulitzer Prizes (among many other journalism awards), far more than any other newspaper.

In 2000, publisher Arthur Sulzberger Jr. was named newspaper publisher of the year by *Editor & Publisher* magazine, the leading publication on the newspaper industry, and The Times was ranked #1 in the publishing industry in *Fortune* magazine's survey of America's Most Admired Companies and the Globally Most Admired Companies. In the global survey, The Times was ranked #1 among all companies for the quality of its products and services and #2 in community responsibility.

Earlier in 2000, Fortune recognized The New York Times Company as one of the 50 best companies for minorities, and in September of 2000, *Working Mother* magazine recognized The New York Times Company as one of the best companies for working mothers.

Tammany Hall Democratic organization, run by "Boss" William Marcy Tweed, in New York City, helped to end Tweed's hold on city politics and became a landmark in American journalism.

In 1896, Adolph S. Ochs, a newspaper publisher from Chattanooga, Tenn., bought The Times, which was then having severe financial difficulties. He took The Times to new heights of achievement, establishing it as the serious, balanced newspaper that would bring readers "All the News That's Fit to Print" (a slogan that he coined and that still appears on the paper's front page). It would do so, he added, "without fear or favor." Mr. Ochs introduced such features as The New York Times Magazine and The Book Review.

On his death in 1935, he was succeeded as publisher by his son-in-law, Arthur Hays Sulzberger, whose grandson, Arthur Sulzberger Jr., is the publisher today. In its extensive coverage of world events throughout the 20th century, The Times came to be known as "the newspaper of record." In 1971, the Supreme Court ruled in favor of The Times's right to publish the so-called Pentagon Papers, government documents concerning the Vietnam War.

And in 1996 The Times entered the dawning digital era, as it launched its acclaimed Web site, NYTimes.com.

Tall Ships Render a Stately Tribute to Independence

HISTORY

The New York Times was founded in 1851 by Henry Jarvis Raymond and George Jones. Its exposé of widespread corruption of the

THE PRODUCT

The New York Times is a seven-day newspaper, with daily coverage of world, national and New York–area news, business and sports, daily weather, news summaries and, of course, the crossword puzzle. The Times has been hailed as "easily the best, most important newspaper in the country" by *Time* magazine. "If it's in The New York Times, it's news," *U.S. News & World Report* has written.

The daily newspaper features special coverage of the media on Mondays, a Science Times section and fashion coverage on Tuesdays, food-related content on Wednesdays, the Circuits section and home-related articles on Thursdays, a two-part Weekend section on Fridays, and extra cultural coverage on Saturdays.

The Sunday Times includes the Arts & Leisure section, The New York Times Magazine, The Book Review, the Week in Review, Travel and Money & Business section.

There are three editions of The Times: New York, Northeast (serving the Washington and New England areas) and National. The Times also publishes online, at www.nytimes.com, which includes The Learning Network, a special component for educators, students and parents (www.nytimes.com/learning).

The New York Times makes content of the paper available to other national and international customers, offers photo reprints to consumers and also offers such special publications as The New York Times Large Type Weekly.

The Times is especially valued not only for its extensive coverage but also for the careful analysis and context it provides.

RECENT DEVELOPMENTS

On June 25, 2000, The New York Times and New York Times Digital launched Continuous News operations, providing updated news and analysis from the reporting staff of The Times throughout the day. During the summer of 2000, The Times published "How Race Is Lived in America," a sweeping, 14-part series of articles that examined the many ways in which issues of race affect daily lives across the country. The ambitious series was a year in the making.

PROMOTION

The New York Times is widely promoted in markets across the country and throughout the New York area. It especially strives to reach "like-minded non-readers," whom The Times has identified as sharing many of the characteristics of its most loyal readers: intellectually and culturally curious, concerned about social issues, career, and their own as well as their children's education.

Among the broad range of promotional tools that The Times uses are image advertising (including its "Expect the World" television campaign, print ads, and billboards) and direct response (including television and direct mail).

The Times has also developed special programs to include various segments of the population, including Chinese-Americans, Hispanics, Asian Indians, and the gay and lesbian communities.

To build brand awareness, The Times has joined with like-minded organizations for targeted joint ventures. It co-produces television specials with ABC News and The National Geographic Channel and publishes "The New York Times Upfront" with Scholastic, Inc.

BRAND VALUES

The Times has a longstanding reputation for integrity and depth of reporting. Many feel that The Times has long set the standard for quality journalism. Readers value The Times because they know that the paper's editors and reporters strive to provide them all the most important news, as well as their prized insights, every day. In an era of ever-more media choices, readers know they can rely on The Times for both substance and style. Advertisers value The Times

because of the closely read, esteemed and timely editorial environment in which their messages will appear and because of the influence and purchasing power of so many Times readers.

THINGS YOU DIDN'T KNOW ABOUT THE NEW YORK TIMES

○ The editorial staff of The New York Times consists of more than 1,000 people. They report, write and edit on three floors in The Times's current building on West 43rd Street in New York City or work in the eight news bureaus reporting to the metropolitan desk, a bureau in Washington, D.C., 11 other news bureaus covering national news, and in 26 news bureaus reporting news from outside the U.S.

○ Times Square was named for The New York Times after the paper moved to the neighborhood in 1905; previously the area was known as Longacre Square. The first Times Square New Year's Eve ball dropped from the Times Tower on December 31, 1907. Designs for a new state-of-the-art Times headquarters in the Times Square area are being created as this book goes to press.

○ The New York Times was the first newspaper to publish a story, and a correct one at that, about the sinking of the Titanic in 1912.

○ The first Sunday crossword appeared in The New York Times Magazine in 1942. The first crossword in the daily paper appeared in 1950.

○ The Times first popularized the Op-Ed page; in 1970 it became the first paper to run opinion pieces by outside writers, placing them on the page opposite its editorials: hence, "op-ed."

○ New York Times food critics spend about $200,000 a year in restaurant bills (tips included).

TOYOTA

Toyota Camry

THE MARKET

No doubt about it—business has been good. A strong U.S. economy made 2000 the best year ever for the American automotive industry, with sales reaching 17,408,842 units. This was a 2.7% increase in sales from 1999, which had previously held the industry record for sales.

As business has increased, so have consumers' demands. Today's competitive market is inspiring diversification and real innovation. SUVs and environmentally friendly vehicles are good examples.

Lately buyers have been calling for more spacious, practical and intrepid vehicles. And so automakers have rushed to diversify their lineups to include sport utility vehicles.

Toyota had long been ready for this shift in consumer expectations. That's no surprise really, since the first Toyota sold in America—the Land Cruiser—was a sport utility vehicle. The company now offers five SUVs, and other automakers are following suit.

Toyota's been quick to spot another development on the horizon. Environmentally conscious vehicles will one day enjoy the popularity that SUVs currently do. And the robust economy of the past few years has presented Toyota with a real opportunity. It's allowed the company to introduce innovative vehi-

cles like the RAV4 EV and the gas/electric hybrid Prius to forward-thinking consumers.

ACHIEVEMENTS

Toyota's reputation for producing affordable, high-quality vehicles is the result of more than just hard work. It's the product of a corporate philosophy developed by the company's founder. Sakichi Toyoda believed that success came from always looking to the future and evolving to meet it. This insistence on continual improvement was called *kaizen*.

There's obviously something to it—the brand continues to grow. In 1958, Toyota sold 288 vehicles in the United States. In 2000, Toyota's U.S. sales reached 1,413,169. By 1997, sales of the Toyota Corolla surpassed those of the Volkswagen Beetle, making the

Corolla the best-selling car in history. And the popular Camry has been the number one-selling car in the U.S. four years running (1997–2000).* This all adds up to secure Toyota's place as the best-selling import brand in America.

Based on R.L. Polk calendar years 1997, 1998, 1999 and 2000 total passenger car registrations.

HISTORY

In 1890 in Yamaguchi, Japan, Sakichi Toyoda founded a business producing automatic looms. His son, Kiichiro, built upon his father's success by developing an automobile for the domestic market.

Toyota was years behind the Western world, but Kiichiro used that to his advantage as he started from scratch. He visited the U.S. and designed his vehicles based on the strongest features of each company he observed. With his guidance, the Toyota Motor Corporation Ltd. was established in August of 1937.

In time, Toyota decided to try the export market. The Land Cruiser was the first product exported to the United States in 1957. Thus, Toyota Motor Sales, U.S.A., Inc. was created.

After evaluating local conditions in the U.S. and building passenger cars to suit them, Toyota's U.S. export market quickly grew. Sales

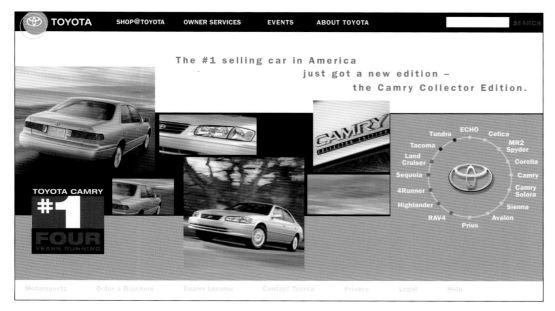

The #1 selling car in America
just got a new edition –
the Camry Collector Edition.

TOYOTA CAMRY #1 FOUR YEARS RUNNING

went from 2,029 units in 1964 to 38,073 units in 1967. This made the United States Toyota's largest export market. In 1968, with the arrival of the Corolla, Toyota's sales more than doubled. That trend continues today as Toyota sales increase.

THE PRODUCT

Toyota vehicles are known for exceptional Quality, Dependability and Reliability. That reputation's been built by using only parts of the highest quality...assembly methods that are continually refined...and people who thoroughly understand and can improve the process. In other words, *kaizen*.

Multi-Model Production demonstrates Mr. Toyoda's philosophy in action. Toyota has developed this method of production in order to foster versatility and precision on the job. It requires that team members be trained in various positions along the assembly line. That way, problems are quickly spotted, and the assembly line can be promptly stopped to make changes. This process also allows for *jidoka,* Toyota's "just in time" method. Parts are produced only as needed, saving time and money on warehousing and inventory.

These methods work. Toyota models consistently place at the top of their class in the

1961 Toyota Land Cruiser

J. D. Power and Associates' Initial Quality Study (IQS). The organization also named eight of Toyota's models the most appealing vehicles in their class for the year 2000.

Kaizen has also led Toyota to broaden its range of vehicles, ensuring that there will be

one to meet the needs of virtually every consumer. The company now produces one of the most comprehensive lineups in the automotive market—seventeen models in all.

RECENT DEVELOPMENTS

In July of 2000, Toyota Motor Sales, U.S.A., Inc. put theory into practice by bringing to the U.S. the world's first mass-produced gasoline/electric hybrid vehicle, the Prius. This hybrid is seen by many as an improvement over current electric vehicles. It produces 90% fewer smog-forming emissions than conventional internal combustion engines, but never needs to be plugged in. The Prius boasts an EPA fuel economy rating of 52 mpg (city) and 45 mpg (highway).

Toyota's recent sales record in the U.S. is also characterized by continual improvement. In 2000, sales were up 9.6% from the year prior. This marked Toyota's fifth consecutive year of record sales. The year 2000 also found Toyota's sales fast approaching those of the Big Three auto manufacturers.

PROMOTION

For over a quarter of a century, Toyota has partnered with Saatchi & Saatchi to market its automobiles in the U.S. There's a clear reason this alliance has been such a long-term success. Toyota's always been willing to embrace the innovations and improvements in marketing communications that Saatchi's put forward.

The advertising and marketing landscape is constantly changing. What was once a monopoly of three television networks is now a vast ocean of cable and satellite-delivered program-

ming. Targeting is more essential than ever. And it's not just in the traditional advertising arena. Toyota and Saatchi have been exploring and delivering interactive programs since 1993 because they offer a one-on-one relationship between consumer and brand. In fact, toyota.com was one of the very first automotive Web sites in the U.S.

Toyota and Saatchi have also been targeting consumers through Lifestyle marketing. Take the recent partnership with Princess Cruises as an example. Toyota placed one of its flagship sedans, an Avalon, on board a Princess Cruise ship. This co-branding did more than just liken one relaxing form of transportation to another. It provided Toyota with a "captive" audience of the very same affluent consumers for whom the car was designed.

So what does the future hold? Well, if the past is any gauge of it, you can bet that Toyota will continue to show enthusiasm for innovative and relevant communications strategies.

BRAND VALUES

From the very beginning, Toyota has prospered based on its core values. Producing some of the highest quality vehicles in the business, Toyota continues to stand apart from the competition.

Just as the founders believed,

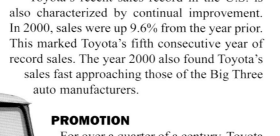

2001 Toyota Prius

kaizen—continuous improvement—has driven Toyota to constantly look ahead, never resting on its many accolades.

These values will continue to ensure Toyota's success and leadership as the automobile industry evolves.

THINGS YOU DIDN'T KNOW ABOUT TOYOTA

○ Toyota was listed on the NYSE for the first time in 1999.

○ The company's first product in 1890 was a wooden handloom.

○ Though the family's name was Toyoda, the company's name was changed to Toyota.

○ The reason for the name change: Toyoda requires ten brush strokes and number ten is not fortuitous. Toyota, on the other hand, uses only eight brush strokes and the number eight suggests growth. The name change must have worked: Toyota is now sold in over 160 countries around the world.

○ Toyota aired the first TV ad in the U.S. by a car importer in 1965.

TOYS "Я" US

THE MARKET

Over $70 billion dollars were spent on toys worldwide in 2000, with almost $30 billion of that from the United States alone, according to the International Council of Toy Industries and the Toy Manufacturers of America.

The toy retail business has also been impacted by the rapid penetration of the Internet among consumers and adoption of online shopping as a new sales channel. Internet toy revenues increased 22 percent in 2000, growing from $650 million in 1999 to $793 million in 2000. And Jupiter Communications projects that online toy sales in the U.S. could reach $2.4 billion—about 7 percent of retail sales—by 2005, hinting at the potential this new sales vehicle holds.

But regardless of the purchasing venue, the toy market is unique for several reasons. More than half of all toy sales occur in the fourth quarter alone, driven by holiday season spending. Furthermore, only a few of the thousands and thousands of toys sold actually become hot sellers, and even fewer remain popular for more than one or two years.

As the world's leading resource for kids, families and fun, Toys "R" Us has more than 1,500 stores worldwide, including Toys "R" Us, Kids "R" Us, Babies "R" Us and Imaginarium. In addition, the company has merchandise on its Internet sites at www.toysrus.com, www.babiesrus.com and www.imaginarium.com.

Total sales for Toys "R" Us increased over six percent to $12.7 billion from 1999 to 2000, giving the company a 15.6 percent share of the U.S. toy industry.

ACHIEVEMENTS

Toys "R" Us was named the #1 specialty retail store in the American Express Top 100 Specialty Stores list, compiled annually by the editors of STORES, the magazine of the National Retail Federation. Toys "R" Us has topped the list nine out of ten times since 1990. Toys "R" Us was also honored as the "Best of Century" retail store in the hard goods category by trade publisher Lebhar-Friedman.

Toyrus.com made amazing strides on the Web as well, capping Holiday 2000 by more than tripling its sales—$180 million—from the year prior. The online toy retailer entered into a groundbreaking alliance with the world's premier online retailer, Amazon.com in August, in which the two companies combined their respective strengths to offer Toyrus.com selection with Amazon.com convenience. As a result, the pairing became the #1 most visited online retail destination in Holiday 2000—more than five times the traffic of its nearest competitor, according to Nielson/NetRatings. Toysrus.com became a reliable source for the hottest toys of the season, and more than 99 percent of purchases were delivered on time for the holidays.

Babies "R" Us reached its own milestone as the millennium began, achieving the one billion dollar sales mark. It is the largest baby product specialty chain in the world. The store's Baby Registry also has the distinction of registering more expectant parents than any other U.S. retailer.

HISTORY

The origin of the world's largest toy store was the decision of 22-year-old Charles Lazarus who, anticipating the baby boom, transformed his father's Washington, D.C., bicycle repair shop into a baby furniture store in 1948. When customers told him they were also looking for baby toys, he began selling them. That policy of determining customer desires by the simple tactic of listening to them was to become a key ingredient in Lazarus' success. In time his selection grew to include toys for older children as well.

He established a "supermarket environment," in which customers could choose what they wanted off the shelves.

In 1957, the store was christened Toys "R" Us, complete with its unmistakable backward "R." By 1966, Lazarus had four toy stores selling $12 million per year. To expand his business, he sold those stores to the large retail conglomerate Interstate Sales. Lazarus continued to run the Toys "R" Us stores, and they prospered. But other Interstate ventures did not work as well and it filed for bankruptcy in 1974. At this point, Lazarus took over the entire company and four short years later he led Interstate out of bankruptcy. The company was renamed Toys "R" Us, Inc.

The company opened the first Kids "R" Us clothing store in 1983. Toys "R" Us began expanding globally in 1984 with stores in Canada, England, and Singapore. Toys "R" Us next acquired The Baby Superstore and merged it with Babies "R" Us, its year-old baby product chain. Toys "R" Us launched its online operations with www.toysrus.com in 1998.

Today, Toys "R" Us continues to meet Lazarus' goals of providing customers with exceptional value and selection. At the same time, the company never forgets its founder's most important rule of business—listening to the customer.

THE PRODUCT

Toys "R" Us is the world's largest retailer of children's products. The company's retail stores feature over 15,000 products that appeal to every guest—infants, teenagers, and even adults. The stores carry a wide array of products including items that are exclusive to Toys "R" Us.

The store offers one-stop shopping for families. Stores stock toys and games for kids and adults ranging from classic standards to the latest innovations. Vast selections of well-known brand names like Barbie and LEGO share the shelves with the latest novelty toys. Toys "R" Us has an extensive selection of family recreational items, and customers buying presents can also find a selection of cards, wrapping supplies, decorations, favors and other party supplies for the big event. Young readers can also choose from a large array of children's books. And for customers young or old, Toys "R" Us features a large selection of video games, computer software and electronic equipment within an area in the store dedicated to those products.

RECENT DEVELOPMENTS

To make its customers' shopping experiences even more enjoyable, Toys "R" Us has been making changes in its stores and other areas of its business.

Its web site, www.toysrus.com, allows customers to search for gifts and purchase products right from their computers. Toysrus.com also launched Babiesrus.com in 2000, bringing access to baby products and the Babies "R" Us Baby Registry to the Internet. In August 2000 Toysrus.com joined in a strategic alliance with Amazon.com dedicated to providing customers with the best shopping experience on the Internet.

Toys "R" Us makes every effort to provide customers with a one-of-a-kind shopping experience. By carrying products that are exclusive to Toys "R" Us, the stores give customers a chance to buy new and exciting products they cannot find anywhere else, in addition to the toy brands known and loved by its customers.

To make stores as customer-friendly as possible, Toys "R" Us launched major initiatives to make shopping more convenient and easier in a more inviting and open environment. Additionally, Toys "R" Us has a renewed commitment to providing a level of service that can't be found anywhere else.

Toys "R" Us has also added Imaginarium to its stores as child development centers and demonstration areas. Toys "R" Us purchased the Imaginarium chain of neighborhood toy stores in 1999.

PROMOTION

From the days when Geoffrey the Giraffe had both children and adults singing "I don't wanna grow up, I'm a Toys "R" Us kid!" he has stood (rather tall) as a foundation of the company's advertising. In 1960 company executives chose the giraffe as their mascot because they liked the idea of having a large, friendly animal represent their large, friendly store. Geoffrey did not get his name, however, until a store associate's suggestion won a contest in 1970.

In-store promotion includes sweepstakes, sponsorships and movie tie-ins. Eager to reach families, Toys "R" Us seeks out marketing projects with many partners and encompassing many areas including entertainment and sports. Past experience has shown the power of sweepstakes and other promotional events to give customers even more reasons to visit the stores.

A newer advertising campaign reminds parents and kids that "There has never been a better time to be a Toys "R" Us Kid." The ads focus on the commitment the company has to families and the value of toys in those relationships.

BRAND VALUES

The essence of the Toys "R" Us brand is all about "kids, families and fun." You only have to watch a child's eyes from the moment they see the Toys "R" Us multi-colored logo to understand the magic of one of retail's most powerful icon brands.

The revitalized Toys "R" Us brand values remain squarely focused on the special relationship the store has with children throughout the world while also working toward being attentive to "Mom's" needs. The company works very hard to be "Mom's Solution."

This is evidenced in Toys "R" Us' increased concentration on learning and child development. The brand values include a firm belief that the products sold should have terrific play value and also help develop children. The exclusive relationships with Animal Planet, Scholastic, Home Depot and "E.T." are excellent examples of this.

Finally, Toys "R" Us is in a unique and special multi-generation position. After all, the very first Toys "R" Us kids are today's parents. The brand is very much a part of the very fabric of family values and family life.

That's why there's never been a better time to be a Toys "R" Us kid!

THINGS YOU DIDN'T KNOW ABOUT TOYS "R" US

- ❍ Geoffrey the Giraffe drives a Geoffreymobile, a double-decker bus that runs on potato chips, and he lives in a New England lighthouse—since it has plenty of headroom!

- ❍ Toys "R" Us' Hospital Playroom Program, established in 1989, has designed, decorated and stocked over 50 playrooms for children in hospitals throughout the United States.

- ❍ Visitors to toysrus.com can access features such as a toy finder, exclusive products, collectible items and toy reviews.

- ❍ Toys "R" Us Children's Fund, Inc., started in 1992, has provided millions of dollars to charities nationwide that promote the health and well-being of children so that all kids can have happier, more fulfilling lives.

Help Is Just Around The Corner™

THE MARKET

Buying a house can be a daunting proposition. While there comes great pride and accomplishment in owning one's own home, it comes at the expense of repairs and renovations. In hometowns all across America, local True Value stores are there to help with exactly the right tools and the expert know-how homeowners need to keep their homes in perfect shape. With True Value, Help Is Just Around The Corner™.

True Value provides its consumers with an affordable and convenient place to get the tools and supplies that they need. True Value is the friendly, neighborhood hardware store that is always happy to point consumers in the right direction. And with locations in every corner of America, there's sure to be one near everyone.

Overall, hardware stores enjoyed a $3.4 billion increase in sales between 1998 and 2001. Sales are expected to increase an additional $1.3 billion by 2003. From these numbers, it's obvious that the hardware store is an important fixture in the neighborhoods of America. True Value hardware stores offer just that — a place where tools, supplies and information are easily available to get homes in perfect working order.

ACHIEVEMENTS

Serving nearly 6,000 independent True Value retailers nationally and internationally, True Value is the largest 100 percent member-owned cooperative in the $159 billion do-it-yourself industry. The True Value name provides lever-

age and buying power for its members who own the co-op and receive stock and cash dividends for their participation, in addition to retail advice and advertising support. True Value offers its members a commitment to their growth. And True Value's products and services are unmatched in the industry.

Beyond the traditional hardware business, True Value offers innovative nursery, commercial/industrial supply and rental programs for its members to help them fulfill the many needs of their various customers. True Value is the largest rental co-op chain in the United States with its Just Ask Rental, Taylor Rental and Grand Rental Station dealerships.

HISTORY

In 1916, 12-year-old John Cotter began working part time in a St. Paul, MN hardware store. By 1928, he was a traveling hardware salesman. Cotter and associate Ed Lanctot began pitching the wholesale co-op idea in 1947 to small town and suburban hardware retailers and by the end of the next year, they had enrolled 25 merchants for $1,500 each.

Cotter became chairman of the new company, Cotter & Company, which created the Value & Service trademark in 1951. This trademark was designed to emphasize the advantages of an independent hardware store. In 1963, acquisitions led to the start of Cotter

& Company's use of the well-known True Value trademark.

The company consolidated in 1995, eliminating its V&S Variety stores and lawnmower factory. Following this, in July of 1997, Cotter & Company became TruServ Corporation (True Value) with the marriage of Cotter & Company (the wholesaler to True Value stores) and ServiStar/Coast to Coast.

TruServ emerged supporting 8,000 independent retailers worldwide as well as boasting $4.0 billion in pro forma wholesale sales and estimated member/retailer sales of $18 billion.

Over the years, True Value has expanded into other brands as well, such as paint manufacturing/sales, garden and nursery sales (Home & Garden Showplace), rental services and sales (Just Ask Rental, Taylor Rental, Grand Rental Station) and commercial/industrial (Commercial Supply Network, Induserve Supply).

THE PRODUCT

True Value's captive label brands have evolved over the years (see above photo) and continue to offer affordability and quality to consumers. True Value Manufacturing is the largest single-site manufacturing facility of latex architectural coatings in North America, producing approximately 45,000 to 50,000 gallons of latex paint everyday.

prices and selection in a cost-effective manner.

True Value sponsors NASCAR and IROC sporting events, as well as maintains a presence on the television broadcasts of those races. Advertising also appears on both network TV and national cable, which helps to increase awareness of the True Value brand.

The brand is also promoted through other vehicles such as Truevalue.com and stadium signage.

BRAND VALUES

The True Value name enjoys strong equity among consumers. Consumers know they can depend on the advice and knowledge the stores provide. True Value members receive training, as well as the marketing and business support

In the manufacturing and distributing division, True Value manufactures exclusive brands for its members, such as True Value E-Z Kare and WeatherAll paints, paint applicators, assorted spray paints and cleaning supplies. Their private label brands include Green Thumb lawn and garden products and Master Mechanic tools.

RECENT DEVELOPMENTS

In 1999, True Value Manufacturing rolled out an upscale premium paint line called Prestige. In 2000, they introduced new Woodsman semi-transparent and solid color acrylic deck and siding stains.

As of March 2000, the company has regional distribution centers located in 17 cities. They have developed a partnership with The Home Service Store, which offers consumers access to a network of qualified contractors and trades people who can perform a number of home repair and improvement tasks.

The company has also experienced exceptional growth in the True Value E-Z Kare and WeatherAll brand paints and launched

Truevalue.com, the largest network of independent retailers online.

Truevalue.com provides a variety of helpful home improvement information including calculators to determine how much paint or wallpaper you'll need by room size, links to ask the expert sites and special savings on many of the over 20,000 items sold on-line.

PROMOTION

True Value advertising positions True Value as the most convenient shopping experience available. The "Help Is Just Around The Corner" tag line embodies the flavor of the locally owned hardware stores while emphasizing the good service consumers have come to expect from True Value.

Circulars are an integral part of the promotion for the brand, getting out the message of great

needed to grow their businesses. As locally owned and operated stores, True Value stores offer a superior shopping experience because the retailers take the time to learn what their customers truly want.

In addition to True Value Paint, the brand value extends to True Value's private labels as well. The Green Thumb and Master Mechanic names are well known to consumers as brands of high quality.

THINGS YOU DIDN'T KNOW ABOUT TRUE VALUE

❍ True Value recently became the official hardware store of the Make-A-Wish Foundation.

❍ A leading consumer-tracking magazine has selected the True Value brand E-Z Kare paint as a "Best Buy" twice.

❍ True Value Manufacturing produces over 2100 colors for interior and exterior paint.

❍ In August 2000, True Value Manufacturing produced its 200 millionth can of latex paint.

❍ Each True Value hardware store is independently owned and operated. There are no corporately-owned stores.

Marines
The Few. The Proud.

THE MARKET

In America, the economy hums. Abroad, the threats retreat. In high schools and at the shopping malls, kids have discovered that 'life skills' can be acquired in the private sector. Increasing numbers of young people choose to find their challenges in college and their rewards in the civilian sector.

The all-volunteer military thus faces a problem that must be addressed: Recruit new members, or America's state of readiness will become extremely vulnerable. For the military services the goal seemed easy enough—recruit 150,000 young Americans in 2000. For the Marine Corps the task was more difficult—sign up 39,500 recruits with less marketing support (1/2 the recruiting force of the U.S. Army), fewer advertising resources (outspent in advertising 5:1 by the Army), and the toughest product to sell (longest boot camp, longer enlistment period, first to fight).

ACHIEVEMENTS

Even though interest in the military was declining, the Marine Corps met the challenge with the same tenacity it has brought to the battlefield. In September of 2000, they exceeded their goal of 39,500 recruits without lowering enlistment standards. Since 1995, the Marine Corps has been the only military service that has met its recruiting goals every year. In addition, they maintained their quality standards which resulted in a 4 percent reduction in boot camp attrition, which was far below all the other military services. And that was for a boot camp that was not only longer, but also more difficult.

At the same time the other services increased their appeal with larger enlistment bonuses and money for college, while they decreased the quality standards for new recruits. The Marine Corps dug in and reinforced their smaller but capable recruiting staff through an intense training program, which included introducing them to event marketing extensions and sponsorships. This introduction provided them with unique opportunities to reach their target market. The combination of hard work, leadership and commitment to quality resulted in attracting some of the most qualified recruits in Marine Corps history

HISTORY

November 10, 1775, is the celebrated birthday of the United States Marine Corps. When the colonies could not work out reconciliation with the Crown, the Colonial Congress decided to take a tougher attitude. A resolution was drafted creating a new military unit called the Continental Marines.

The Marine Corps brand is the result of 226 years of legend, lore, and extraordinary military achievement. Marines were always viewed as the toughest and they proved that on the world's battlefields.

The Marines fought valiantly in the Revolutionary War. They assisted Washington's Army in the second battle of Trenton. Under the command of the illustrious John Paul Jones they made raids on British soil, the first in 700 years. In 1785, at the end of the Revolutionary War, the Continental Marines were disbanded, but 13 years later the Corps was reestablished as President John Adams signed a bill into law.

During the War of 1812 with England, the British burned nearly every public building in Washington, D.C., including the White House and the Capitol. The Marine Barracks, however, were spared the burning out of respect for the Corps.

One of the most famous and memorable battles the Marine Corps ever fought was the Battle of Iwo Jima. More than 30,000 Japanese troops occupied the high ground. Miles of interlocking caves, concrete blockhouses, and pillboxes made their advantage almost impenetrable. Finally, after 36 days of fighting, the tiny island was secured. Just 23 days before, the Marines and Navy Corpsmen had raised the flag on Mt. Suribachi. A moment that was forever captured in the famed Iwo Jima memorial. In the words of Admiral Chester W. Nimitz, "Uncommon valor was a common virtue." Those words live on today. The Marine Corps has courageously defended foreign soil the world over. Since the Persian Gulf Crisis in 1991 through the end of 1998, the Marines have been "sent-in" over 50 times. On the average, the Corps is called upon once every five weeks. Their tenacious spirit and unyielding determination have been captured in such names as "Leathernecks" and "Devil Dogs." The Marines have always been "First to fight" and their legend lives on in the hearts of the American people.

THE PRODUCT

Since the Corps was first formed in 1775 in a small room at Tun Tavern in Philadelphia, it has always been the toughest and most elite branch of all the military services. It has never wavered from this early identity.

The Marine Corps has the longest and by far the most difficult boot camp. Thirteen weeks of tough physical and mental training. It is through this process that some 40,000 young men and women undergo an amazing personal transformation every year that turns them into United States Marines.

Today the Corps is 175,000 strong, the smallest of all the services. Its members are the only ones who stand watch at American embassies throughout the world. And the Marine Band, which was established by Thomas Jefferson in 1803, is known as "The President's Own."

RECENT DEVELOPMENTS

The missions that the Corps conducts today have changed in nature and require a unique set of skills from recruits. To answer this challenge, the Corps recently introduced a 13th week of Marine Corps boot camp, even though it was faced with one of the most difficult recruiting environments in the history of the all-volunteer force. This was done to provide recruits with the moral and mental compass to make decisions in moments of the greatest duress. This 13th week is called "The Crucible" and includes a 48-hour ordeal with little sleep or food. Recruits are subjected to a series of complex mental and physical obstacles.

The Corps has also launched a unique Marine Corps Martial Arts Training Program designed to give new recruits and current Marines a tough edge in situations in which deploying weapons could involve the risk of creating an international incident.

And the new "Strategic Corporal" program is designed to give the power of decision making to small units as they tackle the peace-keeping challenges of the future. All of these initiatives demand a top-quality recruit who can readily adapt and overcome adversity.

PROMOTION

With the advent of "Sword," a 30-second television commercial produced in 1985 that likened the making of a Marine with the making of a sword, the United States Marine Corps embarked on a totally new direction in its national advertising program. As the announcer intoned, "You begin with raw steel. Shape it with fire, muscle, and sweat...", the viewer watched a hot, steel blank being pounded and shaped into the famed Mameluke sword carried by Marine officers.

That spot was followed by a commercial entitled "Knight," where a medieval warrior in armor is knighted and awarded a sword, at which point he transforms into a United States Marine. Three years later, a spot called "Chess" depicted a life-sized white knight on a life-sized chessboard taking the sword into battle and successfully defeating the black king. Thus, the trilogy was complete. Sword is made. Sword is awarded. Sword is taken into battle.

Not only were these spots memorable and extremely effective, they also distinguished the Marine Corps within the military category as well as within the entire teen category of commercials. These commercials have been followed by other striking and successful executions like "Transformation," and "Rite of Passage," which are both fantastic metaphors for Marine Corps boot camp.

Since computers play such a big role in the day-to-day lives of teens, unique web sites, banner ads, and an interactive CD-ROM were also developed to carry the message to the target. Those efforts have been further enhanced with extensive direct mail campaigns and event marketing like ESPN's X-Games and theater advertising, where the Corps sponsored the launch of "Star Wars, The Phantom Menace."

Naturally, the country's premiere leadership school offers only the latest in athletic equipment.

Gym Class

Obviously, this is not your average gym. Sure, we strengthen your body. But we also strengthen your mind. That's how we go about building leaders. Shaping young men and women into confident, determined decision makers. So, like to take a look at the equipment? Call 1-800-MARINES. Or visit us at WWW.MARINEOFFICER.COM. You'll love our new rope climb.

Marines
The Few. The Proud.

BRAND VALUES

For 226 years, the United States Marine Corps has represented the epitome of military virtue. A tough, elite expeditionary force whose members have to earn the right to belong. The motto of the Corps, *"Semper Fidelis"* or *"Always Faithful,"* is a testament to the strong bond that is shared by those who faithfully defend the principles of this nation.

The Marines have always been the first to fight. They have never failed to display perseverance and valor on the battlefield. The Corps' values of honor, courage, and commitment are the hallmarks of membership in this proud and distinguished organization.

Not everyone can be a Marine, but that has made this elite group of men and women what it is today. Or, in the words of the Corps, *"Maybe you can be one of us. The Few. The Proud. The Marines."*

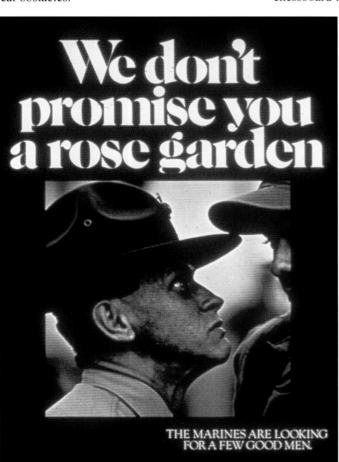

We don't promise you a rose garden

THE MARINES ARE LOOKING FOR A FEW GOOD MEN.

THE MARKET

There's nothing like it. The familiar words, "Mail's here," set the stage for a special ritual in American households from coast to coast. Families stop what they're doing to look through the day's mail, searching for that favorite magazine, the invitation to a special sale or those welcome words from a friend or loved one far away. No other form of communication is so tangible, so immediate and so personal. Only the U.S. Postal Service offers this unique gateway to the household.

The price of a single postage stamp provides access to a delivery network that connects each and every one of America's more than 130 million households and businesses. With retail outlets and post offices in 38,000 locations, the Postal Service covers the map. From money to messages to merchandise, the Postal Service delivers it all, to everyone, everywhere, every day.

ACHIEVEMENTS

A leader in service and customer satisfaction, the Postal Service has established a solid bond of trust with those it serves, bringing special value to its brand. And it is working to extend the value of its brand in a new century, developing new products and services to help its customers communicate better—both in traditional delivery services and new electronic communications.

The growth of online sales creates opportunities for mailers to develop an advertising mix that brings the power of direct mail to Internet sales. That, in turn, means a corresponding rise in package shipments. The Postal Service, with a delivery network unlike any other, is ideally suited to serve this growing market. It is also focusing on other growing markets and has introduced a Spanish-language Web site, www.usps.com/correo.

In embracing new technology, the Postal Service has provided innovative solutions for its customers' communications needs and, at the same time, made it easier for customers to do business with the Postal Service.

HISTORY

In the 225 years since the Continental Congress named Benjamin Franklin the first Postmaster General, the United States and the Postal Service have grown and changed together. The postal system that the Congress created helped bind a fledgling nation together, supported the growth of commerce and ensured a free flow of ideas and information

Today, the Postal Service helps fuel the nation's economy, delivering billions of dollars in financial transactions and more than 600 million messages to a customer base that includes 8 million businesses and 250 million Americans. Yet, despite its size, the heart of the Postal Service remains its local presence and its personal service to people in communities large

and small.

The Postal Service was instrumental in the development of new transportation systems and technologies as it grew to serve an expanding nation. From post roads to highways, and from railroads to air transportation, the Postal Service has led the way in finding better and more economical ways to help the people of America communicate.

That journey through American history is commemorated by the Postal Service though its award-winning and comprehensive postage stamp program, celebrating the people, places, events and ideas that make up the American experience.

THE PRODUCT

Universal mail service is the foundation of everything the U.S. Postal Service does. Postage stamps may be the cornerstone of that foundation, but they are only one of a wide variety of products and services that meet the diverse communications needs of its customers—both consumers and businesses.

Delivery options include city and rural carrier service and post office box delivery, all with forwarding service. Depending on the service selected, mail can be registered, insured and certified with tracking and delivery confirmation options.

Different classes of mail offer customers the level of speed and economy they need. Express Mail, Priority Mail and First-Class Mail get it there fastest. Standard Mail serves the direct-mail industry. Package Services provide an economical way to send parcels and other merchandise items. Publishers and their readers depend on Periodicals Service for delivery of newspapers and magazines. And International Services provide a gateway to the world's markets—with a service structure based on speed of delivery.

The U.S. Postal Service is committed to helping the nation communicate, reliably and securely.

RECENT DEVELOPMENTS

It's an e-world out there and the U.S Postal Service is a part of it. The Internet has opened new avenues for providing postal products and services, and the Postal Service's presence assures Americans a safe and trusted provider for eCommerce transactions.

The Postal Service's USPS eBillPay is a convenient option for receiving and paying bills electronically. PosteCS provides secure online document transmission. USPS' Electronic Postmark adds a welcome level of security to electronic communications. NetPost Mailing Online is the simplest way to prepare and pay for larger mailings, and have them entered into the mailstream—right from home or office. A quick visit to www.usps.com is all it takes.

The Postal Service's Web site offers much more. It's the single best place for information about all things postal: from ZIP codes to postage rates and mailing information; from local post office information to electronic products and services. You can track a package or visit the Postal Store, the online source for postage stamps, stamped cards, stamped envelopes, attractive philatelic gift items—and more. It's just a click away at www.usps.com.

PROMOTION

"Fly Like an Eagle" is the familiar musical and visual theme that helps enhance Postal Service brand awareness across all product lines, as it unifies the organization's advertising and promotional campaigns. The distinctive "whoosh" of the universally recognized postal eagle is now a central feature in Postal Service marketing efforts.

Other companies recognize the value of the Postal Service brand and have joined it in co-advertising ventures. A major credit card company joined the Postal Service in sponsoring a retail sweepstakes that leveraged the U.S Postal Service Pro Cycling Team's back-to-back victories in the challenging Tour de France. The team leader, Lance Armstrong, was the focal point of innovative product advertising on 10,000 Postal Service delivery vehicles and packaging for Priority Mail. Another co-advertising effort featuring America Online, America's leading Internet service

provider, perfectly positioned Postal Service delivery trucks as "The ultimate Internet delivery vehicle," highlighting the comfortable fit of the two service providers.

BRAND VALUES

The Postal Service's brand values, though simple, contribute to an unmatched value proposition: tradition, trust, scope, reliability and affordability. Sending and receiving mail is an experience shared by everyone. Opening and reading the mail is an integral part of daily life in America. It encourages commerce and communication. It connects families and friends, governments and citizens, publishers and readers, businesses and customers, charities and donors. For more than 200 years, the Postal Service brand has delivered for the American people. The strength of its brand values will assure that the organization continues to deliver.

THINGS YOU DIDN'T KNOW ABOUT U.S. POSTAL SERVICE

- Postal operations are funded entirely by the sale of postal products and services, not by tax dollars.

- The Postal Service delivers mail to more than 130 million addresses. This grows by more than 1.5 million new addresses every year. That's the equivalent of adding a city the size of Chicago to its delivery infrastructure.

- The Postal Service handles more than 40 percent of the world's total mail volume.

- In addition to using air, truck, rail and boat, mail is even moved by mule—to and from the bottom of the Grand Canyon.

- The Postal Service operates the nation's largest fleet of alternative-fuel vehicles, using clean fuels such as compressed natural gas and electricity.

- The Postal Service recycled nearly 1 million tons of wastepaper, cardboard, plastics, cans and other material in 1999. These efforts contributed to a cleaner environment *and* resulted in $10 million in revenue, helping to keep the price of postage a world-class bargain.

- The U.S. Mail received the highest security rating in a poll conducted by the Louis Harris organization, beating telephones, faxes, e-mail and the Internet.

THE MARKET

When USA TODAY made its debut in 1982 as a national newspaper, critics thought there was no market for it. There were no national newspapers in America.

Almost twenty years later, USA TODAY has become the largest selling newspaper in the country. The USA TODAY brand now includes: USA TODAY International—an international edition of the newspaper; USATODAY.com—one of the most popular news sites on the internet; USA TODAY *Baseball Weekly*—a weekly magazine for baseball enthusiasts, and USA TODAY LIVE—a broadcast operation between USA TODAY and the Gannett Co., Inc. television stations.

USA TODAY is now a news source known around the world. Americans look to USA TODAY in print, broadcast, or online form for the news they need.

ACHIEVEMENTS

USA TODAY printed 155,000 copies of the newspaper on its first day on sale in 1982. It was a sellout in the area where it was distributed. The newspaper now sells an average of 2.3 million copies per day around the world.

The original dream of the national newspaper has turned into much more. USA TODAY has become a global news source. USATODAY.com serves more than 25 million monthly visitors from all over the world and is an industry-leading news and information Web site. The international edition of the newspaper is printed in five countries overseas and sold in more than 60 countries.

HISTORY

Allen H. Neuharth was the man with the dream of a national newspaper in the U.S. Neuharth was the President and CEO of Gannett Co., Inc. Gannett is one of the largest news and information companies in the United States, owning nearly 100 newspapers and more than 20 television stations. Neuharth had a vision of a national newspaper and assigned four people to study the feasibility of the project. On February 29, 1980, the assignment began as "Project NN"—for national newspaper.

There were many questions that needed to be answered. What production and circulation procedures would have to be put into place in order to get this newspaper to every city across America? How would you market a national newspaper? Would advertisers go for it? These were all things that were studied carefully. After more than a year of exhaustive research, the first prototypes for the newspaper were printed in June of 1981.

This newspaper would be different from any other. It would use bold color and graphics to complement its stories. There would be a lot of sports news and a full page devoted to weather news. Stories would be concise and not jump from page to page. USA TODAY—The Nation's Newspaper, was launched on September 15, 1982. Readers loved it. It was a sellout. The initial launch was in Washington and Baltimore. The next year brought launches in every major U.S. city. The newspaper was well received by readers and the public. The journalism community scoffed at USA TODAY. Critics considered the newspaper to have too much color, too much fluff and not enough hard news. It was nicknamed "McPaper" for its nuggets of information. Despite the criticism, USA TODAY circulation quickly surpassed the one million mark. Readers came and advertisers followed.

USA TODAY's unique look was designed with the baby boomer in mind. It was for those who never knew life without television, had lived in a variety of locations, and had several "hometown teams" they liked to follow. The newspaper was designed for a nation on the go, readers who were traveling for business and pleasure, who would pick up a newspaper in the airport or on the street corner. The TV set-like vending racks made the newspaper stand out among the many newspaper racks on the street. USA TODAY was the first newspaper to recognize the market for selling newspapers to hotels to distribute to their guests. The practice of having a newspaper at your hotel room door in the morning has now become a normal part of most Americans' travel routines. USA TODAY was at the forefront in providing this service to travelers.

USA TODAY was the first newspaper to use satellite technology to manage a national network of presses. The newspaper is edited and composed at USA TODAY headquarters in Virginia and transmitted via satellite to its 36 print sites in the United States.

In 1984, USA TODAY branched outside of the United States. The international edition made its debut in July 1984. Initially, the international edition was printed in the U.S. and flown overseas. Now there are five print sites abroad: London, England; Frankfurt, Germany; Charleroi, Belgium; Milan, Italy; and Hong Kong, Peoples Republic of China. From those five print sites, USA TODAY is

distributed to 60 countries around the world.

USA TODAY *Baseball Weekly* was launched in April, 1991. *Baseball Weekly* is a magazine published each Wednesday and is aimed at baseball enthusiasts across America. More than two million readers turn to *Baseball Weekly* each week to get their baseball news. In April, 1995, USA TODAY went online. The Web site was originally known as USA TODAY Online. The name was later changed to USATODAY.com. The Web site includes content from the newspaper and original content developed by the USATODAY.com staff.

At the Summer Olympic games in Atlanta in 1996, USA TODAY celebrated another first by printing seven days a week in the Atlanta area during the event. USA TODAY dominated coverage with the latest breaking news, scores, and highlights.

All of these firsts and all of these new products have brought USA TODAY to where it is today. USA TODAY is a leader on the American media scene.

THE PRODUCT

The USA TODAY product is news—in all its forms. Whether you want your news from a newspaper or prefer to receive it electronically, USA TODAY is there, in the United States and abroad. The newspaper reaches nearly five million readers each day. The Web site serves more than 25 million monthly visitors' news needs.

USA TODAY has become the source for national news, whether it's print, television, or online. The product is news and information, no matter what form it's packaged in.

RECENT DEVELOPMENTS

The USA TODAY brand has grown and changed with the times over the last two decades. The newspaper launched its most significant redesign in April, 2000.

The production process changed and USA TODAY is now being printed on a slightly smaller paper width. With the size changing, it was a perfect time to redesign some aspects of the newspaper including the font style and size.

The redesign has been well received by readers and the public. A new initiative, USA TODAY LIVE was announced in February 2000. LIVE is the television arm of the USA TODAY brand. This project brings together the newspaper, the Web site and Gannett's television news programs. Television news segments are produced based on USA TODAY content and run on Gannett Co. Inc.'s more than twenty television stations in the U.S. and on USATODAY.com.

PROMOTION

Early promotion of USA TODAY as The Nation's Newspaper included numerous television advertisements to get the word out to the public on this new national newspaper. Some advertisements included such well-known personalities as Willie Mays and Willard Scott in the "I read it every day" campaign.

USA TODAY's current advertising campaign tagline is: "An Economy of Words, A Wealth of Information." The USA TODAY brand is known for its concise and easy-to-read writing style and the current ad campaign plays to those strengths.

USA TODAY has also used strategic product placement in movies and television to heighten the awareness of its products by delivering news racks and newspapers to television and movie productions across the United States.

Mock newspapers are sometimes printed for specific movie scenes in which a newspaper is used.

BRAND VALUES

The USA TODAY mission statement says: USA TODAY is the easy-to-use, comprehensive source of timely news and information edited to inform and entertain today's time-pressed, affluent, and influential people. This mission reflects what USA TODAY does best: keeping the public informed of the news they need to know 24 hours a day, 7 days a week.

With USA TODAY, you truly get an economy of words and a wealth of information.

THINGS YOU DIDN'T KNOW ABOUT USA TODAY

❍ On January 19, 1991, USA TODAY published the first Saturday edition in its history. It was a special edition to cover the start of the Persian Gulf War.

❍ There are more than 100,000 USA TODAY news racks on street corners in the United States.

❍ The electronic content that makes up the newspaper travels more than 44,600 miles through space via satellite each night to all of USA TODAY's print sites.

❍ In September, 1986, USA TODAY became the youngest publication ever parodied by the Harvard Lampoon group.

❍ USA TODAY set a circulation record with 3,251,310 papers sold on September 5, 1997. The issue featured coverage of the death and upcoming funeral of Britain's Princess Diana.

verizon

THE MARKET

The communications industry, in the midst of the fastest and most radical technological change in 100 years, today operates in an era of unprecedented competition. An extraordinary wave of mergers and acquisitions has swept the industry as new players enter the market and established companies expand to provide consumers with a full range of communications services.

By the end of 2001, it's estimated that some 150 million Americans—more than half the U.S. population—will be on-line. Worldwide, the number of on-line users is expected to top 300 million—an increase of 80 percent in the past year alone. U.S. households will spend an average of more than eight hours a week on-line, in part because of the growth of high-capacity access technologies such as Digital Subscriber Line (DSL). In the communications business, data traffic has already surpassed voice traffic; and with data capacity doubling every 90 days as a result of new infrastructure investments, the lead is lengthening rapidly.

Verizon, driven by its belief in the power of networks, the value of customer connections, and the strength of a unified brand, is at the forefront of this dynamic environment and is quickly becoming one of the world's leading communications companies. With its unparalleled national scale in landline and wireless networks and a significant global presence, Verizon is uniquely positioned to capitalize on these growth trends of the new economy and deliver the benefits of communications to everyone.

ACHIEVEMENTS

After two years of negotiations and regulatory hurdles, the FCC approved the $60 billion merger between Bell Atlantic and GTE on June 16, 2000. These two powerful telecommunication companies—each rich in expertise, experience, and aggressive technological foresight—combined to form the ultimate telecommunications resource—Verizon Communications. On July 3, 2000, Verizon began trading on the New York Stock Exchange under the symbol VZ.

From day one, Verizon led the industry with more ways to touch customers and meet their requirements, more cash to fuel growth and innovation, and more investment capital to deploy the technologies of the future than any company before it. Verizon's digital networks already include more fiber optics and more "first mile" assets than any other communications company. These networks, as they continue to develop, will give Verizon the premiere distribution platform for electronic commerce and delivery of a comprehensive suite of

Internet-age services, including high-speed Internet access powered by DSL.

HISTORY

Verizon traces its roots to the late 19th century to such diverse sources as the giant American Telephone and Telegraph Co. (AT&T), which dominated the industry for more than a century, and the tiny independent Richland Center Telephone Co. of Wisconsin. Over the decades, a series of acquisitions, particularly in California, transformed Richland into the General Telephone Corporation.

In 1955, General Telephone merged with Theodore Gary and Co. At the time, these firms were the first and second largest independent telephone companies, respectively, in America. Four years later, General Telephone merged

with Sylvania Electric Products to become General Telephone & Electronics Corp. (GTE).

A new era of communications began in 1984 when the long dominant AT&T was split into seven Regional Bell Operating Companies (RBOCs)—also called "Baby Bells"—including Bell Atlantic (which serviced the mid-Atlantic region) and NYNEX (which serviced the New York and New England regions). In 1991, GTE merged with Contel Communications—at the time, the largest telecommunications deal in history.

In 1997, NYNEX and Bell Atlantic merged to form the second largest telecommunications company in the nation, and retained the Bell Atlantic name, but with a new logo and identity.

In 1998, Bell Atlantic and GTE announced their plans to merge. On April 3, 2000, the joint wireless venture among Bell Atlantic Mobile, PrimeCo, and Vodafone Airtouch was completed, creating Verizon Wireless. On June 30, the Bell Atlantic/GTE merger became official, and the resulting Verizon became the largest local telecommunications company in the United States. GTE Wireless properties were then folded into Verizon Wireless, which became the largest wireless company in the nation as well.

THE PRODUCT

Verizon is the largest provider of wireline and wireless communications in the United States, with more than 109 million access line equivalents and 27.5 million wireless customers. Verizon is also the world's largest provider of print and on-line directory information. A Fortune 10 company with more than 263,000 employees and approximately $63 billion in annual revenues, Verizon has a global presence that extends to 44 countries in the Americas, Europe, Asia, and the Pacific.

Bell Atlantic
and GTE
are now Verizon.

And Ken Konishi's
global IT strategy
won't change a bit.

New name. Same great business solutions.

veri on

Verizon provides a variety of products and services ranging from local, long distance, wireless, data, and video services to Internet access, pay phones, enhanced calling, operator/directory assistance, directory and on-line publishing, and telephones and accessories.

Verizon offers residential consumers a convenient, single source for all at-home communication needs—from long distance and local phone services and features to Internet access, wireless services, and high-speed connectivity.

It offers business customers a superior range of products and services, world-class support, and comprehensive communications solutions. Verizon also provides a vast and complete range of services to federal, state, and local governments.

RECENT DEVELOPMENTS
Verizon is at the forefront of new communication technologies. Through new alliances and product introductions, the company continues to increase its breadth and depth of product and service offerings.

Verizon was the first RBOC to receive FCC permission to offer long distance service. The company set a first-year goal of signing up one million customers for the new service in the state of New York. It reached its goal in seven months and, to mark the occasion, donated $1 million to five charities that positively impact the state. In March 2001, Verizon signed its five-millionth long distance customer nationwide, making it the fourth largest long distance company in the United States.

Verizon business customers can make global connections with three new long distance services—Global Private Line, Frame Relay, and Asynchronous Transfer Mode (ATM)—that promise quick and reliable connectivity to more than 60 countries.

Verizon is launching voice-over DSL, one of the first local phone companies to use this new technology, which will provide high-speed Internet access and support up to 16 separate telephones over a single copper wire for both home and business operations. This new technology will improve broadband access and allow Verizon to offer services beyond standard calling features.

The strategic alliance between Verizon and Radio Shack brought a national, unified approach to wireless offerings for both companies. Verizon Wireless enhanced its national retail presence by offering services in about 75 percent of the Radio Shack chain.

Verizon Wireless also launched the National Mobile Web service, which provides the convenience and mobility of wireless communications with the popular content of the World Wide Web.

PROMOTION
Verizon has become one of the most powerful and recognizable names in the world through a distinctive brand strategy and the effective implementation of a comprehensive brand identity system.

The Verizon brand name is derived from the words "veritas" and "horizon." Veritas, Latin for "truth," represents the company's dedicated approach to providing honest, reliable, and accurate service. Horizon represents the limitless possibilities inherent in Verizon's pioneering spirit and commitment to the future. When joined, these two words form a name that evokes vigor, speed, precision, dependability, and extensive global reach.

On August 1, 2000, the company launched an intense campaign to build brand awareness. James Earl Jones, the highly recognized voice of Bell Atlantic and now spokesperson for Verizon, reassured customers that they could expect the same reliable and dependable service they received in the past. The campaign included TV and radio commercials, as well as print, Internet, and outdoor advertising.

Verizon kicked off 2001 with a powerful nationwide campaign that demonstrated the range of services now available from the new merged company, and how those services can enhance their customers' quality of life. Again, spokesperson James Earl Jones played a key role in the campaign, which utilized TV, radio, print, Internet, and outdoor ads.

BRAND VALUES
Verizon's goal is to be the most respected name in communications and a leader in providing voice, data, and information services in every market it serves, both domestic and international. It seeks to ensure that customers associate the Verizon brand with integrity, respect, imagination, passion, and quality service.

Verizon's promise in this era of technological advancement is to deliver the level of customer care that Internet-age consumers demand: fast, responsive, customized, and reliable communications solutions.

THINGS YOU DIDN'T KNOW ABOUT VERIZON

○ Verizon is the 11th largest employer in the United States, according to April 2001 *Fortune* magazine.

○ Verizon Wireless has a footprint covering 90 percent of the U.S. population and 96 of the top 100 U.S. markets.

○ The Verizon Foundation will invest $70 million in communities from Hawaii to Maine in 2001—placing it among the top 10 largest corporate foundations in the United States.

○ Verizon's SuperPages.com receives 7.7 million contacts per month from approximately 3.4 million unique visitors.

○ Verizon purchased more than $1.3 billion in goods and services from minority- and women-owned suppliers last year, making it a charter member of the elite *Billion-Dollar Roundtable*. The roundtable, a project of *Minority Business News U.S.A.* and *Women's Enterprise Magazine*, includes a select circle of corporations that each spend more than $1 billion annually with minority- and women-owned businesses.

○ Verizon is ranked fourth in the 2001 *Forbes 500* list of America's largest public companies in four categories: sales, profits, assets, and market value.

Westinghouse

THE MARKET

George Westinghouse was an inventive engineer whose intellect probed the frontiers of electricity in the late 19th century on a variety of fronts — generation, transmission, illumination and industrial application. As broad-ranged as his vision was, he never could have foreseen the diversity of businesses that one day would flourish around the globe under the Westinghouse banner.

Nothing then could have hinted that the day would come when Westinghouse would be a name associated with generating systems powered by nuclear energy, with radio and commer-

cial networks heard and seen by millions of people every day, or with sophisticated electronic systems that would help control supersonic aircraft.

Yet these are but a few of the areas that have institutionalized the name Westinghouse as a leader in engineering innovation in consumer, industrial, utility, electronics, and transportation markets. For decades, the Westinghouse brand was most visibly associated with consumer appliances, such as refrigerators and laundry equipment, and with radio and television broadcasting.

As years passed, millions of American families would come to recognize the early slogan "Every House Needs a Westinghouse" and would tune in to Westinghouse Broadcasting's Group W radio stations for news, sports, and entertainment. Less visible but as important

commercially were specialized industrial and governmental markets around the world.

George Westinghouse was at the birth of the electric utility industry in the closing years of the 19th century. His pioneering work in the generation and transmission of electric power was carried on by the business enterprises he founded.

Ground-breaking research in the mysteries of uranium led Westinghouse into a leadership role in the commercial application of the atom in electric power generation and naval ship propulsion. Its expertise extended into challenging assignments in handling and storing radioactive waste at government sites across the U.S.

As skyscrapers rose in cities around the world, elevators and electric stairways with the familiar Westinghouse nameplate moved millions of urban workers to and from their offices (which were cooled by Westinghouse air-conditioning systems) every day. As air traffic increased, Westinghouse captured a leadership position in the horizontal people-mover market at airports in Tampa, Seattle-Tacoma, Atlanta, and other important cities.

ACHIEVEMENTS

Westinghouse has been at the center of a series of remarkable advances in the electric industry and related businesses. George Westinghouse himself was involved in the first successful application of alternating-current electricity, to a lighting system in Great Barrington, Mass., as early as 1886. Two years later, he obtained exclusive rights to important patents developed by inventor Nikola Tesla that made Westinghouse-branded induction motors a key factor in the electrification of manufacturing plants.

Westinghouse also was associated with the first transmission of alternating current power — in Oregon City, Ore., in 1890 — and the lighting of the Colombian Exposition in Chicago in 1893. Westinghouse supplied the first generators when the Niagara Falls were harnessed to produce electricity. The first scheduled commercial radio broadcast was made by Westinghouse's KDKA in reporting the results of the 1920 presidential election--the victory of Warren Harding over James Cox.

In 1937, Westinghouse built the first industrial atom-smasher in a fundamental research program in nuclear physics. Less than two decades later, the first nuclear submarine — the USS Nautilus — went to sea, powered by a Westinghouse nuclear propulsion system. Two years after that, a Westinghouse pressurized-water nuclear reactor went into service at the

nation's first nuclear-electric power plant at Shippingport, Pa.

In yet another historic event, a Westinghouse-designed camera placed on the moon by Neil Armstrong in 1969 relayed pictures back to earth from the lunar landing site.

HISTORY

George Westinghouse was granted a charter for the Westinghouse Electric Company in 1886. In the next few decades, Westinghouse and his associates aggressively promoted the development of electric power across a broad range of applications. Tesla-designed Westinghouse motors revolutionized manufacturing processes, while the landmark successes in Oregon City, Great Barrington, and Chicago's Colombian Exposition laid the groundwork for the nation's electric utility system.

Westinghouse quickly outgrew its first plant in Pittsburgh's Garrison Alley, establishing a plant in nearby East Pittsburgh that continually expanded until the early 1940s, when 25,000 employees were engaged in making equipment in support of the World War II effort.

From its original product lines in motors, generators, and lighting equipment, Westinghouse expanded into scores of related fields — manufacturing and marketing transformers, meters, switchgear, home appliances, circuit breakers, air-conditioning equipment, and elevators.

A modest product development department at the original plant expanded in size and personnel and eventually blossomed into the Westinghouse Research & Development

Center, one of the premier scientific institutions in industry. In 1928, one of the most significant developments in communications was the invention of an iconoscope — the first practical TV camera tube — by Westinghouse scientist Vladimir Zworykin.

As the electrification of the world proceeded, Westinghouse jumped into the emerging market of electric consumer appliances. Laundry equipment, refrigerators, dishwashers and smaller appliances such as toasters, mixers and hair dryers appeared on retail shelves throughout the U.S., and beyond. In 1950, Westinghouse dazzled American consumers with the first self-defrosting refrigerator.

In parallel developments, the Westinghouse Lamp Company grew steadily from the infant days of the light bulb into one of the largest and most innovative producers of lighting products.

From early industrial applications, Westinghouse expertise in motors led the growth of its role in the transit industry, which extended from the trolley-car days to modern urban systems like BART in San Francisco.

From the birth of the industry, Westinghouse was a key supplier of equipment for electric utilities from the first electric turbine-generator station, in Hartford, Conn., at the turn of the century to the atomic power era.

The electronic specialization of Westinghouse scientists and business operations led to the emergence of a strong corporate position in defense systems, especially radar.

From the rudimentary KDKA radio transmitter that first broadcast commercially from a tiny studio near Pittsburgh in 1920, Westinghouse developed and maintained a strong presence in the radio broadcasting industry and, later in television, with stations in key markets from Boston to the West Coast.

THE PRODUCT

Given the historic diversity of its markets, no single product, or family of products, defines the Westinghouse brand. Instead, an array of seemingly unrelated businesses have shared the Westinghouse name. To millions of consumers, certainly, home appliances leap to mind as the core identity of the brand. But to industrial executives, government officials and other specialized buying influences, products as diverse as power generation, transmission, and distribution equipment, aviation electronics, and environmental management services are identified with the Westinghouse name.

RECENT DEVELOPMENTS

From a single corporate umbrella, many of Westinghouse product lines in recent years have become affiliated with leading corporations around the world. Westinghouse Broadcasting, for instance, became part of CBS, a pioneer in the field. In home appliances, Westinghouse will continue as a strong independent brand with a broad product line.

PROMOTION

For more than a century, the Westinghouse name — as a corporation and as a brand identification — has been promoted by creative programs using a variety of media. Traditional print advertising campaigns and radio and television commercials, industrial trade shows, specialized technical forums, world-famous air shows and scientific education programs tailored for young people made Westinghouse a readily identified name around the globe.

"You can be sure…if it's Westinghouse" has endured as the company's slogan for more than a half century as the center of consistent, powerful messages about the quality, reliability, and utility of Westinghouse refrigerators, laundry equipment, toasters, irons, radio and TV sets, and hi-fi equipment.

Westinghouse was identified for many years with the legendary television drama program "Studio One."

Westinghouse was particularly attracted to TV because it provided a way to actually demonstrate Westinghouse consumer products, catching the attention of potential buyers and inviting them to visit their Westinghouse dealers.

A secondary purpose was a corporate one — to show that the company was research-oriented, the maker of advanced products and had the capabilities needed to succeed in major engineering jobs.

During this same period and in succeeding years, Westinghouse undertook major sponsorship programs for college and professional football, convention coverage and election returns for three presidential campaigns, and various variety and drama programs.

BRAND VALUES

Westinghouse began as the name of one of industry's great innovators and business entrepreneurs. In the intervening decades, it established itself as a widely recognized brand name identified with advanced engineering, scientific achievement, and product reliability. "You can be sure…if it's Westinghouse" remains a trusted concept even today.

THINGS YOU DIDN'T KNOW ABOUT WESTINGHOUSE

○ Engineer-Inventor George Westinghouse held a total of 361 patents.

○ Chicago's 1893 Colombian Exposition gave Westinghouse the opportunity to demonstrate the practicality of alternating current. The Exposition was illuminated by about 250,000 lamps — produced in one year in a Westinghouse factory — and involved the use of 350 transformers.

○ Three Westinghouse generators went into service in 1895 harnessing the Niagara River to deliver power to Buffalo, N.Y., 20 miles away. They continued in service for 26 years.

○ Radio's first scheduled commercial operation was the Westinghouse broadcast of the 1920 Harding-Cox election returns from a tiny 100-watt transmitter of station KDKA in East Pittsburgh, Pa.

○ A Westinghouse lunar camera enabled millions of TV viewers on earth to watch man's first steps on the moon in 1969.

○ The Science Talent Search, a nationwide science and math competition for high school seniors sponsored by Westinghouse for more than 50 years, produced five winners who went on to win Nobel Prizes and two who won Fields Medals, the top prize in mathematics.

THE MARKET

Over the past 20 years, World Wrestling Federation Entertainment, Inc. (WWFE) has become one of the most universally recognized brands in the entertainment industry. It has succeeded in crafting a weekly action-adventure soap opera that has attracted audiences worldwide, and has created Superstars—such as Stone Cold Steve Austin and The Rock—who have quickly become household names.

An integrated media and entertainment company, World Wrestling Federation Entertainment has built its name on the development, production and marketing of television programming, pay-per-view specials and live events, as well as the licensing and sale of branded consumer products.

WWFE's unique product—The World Wrestling Federation—combines thrilling athleticism with exciting storylines and dynamic characters. Every week, more than 20 million U.S. households tune in to watch nine hours of WWFE programming across The National Network (TNN), UPN, MTV and syndicated programming. Its appeal is strongest among the critical demographic of teens, a group that spends $153 billion annually, and young adults.

But it is the live event that is truly the starting point for all great things that follow. In 2000, the company produced more than 200 live events at arenas around the United States and Canada. The company also sold out two shows in the United Kingdom.

The enterprises of WWFE are constantly expanding. To date, the company has launched its own record label—SmackDown! Records, a drag racing team, and an entertainment complex in the heart of New York's Times Square.

ACHIEVEMENTS

As clear indications of the success of the WWFE brand, the numbers speak for themselves:
• An 800 percent increase in branded merchandise sales over the past four years. This takes into account the 110 domestic and international licensee partners in sports apparel, action figures, video games, publishing and music, as well as other product areas appealing to the core young adult demograpic.

• Television programs and pay-per-view events seen in more than 130 countries, and broadcast in 11 languages.
• The company's 12 annual pay-per-view programs generated 6.8 million buys in fiscal year 2000—over one million alone for WrestleMania in April 2000.
• Six of the top ten home videos in the recreational sports category "*Billboard*," (March 2001) are World Wrestling Federation Home Videos. In 2000, the company shipped more than 30 titles on VHS and DVD formats.

However, even with all of the achievements the company has as a whole, it is the World Wrestling Federation Superstars who have earned the respect of millions and millions of fans worldwide. Even Hollywood has taken notice of their star power. For instance, The Rock has hosted NBC's Saturday Night Live and made his feature film debut in "The Mummy Returns." Stone Cold Steve Austin has appeared on CBS's "Nash Bridges," and Chyna has appeared on several episodes of NBC's "3rd Rock from the Sun."

In addition to the on-air personalities that have become part of mainstream America, some of the World Wrestling Federation Superstars have brought their personal stories to life in best-selling autobiographies. Mick "Mankind" Foley has written two autobiographies—"Have a Nice Day!" and "Foley is Good"—both of which reached the #1 spot on the New York Times Bestseller list. The Rock's autobiography also landed atop the New York Times Bestseller and stayed on the chart for 20 weeks. More best-selling books quickly followed including, "If They Only Knew"—Chyna's autobiography,—"Can You Take the Heat?"—a compilation of the World Wrestling Federation Superstars favorite recipes, "The History of Wrestlemania," and "Mick Foley's Christmas Chaos," a children's holiday book penned by the man himself.

HISTORY

Vincent K. McMahon, chairman of the board of World Wrestling Federation Entertainment, Inc., is a third generation promoter who has made the World Wrestling Federation the global phenomenon it is today. As a pioneer in the television syndication business, a recognized television personality throughout the world, a visionary promoter and a fearless marketer, he continues to make his presence known as a leader within the broadcast and entertainment industries. Vince's wife, Linda, is CEO of WWFE. They have two adult children - Shane, president of WWF New Media, and Stephanie, director of the Creative Team, and a daughter-in-law, Marissa McMahon, who is director of publicity for the company.

In 1980, Titan Sports was incorporated and, in 1982, Vince purchased the Capitol Wrestling Corporation from his father. With this purchase, Vince saw the opportunity to take what had always been a regional operation, and gave the World Wrestling Federation a much broader appeal.

However, it was one event in 1985 that changed the face of sports-entertainment forever. That year, WWFE (then known as Titan Sports) presented its first WrestleMania at Madison Square Garden. The fans responded resoundingly. WrestleMania proved the viability of using a live event as a catalyst for revenues stretching far beyond the attendance gate.

Sports-entertainment had gone mainstream, opening up infinite possibilities in merchandizing and licensing opportunities. Towards the end of the '80s, pay-per-view television became a key source of revenue, bringing exciting action into households around the world and building brand name recognition in the process. Licensees and advertisers viewed the company as an even more attractive investment now that it had begun marketing itself as entertainment.

As the world marveled at the company's strides, the McMahons kept looking ahead, eventually transforming WWFE into a multi-dimensional company unlike any other.

THE PRODUCT
World Wrestling Federation programming features ongoing storylines that center around a cast of colorful, larger-than-life characters. Along with writers from diverse entertainment backgrounds, Vince McMahon heads the World Wrestling Federation's creative team. Among the long-term goals of this creative process are the licensing and merchandising of the performers' likenesses and catch phrases.

WWFE produces two flagship programs that carry the storylines on a weekly basis: "WWF RAW IS WAR," the number-one rated weekly program on cable television, and WWF "SmackDown!," the top-rated program on

As part of its campaign to diversify the company's core business, WWFE created SmackDown! Records. Music has always played a major part of the World Wrestling Federation live event and recent World Wrestling Federation compilation releases have sold more than a million copies In February 2001 the first CD from SmackDown! Records landed on store sheves.

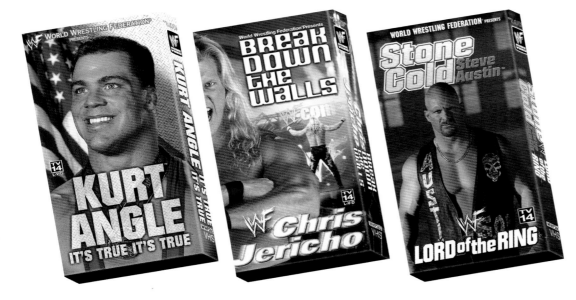

UPN. Additional programs, including "Sunday Night Heat," "Superstars," "Livewire," "Metal" and "Jakked" round out the company's programming options.

RECENT DEVELOPMENTS
World Wrestling Federation Entertainment set its sights on laying the smackdown on Wall Street. In October 1999, the company underwent a successful initial stock offering, and is now featured on the New York Stock Exchange (NYSE) under the symbol WWF.

WWF The Music Volume 5 debuted at #2 on the Billboard Top 200 and shipped more than 1. 5 million copies worldwide.

WWFE has also had an impact on National Hot Rod Association drag racing, unveiling dragsters named after World Wrestling Federation Superstars The Rock, Stone Cold Steve Austin, Kane, Cactus Jack, and Triple H.

In 1999, New York's Times Square became home to WWF New York—the company's first entertainment complex and restaurant. The facility also houses a merchandise store and a

soundstage for television production and concerts. "Sunday Night Heat", which airs on Sunday nights on MTV, is broadcast live from the entertainment complex.

Always looking to strengthen its portfolio of brands, WWFE accquired the World Championship Wrestling (WCW) brand in March 2001. The acquisition adds a solid list of athletes and performers to the roster and gives the company the unique opportunity to build new revenue streams by potentially having more live events, more programming, and more advertisers and sponsors. And in typical WWFE fashion, the acquisition will allow the company to add more diversity and creativity to their storylines.

PROMOTION
No entertainment company has utilized television as effectively as the World Wrestling Federation. Cliffhangers are a staple of its television programs. Fans are urged to attend live events or order pay-per-views in order to satisfy their curiosity about the outcome of the numerous exciting storylines going on simultaneously at any given time. There are no reruns, so viewers are tuning into original-and often live-programming 52 weeks a year.

The World Wrestling Federation's groundbreaking innovations in pay-per-view television established it as an entity people would pay to watch. Similarly, it has taken optimum advantage of more recent technology to further advance its brand.

WWF.com receives more than 8.1 million unique visitors and 240 million page views per month. Additionally, more than eight million video streams are downloaded every month, making WWF.com one of the leading providers of streaming video on the Internet.

The company also promotes its product through two monthly publications. "World Wrestling Federation Magazine" and "RAW Magazine" have a combined reach of nearly 7.5 million readers last year.

BRAND VALUES
WWFE's incredible success derives from its ability to give consumers an affordable and exciting entertainment experience. The company literally exhilarates its audience by presenting a unique spectacle with a trademark "Attitude" that fans have grown to recognize and identify with the WWFE product.

THINGS YOU DIDN'T KNOW ABOUT WWFE

- 93,173 fans attended WrestleMania III at Michigan's Pontiac Silverdome in 1987—an indoor attendance record that still stands.

- At WrestleMania 2000 at Anaheim's Arrowhead Pond, merchandise sales averaged $19 per patron.

- On April 1, 2001, 67,925 fans filled Houston's Reliant Park (formerly the Astrodome) to witness Wrestlemania X-Seven, the largest crowd ever assembled at the famous domed stadium.

THE MARKET

Yogurt has been a staple for centuries in Europe and the Near and Middle East, but it didn't reach the U.S. until the 1930s. In the 1960s, yogurt started gaining popularity, and in the 1970s, U.S. consumption increased 200 percent. Today, yogurt is a staple in two-thirds of American households. Yoplait, the nation's leading brand of yogurt, has been instrumental in growing the U.S. market.

Yogurt is popular among consumers because it's nutritious, makes a satisfying light meal or snack and tastes great. The biggest factor that affects consumers' buying decisions is taste. Yoplait yogurt's exquisite French taste has made it a popular choice worldwide.

Research shows that about half of yogurt lovers eat yogurt at lunch or as an afternoon snack. It seems that heavy yogurt eaters are most likely to eat yogurt as part of their meal. People who eat yogurt less frequently are more evenly split between eating yogurt at mealtime or as a snack. Curiously, women tend to eat yogurt in the morning or afternoon, whereas men eat yogurt at night for an evening snack.

Yogurt consumed by adults is split 60/40, with women eating more than men. For women, yogurt represents a means of taking good care of themselves. Kids also are enjoying yogurt at increasing levels. This is driven in part by the introduction of more kid-targeted yogurt offerings. Moms have discovered that serving kids yogurt is an easy way to ensure they're getting the calcium they need.

ACHIEVEMENTS

The U.S. yogurt industry is a $2-billion dollar industry, and Yoplait is the top-selling brand. Several factors have contributed to the success of the core Yoplait brand, including its easily recognized, inverted-cone shaped cup that makes it stand out on the dairy case shelf. Other strong attributes of the brand include its unique texture and taste, the upscale image conveyed by the packaging design and its compelling marketing communications. Consumers perceive Yoplait yogurt as sophisticated, yet approachable.

In the 1990s, Yoplait recognized that while kids like yogurt, they would like it even more if flavors catered to their tastes. Yoplait introduced Trix yogurt for kids in 1992 and current-ly offers Yumsters and Go-Gurt yogurt as well. These brands allow Yoplait to claim itself as the No. 1 choice in yogurt for kids.

For more than 15 years, Yoplait has been a champion for women's wellness issues. During the past several years, Yoplait has directed a more intense focus on the issue of breast cancer, dedicating a television advertisement, print advertisement, and other promotion to this very important cause.

HISTORY

Developed in France during the early 1960s, Yoplait yogurt was created by SODIMA, a dairy cooperative with headquarters near Paris. SODIMA invented the special process that

makes Yoplait distinctive from other yogurts. Yoplait quickly became a favorite with the French people, and SODIMA decided to expand into other countries. Plans were made for a six-week test run in the U.S.

In January, 1976, the first container of Yoplait rolled off the line of the Michigan Cottage Cheese Company in Reed City, Michigan. The test results exceeded their wildest expectations. By the end of the month, the Reed City plant could not meet product demand.

As one of the fastest-growing items in the supermarket, Yoplait attracted the attention of General Mills, Inc. General Mills was interested in adding a high-quality yogurt to its product line and saw Yoplait as a new way to meet these requirements. Yoplait was a healthful product, delicious, distinctive and reasonably priced.

In October 1977, General Mills acquired the American Yoplait franchise and two Michigan Cottage Cheese plants. With the license from SODIMA and assets from Michigan Cottage Cheese, General Mills established a separate corporate subsidiary, Yoplait USA, Inc. Today, Yoplait is manufactured at four production plants across the country.

THE PRODUCT

The Yoplait brand has repeatedly met the lifestyle demands of consumers, especially in regard to great taste, texture, flavor, variety, convenience and health.

Original Style Yoplait Yogurt continues to be made from the original French recipe. The creamy yogurt has fruit mixed evenly throughout. Originally available in 12 flavors, new varieties are launched every season. Currently, consumers can choose from more than 25 flavors. The most popular flavors are Strawberry, Peach and Strawberry Banana. Yoplait also offers indulgent flavors, such as Key Lime Pie and Orange Crème.

In 1981, General Mills introduced Custard Style Yoplait Yogurt, featuring a rich, creamy texture, like fine custard. The yogurt is mixed with a fruit puree and natural fruit flavors. Popular flavors include Custard Vanilla, Custard Strawberry and Custard Banana.

Yoplait USA launched a nonfat yogurt in 1987. Yoplait Light, initially marketed as Yoplait 150, is available today in 15 flavors. Three flavors introduced

in 2000 include Very Vanilla, Passion Fruit Banana, and Orange Créme.

The Yoplait family includes two yogurt cup products marketed to kids:

Yumsters, a creamy yogurt with added calcium packaged in kid-sized, four-ounce cups, which is popular with children under age 5, and Trix, four-ounce cups of creamy yogurt in flavors inspired by General Mills' popular Trix cereal, is marketed to kids under age 8.

Both sub-brands are sold in multi-packs.

RECENT DEVELOPMENTS

Yoplait took yogurt for kids to a whole new playing level in the fall of 1998 when it introduced Go-Gurt, the first ever yogurt in a tube. Go-Gurt is creamy and delicious yogurt in a squeezable tube that lets kids enjoy it without a spoon. Go-Gurt yogurt's unique formulation keeps it creamy and delicious, whether it is refrigerated, frozen or thawed. Conveniently sized to fit into a lunchbox, frozen Go-Gurt can be packed in the morning and kids can eat it later for lunch or snack. Go-Gurt is available in the flavors kids love, including Strawberry, Strawberry-Banana and Watermelon.

General Mills supported the launch of Go-Gurt with TV spots that encourages kids to "Lose the Spoon" if they wanted to be cool, as well as sampling at children's events. The product was hugely successful, driving the Yoplait kid segment of the yogurt market volume by almost 50 percent over the previous years. Go-Gurt reeled in several awards for General Mills, including packaging, product innovation, and television advertising.

The success of Go-Gurt spurred the development of a portable yogurt for grown-ups: Yoplait Exprèsse. It combines the portability of a tube with great tasting adult flavors, such as Mixed Berry, Lemon Burst, and Key Lime. Like Go-Gurt, Exprèsse can be eaten frozen, thawed or refrigerated.

PROMOTION

As part of its commitment to fight breast cancer, Yoplait is the national series presenting sponsor of the Susan G. Komen Foundation Race for the

Cure®, providing significant financial support. Proceeds from the race fund both national research and local community programs that support breast health education, screening and treatment. The Komen Race for the Cure® is the largest series of 5K run and fitness walks in the world. Yoplait has a presence at each race, and at many of the races provides product sampling, kid activities and post-race massages for participants.

Yoplait also has supported the breast cancer cause with its "Save Lids to Save Lives" pink-lid redemption program. This program offers consumers an opportunity to help raise over $1 million to fight breast cancer. In 2000, Yoplait gave a guaranteed donation of $550,000 to the Komen Race for the Cure®, plus 10 cents for every pink lid received from consumers between September 1 and December 1, 2000, up to a maximum of $500,000, to the Susan G. Komen Breast Cancer Foundation. This contribution will support the Komen Foundation's

mission to eradicate breast cancer as a life-threatening disease by advancing research, education, screening, and treatment.

Yoplait also has been a sponsor of the 1996 and 1998 Olympic Games. To promote its sponsorship of the 1996 Olympics, Yoplait featured a "Flip and Win Olympic Sweepstakes," where a lucky consumer won a significant cash prize by purchasing the cup with the winning lid.

Yoplait promoted its sponsorship of the 1998 Olympics with a "Go for Gold" lid promotion and by featuring figure skating champion Michelle Kwan on its packaging.

National print and television advertising campaigns throughout the years have positioned Yoplait yogurt as a healthy food choice and emphasized the brand's unique taste and texture.

BRAND VALUES

Yoplait USA summarizes the values of the Yoplait brand in this single statement: "Yoplait is the yogurt of singularity, exquisite taste and sophistication that celebrates a joy of life."

THINGS YOU DIDN'T KNOW ABOUT YOPLAIT

○ In the U.S. alone, Yoplait produces 8 million packages of yogurt a day.

○ Yoplait U.S. facilities use 650 million pounds of milk in a year to produce yogurt.

○ That's equivalent to 75 million gallons— or 1.3 billion 8-ounce glasses of milk. It takes 30,000 cows per year (working 24 hours a day) to produce that much milk.

○ 75,000 miles of Go-Gurt tubes have been sold in the past year, enough to circle the globe 3 times.

○ Yoplait is currently sold in 47 countries and is the No. 1 or 2 brand in 37 of those countries.

Brand equity

Brands are everywhere. In this book there are many great brands from different sectors of industry, with different target audiences and different owners. What key element links them all? It is that they all add fundamental value to their owners. This is what brand equity is all about. Consumer perception is always the key in marketing, but brand equity allows us marketers to take a corporate perspective for a change. What does branding do for us, what do we get from developing a great brand? In economic terms, the answer is simple. Brands impact on both the demand and supply curves.

On the demand side, brands enable a product to achieve a higher price at a given sales volume. Strong brands can also increase sales volumes and reduce churn rates. Price and volume impacts are often achieved at the same time.

Strong brands also establish more stable demand, through their relationship with consumers. They establish barriers to entry. The relationship with consumers is due to both functional and emotional attributes. On the functional side, brands ensure recognition and further aid the purchase decision through a guarantee of quality. From an emotional perspective, they satisfy aspirational and self-expression requirements. This is most evident in luxury and fashion sectors.

A further benefit of branding, which has increased in importance in recent years, is the ability to transfer the equity or values associated with a brand into new product categories. In order for brand stretching to be effective, it is necessary that the core values of the brand are image, rather than product, based.

Whilst there are numerous examples of successful brands that have achieved significant price premiums or higher volumes, the impact of branding on the supply curve is often ignored. Brands tend to shift the supply curve downwards due to the following reasons:

- Greater trade and consumer recognition and loyalty. This results in lower sales conversion costs and more favorable supplier terms.
- Lower staff acquisition and retention costs.
- Lower cost of capital.
- Economies of scale achieved through higher volumes.

There is an increasing body of research supporting the fact that successful brands add corporate value. There are, of course, examples of successful brands that have fallen from grace and branding initiatives that have failed. The challenge is to identify how your brand impacts on the business model, and to monitor whether marketing strategies are successful in adding value to the brand.

WHAT IS BRAND EQUITY?

There has been much debate about the term and while there is, as yet, no common definition for the conceptualisation or measurement of brand equity the principle is rapidly gaining acceptance.

It is important to note the difference between a brand and brand equity. A brand is what the customer buys. Brand equity is what the company owns. Brand equity represents the continuing value to the owner of that brand, i.e. value generated from customer loyalty and its influence on future sales. Brand equity is not a financial value, although brand equity as an asset may have a financial value attached to it in the same way that a property portfolio may have.

The term brand equity is often misunderstood. It has been mistaken for a variety of other brand terminologies such as brand description, brand measurement and brand value. Whilst these three terms describe aspects of brand equity, not one of them represents brand equity as such.

To help clear up some of the confusion, let me explain those three terms as companies and academics often use them. Brand description relates to the images, associations and beliefs consumers have about particular brands. This could be that the brand is dynamic, that it represents professionalism or even that the brand is a certain color. These images are important to consumers' perception of the brand (and therefore purchase decision) and need to be understood and managed to ensure that the positioning of the brand maximizes market potential.

Brand measurement relates to brand value. These measurements include price elasticity, demand volume, purchase frequency and attitudes or awareness levels, among others. These measurements aid management's understanding and alert management to potential changes in the market.

The third aspect of branding is financial evaluation of brands as separate assets, simply referred to as 'brand value'. This provides management with a real dollar figure; how much the brand is worth and what it contributes to shareholder value.

These three elements combined help us to understand brand equity. There is widespread belief that for every brand there is a pattern and a structure in the underlying 'brand equity' data which, if properly understood, could be used to better manage brand health and value. If only connections could be made between apparently unconnected data, it should be possible to solve all manner of fundamental marketing problems.

A great deal of effort has been wasted and confusion created in trying to find an answer. Many branded goods companies and market-

David Haigh is CEO of Brand Finance, a leading independent global brand valuation and evaluation consultancy.

David can be reached at:
d.haigh@brandfinance.com,
or visit
www.brandfinance.com .

ing academics remain busy attempting to solve the 'brand equity' puzzle. Consequently there are numerous teams working in parallel, with much duplication of effort. Leading market research and marketing consultancy organizations are also carrying out detailed and expensive research.

Unfortunately, finding the answer is hindered by a lack of agreement about what 'brand equity' actually is; which are the most important 'brand equity' measures; and what are the most likely causal relationships between them. One of the most significant problems is the drive to reduce complex branding issues to simple or even single measures of 'brand equity' which can then be compared easily.

For example, some have suggested that brand valuation might be the answer to finding a single measure of 'brand equity'. Most professional brand valuers however regard brand valuation as just one aspect of brand measurement, which works side by side with and must be seen in the context of other measures.

The word 'equity' has been borrowed from finance. It was borrowed to change the perception of brands by businesses. The idea is to share responsibility for the brand between the finance and marketing functions. The marketing department will always have responsibility for the creative aspects of brand building, maintenance and support. But as brands grow in importance, ensuring that return on brand (as an asset) is measured, monitored and maximized is the responsibility of both marketers and financiers.

The problem is that brands are often seen as the creative "fluffy" side of corporations, detached from their hard financial aspects. What brand equity as a term and a theory offers companies is an opportunity to bridge

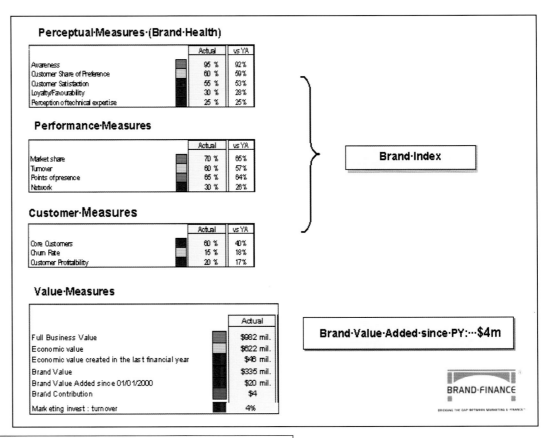

Perceptual Measures (Brand Health)	Actual	vs YA
Awareness	95 %	92%
Customer Share of Preference	60 %	59%
Customer Satisfaction	55 %	53%
Loyalty/Favourability	30 %	28%
Perception of technical expertise	25 %	25%

Performance Measures	Actual	vs YA
Market share	70 %	65%
Turnover	60 %	57%
Points of presence	65 %	64%
Network	30 %	26%

Customer Measures	Actual	vs YA
Core Customers	60 %	40%
Churn Rate	15 %	18%
Customer Profitability	20 %	17%

Value Measures	Actual
Full Business Value	$982 mil.
Economic value	$622 mil.
Economic value created in the last financial year	$46 mil.
Brand Value	$335 mil.
Brand Value Added since 01/01/2000	$20 mil.
Brand Contribution	$4
Marketing invest : turnover	4%

Brand Index

Brand Value Added since PY: $4m

BRAND FINANCE

the gap between the marketing and finance disciplines. It supports the notion that branding is a creative practice that, if done successfully, generates financial returns for companies and their shareholders.

Brand equity is really a combination, as we mentioned, of many different factors. So while point of time brand valuations are useful for balance sheet or tax planning purposes, at a strategy level brand valuation should be only one output in a more thorough process. That process increases our understanding of brand equity at an individual company level.

It is important to develop an understanding of what the brand is contributing to the business, how that changes over time and what variables affect that change. For example it is important to understand the correlation between, say, marketing expenditure, customer loyalty and brand value or between market penetration, sales growth and perceived quality. The drive to create more simplistic models by consultancies in a bid to achieve commercial populism is misguided. The key is turning potentially complex relationships into a set of visible measures that enable brand owners to track, predict and explain changes in brand equity.

There is no simple measure of 'brand equity'. There are several measures which, taken together, inform management decision-making. What major companies are beginning to realize is that all of the measures

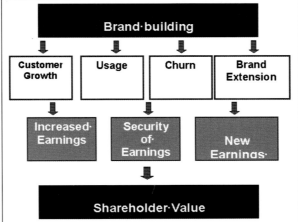

available need to be gathered, reviewed and prioritized in a structured brand audit and considered as a whole in the brand evaluation process. Ideally data should be statistically analyzed to find persuasive if not definitive relationships which can be tested empirically.

Among these measures there is a place for the consumer-oriented approaches like Y&R's Brand Asset Valuator or AGB Taylor Nelson's BrandVision. There is also a place for the type of financial analysis pioneered for balance sheet valuations.

Inevitably there have to be strong commercial reasons for the development and use

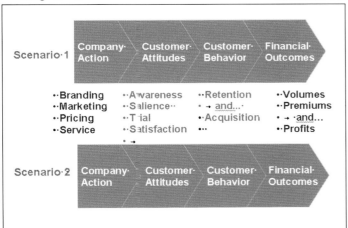

of brand tracking and valuation methods. If a model were to be produced which was almost foolproof in its predictive qualities, then its value to both finance and marketing professionals would be infinite.

To this end more and more companies are building brand monitoring and forecasting systems with large volumes of detailed research and financial data incorporating brand equity and brand value measures. The search for a perfect solution goes on.

BRAND EQUITY TRACKING

Brands will be major drivers of corporate value in the 21st century. Investors and business leaders have recognized this. Financial managers and planners are increasingly using brand equity tracking models to facilitate business planning. They should go one step further. Investors need and want greater disclosure of brand values and marketing performance. Financial managers should play a leading role in ensuring that such information is adequately communicated to investors, rather than waiting for statutory disclosure

requirements to catch up with reality.

Having detailed information on the brand, not just a brand value in dollar terms (value measures) but also information on perceptual, performance and customer measures can aid the investor relations function. By utilizing detailed brand equity trackers it is possible to show the investment community the contribution of the brand as well as its actual value.

Other key areas in which a greater understanding of brand equity aids company performance includes the setting of marketing budgets, resource allocation, internal communication and brand performance tracking.

Many organizations suffer from a surplus rather than a lack of market and consumer information. Unfortunately, much of this is gathered and stored in isolation. The old functional boundaries of a bygone era still prevent the effective flow and integration of information. Even if brand tracking data makes it onto the intranet or a shared directory, it tends to remain in 'research speak' and tends not to be used by financial and strategic planners.

SO, WHAT IS BRAND EQUITY?

Brand equity is a recognition of the importance of branding. It is a recognition of brands as assets, similar to a factory or other plant, and it is recognition of brands as items of significance which need to be managed and monitored carefully to ensure returns are maximised in the long-term.

What marketers, and brand owners need to ensure is that adequate data is collected centrally and regularly, that the relationship between the data variables are understood, that the real dollar value of the brand is understood and that it is monitored. It may seem a simple argument but it is one that has yet to be won.